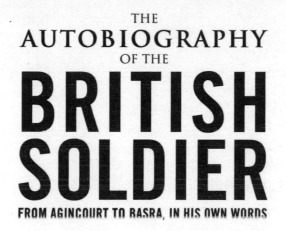

THE
AUTOBIOGRAPHY
OF THE
BRITISH
SOLDIER

FROM AGINCOURT TO BASRA, IN HIS OWN WORDS

THE
AUTOBIOGRAPHY
OF THE
BRITISH
SOLDIER

FROM AGINCOURT TO BASRA, IN HIS OWN WORDS

John Lewis-Stempel

headline
review

First published in 2007
by HEADLINE REVIEW

An imprint of Headline Publishing Group

1

Cataloguing in Publicaton Data is available from the British Library

ISBN 978 07553 1581 9

Typeset in Baskerville and Swis721 by Avon DataSet Ltd,
Bidford on Avon, Warwickshire'

Designed by The Flying Fish Studio Ltd

Printed and bound in Great Britain by
Mackays of Chatham plc, Chatham, Kent

Headline's policy is to use papers that are natural, renewable and recyclable
products and made from wood grown in sustainable forests. The logging and
manufacturing processes are expected to conform to the environmental
regulations of the country of origin

HEADLINE PUBLISHING GROUP
A division of Hachette Livre UK Ltd
338 Euston Road
London NW1 3BH

www.reviewbooks.co.uk
www.hodderheadline.com

'One night in particular I remember, and that was the night we took the quarries. That night we had a hard tussle and lost a lot of our poor fellows, the enemy turning out in very strong force. But eventually we drove them back and succeeded in taking the quarries, although both sides lost heavily. In this attack I had a brother killed, belonging to the 7th Royal Fusiliers. I knew he was in the engagement, and after it was over made enquiry and finding no trace of him, next day – the flag of truce being hoisted – I went out amongst the dead to search for the body, in this being successful. Obtaining a pick and spade I buried him alone, the other bodies being placed in heaps. I had another brother belonging to the marines, also engaged in this action, but he fortunately escaped. It is after the battle when the field is strewn with the dead and wounded, that the full horror of war makes itself felt; a horror which words but feebly express, and entirely fail to describe, were you bold enough to attempt to describe such scenes; but the soldier has no place for fine feeling, and at the call of duty he must do or die, and leave the sentiment for others.'

Private Parsons finds his brother's body on the battlefield, Sebastopol, 8 June 1855

For Freda, Tristram and Penny, in the hope that you are spared such things.
And for the British soldier, who fought that you might be.

CONTENTS

INTRODUCTION

Agincourt. Blenheim. Waterloo. The Somme. Dunkirk. Mount Longdon. Basra. One man fought in all these battles, separated as they are by decades, even centuries. It's a curiosity but, take away the kit, and the archer at Agincourt and the SA80-carrying 'tom' in Iraq is fundamentally the same fighting man. The British soldier.

Here is the British Soldier's autobiography, from enlistment to death, with all the trudging, fighting and bivouacking across the globe in between, told in his own words. It is a life story of glory and honour – with Rorke's Drift, Albuera and Kohima on the C.V. it could not be otherwise – but like the painting for which cavalryman Oliver Cromwell once sat, it is a 'warts and all' picture. So, T*he Autobiography of the British Soldier* does not omit the soldier's chronic tippling, or his long habit of larceny. 'If God were a soldier,' one Englishman at Agincourt is reputed to have said, 'he'd be a plunderer too.'

The merits – and frailties – of the British soldier predate Agincourt in 1415. If sheer unflinching bravery were a startline, the British soldier's story might begin with the Saxon shield wall at Maldon in 991, or with Harold's housecarls on Hastings hill in 1066, hung over as they were from the eve of battle's carousing. On the other hand, the purist might claim that the British soldier did not exist before the formation of the standing army in 1645. Or even the founding of 'Britain' by the act of Union in 1707.

But Agincourt is the true birth date of the British soldier, and not solely because of the heroic stand there of the few against the many that has come to inspire and define the British at war ever since. At Agincourt, the professional soldier begins to supercede the feudal, part-time warrior ('soldier' being a corruption of the old French *soude*, to be paid). At Agincourt, for all the magnificence of the English longbow, gunpowder is making its entrance, a new age of war is beginning. At Agincourt, the first voices of the 'common' fighter begin to be heard. At Agincourt, the English and Welsh – no matter their rank – are bound together in patriotic ideology, an almost unknown phenomenon at the time.

Patriotism is the iron inner armour of the British soldier. For six hundred years the British soldier has conceived of himself as superior to the enemy purely by the virtue of having been born in the isles. As a rule of thumb, the British soldier in the Napoleonic Wars considered himself worth at least five 'Johnny Crapauds'. Loathsome it might be, but such national arrogance wins wars. At Singapore in 1942 a Japanese officer, Colonel Tsuji, asked the surrendering British why they had not destroyed the town. A junior British officer replied: 'Because we will return again . . . We may be defeated 99 times, but in the final round . . . we will win that.'

There is, of course, more to the British way of soldiering than insolent patriotism. The Germans concluded at the end of the First World War that it was the British sense of humour which allowed them to endure where the *Feldgrau* faltered. The British soldier certainly has his witty moments, as the wag who scrawled, 'This is another fine mess you've got me into, Stanley' in the Falklands capital in 1982 attests. More seriously, like the Romans, the British have never shied away from violence and close-quarters killing. Corporal Jones' cry in *Dad's Army* 'They don't like it up 'em!' wasn't just a funny one-liner; it was an historical truth summating the efficacy of the British bayonet charge. In truth, it is hard to evade the conclusion that the 'warrior race' is precisely that; the British are natural born warriors.

Congenitally keen on fighting, the British have never much minded whom they war against: the French, 'natives', 'Johnny Rooskie', the 'Hun', the Japanese, Koreans, 'Argies', whomever, have all seamlessly succeeded each other as 'the enemy'. The British soldier, like the people from which he comes, is not a believer in abstract causes. Only twice in his long career has the British soldier been possessed by politics: in the English Civil War of the 1640s and, more thoughtfully, in the Second World War. Born to fight, the British soldier is also the ultimate mercenary.

Lacking political passion – which so easily slides into righteous hate – the British soldier tends to treat his foe with common humanity. There has been the odd moral blemish on the conduct record, the running amok at Badajoz in the Peninsular War comes storming unwillingly to mind, but as Sir John Fortescue observed in his 1930 *History of the British Army*, that army 'will be remembered best not for its countless deeds of daring and invincible stubbornness in battle, but for its lenience in conquest and its gentleness in domination'. The policing of post-Sadaam Iraq, where the British trod softly softly and the Americans strutted like rulers, gives the only proof needed.

Despite his record of grace in peace and victory in battle, the British public has long been ambivalent towards the soldier. As the soldiers themselves used to sing:

> *When war is proclaimed and the danger nigh,*
> *'God and our soldiers' is the people's cry*
> *But when peace is proclaimed and all things righted*
> *God is forgot and the soldier slighted.*

The love–hate affair with the soldier is easily explicable. Most soldiers, historically, have been recruited from the bottom of the social pile, enlisting because of the 'compulsion of destitution' rather than the desire for service. Soldiers have been press-ganged, soldiers have also been pulled out of prison and into uniform. (Conscription has generally been avoided in Britain, because it conflicts with the national notion of individual liberty.) As late as 1877, enlisting in the 'brutal and licentious soldiery' was regarded as so shameful that Mrs Robertson told her son that she would rather see him dead than in a red coat. Willie joined up anyway, and made the long and original journey from private to field marshal, Chief of the Imperial General Staff.

Then there is the curious anti-militarism of the British. They like to fight, but where other nations parade their armed might, the British keep the army to the bare minimum. Even then, the British soldier has been treated abysmally. Before the First World War around 80 per cent of soldiers who died on service did so from disease and neglect. Rifleman Harris, returning stricken with 'ague' from Walcheren in 1809, was unloaded by fellow soldiers. 'I never beheld men more moved than they were at our helpless state,' he later wrote.

The life, feelings, experiences of the British soldier are seldom what the outsider expects to find. Harris' comrades' emotion is hardly the stuff of 'brutal' soldiery. In these pages the British soldier's closed, inner world, as well as his public duty, is revealed in full, taken as they are from his letters, diaries and memoirs. Such sources are scarcer in the far past for the simple reason that few soldiers were able to write. There is a more arcane reason, too. Before the seventeenth century the soldier was less reflective, seeing himself as God's cipher, not a man with an individual destiny. One reflection loops in the mind of the literate, thoughtful, modern British soldier. His isolation. On returning home from combat in 1982, Lance-Corporal Vince Bramley finds that even his wife, when he tried to describe his Falklands war, 'couldn't understand me at all. I never said anything again'. The Agincourt archer came from a society where bloody violence, be it village brawl or the slaughtering of swine in the town square, was the weft of everyday existence. In modern times the soldier's job, with its necessary end business of killing, is removed from anything his peers and the public know. Which makes his mental burden greater than that of his Agincourt self.

Otherwise the swearing, stubborn, sentimental, mocking, modest, hardcase, impudent, courageous British soldier is much as he ever was. If you want a war won, he's your man. How many wars, after all, has he ever lost?

The Autobiography of the British Soldier is emphatically not a history of Britain at war, not even of the British army. It is an eye-witness account of the soldier's lot and life, in war and in peace, in the last six hundred years. Inevitably the commands of space mean that some battles are omitted, and the mechanics of warfare are given in only bare necessary detail. However, if you want to know what it felt like to stand in an infantry square at Waterloo, to bury your brother's body in the Crimea, to rob a French corpse at Vimeiro, to be operated on in a field hospital in 1917, to be drunkenly tricked into taking the queen's shilling by a Victorian recruiting sergeant, to dress for parade in the Georgian army (with hair so tightly tied back that you can't close your eyes), to charge with the Royalist cavalry at Edgehill, to sing irreverent daft songs as you march ('I don't want to be a soldier/I don't want to go war/Have a banana!'), to write a last letter home to your son from the trenches before you go over the top to your death, to guiltily get through a battle in one piece, to jump out into the night over Normandy on D-Day, to be the thin red and khaki line that saved Europe from totalitarianism on three occasions (the Napoleonic Wars, the First and Second World Wars) then you will.

Soldier. A salute.

John Lewis-Stempel, Herefordshire, June 2007

ACKNOWLEDGEMENTS

They also served: My wife, Penny, who held the fort and patrolled the manuscript with her usual intelligence; Emma Daffern, for research above and beyond the call of duty; Andrea Henry and Bernard Dive at Headline; Julian Alexander, Mark Lucas, Katie Mankin, Petra Lewis at LAW; Sally Sergeant; Kathryn Fox for book spotting; the staff at Hereford and Monmouth libraries; the staff at the Imperial War Museum; Joyce and Eric Lewis, for logistics, this time, last time, every time.

AGINCOURT
THE VIEW FROM THE RANKS
FRANCE, 25 OCTOBER 1415

Fought in pursuance of Henry V's claim to the French throne, the Battle of Agincourt was the first of the great British victories over impossible odds. Ravaged by dysentery – the soldier's occupational disease before the twentieth century – hunger, and a forced tramp over 200 miles of northern France, Henry's force was down to 5,000 men when it was trapped by the French in the sodden defile between Agincourt and Tramecourt woods. The French army numbered as many as 20,000.

Henry's army, however, held three trumps: its yew longbows which were quicker, longer-reaching, than the French crossbow; its innovative 'palings' (stakes) which served as defence against horse-soldiers; and its patriotism, which fervoured up the troops to face – and beat – adversity. While other nations struggled to find an identity, the English had already convinced themselves that they were God's other chosen people.

The lie of the land also favoured Henry's force: the narrowness of the Agincourt dingle meant that the French could not easily bring their superior numbers to bear. Indeed, they crushed each other in the rush to battle. And then again in the retreat.

The author of the account of Agincourt which follows was a priest in Henry's force; the army chaplain has a long pedigree.

And when on the following day, Thursday, we were descending the valley towards the River of the Swords, the king was told by scouts and cavalry skirmishers that there was a powerful adversary numbering many thousands on the other side of the river, almost a league to our right. We therefore crossed the river as fast as we could, and when we reached the crest of the hill on the other side, we saw emerging from the valley about a mile from us hateful swarms of Frenchmen, who appeared to us to be an incomparable multitude in their columns, lines and divisions. They took up their position just over half a mile ahead of us, filling a broad field like an innumerable swarm of locusts, having a small valley between us and them.

Meanwhile our king was encouraging his army courteously and bravely, marshalling them into lines and wings, as if they were to go at once into battle. And then everyone who had not previously cleared his conscience by confession, put on the armour of penitence ... And among other sayings which I noted then, a certain knight, Sir Walter Hungerford, wished to the king's face that in addition to the small band which he had there he could have had ten thousand of the better archers of England, who would have been glad to be with them. The king replied: 'Thou speakest as a fool, for by the God of Heaven in whose grace I trust and in whom is my firm hope of victory, I would not have one more than I have, even if I could ... Dost thou not believe that the Almighty can through this humble little band overcome the pride of these Frenchmen, who boast of their numbers and their strength?' ...

And when the enemy in position saw and considered the disposition and fewness of our troops, they betook themselves to a field beyond a certain wood, which lay near to the left between us and them, where was our road to Calais. So our king, thinking that they might go round the wood to attack him along the road, or else might go round woods further away in the neighbourhood and surround us from all sides, at once moved his lines and he always stationed himself to face the enemy ...

And when at last we were at the last rays of light, and darkness fell between us and them, we still stood in the field and heard our foes, everyone calling as the manner is, for his comrade, servant and friend, dispersed by chance in so great a multitude. Our men began to do the same, but the king ordered silence throughout the whole army, under penalty of the loss of horse and harness in the case of a gentleman ... and of the right ear in the case of a yeoman or below, with no hope of pardon, for anyone who might presume to break the king's order. And he at once went in silence to a hamlet nearby, in a place where we had only a few houses; most of us had to rest in gardens and orchards, through a night of pouring rain. And when our enemies considered the quietness of our men and our silence, they thought that we were struck with fright at our small numbers and contemplated flight during the night; so they established fires and strong watches throughout the fields and routes. And as it was said they thought they were so sure of us that they cast dice that night for our king and nobles.

And on the morrow, Friday the feast of Saints Crispin and

Crispinian, 25 October, the Frenchmen, at dawn, organized themselves into lines, battles, and wedges, and took up their position facing us in the field called Agincourt, through which lay our route to Calais, in terrific multitude; and they set squadrons of horsemen in many hundreds on either side of their front lines, to break our line and the strength of our archers. The front line was composed of dismounted men made up of all the noblest and choicest of their forces, who in the forest of spears . . . were by estimation thirty times more numerous than our men. But their rear lines . . . were all on horseback . . . and compared with our men they were an innumerable multitude.

And meanwhile our king prepared himself for the field, after hearing lauds and masses and . . . arranged his small numbers in one 'battle', placing his vanguard as a wing to his right with the Duke of York in command and the rearguard as a wing to his left under Lord Carnoys. Interspersed among the line were wedges of archers, whom the king ordered to affix stakes in front of them, as he had ordered earlier, to stop the attacks of the horsemen . . .

And when much of the day had been consumed . . . and both armies had stood and had not moved a foot, the king, seeing that the opposing army was abstaining from the attack which had been expected . . . either to cause us to break our order, or to strike terror into our hearts because of their numbers, or . . . because they expected more reinforcements to arrive, and knowing that our shortage of food would conquer us by hunger, ordered his men to move towards the enemy, sending orders to the baggage-train of the army to follow up close so that they should not fall as booty to the enemy . . . After the king had estimated that all his baggage had come up to his rear, he advanced towards the enemy, with his men, in the name of Jesus . . . and of the glorious Virgin and St George, and the enemy moved towards him.

And when they came near enough to attack, the French horsemen posted on the sides rushed against our archers on both flanks of our army; but quickly, God willing, they were compelled to retreat by the showers of arrows and to flee behind their lines . . . except the large numbers whom the points of the stakes or the sharpness of the arrows stopped from flight by piercing the horses or the horsemen. The crossbowmen of the enemy, who were behind the men at arms and on their flanks, fell back in face of the strength of our archers after the first draw, which was too hasty and injured only a few of our men . . . But the French nobles who had first approached in line, just as they had come from their muster nearby . . . divided themselves into three columns, either for fear of the arrows . . . or to penetrate more quickly our force to the banners, attacked our forces at the three places where there were banners; and at the first clash they met our men with such a fierce impact that they were compelled to fall back for almost the distance of a lance . . . And then the battle grew hotter and our archers shot . . . their arrows through the flanks of the enemy, the battle continually renewing. And when their arrows were exhausted, they seized axes, swords and lances from those who were lying on the ground, and beat down, wounded and killed the enemy with them . . . And the just Judge who wished to strike down the proud multitude of the enemy with the thunderbolts of vengeance . . . broke their power . . . No one had time to receive them as captives, but almost all of them without distinction of persons, when they fell to the ground, struck down by our men or by those following them, I know not by what hidden judgement of God, were killed without intermission . . . For when some of them slain at the start of the engagement fell in front, such was the indisciplined violence and pressure of the host behind that the living fell on the dead, and others falling on the living were killed in turn; and so in the three places where there was a concentration of our forces, the piles of dead and those crushed in between grew so much that our men climbed on these heaps which grew higher than a man and slew those below with swords, axes, and other weapons. And when at last after two or three hours the vanguard was cut up and worn out, and the rest were forced into flight, our men began to sort these heaps and separate the living from the dead, intending to keep the living as property to be ransomed. But behold! at once, we know not by what wrath of God, a cry arose that the enemy's rearguard of cavalry, in overwhelming numbers had repaired the enemy line . . . and was coming against our small and tired band. And so they killed their prisoners with swords . . . without any distinction of persons, except for the Dukes of Orléans and Bourbon and other illustrious persons in the royal entourage, and a few others, lest the captives should be our ruin in the coming battle.

> But after a little while the troops of the enemy, having tasted the bitterness of our weapons, and at our king's approach, left the field of blood to us . . .

On this 'field of blood' French losses were between 7,000 and 10,000 killed; perhaps a 100 English and Welsh lay dead in the Agincourt mud.

Agincourt served to inspire – if not define – the British soldier for the next 600 years: small numbers, long odds. As late as 1803 Agincourt was used in recruitment posters for the British army; during World War II, Agincourt, as burnished by Shakespeare, was patriotically held up before the nation in a government-backed 1944 film of *Henry V*. In it, Laurence Olivier delivers the Shakespearean version of Henry's pre-battle speech at Agincourt, with its promise:

> We few, we happy few, we band of brothers;
> For he today that sheds his blood with me
> Shall be my brother; be he ne'er so vile,
> This day shall gentle his condition;
> And gentlemen in England now a-bed
> Shall think themselves accurs'd they were not here,
> And hold their manhoods cheap while any speaks
> That fought with us upon Saint Crispin's day.

If English soldiers were brothers in arms, few of the 'vile', the lowly, would be given a helping hand by the crown when their services were no longer required. The lot of the dismissed soldier would be, invariably, poverty. Even begging.

'for . . . service never yit recompensed ne rewarded'
THOMAS HOSTELL

PETITION OF AN AGINCOURT VETERAN, 1422

A plea for alms, sent to Henry V.

To the Kyng our Sovereign Lord
Beseecheth meekly your poure liegeman and humble horatour [petitioner], Thomas Hostell, that in consideration of his service doon to your noble progenitors of full blessed memory Kyng

Henri the iiijth, and King Henri the fift, whoos soules God
assoille; being at the Siege of Harflewe, there smitten with a
springolt [dart] through the hede, losing his oon eye, and his
cheke boon broken; also at the Battle of Agingcourt, and after at
the taking of the carracks on the See, there with a gadde of yren
[iron] his plates smitten into his body and his hand sore hurt,
maimed and wounded; by meane whereof he being sore feebled
and debrused, now falle to greet age and poverty; greatly
endetted; and may not helpe himself; having not wherewith to be
sustained ne relievd, but of men's gracious almesse [alms], and
being for his said service never yit recompensed ne rewarded, it
plese your high and excellent Grace, the premises tenderly
considered, of youre benign pitee and grace, to releve and
refresh your said poure horatour, as it shall plese you, with your
most gracious Almesse at the reverence of God and in werk of
charitee, and he shall devoutly pray for the soules of your said
noble progenitors, and for your moost noble and high estate.

Hostell was assuredly an ex-professional soldier, a man who served fixed-term
contracts for a captain, usually a local noble or a knight; in turn, the captain was
contracted and paid by the crown. The 'wages of war' for soldiers were middling: 1s
a day for a mounted man-at-arms, 6d for a mounted archer, 3d for a foot archer and
2d for a spearman. A labourer, by contrast, earned 4d.

Not all soldiers in a country which was still feudal, like Britain in the 1400s, were
professionals. All freemen owed an obligation to serve the crown for up to 60 days
a year. Men raised under such shire-levies (which dated back to the *fyrds* of Anglo-
Saxon times) tended to be unwilling and untrained. Even un-equipped; in the
hundred of Ewelme one muster found that only a third of men had weapons or
armour. The future of soldiering belonged to the professional.

For whom, as the fifteenth century wore on, work became plentiful. There were
many who would pay for his martial services. Foreign princelings had a liking for
medieval English soldiers; after all, who had been seasoned more in the battlefield
arts having fought the French for year upon year? The mercenary life not only offered
a daily wage; it also offered the fifteenth-century version of the lottery win; the
chance of lucre on a massive scale. It had happened to Sir John Hawkwood, the
son of an Essex tanner, whose Italian jobs had earned him a castle; it might happen
to any man jack.

And there was also employment closer to home, as England slipped ineluctably
into the dynastic struggle known as the 'Wars of the Roses', 1455–1485, between

the Yorkist (White Rose) and Lancastrian (Red Rose) claimants to the country's throne.

─────◆─◆◆─────

'the second gun of iron . . . so belaboured the place that
stones of the walls flew into the sea'
WILLIAM GREGORY, JOHN WARKWORTH

WAR OF THE ROSES
GUNS AND THE WARS OF THE ROSES
1461–4

Gunfire first sounded in Britain in 1327 when the English marched north of the border with 'crakys' (cannon); but the British were slow to realize the potential of gunpowder. The French were not; it was their supremacy in artillery in the mid fifteenth century which enabled them to win back Henry V's gains in the Hundred Years War (1337–1453). The unreliability of early cannon, as recorded by Gregory during the Second Battle of St Albans in 1461, only served to reinforce the British prejudice against gunpowder, and their patriotic preference for the bow:

The lords in King Henry's party pitched a field and fortified it very strongly, and like unwise men broke their array and field and took another, and before they were prepared for battle the queen's party was at hand with them in the town of St Albans, and then everything was to seek and out of order, for their scouts came not back to them to bring tidings how near the queen was, save one who came and said that she was nine miles away. And before the gunners and Burgundians could level their guns they were busily fighting, and many a gun of war was provided that was of little avail or none at all; for the Burgundians had such instruments that would shoot both pellets of lead and arrows of an ell in length with six feathers, three in the middle, and three at one end, with a very big head of iron at the other end, and wild fire, all together . . . In time of need they could not shoot one of them, for the fire turned back on those who would shoot these three things. Also they had nets made of great cords of four fathoms long and four feet wide, like a hedge, and at every second knot there was a nail standing upright, so that no man could pass over it without a strong chance of getting hurt. Also they had a pavise borne as a door, made with a staff folding up and down to set the pavise where they like, and loop holes with shooting windows to shoot out at . . . And when their shot was spent and finished, they cast the pavise before them; then no man might come over the pavise because of the nails that stood upright, unless he wished to do himself a mischief. Also they had a thing made like a lattice full of nails as the net was, but it could be moved as a man would: a man might squeeze it together so that the length would be more than two yards long, and if he wished, he might pull it wide, so that it would be four square. And that served to be at gaps where horsemen would enter . . . And as the real opinion of worthy men who will not dissemble or curry favour for any bias, they could not understand that all these devices did any good or harm, except on our side with King Henry. Therefore they are much neglected, and men betake themselves to mallets of lead, bows, swords, glaivers, and axes. As for spearmen, they are only good to ride before the footmen and eat and drink up their victuals, and many more such fine things they do. You must hold me excused for these expressions, but I say the best; for in foot soldiers is all the trust.

The Chronicler John Warkworth recorded a more successful example of the revolution in arms at the Siege of Bamborough in 1464:

Also, my said lord of Warwick, and his brother the Earl of Northumberland, the 25th day of June, laid siege unto the Castle of Bamborough, there being within Sir Ralph Grey, with such forces as attended him to keep the said castle against the power of the king and my said lord. And then my lord lieutenant had ordained all the king's great gun, and London the second gun of iron; which so belaboured the place that stones of the walls flew into the sea. *Dysyon*, a brazen gun of the king's, smote through Sir Ralph Grey's chamber many times. Edward and Richard Bombartell and other men of the king's ordnance with men at arms and archers, won the castle of Bamborough by assault, in spite of Sir Ralph Grey, and took him, and brought him to the king at Doncaster, and there he was executed . . .

The coming of gunpowder was not restricted to artillery; smaller firearms also made their presence felt. When landowner John Paston of Norfolk decided in July 1468 to hire four soldiers to protect the family estate – the Wars of the Roses bred lawlessness – he reported that they 'can well shoot both guns and cross-bows'.

Even so, the gunpowder revolution only made stuttering progress in Britain; as late as the 1540s the borderers of Scotland were reported to have run from the novel noise of gunfire. The blood that was spilled in the Wars of the Roses tended to be caused by bow, sword and spear. And sometimes the blood of Englishmen leached in fantastic quantity; the Battle of Towton, 27 March 1461, waged a day long in a snowstorm, caused 28,000 casualties.

In such engagements the lion's share of fighting was done by the private armies of the nobles; these were made up of disbanded veterans of the Hundred Years War. Or local retainers who fought in return for 'Livery [uniform] and Maintenance'. Men like Henry Vernon.

⏺

'Henry, I pray you, fail not now'
RICHARD, EARL OF WARWICK

THE WARS OF THE ROSES
HENRY VERNON IS SUMMONED TO THE FIELD
25 MARCH 1471

Warwick, the mighty 'Kingmaker' of England, calls his retainer Vernon to war:

Right trusty and right well-beloved, I greet you well, and desire and heartily pray you that inasmuch as yonder man Edward, the king's our sovereign lord great enemy, rebel, and traitor, is now late arrived in the north parts of this land and coming fast on southward accompanied with Flemings, Easterlings, and Danes, not exceeding the number of all that he ever hath of 2,000 persons, nor the country as he cometh nothing falling to him, ye will therefore, incontinent and forthwith after the sight hereof, dispose you toward me to Coventry with as many people defensibly arrayed as ye can readily make, and that ye be with me there in all haste possible, as my very singular trust is in you, and as I may do thing to your weal or worship hereafter. And God keep you. Written at Warwick the 25th day of March.

Henry, I pray you, fail not now as ever I may do for you.

Th' Earl of Warwick and Salisbury, Lieutenant to the king our sovereign Lord Henry the Sixth.

R. WARWICK

Three weeks later Warwick's Lancastrian army encountered Edward IV at Barnet.

'the mist was so thick, that a man might not perfectly judge one thing from another'
JOHN WARKWORTH

THE WARS OF THE ROSES
FOG AND TREACHERY: THE BATTLE OF BARNET
14 APRIL 1471

Like many a medieval battle, that fought in fog at Barnet in Spring 1471 lapsed into utter confusion when Warwick's Lancastrians mistook a private badge for Edward's 'sun and rays' insignia – and attacked their own centre.

And upon Easter Even, he [Edward IV] and all his host went toward Barnet . . . [and] it happened that he, with his host, were entered into the town of Barnet, before the Earl of Warwick and his host. And so the Earl of Warwick, and his host, lay without the town all night, and each of them loosed guns at other all the night. And on Easter day in the morning, the fourteenth of April, right early each of them came upon [the] other; and there was such a great mist, that neither of them might see the other perfectly. There they fought from four of clock in the morning, unto ten of clock the forenoon. And divers times the Earl of Warwick's party had the victory, and supposed that they had won the field. But it happened so, that the Earl of Oxford's men had upon them their lord's livery, both before and behind, which was a star with streams, which [was] much like King Edward's livery, the sun with streams; and the mist was so thick, that a man might not perfectly judge one thing from another; so the Earl of Warwick's men shot and fought against the Earl of Oxford's men, thinking and supposing, that they had been King Edward's men; and anon the Earl of Oxford, and his men, cried 'treason! treason!' and fled away from the field with eight hundred men.

The Lord Marquis Montague was agreed, and appointed with King Edward, and put upon him King Edward's livery; and a man of the Earl of Warwick's saw that, and fell upon him, and killed him. And when the Earl of Warwick saw his brother dead, and the Earl of Oxford fled, he leaped on horseback and fled to a wood by the field of Barnet, where was no way forth; and one of King Edward's men had espied him, and one came upon him, and despoiled him naked. And so King Edward got that field. And there was slain of the Earl of Warwick's party, the Earl himself, Marquis Montague, Sir William Tyrell, Knight, and many others. The Duke of Exeter fought manly there that day, and was greatly despoiled, and wounded, and left naked for dead in the field, and so lay there from seven of clock, till four afternoon, which was [his body] taken up and brought to a house by a man of his own, and a leech brought to him and so afterwards brought into sanctuary at Westminster.

There was nothing unusual in a knight like Warwick fighting on foot; it was the English way of warfare for armoured knights in the fifteenth century. (Plate armour weighed up to 60 pounds a suit; the best was made in Milan.) Invariably these 'men-at-arms' fought alongside billmen in the central 'battle' (division), with a 'battle' of archers on either wing.

The Wars of the Roses spluttered on their violent course until 1485, when Henry VII killed Richard III, the crouch-back murderer of the Princes in the Tower, and established the Tudors on the throne of England.

His victory at Bosworth notwithstanding, Henry VII was utterly uninterested in war and much preferred finance, hence his reputation as 'the best businessman ever to sit on the throne of England'. But he did make one military innovation. Sensible of his own protection, he: 'constituted and ordained a certayne number . . . of good archers . . . [and] diverse other persons being hardye, strong and of agilitie to give dayly attendance on his body, whome he named Yomen of the crowne . . . men remembre not anye king of Englande before that tyme which used such a furniture of dayle soldiers'.

Founded in 1487, the Yeomen of the Guard is the world's oldest extant military unit.

*'Frenchmen call this battle the Journey of Spurs –
because they ran away so fast on horseback'*
EDWARD HALL

THE JOURNEY OF SPURS
GUINEGATE
FRANCE, 16 AUGUST 1513

On succeeding to the throne, Henry VIII revived the traditional English habit of warring with France. Where his father had enjoyed counting money, Henry VIII wanted to count military glories. He was not alone; the chivalric ideal of honour through combat died hard amongst the British aristocracy. What Henry lacked was 'small folk' – foot soldiers, gunners, cooks, builders – since the part-time county levies would not and could not serve abroad. So Henry recruited, via his nobles and self-styled 'captains', 25,000 volunteers; these, however, were mostly old-fashioned bowmen and billmen. For more modern soldiers, arquebusiers (musket men) and pikemen, Henry had to resort to hiring German and Burgundian mercenaries.

The campaign in France was successful enough, starting with the siege, and eventual capture, of Terouenne (Thérouanne). Humphrey Rudyng was there:

> The walls of Terouenne are sore beaten with guns, and many houses are broken and destroyed. Great trenches have been made on our part . . . The Frenchmen daily make 'skryes' [sorties] outside the walls, and make decoys to bring Englishmen out of the trenches and into their gunshot. Men have been slain on both parts, the more part Frenchmen. On Saturday, St Kenelm's Eve, six thousand Frenchmen showed themselves upon a hill-side . . . Sir Rice ap Thomas set a wing of his spearmen upon them, and so put them to flight, slew three, drowned two, and took four live prisoners. On Sunday, St Kenelm's Day, Frenchmen showed themselves on the south part of Terouenne in the afternoon . . . but our men drove them in at the gates, and galled them with arrows . . . On Monday after St Kenelm's Day, Frenchmen countermined upon our miners, and with gunpowder and wildfire burned two of our miners to death. Three others of them lie burned, more likely to die than to live.

A French attempt to relieve Terouenne was intercepted at Bomy by the English on 16 August 1513; so enthusiastically did English men-at-arms (now, under Henry's insistence, horsed) tackle the French cavalry that the latter quit the field in indecent haste: the affair known as the Journey, or Battle, of Spurs.

Then every man prepared himself to battle, resorting to the standard; the horsemen marched before the footmen by the space of a mile, till came couriers bearing tidings that the French army approached. The king bad set forward and to advance his banner in name of God and St. George. The Almaynes seeing this – to what purpose it was not known – suddenly embattled themselves on the left hand of the king and left the breast or front of the king's battle bare. As the king was thus marching forward toward the battle, to him came the Emperor Maximilian with thirty men of arms, he and all his company armed in one suit with red crosses. Then by the counsel of the emperor, the king caused certain pieces of small ordnance to be laid on the top of a long hill or bank for the out-scourers. Thus the king's horsemen and a few archers on horseback marched forward. The king would fain have been afore with the horsemen, but his council persuaded him the contrary; and so he tarried with the footmen accompanied with the emperor.

The Frenchmen came on in three ranks, thirty-six men's thickness, and well they perceived the king's battle of footmen marching forward. The earl of Essex, captain of the horsemen, and sir John Peche with the king's horsemen and the Burgundians to the number of eleven hundred, stood with banner displayed in a valley. The lord Walonne and the lord Ligny and their band to the number of four hundred horsemen severed themselves and stood aside from the Englishmen; so then the Englishmen were but seven hundred. Yet they with banner displayed removed up to the top of the hill, and there they met, with sir John Guilford, a hundred tall archers on horseback, which had ascried the Frenchmen. Now on the top of the hill was a fair plain of good ground, on the left hand a low wood, and on the right hand a fallow field. The lord Walonne and the Burgundians kept them aloof. Then appeared in sight the Frenchmen with banners and standards displayed. Then came to the captains of the Englishmen of arms, an English officer of arms called Clarencieux, and said: 'In God's name set forward, for the victory is yours, for I see by them they will not abide, and I will go with you in my coat of arms.' Then the horsemen set forward, and the archers alighted and were set in order by an hedge all along a village side called Bomy. The Frenchmen came on with thirty-three standards displayed, and the archers shot apace and galled their horses; and the English spears set on freshly, crying: 'St. George!' and fought valiantly with the Frenchmen and threw down their standard. The dust was great and the cry more, but suddenly the Frenchmen shocked to their standard and fled, and threw away their spears, swords, and maces, and cut off the bards of their horses to run the lighter. When the hinder part saw the former fly, they fled also, but the sooner for one cause which was this: as the English horsemen mounted up the hill the stradiates were coming downwards on the one side of the hill before the French host, which suddenly saw the banners of the English horsemen and the king's battle following upward. Weening to them that all had been horsemen, then they cast themselves about and fled. The Frenchmen were so fast in array that the stradiates could have no entry, and so they ran still by the ends of the ranks of the French army. And when they behind saw the fall of their standards and their stradiates in whom they had great confidence return, they that were farthest off fled first. Then up pranced the Burgundians and followed the chase. This battle was of horsemen to horsemen, but not in equal number, for the Frenchmen were ten to one, which had not been seen before-time, that the English horsemen gat the victory of the men of arms of France. The Frenchmen call this battle the Journey of Spurs – because they ran away so fast on horseback.

⟹•⟸

'my broder . . . burnt and destroyed the Town of Rowcastell'
LORD DACRE

SCORCHED EARTH, AMBUSH AND SHEEP STEALING
THE DACRES GO ON A BORDER FORAY
SCOTLAND, 13 NOVEMBER 1513

Dacre was the Warden of the Marches in the early reign of Henry VIII; border skirmishing between Scots and English was endemic, but it was given an added piquancy after the Scots had been slaughtered by English bills at Flodden Moor on 9 September 1513, the English levies desperate to get the fight over and get home. The beer had given out three days before.

Please it your Highness to knowe ... Upon Thuresday last I assembled your subgietts in Northumberland to the nombre of a thousand horsmen, and rode in at Gallespeth and so to the water of Kale two myle within Scotland, and there set furth two foreyes [forays]; my broder Philipp Dacre with CCC. men which burnt and destroyed the Town of Rowcastcll with all the cornes in the same and thereabouts, and wan two towers in it, and burnt both rofe [roof] and flores [floors]: and Sir Roger Fenwike with CCC. men burnt the Town of Langton and destroyed all the cornes therein ... And I come with a stale [ambush] to a place called the Dungyon, a myle from Jedworth, and so went to the Sclater furd [ford] on the water of Bowset, and there the Scotts persewed us right sore, there bekered [bickered] with us, and gave us hand stroks; there come three standards to bak theym, that is to say David Karr of Fernehirst and the laird of Boudgedworth upon the one side, and the sheriff of Tevidale on the other side, with the nombre of DCC. Men or mo[re]. The laird of Walghope was hurt there with one arrowe and his hors slane; Mark Trumbrill was stricken with a spere and the hede [of it] left in hym, his hors was won, and diverse Scotesmen were hurt there. And so we come forwards, where we saw my broder Syr Cristofer Dacre with his oste [host] arrayed at a place called the Bellyng, which was to us no litill comfort, and to hym gret gladnes seying the small power we were of at that tyme ... We had not rydden above the space of a myle when we saw the Lord Chamberlane appere in our sight with ijM. men, and four standards; the other thre standards resorted to hym and so the countre drew fast to theym. We put us in arreye and come homewarde and rode no faster then nowr [our] shepp [sheep] and swyne that we had won wold dryve, which was of no great substance, for the countre was warned our comyng and bekyns [beacons] burnt fro mydnyght forward. And when the Scotts had geven us overe we retourned home and come in at the Redeswyre. I come to Harbotill at mydnyght; my broder Syr Cristofer lay that night at the towne of Otterburne, and upon the morne to Hexham, and his folks in other townes upon the water of Tyne, and, on the third day at home, as many as might git.

'Bot for all that, as ye se, he lieth under thys stone'
SIR MARMADUKE CONSTABLE

A SOLDIER'S GRAVESTONE EPITAPH
FLAMBOROUGH
YORKSHIRE, 1518

Here lieth Marmaduke Cunstable, of fflaynborght, knyght,
Who made advento[re] into ffrance, and for the right of the
    same
Passed over with kynge Edwarde the fourtht, yt noble kynght;
And also with noble king Herre [Henry], the sevinth of that
    name.
He was also at Barwick, at the winnyng of the same,
And by ky[n]g Edward chosy[n] Captey[n] there first of any
    one;
And rewllid [ruled] and governid ther his tyme without blame.
Bot for all that, as ye se, he lieth under thys stone.

At Brankisto[n] feld, wher the kyng of Scottis was slayne,
He, then being of the age of thre score and tene,
With the gode duke of Northefolke yt jorney he hay tayn
And coragely avau[n]cid hy[m]self emo[n]g other, ther and
    then,
The ky[n]g being i[n] Frau[n]ce with grete nombre of
    Y[nglesh]men
He, nothing hedyng [hiding] his age ther but jeopyde hy as on
With his sonnes, brothe[r], sarvantt[s], and kynnismen,
Bot now, as ye se, he lyeth under this stone.

The 'Brankisto[n]' referred to is Branxton, north-east England, the epicentre of the battle of Flodden. Constable, who led one of the English divisions, was, as he says, around seventy then. Old soldiers in Tudor times fought until death or decrepitude overtook them; Constable's commander at Flodden, the wily Duke of Norfolk (the Earl of Surrey), had been nearly 80 at the time of his finest hour.

Such long life was the almost exclusive preserve of the aristocracy, as was their greater length of body. So too a personal war memorial in a church or cathedral.

———————

'the French followed at our heels . . . and we, to save our
lives . . . shot off one haragaboze'
THOMAS CHURCHYARD

THOMAS CHURCHYARD
UNDER SIEGE AT GUISNES
FRANCE, 11–22 JANUARY 1558

Guisnes was an outpost of Calais, the last English possession on French soil; Calais' fall to the French was a national disaster for Tudor England. Queen Mary, who succeeded her father Henry VIII as monarch, cried that when she died 'Calais' would be found engraved on her heart.

Thomas Churchyard, poet and soldier, was in the Guisnes outpost when the final French assault came. Holding the fort with the English were Spaniards – allies of England after Mary's marriage to Phillip of Spain – and Burgundian mercenaries.

Everyman was occupied with his own business and charge; that no person might be spared from his place . . . Monsieur D'Andelot [a French captain] . . . with 2000 soldiers, entered the Mary Bulwark, who slew the Spaniards . . . and forced as many Burgundians and English as were left alive, which were but 15 (Captain Andrea, Captain Lambert, and Myself; with twelve common soldiers) out of 400, to leap down the dykes, and so scramble for their lives; and to creep into a hole of a brick wall that my Lord Grey had broken out to receive such as escaped from the assault. But when we had entered the hole in the wall, the French followed at our heels and we, to save our lives, turned again, bending pikes against the passage, and so shot off one haragaboze; by which means, the enemy followed no further.

And yet we were in as great distress as before. For we were between two gates: and at the gate we should have entered, were two great cannon, ready charged to be shot off; to drive them back that would have set fire on the gate. And the cry and noise was so great and terrible, on all sides, that we could not be heard to speak. But, as God would [have it], Master Lewis Dive . . . heard my voice. Then I plied the matter so sore, for life; so that, with much ado, Master Dive received us into the heart of the Castle. And yet, in the opening of the gate, the French were like to enter pelley melley with us, if a cannon shot had not made [taken] place, while the gate was a shutting.

But now, we were no sooncr come before my Lord Grey but all the soldiers cried, 'Yield up the Castle, upon some reasonable composition!' And when the soldiers saw they could not have the Castle yielded, they threatened 'to fling my Lord Grey over the walls!' and that was determined, if my Lord had not prevented them with a policy. Whereupon the Captains were called together and there agreed to send me to Monsieur De Guise with an offer, that 'If we might all march, with bag and baggage, ensign displayed, and six pieces of ordnance, we would yield the Castle into the hands of the French'.

Now it was night, and I must be let out . . . but neither Drum nor Trumpet went with me: because a Trumpeter was slain as he sounded to have a parley; and, as I heard say, a Drum that would have followed me was shot in the leg. But there was no remedy – I must wade over the water, in which lay certain galthroppes, as they term them, which were great boards, full of long spikes of iron; on the which, having good boots and a stay in my hand, I was taught daintily to tread: and the night was so dark, that the enemy might not take any good mark of me, albeit they shot divers times.

At length, Churchyard reached the camp of the French commander, and after a protracted parley the English capitulated.

Calais was lost, but the English desire for a piece of France was an historical reflex. In 1563, under pressure from her advisors, Elizabeth, the Virgin Queen, interfered in the French civil war on behalf of the Huguenots (Protestants) – and in the hope of securing a corner of the country. But no sooner did an English army cross the Channel than the Huguenots made peace with their Catholic tormentors, leaving the English expeditionary force under Dudley, Earl of Warwick, stranded in Havre de Grace, amidst plague and 'Papist' demi-culverins (cannon of four-and-a-half-inch bore). Among the besieged was William Cothe.

'there was never the lyke misery . . . I thinke never to see Englonde agayne'
WILLIAM COTHE

A SOLDIER'S LETTER
HAVRE DE GRACE
FRANCE, JULY 1563

Cothe writes to Sir William Seintloe, Knight Captin to the Garde for the Quene's Majesties:

Right Worshipful Sir
. . . truly we have not left within our town and fort 2 thousand able men . . . we have skant men enough to bury our dead carkases, there dyeth Viixx and odd every day . . . I assure you by the report of such as have travayled, there was never the lyke mysery in any towne, my pen is scarce able to towche [it] . . . Who wold have thought that we should have been besiegcd vii or viii weekes, without relief, knowing that the plague hath and doth dayly so miserably devour us. If it be lost, the quene shall lose not only great honour, but suche a company [of men] withall as I am out of hope to see again brought up in my tyme . . . As for my part I thinke never to see Englond agayne, unless God so miraculously deliver us, in whom is all our trust. Dick Saunders is killed, so is our water-bayly, whose braynes were struck out [by cannon fire] going in the streets, the master of the ordennance is hurt of the face and foote. Head is hurt in the thighe, so is Captain Sawle, and Wekes with many others. Thus with my humble commendations to my very good lady, for this tyme I commyt you unto God, who preserve you, from the most miserable New Haven [Havre de Grace].

The survivors of Dudley's expedition returned home in 1564. Cothe is not thought to have been among them.

In the annals of Elizabeth's reign, the triumphs of the sea-dogs Raleigh, Drake, Hawkins and Howard loom bright. The long struggles of the soldier in the muddy Netherlands, supporting fellow Protestant Dutchmen against the Spanish, are all but forgotten – save for the much-storied demise of Sir Philip Sidney at Zutphen in 1586. Lying mortally wounded from a musket wound to his thigh, Sidney passed over his precious drink to a poor wounded soldier saying, 'Thy necessity is yet greater than mine!'

Quite possibly, Sidney's drinking companion in death had been pressed into service; the authorities of Elizabethan England offloaded, in the words of one professional soldier, Captain Rich, 'every idle fellow . . . drunkard, or seditious quarreller . . . privy picker or such a one that hath some skill in stealing a goose' into the Queen's expeditionary forces. Others went too, professionals, and patriotic volunteers from the 'trained bands', the best elements of Elizabeth's revamped part-time shire-levies, but the bulk were from the bottom layers of society.

Not, of course, that bad men made bad soldiers. When trained the self-same 'scum and dregs' beat the Spanish – reputed to be the best troops in Renaissance Europe – in a straightforward infantry battle in the dunes of Nieuport in July 1600. They did so with arquebus and pike; the long reign of the longbow was definitively over. Soldiers from the Netherlands campaign even petitioned the authorities for relief because they had gone deaf from the 'noyse of gonne shottes'.

<hr />

'Thus fortune tossed me up and down'
SYDNAM POYNTZ

AN ENGLISH MERCENARY ABROAD
C 1624–7

Poyntz was one of the 40,000 or so Britons who went abroad as mercenaries during the Thirty Years War, which ravaged Europe between 1618–48. Few, if any, memoirs illustrate more vividly than Poyntz's the vertiginous ups and downs, and the cheap loyalties, of the mercenary's career. Poyntz served initially under the Protestant soldier of fortune Count Mansfeld:

> . . . when I began to first as many others did to follow after Mansfield [Mansfeld] like mad folks we . . . found such plenty of all things for back and belly that heart could desire . . . but at length we had a Cross of fortune, for Tilly met with us and stripped us naked of all Canon, Ammunition and whatsoever we had, yea with the death of most but those that saved their lives by running away: yet at length our Army was increased again by the [German] Protestant Princes through whose plentiful Countries we had marched; that at the time when we met with Bethlem Gabor we were got to 30 thousand which . . . came to nothing,

and worse than nothing by the death of Mansfield and Weymar, and most of many brave soldiers fell into miserable captivity where we were stripped of all that we got in that long journey, but lost in an hour, and made slavish Slaves [by the Turks] & nightly chained by the feet to a great log after our sharpe days Labour . . . [I] fell to my drudgery hoping once for a light night as they say and went merrily to my Worke and strove to get the language and now & then some money by hook or by crook & hid it in odd corners: so after 2 or 3 years patience, opportunity fell that I got away and some 40 miles but was brought back with a vengeance and had 300 blows on my feet which cooled my running for one year. But God at length did prosper my intentions, for I got a brave horse which at length brought me to the skirts of Christendom, but fortune threw me again on my back: [I] met with thieves [who] got all my little Money and horse and all: O how that went to my heart to part with my horse, which had brought me out of the Devil's Mouth, and so near Christendom, [by which] I mean Austria . . . After all these Crosses the Sun began to shine clearly upon me . . . I light upon a poor Franciscan, an Englishman by name A. More, and somewhat allied by marriage to our name in Sussex. Then I rise by fortunes from a Lieutenant to a Captain of a troop of Horse in Saxon[y]'s Army, but being taken Prisoner by the Imperialists I lost again all that I had under the Saxon Duke. Thus fortune tossed me up and down, but I sped better than I expected; for I was taken Prisoner by Count Butler with whom after I got in favour he raised me extremely [well]: for by his favour he got me my first Wife, a rich Merchants daughter, who though we lived not two years together, she dying in child-bed to my great grief, yet she left me rich, and she was of an humble condition and very housewifely . . . and if she had lived but half a year longer I had come to greater Wealth: for within that time . . . her Father and Mother . . . died, and left a World of Wealth which came [went] to strangers, having no child or childs child; and not content with this Count Butler got me another Wife, rich in Land and money, but of a higher birth and spirit, and therefore would live at a higher rate than our means would well afford, for no Lady in this Land wore better clothes than she did, beside her Coach and 6 Coach-horses which with Attendants answerable to it would be very expensive . . . But

I . . . got to be by Count Butler's favour Sergeant Major of a troop of 200 horse but I was to raise them at my own charge, which was no small matter for me to do . . . but fortune turned against me again for in that cruel bloody Battle wherein the King of Sweveland was killed, my horses were either killed or ran away . . . At the beginning great store of prisoners were taken on both sides, I myself was taken prisoner three times but twice I was rescued by my fellows: the third time being taken hold of by my belt, having my sword in my hand, I threw the belt over my Ears and rescued myself. I lost three horses that day being shot under me, and I hurt under my right side and in my thigh, but I had horses without masters enough to choose and horse myself . . . all that I could do, was with my sword without a scabbard, and a daring Pistol but no powder nor shot: my last horse that was shot almost killed me for being shot in the guts, as I think, he mounted on a sudden [moment] such a height, yea I think on my conscience two yards, and sudden fell to the ground upon his bum, and with his sudden fall thrust my bum a foot into the ground and fell upon me and there lay grovelling upon me, that he put me out of my senses. I knew not how I was, but at length coming to myself, with much a do got up, and found 2 or 3 brave horses standing fighting together. I took the best, but when I came to mount him I was so bruised & with the weight of my heavy Armour that I could not get my leg into the saddle that my horse run away with me in that posture half in my saddle and half out, and so run with me till he met up with Picolominie coming running with a Troop of horse and my horse run among them that I scraped very narrowly of being thrown clean off but at length got into my saddle full of pain and could hardly sit, and followed the Troop having nothing but a daring Pistol and a naked Sword.

No more Prisoners were taken that day, every one strove to save himself. Here fortune left me almost bare again, and well she left me at so bloody a battle with life. But this loss I did prettily well recover that Winter being billeted in Austria among rich Boores, by hook or by crook, I got me strong in horse and men as I thought any had: but it fell out that so with continual marching this spring from one side of Germany to the other, to help the miserly Duke of Saxon[y] against the Sweve: and from thence back again to Lorraine from whence we went at first to Gallas who lay there entrenched with the Army, and the famine we endured so long there, my Troop grew so short & poore & the Country grown so poor that nothing was to be got amongst the Boores upon whom always lay the Commanders hopes, whilst they were in good plight, for we might be our own carvers, for we had no other pay: these failing, my thoughts were in despair of ever raising my company again: And I had almost £2000 in my purse with me at that time, yet I considered it would go hard to part with my ready Money, and nothing to be got, and I knew not how things stood at home, and to go empty handed home would not do so well, considering also I had left a costly Wife at home: and having been almost a whole year in Wars, I set up rest of my going home, and me thought a private life after these wandering wearisome marches did relish sweetly in my thoughts, and so after a long march I came near home, where I hear the true trial of fortunes mutability, which was that my Wife was killed & my child, my house burned and my goods all pillaged: My Tenants and Neighbours all served in the same sauce, the whole Village being burned; neither horse, Cowe, sheep nor Corne left to feed a Mouse. This when I come home I found true some poor people got into the ruins living with roots . . . here was little comfort for me to stay here: I presently determined to go see my dear friend Count Butler . . . but my hopes were turned upside down, for it was my good hap to see him, but he was dying, which struck more near to me, or as much as my own loss . . . but yet it somewhat revived him and what show of love a dying man can express, he did grasping my hand with all his strength and calling for his Will gave me a thousand pound therein and not long after having received his Viaticum with a great silver Crucifix in his hand in my Armes yielded up the Ghost. I had thought my heart would have burst with grief, but could get no tears out of my stony heart: but to my own heart I cried Spes et Fortuna Valete, my hopes and fortune farewell, who if he had lived I had had fortune almost at my beck; but he being dead about the £1000 he gave me his Wife being the Executrix and not so friendly to me as she might have been . . . kept me so of delays, and at last . . . away I went for England loosing my friend and his gift.

'It will kill a man to serve in a whole cuirass'
SIR EDMUND VERNEY

ARMS, ABSENCE AND MEDICINE
THE WORRIES OF A FATHER SOLDIER
YORK, 1 APRIL–4 JUNE 1639

Verney writes to his son, Ralph, whilst on active service against the Scots in the Bishops' Wars (1639–40). The latter were caused by Charles I's attempt to foist the Anglican settlement north of the border, where Presbyterianism held sway.

29 April 1639

Our army is but weak; our purse is weaker; and if we fight with these forces & early in the year we shall have our throats cut; and to delay fighting long we can not for want of money to keep our Army together. I dare say there was never so raw, so unskilful and so unwilling an Army brought to fight ... truly here are many brave Gentlemen that for point of honour must run such a hazard. For my own part I have lived till pain and trouble has made me weary to do so; and the worst that can come shall not be unwelcome to me; but it is a pity to see what men are like to be slaughtered here.

Last night there came certain news that Aberdeen is delivered up too, without so much as a bloody nose; so that to me it seems apparent that they have only pretended to make a party for the King there to cozen him of arms, munition, and money, to weaken us and strengthen themselves; for they were 6000 men well armed, in a reasonable defensive town, well victualled, and yet never struck one blow for it. So now all Scotland is gone. I would it were under the sea, for it will ask a great time, and cost much blood, to reduce them again.

I am infinitely afraid of the gout, for I feel cruel twinges, but I hope to starve it away, for God willing, I will drink but once a day. I pray put your mother in mind to send me those papers of powder I gave her to keep for me, for they are excellent to prevent the gout. As I came hither I was in so much hope of a peace that I bought a fine hunting nag by the way. I would I had my money in my purse again, for I fear I shall not hunt in haste again.

I have not yet seen my armour, for it is at Newcastle, but I believe there is never a long gauntlet sent with it. It will kill a man to serve in a whole cuirass. I am resolved to use nothing but back, breast, and gauntlet. If I had a pot for the head that were pistol proof, it may be I would use it, if it were light; but my whole helmet will be of no use to me at all. I pray go or send about this the next day after you receive this letter. Say nothing to your mother, it may give her causeless fears.

York, 1 April 1639

Since Prince Henry's death I never knew so much grief as to part from you; and truly, because I saw you equally afflicted with it, my sorrow was the greater. But, Raph, we cannot live always together. It cannot be long ere by course of nature we must be severed, and if that time be prevented by accident, yet we must resolve to bear it with that patience and courage as becomes men and Christians; and so the great God of heaven send us well to meet again, either in this world or in the next . . .

4 June 1639

. . . When my pot [helmet] is done let it be quilted and lined, and sent to me, for here is no hope at all of peace, and we are like to have the worst of the war which makes the Scots insufferably proud and insolent, insomuch that every Englishman's heart is ready to break with rage against them here.

Verney was unusual among mid-17th-century English gentlemen in having experience of war, for King Charles I had assiduously kept England aloof from the struggles on the continent. Only one in five gentlemen and peers had combat experience; in King Henry VIII's day, only a century before, every able-bodied aristocrat had been bloodied on the battlefield. There were widespread complaints that England had been too long without war to temper and fortify its people. England was 'overgrown with peace' declared a Twelfth Night masque in 1640.

All that was about to change, for England was to be ripped apart by the Civil War.

———◆◆◆———

'Our gunner tooke theire owne bullet, sent it to them againe,
and killed a horse and a man'
SERGEANT NEHEMIAH WHARTON

ENGLISH CIVIL WAR
NEHEMIAH WHARTON SKIRMISHES,
STARVES AND PLUNDERS
AUGUST 1642

The breach between the Catholic-loving, absolutist King Charles and the Puritan-Inclining, liberty-loving Parliament became definitive on 4 January 1642, when the King tried to arrest five members of the House of Commons. Charles's attempted coup caused mass protests on the streets of London, forcing him to quit the capital for Nottingham, where he raised his standard – effectively declaring war on his own country. Parliament sought to protect itself by calling up troops through the Militia Ordinance (these usually proved pitiably useless, and it relied instead on volunteers, paid out of its own coffers); Charles sent out 'commissioners of array' to raise forces from the shires loyal to him, these located mainly in the West and North. While these arrays garnered some recruits ultimately King Charles would depend on mercenaries from abroad; Prince Rupert of the Rhine ventured to England in August to aid Uncle Charles, along with a useful 100 professional German and Dutch officers.

There would be few set-piece battles. The war these volunteers, militia and mercenaries would fight for nigh on a decade would be, above all, a war of siege and skirmish.

Sergeant Nehemiah Wharton served with Colonel Denzil Holles' Regiment in the parliamentary army of Robert Devereux, Earl of Essex.

August 17, our companies, after they had taken sixe delinquents and sent them to London, returned to Alesbury this day; we retained two feild pieces and two troopes of horse, with other necessaries for warre. Wensday morning, a Warwickshire minister, which the Calualleres had pillaged to the skin, gave us a sermon. After noone our regiment marched into the field and skirmished. Thursday morning another sermon was given us. After noone our regiment marched into the feild, but by reason of foule weather were immediately definished. This night our regiment was commanded to march the next morninge by four of the clock under our Leiftenant Colonell, but our sargeants refused to surrender their halberts, and the souldiers their armes, and not to march. Friday, very early in the morninge, our Lieftenant Colonell was cashiered, for which I give you hearty thanks, and Sergeant-Major Quarles imployed in his roome, whereat both commaunders, officers, and souldiers exceedingly rejoysed. This morninge wee cherfully marched towards Buckingham in the rear of Colonell Chomlcy's regiment, by reason whereof we could get no quarter there, but were constrained to quarter ourselves about the countrey, whereupon I and three gentlemen of my company visited that thrice noble gentleman Sr Richard Inglisby, where his owne table was our quarter, and Sergeant-Major Burrif, and his sonne Captaine Inglisby, and several other noble gentlemen were our comrades.

Saturday, early in the morning, I departed hence and gathered a compliete file of my owne men about the countrey, and marched to Sir Alexander Denton's parke, who is a malignant [i.e. Royalist] fellow, and killed a fat buck, fastened his head upon my halbert, and commanded two of my pickes to bring the body after me to Buckingham, with a guard of musquetteers comminge theither. With part of it I feasted my captaine, Captaine Parker, Captaine Beacon, and Colonell Hamden's sonne, and with the rest severall leiftenants, enseignes, and serjeants, and had much thankes for my paincs. This day Sergeant Major our Generall came unto us, and declared the commaund given him over our regiments. Sunday morninge wee marched from Buckingham into Northamptonshire, a longe and tedious jorney, wantinge both bread and watei, and about ten at night came unto Byfeild in dispight of our enemies, at which towne we could get no quarter, neither meate, drinke, nor lodginge, and had we not bin suplyed with ten cart loade of provision and beare from Banbury, many of us had perished. This night our company was commanded to guard the towne all night, whiche after a longe and tedious marche, was very grevious unto me. Monday morninge wee marched into Warwickshere with about three thousand foote and four hundred horse, until we came to Southam. In the way we tooke two Calvalleres spies. This is a very malignant towne, both minister and people. We pillaged the minister, and tooke from him a drum and severall armes. This night our soildiers, wearied out, quartered themselves about the towne for foode and lodginge, but before we could eat or drinke an alarum cryed 'arme, arme, for the enemy is commenge,' and in halfe an hower all our soildiers, though dispersed, were cannybals in armes, ready to encounter enemy, cryinge out for a dish of Calvellaers to supper. Our horse were quartered about the countrey, but the enemy came not, whereupon our soildiers cryed out to have a breakefast of Cauallers. We barecaded the towne, and at every passage placed our ordinance and watched it all night, our soildiers contented to lye upon hard stones. In the morning early our enemise, consisting of about eight hundred horse and three hundred foote, with ordinance, led by the Earl of Northampton, the Lord of Carnarvan, and the Lord Compton and Captn Legge, and other, intended to set upon us before we could gather our companies together, but beinge ready all night, early in the morninge wee went to meet them with a few troopes of horse and sixe feild pieces, and beinge on fier to be at them wee marched thorow the coarn and got the hill of them, wherupon they played upon us with their ordinances, but they came short. Our gunner tooke theire owne bullet, sent it to them againe, and killed a horse and a man. After we gave them eight shot more, whereupon all their foote companies fled and offered their armes in the townes adjacent for twelve pence a peece.

Ther troopse, whelinge about, toke up their dead bodies and fled; but the horse they left behind, some of them having ther guts beaten out on both sides. One drummer, being dead at the bottom of the hill, our knapsack boyes rifled to the shirt, which was very louzy. Another drummer wee found two miles of, with his arme shot of, and lay a dieinge. Severall dead corps wee found in corne feilds, and amongst them a trumpeter, whose trumpet our horsemen sounded into Coventry. Wee tooke severall prisoners, and amongst them Capt. Legge and Captaine Clarke. From thence wee marched valiantly after them toward Coventry, and at Dunsmore Heath they threatned to give us battaile, but we got the hill of them, ordered our men, and cryed for a messe of Caiualleres to supper, as we had to breakefast; but they all fled, and we immediately marched into Coventry, where the countrey met us in armes and welcomed us, and gave us good quarter both for horse and foote.

Wharton's unpopular commanding officer, Lieutenant-Colonel Brideman, was eventually removed from his post.

Not many NCOs were as literate as the keen, shaven-headed Wharton, a former apprentice who wrote regularly to his old master, Mr Willingham, in London. On 3 September 1642 Wharton informed Willingham that 'we officers wet our halberds with a barrel of strong beer called "old Hum" which we gave to our soldiers'. On a darker note he recounted the fate of a 'whore' who had followed the army from London: 'The soldiers took her and led her about the city, set her in the pillory and afterwards in the cage. Then they ducked her in the river, and at last banished her'. Later Wharton marched on Hereford, the exertions and cold killing one of his men en route. Wharton's letters end just before the battle of Edgehill; the presumption must be that Wharton was killed there when the Royalist cavalry burst through the red-coated ranks of Colonel Denzil Holles' Regiment.

'two foot regiments . . . made us hasten as fast back as we had pursued'
SIR RICHARD BULSTRODE

EDGEHILL
A CAVALIER IN ACTION
23 OCTOBER 1642

Edgehill in Warwickshire was the first major battle of the English Civil War. The opposing sides had about 14,000 men apiece; one royalist officer, Sergeant-Major-General Sir Jacob Astley, seeing the parliamentarian hordes before him, raised his hands in prayer: 'O Lord, thou knowest how busy I must be this day: if I forget thee, do not thou forget me.'

He did not. Nor did he forget Astley's fellow royalist, Sir Richard Bulstrode, adjutant with the Prince of Wales' Regiment of Horse:

> Our whole army was drawn up in a body, the horse three deep in each wing, and the foot in the centre six deep. The Prince of Wales' regiment was on the right wing, which was commanded by Prince Rupert, and Colonel Washington was with his dragoons upon our right. In the centre was the infantry, commanded in chief by General Ruthven, and under him, by Sir Jacob Astley. The Earl of Lindsey marched on foot, in the head of the regiment of the royal foot guards, with his son, the Lord Willoughby, and Sir Edmund Verney carried the Royal Standard. The left wing of

our horse was commanded by Commissary-General Wilmot, with Lieutenant-Colonel Edward Fielding and some other principal officers; and Lieutenant-Colonel George Lisle, with Lieutenant-Colonel John Ennis were in the left wing, with a regiment of dragoons, to defend the briars on that side, and we had a body of reserve, of six hundred horse, commanded by the Earl of Carnarvon. When our army was drawn up at the foot of the hill and ready to march, all the generals went to the King (who intended to march with the army) and desired he would retire to a rising ground, some distance from thence, on the right, with the Prince of Wales and the Duke of York (having his guard of Pensioners on horseback with him) from whence he might see the issue of the battle and be out of danger, and that otherwise the army would not advance towards the enemy. To which the King (very unwillingly) was at last persuaded.

Just before we began our march, Prince Rupert passed from one wing to the other, giving positive orders to the horse, to march as close as was possible, keeping their ranks with sword in hand, to receive the enemy's shot, without firing either carbine or pistol, till we broke in amongst the enemy, and then to make use of our firearms as need should require, which order was punctually observed.

The enemy stayed to receive us in the same posture as was formerly declared; and when we came within cannon shot of the enemy, they discharged at us three pieces of cannon from their left wing, commanded by Sir James Ramsey; which cannon mounted over our troops, without doing any hurt, except that their second shot killed a quarter-master in the rear of the Duke of York's troop. We soon after engaged each other, and our dragoons on our right beat the enemy from the briars, and Prince Rupert led on our right wing so furiously, that, after a small resistance, we forced their left wing, and were masters of their cannon; and the Prince being extremely eager of this advantage (which he better knew how to take than to keep) was not content with their cannon, and keeping their ground, but eagerly pursued the enemy, who fled on the other side of Kineton towards Warwick. And we of the Prince of Wales' regiment (who were all scattered) pursued also, till we met with two foot regiments of Hampden and Holles, and with a regiment of horse coming from Warwick to their army, which made us hasten as fast back as we had pursued.

In this pursuit I was wounded in the head by a person who turned upon me and struck me with his pole-axe, and was seconding his blow, when Sir Thomas Byron being near, he shot him dead with his pistol, by which means I came back. In fine, by meeting these three regiments, we were obliged to return back to our army and then found our great error, in leaving our foot naked who were rudely handled by the enemy's horse and foot together in our absence, who fell principally upon the King's royal regiment of foot guards, who lost eleven of thirteen colours, the King's Standard-Bearer, Sir Edmund Verney, killed, and the Royal Standard taken, which was presently retaken by Captain John Smith, who was knighted for it that night by the King, under the Standard Royal and made a banneret with the usual ceremonies; and had afterwards a large medal of gold given him, with the King's picture on the one side, and the banner on the other, which he always wore to his dying day, in a large green watered ribband, cross his shoulders . . .

Now, when we returned from following the enemy, the night came soon upon us, whereas, in all probability, we had gained the victory, and made an end of the war, if we had only kept our ground after we had beaten the enemy, and not left our foot naked to their horse and foot. And, to add to our misfortune, a careless soldier, in fetching powder (where a magazine was) clapt his hand carelessly into a barrel of powder, with his match lighted betwixt his fingers, whereby much powder was blown up and many kill'd . . .

On Monday morning, being next after the battle, several parties were sent down to view the dead, the greatest part of the enemy having retired in the night to the town of Kineton, which was near them; and Mr Adrian Scroop having seen his father fall (being much wounded) desired the Duke of Lennox to speak to the King, that one of his coaches might go with him, to bring up his father's body; which being granted, he found his father stripped, with several very dangerous wounds, and that he was alive. Whereupon he lap'd him up in his cloak, and brought him in the coach, where he was presently dressed by the King's chirurgeons, and by their care and skill was cured, and lived many years after, tho' he had seventeen wounds, and had died upon the place, but that the coldness of the weather stopp'd the bleeding of his wounds, which saved also several other men's lives that were wounded.

Prince Rupert's ill-disciplined (cavalier, even) pursuit of the Roundheads into Kineton probably cost the royalists a victory. In the event, Edgehill ended in a draw. Sir Edmund Verney, killed clutching the Royal Standard so firmly his fingers had to be prised from it, had perhaps welcomed death. To his grief his beloved son Ralph had declared for Parliament.

The Verneys were not the only ones to find relationships divided by the sword.

'but I must be true to the cause wherein I serve'
SIR WILLIAM WALLER

FRIENDS BY THE SWORD DIVIDED
16 JUNE 1643

In this moving communication, the parliamentarian Waller writes to his friend Sir Ralph Hopton, a royalist.

To my noble friend Sir Ralph Hopton at Wells,
Sir,
  The experience I have had of your worth and the happiness I have enjoyed in your friendship are wounding considerations when I look upon this present distance between us. Certainly my affections to you are so unchangeable that hostility itself cannot violate my friendship to your person, but I must be true to the cause wherein I serve ... I should most gladly wait on you according to your desire, but that I look upon you as you are engaged in that party beyond a possibility of retreat and consequently incapable of being wrought upon by any persuasion. And I know the conference could never be so close between us, but that it would take wind and receive a construction to my dishonour. That great God which is the searcher of my heart, knows with what a sad sense I go upon this service and with what a perfect hatred I detest this war without an enemy, but I look upon it as *opus domini*, which is enough to

silence all passion in me. The god of peace in his good time send us peace and in the meantime fit us to receive it. We are both upon the stage and must act those parts that are assigned us in this tragedy. Let us do it in a way of honour and without personal animosities. Whatsoever the issue be, I shall never willingly relinquish the dear title of your most affectionate friend and faithful servant,

William Waller.

The two friends met in battle three weeks later at Lansdown Hill, outside Bath. A Roundhead charge was repulsed by Cornish pikemen, who then marched up the hill to capture Waller's cannon. Following them up was the royalist captain Richard Atkyns:

As I went up the hill, which was very steep and hollow, I met several dead and wounded officers brought off, besides several running away, that I had much ado to get up by them. When I came to the top of the hill I saw Sir Bevil Grenville's stand of pikes, which certainly preserved our army from a total rout with the loss of his most precious life. They stood as upon the eaves of a house for steepness, but as unmoveable as a rock. On which side of this stand of pikes our horse were, I could not discover, for the air was so darkened by the smoke of the powder that for a quarter of an hour together (I dare say) there was no light seen, but when the fire of the volleys of shot gave, and 'twas the greatest storm that I ever saw, in which thought I knew not whither to go, nor what to do, my horse had two or three musket bullets in him immediately, which made him tremble under me at a rate, and I could hardly with spurs keep him from lying down, but he did me the service to carry me off to a led horse and then die.

Just over a week later, the armies of Waller and Hopton engaged once more, this time outside Devizes. Once again Richard Atkyns was there:

'he was too well armed all over for a pistol bullet to do him any hurt'
CAPTAIN RICHARD ATKYNS

THE DIFFICULTY OF KILLING SIR ARTHUR HESELRIGE
ROUNDWAY DOWN
13 JULY 1643

We lost no time but marched towards the enemy, who stood towards the top of the hill; the foot in the middle between two wings of horse, and the cannon before the foot . . . The charge was so sudden that I had hardly time to put on my arms. We advanced at a full trot three deep and kept in order. The enemy kept their station and their right wing of horse, being cuirassiers, were I'm sure five if not six deep, in so close order that Punchinello himself, had he been there, could not have gotten in to them . . .

'Twas my fortune in a direct line to charge their General of Horse which I supposed to be so by his place. He discharged his carbine first but at a distance not to hurt us, and afterwards one of his pistols, before I came up to him and missed with both. I then immediately struck into him, and touched him before I discharged mine; and I'm sure I hit him, for he staggered and presently wheeled off from his party and ran . . .

I pursued him, and had not gone twenty yards after him, but I heard a voice saying, ''Tis Sir Arthur Heselrige – Follow him!' But from which party the voice came I knew not, they being joined, nor never did know till about seven years since. But follow him I did and in six score yards I came up to him, and discharged the other pistol at him, and I'm sure I hit his head for I touched it before I gave fire and it amazed him at that present, but he was too well armed all over for a pistol bullet to do him any hurt, having a coat of mail over his arms and a headpiece (I am confident) musket proof, his sword had two edges and a ridge in the middle, and mine was a strong tuck. After I had slackened my pace a little, he was gone twenty yards from me, riding three quarters speed and down the side of a hill, his posture was waving his sword on the right and left hand of his horse, not looking back to see whether he were pursued or not, (as I conceive) to daunt any horse that should come up to him.

In about six score more yards I came up to him again (having a very swift horse that Cornet Washnage gave me) and stuck by him a good while, and tried him from head to the saddle and could not penetrate him nor do him any hurt. But in this attempt he cut my horse's nose, that you might put your finger in the wound, and gave me such a blow on the inside of my arm amongst the veins that I could hardly hold my sword. He went on as before and I slackened my pace again and found my horse got up to him again, thinking to have pulled him off his horse. But he having now found the way, struck my horse upon the cheek, and cut off half the headstall of my bridle; but falling off from him, I ran his horse into the body and resolved to attempt nothing further than to kill his horse; all this time we were together hand to fist.

In this nick of time came up Cornet Holmes to my assistance (who never failed me in time of danger), and went up to him with great resolution, and felt him before he discharged his pistol, and though I saw him hit him, 'twas but a flea-biting to him. Whilst he charged him, I employed myself in killing his horse, and ran him into several places, and upon the faltering of his horse his headpiece opened behind, and I gave him a prick in the neck, and I had run him through the head if my horse had not stumbled at the same place. Then came in Captain Buck, a gentleman of my troop, and discharged his pistol upon him also, but with the same success as before, and being a very strong man, and charging with a mighty sword, stormed him and amazed him, but he fell off again. By this time his horse began to be faint with bleeding, and fell off from his rate, at which said Sir Arthur, 'What good will it do you to kill a poor man?' Said I 'Take quarter then', with that he stopped his horse and I came up to him, and bid him deliver his sword, which he was loathe to do. And being tied twice about his wrist, he was fumbling a great while before he would part with it. But before he delivered it, there was a runaway troop of theirs that had espied him in hold. Says one of them 'My Lord General is taken prisoner!'; says another, 'Sir Arthur Heselrige is taken prisoner! Face about and charge!' With that they rallied and charged us, and rescued him; wherein I received a shot with a pistol, which only took off the skin upon the blade bone of my shoulder.

This story being related to the King at a second or third hand, his answer was, 'Had he been victualled as well as fortified, he might have endured a siege of seven years'. His horse died in the place, and they horsed him upon another and went away together . . .

Possibly Sir Arthur was wearing full armour, although most cavalrymen of the Civil War preferred just a metal helmet and breastplate, trusting that this allowed greater freedom of movement. Under the breastplate was invariably worn an ox-hide coat, which was surprisingly effective in stopping sword strokes, even musket shots.

'For God's sake . . . come home'
SUSAN OWEN

A LETTER TO A SOLDIER HUSBAND
LONDON, 5 SEPTEMBER 1643

Owen's husband, John, served with the 'trained bands' of the London parliamentary militia; he took part in the raising of the siege of Gloucester, a success which helped turn the war in Parliament's favour.

Most tender and dear heart, my kind affection remembered unto you. I am like never to see you more I fear, and if you ask the reason why, the reason is this, either I am afraid the Cavaliers will kill you or death will deprive you of me, being full of grief for you, which I fear will cost me my life. I do much grieve that you be so hard-hearted to me. Why could you not come home with Master Murphy on Saturday? Could not you venture as well as he? But you did it on purpose to show your hatred to me. There is none of our neighbours with you that has a wife but Master Fletcher and Master Norwood and yourself. Everybody can come but you. I have sent one to Oxford to get a pass for you to come home, but when you come you must use your wits. I am afraid if you do not come home, I shall much dishonour God more than you can honour him. Therefore if I do miscarry, you shall answer for it. Pity me for God's sake and come home. Will nothing prevail with

you? My cousin Jane is now with me and prays for your speedy
return. For God's sake come home. So with my prayer for you I
rest your loving wife.
Susan Owen

'a perfect manumission from the hated life I had lived . . . among soldiers'
ADAM MARTINDALE

THE RELUCTANT SOLDIER
1644

By 1643 both sides in the Civil War had resorted to conscription. Martindale, as a
schoolmaster, was exempted from the draft to the parliamentary army but, under
pressure from family and his Lancashire Puritan community, he joined the ranks.
Reluctantly.

I was therefore well content to come down a peg lower, accepting
of the chief clerk's place in the foot regiment, which place
(though below the other for profit and credit) gave me better
content; for now I lived in peace, and enjoyed sweet communion
with the religious officers of the company, which used to meet
every night at one anothers' quarters, by turns, to read scriptures,
to confer of good things, and to pray together. My work also was
easy enough, and such as gave me time for my studies, being only
to keep a list of the officers' and soldiers' names, and to call them
upon occasion. Nor was I to carry either musket, pike, halberd, or
any other weapon, only for fashion sake I wore a sword, as even
ministers in those days ordinarily did.

But in this condition I remained not long, for the quarter-
master of the troop being no scholar, would needs have me into
it, to assist him in making tickets, though under the name and
notion of clerk of the troop, to whose office, in strictness, it
belonged not. But that work was not great; and the rest of my
employment was much-what the same with that in the company. I
was not by my office either to wear armour, or buff-coat; to stand
upon guard, or to ride out as a scout. And accordingly I was not
furnished with a charging-horse, war-saddle, pistols, holsters, or
carbine, but only with a little hackney, and an ordinary saddle and

bridle to ride along with the rest; and here also I had the comfort and benefit of some devout persons' company. After some time, Mr Thompson, the chaplain of the regiment, was sent to us to tender to us the Covenant and to satisfy any that should make scruple, which he did so effectually, that I think not one refused it.

In this easy employment of clerk of the troop and deputy quarter-master, I continued till the taking of Liverpool by Prince Rupert; in which space of time, the garrison at Lathom making some sallies out in the night, did such exploits as the colonels for the parliament took for unsufferable affronts, and laid siege to it. This was instrumental to bring an old house upon our heads: for the prince going to raise the siege at York, (where he received a great overthrow) the Earl of Derby brought him through Lancashire, where his army, after two smart repulses, took Bolton by storm (the works having been sleighted, and in very bad order) putting about one thousand eight hundred to the sword. Then spreading themselves up and down the country, made woeful work wherever they came. My brother Henry was so lately married, that he easily secured those few goods he had, together with himself and his wife, in the garrison at Warrington. My brother Thomas secured himself and some choice goods there also, but the rest, together with his poor wife and children, were at the mercy of his enemies, who were so severe that they scarcely left his family anything in the world to subsist on. But his great stock of cattle were seized upon by a great papist in the neighbourhood, intentionally for his own use, but eventually for my brother. But my poor father fared much worse, for they took the old man prisoner, and used him most barbarously, forcing him to march in his stockings, without shoes, and snapping his ears with their firelock-pistols. His house they plundered of everything they thought worth carrying away, in carts which they brought to his door to that purpose, and were sore troubled (good men!) that the walls being stone, and the roof well shot over within, they could fasten no fire upon the house, though they several times essayed so to do. His stock of cattle they wholly drove away, and he never had an hoof again, amongst which was an excellent colt, almost ready for service, which, in regard of its high mettle and curious shapes, resembling its dam, which was a gallant mare, he valued an high rate. This, being exceeding hard to be taken, they were resolved to shoot, (out of perfect malice to him,) but at last, with difficulty, they caught her, and away she went with the rest . . .

When Liverpool was surrendered upon terms of free-quarter, though Rupert's men, upon their first entrance, did (notwithstanding these terms) slay almost all they met with, to the number of three hundred and sixty and, among other, divers of their own friends, and some artificers that never bore arms in their lives, yea, one poor blind man; yet the first that I met with offered me quarter before I asked.

Though I lost there, in a manner, all I had, viz.: my mare, books, money, and clothes, and my relations were in such distress as even now I declared, I was sufficiently provided for, and my spirit cheerfully supported throughout a tedious imprisonment of about nine weeks, though I neither knew where I should be supplied for a week beforehand, nor by what means I could expect deliverance.

When I was at last set at liberty, a free-school was vacant, and (as it were) waiting for me, in Over Whitley, in Cheshire, with which I closed when I lacked a few weeks of twenty-one years old; and this was a perfect manumission from the hated life I had lived about two years among soldiers; though mine office was all along to employ my pen, not my sword, and to spend ink, not spill blood.

For every Adam Martindale there was an Englishman who discovered he rather liked soldiering. Sir William Waller, though he loathed the Civil War, 'this war without an enemy', tried to enlist as a Venetian mercenary when Parliament dispensed with his services; even the King, sensitive and delicate, found that soldiering in the field put him in rude health.

———⇒•⇐———

'Q. What are the principall things required in a Souldier?
A. That he be religious'

ANONYMOUS

THE SOLDIER'S CATECHISM

1644

Composed in 1644 for Parliament's army, those 'that have taken up Armes in this cause of God and his people, especially the common soldiers'.

Q. What profession are you?
A. I am a Christian and a souldier.
Q. Is it lawfull for Christians to be souldiers?
A. Yea doubtlesse; we have Arguments enough to warrant it.
  1. God calls himself a man of war, and Lord of Hosts.
  2. Abraham had a Regiment of 318 Trained men.
  3. David was employed in fighting the Lords battles.
  4. The Holy Ghost makes honourable mention of Davids worthies.
  5. God himself taught David to fight.
  6. The noble gift of valour is given for this purpose.
Q. What are the principall things required in a Souldier?
A. 1. That he be religious and godly.
  2. That he be courageous and valiant.
  3. That he be skilfull in the Militarie Profession . . .
Q. What is the reason then there be so many lewd and wicked men in the Parliament's Army?
A. 1. Because Commanders in Chief are not more carefull in choosing godly officers.
  2. Because honest religious men are not more forward to put themselves in this service of God and his Church.
  3. Because Order and Discipline is not more strictly executed by Superiours.
  4. Because Officers in Towns and Counties aim to presse the scumme and refuse of men, and so by easing themselves pesture our Armies with base conditioned people . . .
Q. What are the principall enemies to courage and valour?
A. 1. Want of experience; fresh-water souldiers are commonly faint-hearted souldiers; whereas they that have been used

to the Warres are usually of undaunted spirits.
2. Want of metall: some mens spirits are naturally so low and base, that they will never prove good souldiers. As it is with cocks so it is with men . . .
3. Want of Faith . . .
4. Want of Innocency and a good conscience . . .
5. Want of wisdome and consideration: for surely if men would seriously consider the evills of cowardice and the excellency of valour, it would make them abhorre the one and be ambitious of the other . . .

Q. What should be done to make souldiers skillful in their art?
A. 1. Officers should be very diligent on teaching and exercising their men.
2. Common souldiers should make it their business to learn and get what cunning they can.
3. Every souldier should seeke to God by prayer, that he would instruct and teach them: for it is the blessing of God that makes men profit in any profession.
4. Both Commanders, Officers and common Souldiers may advantage themselves by reading and observing what hath been written by eminent Souldiers, of this Art.

Q. How ought commanders and officers to carry themselves towards their souldiers?
A. 1. Religiously . . . lovingly . . . discreetly . . . justly . . .

Q. How should inferior Souldiers demeane themselves towards their Commanders and Officers?
A. 1. They must acknowledge and honour them as Superiours and account them as men set over them by the providence of God and wisdome of the State.
2. They must be exactly obedient to their command evern for conscience sake. Ro. 13.5. Of all men Souldiers are most strictly tied to obedience, the want whereof may prove of very dangerous consequences.

Q. What is your opinion of those Souldiers that run away from their Colours?
A. 1. Such are, by Martiall Law, to suffer death, and surely, they deserve it. . . .

As the authors of 'The Soldier's Catechism' hoped, the parliamentary army was more 'Godly', more moral, than its royalist opponent. Even royalist officers allowed it. Whereas the Roundheads (as Parliament's soldiers were dubbed in reference to their pudding-basin haircuts) were seemingly never charged with rape, royalist forces made it a stock-in-trade. Just one instance will serve, their occupation of Puritan Birmingham:

> Having thus possessed themselves of the town, they ran into every house cursing and damning, threatening and terrifying the poor women most terribly, setting naked swords and pistols to their breasts . . . They beastly assaulted many women's chastity, and impudently made brags of it afterwards, how many they had ravished; glorying in their shame. Especially the French [mercenaries] among them were outrageously lascivious and lecherous . . . That night few or none [of them] went to bed, but sat up revelling, robbing and tyrannizing poor affrighted women and prisoners, drinking drunk, healthing upon their knees, yea, drinking drunk healths to Prince Rupert's dog.

Some sins, however, were common to both sides. Royalist and Roundhead alike plundered civilians. In Oxfordshire, labourer Thomas Tasker petitioned a parliamentary committee for the return of his goods:

> Your petitioner, being a poor man and aged, in December 1644, in the middle of the night, a party of major Purefoy's soldiers . . . came into his house and violently took away the most part of his household goods, to the value of £10 or upwards and also took away your petitioner to Compton where he was unjustly imprisoned . . . They [the soldiers] had in money 10s, 7 pairs of sheets, 3 brass kettles, 2 brass pots, 5 pewter dishes and other small pewter, 4 shirts, 4 smocks, other small linens, 2 coats, 1 cloak, 1 waistcoat, 7 dozen of candles, 1 frying pan, 1 spit, 2 pairs of pot hooks, 1 peck of wheat, 4 bags, some oatmeal, some salt . . . a basket full of eggs . . . pins, bowls, dishes, spoons, ladles, drinking pots and whatsoever else they could lay their hands on . . .

One civilian, Henry Townshend in Worcester, despairing of the depredations of the royalist soldiery garrisoned there (which included dismantling citizens' houses to sell for liquor), suggested that good Christians insert in their Litany: 'From the plundering of soldiers, their Insolency, Cruelty, Atheism, Blasphemy and Rule over us, *Libera nos Domine*.'

The crimes of the soldiers were not restricted to civilian targets. Atrocities on the battlefield became common as the war wore on. Edmund Ludlow, the Roundhead cavalryman, recounts an incident from 1644.

In the mean time Sir Francis Doddington had caused the two men that he had taken at Warder to be hanged, upon pretence that they ran away from him; and having brought some pieces of cannon before Woodhouse, made a breach so considerable in the wall, that the besieged were necessitated to surrender at mercy, but they found very little, for they were presently stripped of all that was good about them: and Sir Francis Doddington being informed by one Bacon, who was parson of the parish, that one of the prisoners had threatened to stick in his skirts, as he called it, for reading the Common-Prayer, struck the man so many blows upon the head, and with such force, that he broke his skull, and caused him to fall into a swound; from which he was no sooner recovered, but he was picked out to be one of the twelve which Sir Francis had granted to Sir William St. Leger to be hanged, in lieu of six Irish rebels who had been executed at Warum by Col. Sydenham, in pursuance of an order from the Parliament to give them no quarter. These twelve being most of them clothiers, were hanged upon the same tree; but one of them breaking his halter, desired that what he had suffered might be accepted, or else that he might fight against any two for his life . . .

'*Sir, God hath taken away your eldest Son by a cannon-shot*'
COLONEL OLIVER CROMWELL

CIVIL WAR
DEATH OF A NEPHEW AT MARSTON MOOR
2 JULY 1644

Oliver Cromwell was 43 before he took up arms and raised a horse regiment for the Eastern Association of the parliamentary army in 1642. If he was late to warring, he made up for inexperience by being a natural commander of men; one moreover, who selected on ability not class: 'I had rather have a plain russet-coated captain that knows what he fights for, and loves what he knows, than that which you call a gentleman and is nothing else'.

Cromwell was also an instinctive battlefield tactician; it was the counter-strike by Cromwell's cavalry 'Ironsides' that enabled Parliament to win the biggest battle of the Civil War, that at Marston Moor on a late summer's evening in 1644. But for Cromwell's family, the victory was touched by tragedy. He writes to his brother-in-law, Colonel Valentine Walton.

It's our duty to sympathize in all mercies; and to praise the Lord together in chastisements or trials, that so we may sorrow together.

Truly England and the Church of God hath had a great favour from the Lord, in this great Victory given unto us, such as the like never was since this War began. It had all the evidences of an absolute Victory obtained by the Lord's blessing upon the Godly Party principally. We never charged but we routed the enemy. The Left Wing, which I commanded, being our own horse, saving a few Scots in our rear, beat all the Prince's horse. God made them as stubble to our swords. We charged their regiments of foot with our horse, and routed all we charged. The particulars I cannot relate now; but I believe, of Twenty-thousand the Prince hath not Four-thousand left. Give glory, all the glory, to God . . .

Sir, God hath taken away your eldest Son by a cannon-shot. It brake his leg. We were necessitated to have it cut off, whereof he died.

Sir, you know my own trials this way: but the Lord supported me with this, That the Lord took him into the happiness we all pant for and live for. There is your precious child full of glory, never to know sin or sorrow any more. He was a gallant young man, exceedingly gracious. God give you His comfort. Before his death he was so full of comfort that to Frank Russel and myself he could not express it, 'It was so great above his pain.' This he said to us. Indeed it was admirable. A little after, he said, One thing lay upon his spirit. I asked him, What that was? He told me it was, That God had not suffered him to be anymore the executioner of His enemies. At his fall, his horse being killed with the bullet, and as I am informed three horses more, I am told he bid them, Open to the right and left, that he might see the rogues run. Truly he was exceedingly beloved in the Army, of all that knew him. But few knew him; for he was a precious young man, fit for God. You have cause to bless the Lord. He is a glorious Saint in Heaven; wherein you ought exceedingly to rejoice. Let this drink up your sorrow; seeing these are not feigned words to comfort you, but the thing is so real and undoubted a truth. You may do all things by the strength of Christ. Seek that, and you shall easily bear your trial. Let this public mercy to the Church of God make you to forget your private sorrow. The Lord be your strength: so prays

    Your truly faithful and loving brother

My love to your Daughter, and my Cousin Perceval, Sister Desborow and all friends with you.

Among the 4,000 royalist victims at Marston Moor was Prince Rupert's poodle dog, Boy. The prince himself, his horse shot from under him, hid in a bean field before fleeing.

'therefore put us not of with the cocking of a pistol'
THOMAS WEBB, WILLIAM SEDWELL ET AL

SOLDIERS DEMAND THEIR PAY

NORTHAMPTONSHIRE, 14 APRIL 1645

A letter to the parliamentary commander Sir William Luke from his men.

Wee are fully resolved that you are not ignorant of our wants and grievances, in regard that our pay is soe long kept from us; and who is the occasion, it is unknowne to us. In the meane tyme wee find many commaunds from your Honor which except speedily redressed will prove very disadvantagious to the State. As for those that concerne our dutyes in martiall discipline, it is best knowne to your Honor how ready wee have beene to obay; but for those that concerne our quartering in the country, wee may have just cause to feare that the people may rise and cutt our throates, if an enemy approach from whom they may expect some releife from such oppression; as by their continuall murmering appeares that their grievances are soe great that their generall expressions are that wee eate the meate out of their childrens mouthes, they paying their contribution and wee neither receiving any pay to give some small satisfaction for quarter, nor they expecting any abatement out of their taxe, having beene soe long deceived by fayre promises; which is probably as greate oppression to the country as Pharoh's demaunding the full tayle of bricke, without allowance of straw. Your Honor may bee pleased to consider the crye of the Country which is dayly in our eares, and our wants likewise, which wee are very sensible is likely to bee greater if wee march further without mony. Wee are not ignorant of the extraordinary sums of mony that are allowed by the Parliament for the payment of the garrison, which wee conceive should amount to above four weeks pay in four months at 14s. per weeke; and the most of us paying a months quarters out of it, our desire is that yor Honor would speedily redresse it, considering that wee can neither have apparell for our selves nor necessarye for our horse, noe nor soe much as powder and bullett, from the garrison, although to secure it from the approach of the enemy, without mony or security; and finally wee desire that your Honor may understand, that, if upon this reasonable declaration, wee cannot have our pay upon reasonable tearmes, that wee shall more fully declare our selves, and appeale to the honorable the High Court of Parliament. In the meane tyme until wee have an answer from your Honor wee rest at our quarters at Cosgrave. . . .

Our demaunds is ten weekes pay at the least, and therefore put us not of with the cocking of a pistol, or stearne threatening, as upon the like occasion hath beene formerly.

Small pay or no pay were the bugbears of the Civil War soldier.

For Roundhead soldiers finances were destined to improve, however. In April 1645, at Cromwell's urging, the flagging militias of Parliament were replaced by a professional, trained army. One, moreover, that was paid properly, out of taxation.

And so Britain's first standing army was born.

Numbering some 22,000 men, the 'New Model Army' was Cromwell's Ironside division writ large: command was centralised and promotion was by merit; one cavalry colonel, Thomas Shelbourne, was a former shepherd.

Cohering the New Model Army was religious purpose; the Soldier's Catechism was alive and well within it. There was also a distinct undertow of political radicalism headed by the Leveller Colonel Lilburne. Britain's first standing army was an ideological army; not until the Second World War, when troops overwhelmingly voted Labour in 1945, would Britain see another.

'Eleven huge granadoes like so many tumbling demi-phaetons'
RANDLE HOLME

INFERNO
INSIDE THE SIEGE OF CHESTER
1645–6

Any lingering hope the King had of defeating Parliament was dashed to death by the New Model Army at Naseby, Leicestershire, on 14 June 1645. The rest was mere, but brutal, mopping up of such exasperating royalist holdouts as Chester, which was treated to blockade and barrages of mortars (granadoes). Witness to life – and death – on the receiving end of Roundhead siege warfare was Randle Holme, a Chester merchant:

> December 10 1645: Eleven huge granadoes like so many tumbling demi-phaetons threaten to set the city, if not the world, on fire. This was a terrible night indeed, our houses like so many split vessels crash their supporters and burst themselves in sunder through the very violence of these descending firebrands ... another Thunder-crack invites our eyes to the most miserable spectacle that spite could possibly present us with – two houses in the Watergate skippes [hit] ... the whole fabric is in perfect chaos ... The grandmother, mother and three children are struck stark dead and buried in the ruins of this humble edifice, a sepulcher well worth the enemy's remembrance.

The Roundhead blockade was also taking its toll:

> December 17 1645: Poor in very great want and many that have lived well formerly go a begging – little bread or beer left. The Welsh soldiers [in the garrison] almost famished. Not above 20 cattle in City. They are expecting relief and they will shortly make a sudden sally out through Eastgate and Northgate and their sally port under the Sadler's Tower. 3,000 fighting men in City, one

half Welsh, about 50 horse. The poor people and soldiers willing the city should be delivered up.

In January 1646 troops in the Welsh companies mutinied. 'On Thursday last,' recorded Lieuteant Philemon Mainwaring of the Chester garrison, 'in evening at the Parade 300 Welshmen laid down their arms and told Lord Byron unless he would afford them more meat they would do no more duty, but would rather choose to stand to the mercy of the enemy than to be starved in town.' There was no more meat. Chester duly capitulated.

. By now the royal game was up, and the king surrendered in June 1646. It fell to Cornet Joyce to take the king prisoner. When the king asked by what authority he was being arrested, Joyce informed him 'the soldiery of the army'. 'What commission do you have?' taunted the king. 'Here,' answered Joyce, pointing to the mounted troopers behind him.

Charles I had learned nothing from his defeat. In a fit of delusion he re-opened the Civil War in 1648. If anything the second bout of the Civil War was more bloody than the first.

'our men . . . were ordered by me to put them all to the sword'
LIEUTENANT-GENERAL OLIVER CROMWELL

THE STORMING OF DROGHEDA
10–11 SEPTEMBER 1649

Fearing that Ireland would be used as a launch pad for a royalist invasion of the mainland, Cromwell crossed to Ireland, where his ruthlessly efficient army captured the garrison at Drogheda, a seaport on the Boyne. An estimated 4,000 defendants were slaughtered.

For the Honourable William Lenthall Esquire, Speaker of the Parliament of England: These.

Dublin
17th September, 1649

Sir,

. . . Upon Tuesday the 10th instant, about five o'clock in the evening, we began the Storm; and after some hot dispute we entered, about seven or eight hundred men; the enemy disputing it very stiffly with us. And indeed, through the advantages of the place, and the courage God was pleased to give the defenders, our men were forced to retreat quite out of the breach, not without some considerable loss; Colonel Castle being there shot in the head, whereof he presently died; and divers officers and soldiers doing their duty killed and wounded. There was a Tenalia to flanker the south Wall of the Town, between Duleek Gate and the corner Tower before mentioned; – which our men entered, wherein they found some forty or fifty of the Enemy, which they put to the sword. And this 'Tenalia' they held: but it being without the Wall, and the sally-port through the Wall into that Tenalia being choked up with some of the Enemy which were killed in it, it proved of no use for an entrance into the Town that way.

Although our men that stormed the breaches were forced to recoil, as is before expressed; yet, being encouraged to recover their loss, they made a second attempt; wherein God was pleased so to animate them that they got ground of the enemy, and by the goodness of God, forced him to quit his entrenchments. And after a very hot dispute, the Enemy having both horse and foot, and we only foot, within the Wall – they gave ground, and our men became masters both of their retrenchments and of the Church; which, indeed, although they made our entrance the more difficult, yet they proved of excellent use to us; so that the Enemy could not now annoy us with their horse, but thereby we had the advantage to make good the ground, that so we might let in our own horse; which accordingly was done, though with much difficulty.

Divers of the Enemy retreated into the Mill-Mount: a place very strong and difficult of access; being exceedingly high, having a good graft, and strong palisadoed. The Governor, Sir Arthur Ashton, and divers considerable Officers being there, our men getting up to them, were ordered by me to put them all to the sword. And indeed, being in the heat of action, I forbade them to spare any that were in arms in the Town: and, I think, that night they put to the sword about 2000 men; – divers of the officers and soldiers being fled over the Bridge into the other part of the Town, where about 100 of them possessed St. Peter's Church-steeple, some the west Gate, and others a strong Round Tower next the Gate called St. Sunday's. These being summoned to yield to mercy, refused. Whereupon I ordered the steeple of St. Peter's Church to be fired, when one of them was heard to say in the midst of the flames: 'God damn me, God confound me; I burn, I burn.'

The next day, the other two Towers were summoned; in one of which was about six or seven score; but they refused to yield themselves: and we knowing that hunger must compel them, set only good guards to secure them from running away until their stomachs were come down. From one of the said Towers, notwithstanding their condition, they killed and wounded some of our men. When they submitted, their officers were knocked on the head; and every tenth man of the soldiers killed; and the rest shipped for the Barbadoes. The soldiers in the other Tower were all spared, as to their lives only; and shipped likewise for the Barbadoes.

I am persuaded that this is a righteous judgement of God upon these barbarous wretches, who have imbrued their hands in so much innocent blood; and that it will tend to prevent the effusion of blood for the future. Which are the satisfactory grounds to such actions, which otherwise cannot but work remorse and regret. The officers and soldiers of this Garrison were the flower of their army. And their great expectation was, that our attempting this place would put fair to ruin us . . . And now give me leave to say how it comes to pass that this work is wrought. It was set upon some of our hearts, That a great thing should be done, not by power or might, but by the Spirit of God. And is it not so, clearly? That which caused your men to storm so courageously, it was the Spirit of God, who gave your men courage, and took it away again; and gave the Enemy courage, and took it away again; and gave your men courage again, and therewith this happy success. And therefore it is good that God alone have all the glory . . .

Your most obedient servant,

OLIVER CROMWELL

The war in Ireland was profitable, too. Seized Irish lands were doled out to 33,000 English soldiers, creating a Protestant ascendancy in Northern Ireland that would last for four centuries.

After Ireland, Cromwell – in his finest battlefield hour – crushed the pro-royalist Scots at Dunbar in 1650. The Scots, said Cromwell, 'fell like stubble to our swords'; they assuredly fell like stubble – but to musket fire. Cromwell was a military innovator, quick to see the advantage of the new fangled flintlock over the matchlock, with its burning cord which so often failed. In his dawn attack at Dunbar, most of the Scots didn't even have their matchlocks lit when the New Model Army opened fire with their hi-tech flintlocks.

By now Our Chief of Men was not only commander of the army, but ruler of Britain in what was, to all intents and purposes, a military dictatorship. A soldier's republic.

Like so many other British soldiers, Cromwell fell not to enemy steel but to disease. He was defeated by bronchitis in September 1658. For want of the greater evil of anarchy, the army, the only power in the land, invited the Stuarts back to England's throne. Soldiers had ended the monarchy; soldiers restored it.

The terror of Civil War and military dictatorship left a burdensome legacy for the British soldier. The public disliked and dreaded him.

Charles II, doubtless, shared the sentiment, but his throne needed protection from the simmering anger of old Commonwealth devotees. The solution was politic if ironic.

In the morning of 14 February 1661 two regiments of the New Model Army laid down their weapons as Commonwealth soldiers – and picked them up in the royal service. (One of the regiments, General Monck's Regiment of Foot, known as 'Coldstreamers', survives to this day as the Coldstream Guards.) Soon after, other regiments were added to the army, including the men who had guarded Charles II in exile, later designated the Grenadier Guards.

Initially, officers in the new post-Restoration army were promoted by merit, but within a decade commissions were put up for sale. There was no quality control; the commission went to whichever aristocrat or gentleman's son could afford it. A colonelcy in the First Foot-guards in 1681 cost £5,000. The purchaser would hope to recoup his outlay by plundering or racketeering. Generally, he would succeed.

The reign of Charles II lasted until 1685, when he was succeeded by his brother, James II, who assiduously built up the strength of the army to 34,000 men. Many of these were crammed into garrison towns such as York, where the luckless Sir John Reresby MP was governor and garrison commander.

'my own lieutenant, one Mr Butler . . . had sold some of my soldiers'
Sir John Reresby

MURDER, MUTINY AND MAYHEM
THE TRIBULATIONS OF A GARRISON COMMANDER
York, 1686–7

26 August 1686 . . . The tattoo was beaten every night by five drums at ten o'clock, at which hour every soldier was to go to his quarters, or be punished if found after that hour in the streets by the patrol that went the round of the streets to see that good order was kept.

No soldier was suffered (nor indeed citizen) to go out of the gates in the daytime with firearms, dogs, or engines for the destruction of game, except gentlemen or officers, or such as had leave in writing from myself. I did not suffer any quarters to be given without my allowance, and where I found the magistrates did oppress I relieved as I thought fit . . . I punished such soldiers very severely against whom any complaint was made out to be just, which being done at the first prevented many disorders. There was one that was accused of a felony. I presently turned him over to be punished by the civil magistrate . . .

There happened a dispute between me and my own lieutenant, one Mr. Butler, who, being . . . not very easy in his fortune, and extravagant in his expenses, had sold some of my soldiers whilst he was at Hull with the company; that is he had taken money to set them at large, and entertained others in their room without my knowledge or consent. When I told him of this he justified himself in it, said that other lieutenants had done the same thing. I told him that was no rule to me, that it was me only that was to answer to the king for my company, which was impossible if he modelled it at his pleasure, and enlarged old disciplined men for money and took novices and inexperienced in their stead, and therefore expected that he begged my pardon and owned his error. This he denied to do, so that I sent to confine him and resolved to suspend him the next day, and the rather because he pretended to have some letters from me by which he was able to make out something to my prejudice. But the next morning he came and offered me to submit himself, which I would not accept till he brought me those letters and gave them into my hands, with great promises of repentance and of better carriage.

12 November . . . I had several complaints from the citizens against officers and soldiers for taking money for quarters, and giving ease to such as feed them the best. For this crime a Scotchman of my Lord Huntingdon's regiment was punished at a council of war, to lie at the marshal's for three days, to ride the wooden horse every day at the relief of the guard with a paper upon his breast expressing his crime. I confined two commissioned officers, one for lying out of the garrison without acquainting me with it, the other for quarrelling with and misusing a citizen, and afterwards committing him by his own authority to the guard with a file of musketeers. I committed another to the dungeon for beating a constable, and punished several for leaving the guard without leave and neglect of their duty . . . Every day some disorder or other was committed, though none passed unpunished either by judgment of a council of war or my own appointment, to the satisfaction of the city . . .

5 December. I committed three soldiers to the guard, and then sent them to my lord mayor, two of them for suspicion of robbing a man of a gun and a pair of stockings in the highway, another for cutting cloth out of some tenters. Two more were concerned in the last felony, but they ran away before they could be caught, and so committed one felony by deserting to escape the punishment of another. I caused a hue and cry to be sent after them . . .

7 February 1687. That afternoon as I was going to visit the main guard, seeing a great crowd and disorder in the streets, I found it was occasioned by six soldiers, three of each regiment, who had quarrelled and fought, two of them being fresh killed upon the place, and a third desperately wounded. I took all the speedy care to get the last man dressed by a surgeon, and to pursue the murderers that had escaped. One of them we soon took. For the other two I doubled the guards, and caused search to be made for them that night, but ineffectually.

19 August. I had notice from my first lieutenant that my company was on their march towards York as far as Doncaster, all the men returning safe but three since the time they went from

thence. One was discharged, another deserted, and the third, quarrelling upon the road with some reapers of corn, was cut into brains with a scythe or reaping-hook by one of them after he had killed one and wounded several of them, so that he died upon the place before the rest of the company overtook him . . .

4 September . . . Some soldiers in my company committed a robbery, and three others mutinied upon the guard and broke the leg of the sergeant that commanded. I gave the king an account.

30 December . . . A court-martial sitting at York upon the three mutineers according to his Majesty's order, the sentence so very severe that I acquainted the king with it, not presuming to mitigate it without his leave, the court having sat by his own appointment. But the king would not have it moderated in the least.

While Reresby was preoccupied with his York garrison, the country underwent a 'Glorious Revolution'. Unable to further stomach James II's Catholicism – which had extended to forcing Catholic officers upon the army – his subjects invited his Protestant son-in-law, William of Orange, onto the English throne. James' army concurred, even colluded, in the political manoeuvring; the deposed monarch fled to the continent.

The revolution of 1668 was 'Glorious' because it established constitutional monarchy (in which, incidentally, Parliament not the crown controlled the army) without the shedding of blood.

But blood was shed, to a massive degree, when James II tried to use Ireland as a base for another tilt at the crown:

'screwing their swords into their muskets, received the charge with all imaginable bravery'
CHAPLAIN ROWLAND DAVIES

THE BATTLE OF THE BOYNE
1 JULY 1690

Fought on the river Boyne, north of Dublin, this was the battle that secured control of Ireland for the English Protestant monarchy of William and Mary. William, in addition to outnumbering James II, made sure of victory by a cavalry movement that enveloped the opposition. Davies was chaplain to one of William's cavalry regiments.

> June 30th – At two in the morning we decamped again, and marched towards Drogheda, where we found King James encamped on the other (side) of the Boyne; we drew up all our horse in a line opposite him within cannon-shot, and as his Majesty passed our line they fired six shot at him, one whereof fell and struck off the top of the Duke of Wurtemberg's pistol, and the whiskers off his horse, and another tore the King's coat on the shoulder. We stood open during at least twenty shot, until, a man and two horses being killed among the Dutch Guards, we all retired into a trench behind us, where we lay safe while much mischief was done to other regiments, and in the evening drew off and encamped behind the hill.
>
> July Ist – About six in the morning the Earl of Portland marched up the river almost to the bridge of Slane, with the right wing, consisting of twenty-four squadrons of horse and dragoons and six regiments of foot, and at two fords we passed the river where there were six squadrons of the enemy to guard the pass; but, at the first firing of our dragoons and three pieces of cannon that marched with us, they all ran away killing nothing but one of our dragoon's horses. As soon as we passed the river, we saw the enemy marching towards us, and that they drew up on the side of a hill in two lines; the river on their right, and all their horse on the left wing: their foot appeared very numerous, but in horse we far exceeded. Whereupon the Earl of Portland drew us up also in two lines, intermixing the horse and foot by squadron and battalion, and sent away for more foot to enforce us; and thus the armies stood for a considerable time, an impassable bog being between them. At length six regiments of foot more joined us, and we altered our line of battle, drawing all our horse into the right wing; and so outflanking the enemy we marched round the bog and engaged them, rather pursuing than fighting them, as far as Duleek. In the interim Count Solmes with the foot forced the pass under our camp and marched over the river with the Blue Dutch regiment of Guards; no sooner were they up the hill but the enemy's horse fell on them, ours with the King being about half a mile lower passing at another ford. At the first push

the front rank only fired and then fell on their faces, loading their muskets again as they lay on the ground; at the next charge they fired a volley of three ranks; then, at the next, the first rank got up and fired again, which being received by a choice squadron of the enemy, consisting mostly of officers, they immediately fell in upon the Dutch as having spent all their front fire; but the two rear ranks drew up in two platoons and flanked the enemy across, and the rest, screwing their swords into their muskets, received the charge with all imaginable bravery and in a minute dismounted them all. The Derry Regiment also sustained them bravely, and as they drew off maintained the same ground with a great slaughter. His Majesty then came up and charged at the head of the Enniskilling horse, who deserted him at the first charge, and carried with them a Dutch regiment that sustained them; but the King's blue troop of Guards soon supplied their place, and with them he charged in person and routed the enemy, and coming over the hill near Duleek appeared on our flank, and, not being known at first, made all our forces halt and draw up again in order, which gave the enemy time to rally also, and draw up on the side of the hill, a bog and river being between us, and then they fired two pieces of cannon on us, but did no mischief; but, as soon as our foot and cannon came up, they marched on, and we after them, but, our foot being unable to march as they did, we could not come up to fight again, but, on the night coming on, were forced to let them go; but had we engaged half an hour sooner, or the day held an hour longer, we had certainly destroyed that army. However we killed the Lord Dungane, Lord Carlingford, Sir Neal O'Neal, and about three thousand others, and lost Duke Schomberg, Dr. Walker, Colonel Caillimotte, and about three hundred more. We took Lieutenant-General Hamilton and several officers and soldiers prisoners, and, it being very dark, were forced to lie in the field all night with our horses in our hands.

July 2nd – In the morning as soon as it was light we returned to Duleek, where our foot was, and sent a detachment to bring up our baggage from the last camp. In the afternoon six troops of horse and three regiments of foot that came from Munster to join King James appeared on the flank and alarmed us, and, sending

two spies to discover who we were, we took and hanged them, the rest marching back without any engagement.

It was during the Irish campaign that another chaplain, Story, noted of the English: 'It is observable that . . . what blunts the courage of all nations commonly whets theirs – I mean the killing of their fellow soldiers before their faces'.

Story was perspicacious. Despite the superseding of the pike by the flintlock musket everywhere on the late 17th- early 18th-century battlefield, warfare still took place 'up close and personal'. Serried lines of soldiers, to employ their muskets, marched to within 100 yards of each other before firing; the winner was the side that by drill and by temperament could endure the more and inflict the higher casualties.

Or have the stomach to use the bayonet. At the Boyne, the plug bayonet was still in use, but its clear limitation – it fitted into the end of the musket, preventing its use as a firearm – ensured it was phased out in favour of the socket bayonet by 1693. Fitted to the outside of the barrel with a twist action (as in the 'bayonet fitting' of the modern light bulb), the socket bayonet allowed every foot soldier to be simultaneously musketeer and pikeman.

As the British were destined to discover, other armies did not have the same appetite for cold steel. Over the next century many an enemy, their lines weakened by musket fire, would be broken by a British bayonet charge coming through the smoke of battle.

After the Boyne, William III took the English army on tour to the Low Countries, fighting the French at Steenkirk, Neerwinden and Namur, but outnumbered, desultorily commanded and hardly provisioned the troops became disconsolate. Molyneux Bunny wrote from Flanders to his uncle in Yorkshire: 'For I must deal plainly with you I am very weary of a souldier our pay is very small and we have much to do to live . . .'

The pay was, indeed, small. A soldier after the Restoration in 1660 earned 8d a day, almost all of which was taken back from him for subsistence and 'off reckonings'. He was also expected to serve for what was effectively life. Neither could it be said that soldiering in the late 17th century was an esteemed occupation; one contemporary newspaper, the London *Spy*, thought that the soldier 'is generally beloved of two sorts of companion, in whores and lice, for both these Vermin are great admirers—'

Unlike its absolutist neighbours, Britain ruled out conscription to the regular army. Somehow, volunteers had to be enticed into this most unenticing of institutions.

Such was the job of recruiting officer.

'I must say that never in my life have I seen a man better built.'
LIEUTENANT GEORGE FARQUHAR

THE RECRUITING OFFICER
THE MIDLANDS
1704–5

The playwright Farquhar scarcely exaggerates in his depiction of the sly methods – blarney, booze, and the promise of booty – used to secure volunteers for the army in his stage comedy *The Recruiting Officer*, 1706; as Lieutenant Farquhar he had been the recruiting officer for the Earl of Orrery's regiment of foot.

Act I, Scene i

The Market-place

DRUMMER *beats the 'Grenadier March'*

Enter SERGEANT KITE, *followed by the* MOB

KITE (*Making a speech*)

If any gentlemen soldiers, or others, have a mind to serve Her Majesty, and pull down the French king; if any prentices have severe masters, any children have undutiful parents; if any servants have too little wages, or any husband too much wife; let them repair to the noble Sergeant Kite, at the Sign of the Raven, in this good town of Shrewsbury, and they shall receive present relief and entertainment. – Gentlemen, I don't beat my drums here to ensnare or inveigle any man; for you must know, gentlemen, that I am a man of honour. Besides, I don't beat up for common soldiers; no, I list only grenadiers, grenadiers, gentlemen – pray, gentlemen, observe this cap – this is the cap of honour, it dubs a man a gentleman in the drawing of a tricker; and he that has the good fortune to be born six foot high was born to be a great man. (*To one of the Mob*) Sir, will you give me leave to try this cap upon your head?

MOB

Is there no harm in't? Won't the cap list me?

KITE

No, no, no more than I can – conic, let me see how it becomes you.

MOB

Are you sure there be no conjuration in it, no gunpowder plot upon me?

KITE

No, no, friend; don't fear, man.

MOB

My mind misgives me plaguily – let me see it. (*Going to put it on*) It smells woundily of sweat and brimstone; pray, Sergeant, what writing is this upon the face of it?

KITE

'The Crown, or the Bed of Honour'.

MOB

Pray now, what may be that same bed of honour?

KITE

Oh, a mighty large bed, bigger by half than the great bed of Ware, ten thousand people may lie in't together and never feel one another.

MOB

My wife and I would do well to lie in't, for we don't care for feeling one another – but do folk sleep sound in this same bed of honour?

KITE

Sound! Aye, so sound that they never wake.

MOB

Wauns! I wish again that my wife lay there.

KITE

Say you so? Then I find, brother–

MOB

Brother! Hold there, friend, I'm no kindred to you that I know of, as yet – look'ee, Sergeant, no coaxing, no wheedling, d'ye see; if I have a mind to list, why so – if not, why 'tis not so – therefore take your cap and your brothership back again, for I an't disposed at this present writing – no coaxing, no brothering me, faith.

KITE

I coax! I wheedle! I'm above it. Sir, I have served twenty campaigns. But sir, you talk well, and I must own that you are a man every inch of you, a pretty, young, sprightly fellow – I love a fellow with a spirit, but I scorn to coax, 'tis base; though

I must say that never in my life have I seen a man better built; how firm and strong he treads, he steps like a castle! But I scorn to wheedle any man – come, honest lad, will you take share of a pot?

MOB

Nay, for that matter, I'll spend my penny with the best he that wears a head, that is, begging your pardon, sir, and in a fair way.

KITE

Give me your hand then; and now, gentlemen, I have no more to say but this – here's a purse of gold, and there is a tub of humming ale at my quarters; 'tis the Queen's money and the Queen's drink. She's a generous queen and loves her subjects – I hope, gentlemen, you won't refuse the Queen's health?

ALL MOB

No, no, no.

KITE

Huzza then! Huzza for the Queen, and the honour of Shropshire!

ALL MOB

Huzza!

KITE

Beat drum.

Exeunt, drummer beating the 'Grenadier March'
Enter PLUME *in a riding habit*

PLUME

By the Grenadier March that should be my drum, and by that shout it should beat with success – let me see – (*looks on his watch*) – four o'clock – at ten yesterday morning I left London – a hundred and twenty miles in thirty hours is pretty smart riding, but nothing to the fatigue of recruiting.

Enter KITE

KITE

Welcome to Shrewsbury, noble Captain: from the banks of the Danube to the Severn side, noble Captain, you're welcome.

PLUME

A very elegant reception indeed, Mr Kite, I find you are fairly entered into your recruiting strain – pray, what success?

KITE

I have been here but a week and I have recruited five.

PLUME

Five! Pray, what are they?

KITE

I have listed the strong man of Kent, the king of the gypsies, a Scotch pedlar, a scoundrel attorney, and a Welsh parson.

PLUME

An attorney! Wert thou mad? List a lawyer! Discharge him, discharge him this minute.

KITE

Why, sir?

PLUME

Because I will have nobody in my company that can write; a fellow that can write, can draw petitions – I say, this minute discharge him.

KITE

And what shall I do with the parson?

PLUME

Can he write?

KITE

Umh – he plays rarely upon the fiddle.

PLUME

Keep him by all means. But how stands the country affected? Were the people pleased with the news of my coming to town?

KITE

Sir, the mob are so pleased with your honour, and the justices and better sort of people are so delighted with me, that we shall soon do our business. But, sir, you have got a recruit here that you little think of.

PLUME

Who?

KITE

One that you beat up for last time you were in the country: You remember your old friend Molly at the Castle?

PLUME

She's not with child, I hope.

KITE

No, no, sir; she was brought to bed yesterday.

PLUME

Kite, you must father the child.

KITE

Humph – and so her friends will oblige me to marry the mother.

PLUME

If they should, we'll take her with us, she can wash, you know, and make a bed upon occasion.

KITE

Aye, or unmake it upon occasion. But your honour knows that I'm married already.

PLUME

To how many?

KITE

I can't tell readily – I have set them down here upon the back of the muster-roll. (*Draws it out*) Let me see – *Imprimis*, Mrs Sheely Snickereyes, she sells potatoes upon Ormonde Quay in Dublin – Peggy Guzzle, the brandy-woman at the Horse-guard at Whitehall – Dolly Waggon, the carrier's daughter in Hull – Mademoiselle Van-bottom-flat at the Buss – then Jenny Oakum, the ship-carpenter's widow at Portsmouth; but I don't reckon upon her, for she was married at the same time to two lieutenants of marines, and a man of war's boatswain.

PLUME

A full company – you have named five – come, make 'em half a dozen, Kite. Is the child a boy or a girl?

KITE

A chopping boy.

PLUME

Then set the mother down in your list, and the boy in mine; enter him a grenadier by the name of Francis Kite, absent upon furlough – I'll allow you a man's pay for his subsistence; and now go comfort the wench in the straw.

KITE

I shall, sir.

But the British army was not entirely a force of volunteers, persuaded there by their own desires or Sergeant Kite's wiles. Some in the ranks were there by compulsion; in 1696 insolvent debtors were forcibly enlisted and in 1702 convicted felons were offered a place in His Majesty's army instead of detention at His Majesty's pleasure. The following year all those without 'visible means of support' found themselves on parade.

If the human material seemed unprepossessing, it was not. Drilled, and given to violence and an overweening racial self-belief that almost all foreigners complained of, the British soldier was about to create a legend of valour and victory.

All he needed was a red coat and leadership. He was given both by John Churchill, Duke of Marlborough.

'The bravery of all our troops on this occasion cannot be expressed'
CAPTAIN-GENERAL JOHN CHURCHILL, DUKE OF MARLBOROUGH

BLENHEIM
THE COMMANDER'S VIEW
BAVARIA, 13 AUGUST 1704

It might be said of the 'sickly Stuart' dynasty that they saved the best till last; it was under the diminutive, ultra-patriotic, unswervingly Protestant Queen Anne that Britain enjoyed her greatest military victories on land since the days of Henry V.

If Anne was the figurehead and the inspiration, the architect of the victories in the War of the Spanish Succession was John Churchill, Duke of Marlborough. Appointed Captain-General of British forces in 1702, Marlborough was a martinet who ruled that 'whoever is taken [found] fishing Ponds . . . shall suffer death'. Yet Marlborough also had a sympathy for the ranker untypical of the age; It was Marlborough who increased the soldier's rations; it was Marlborough who brought in a system of camp sanitation; it was Marlborough who made the red coat the standard dress of the British Infantryman. The men affectionately nicknamed Marlborough 'Corporal John'.

Marlborough, marching his redcoats through the Rhineland in Summer 1704 at a speed the French thought impossible, caught them unprepared at Blenheim, on the river Danube. Facing Marlborough's 50,000 British and Austrian troops were 60,000 Franco-Bavarians.

Sir: I gave you an account on Sunday last of the situation we were then in, and that we expected to hear the enemy would pass the Danube at Lawringen, in order to attack Prince Eugene at eleven of the clock that night. We had an express from him, that the enemy were come, and desiring he might be reinforced as soon as possible. Whereupon I ordered my Brother Churchill to advance at one of the clock in the morning with his two battalions, and by three the whole Army was in motion; for the greater expedition, I ordered part of the troops to pass over the Danube, and follow the march of the twenty battalions; and with most of the Horse and the Foot of the First Linc, I passed the Lech at Rain, and came over the Danube at Donawert. So that we all joined the prince that night, intending to advance and take this Camp at Hochstet: in order whereto we went out early on Tuesday with forty squadrons to view the ground, but found the enemy had already possessed themselves of it.

Whereupon we resolved to attack them, and accordingly we marched between three and four yesterday morning from the Camp at Munster, leaving all our tents standing. About six we came in view of the enemy, who, we found, did not expect so early on onset. The cannon began to play about half an hour after eight. They formed themselves in two bodies, the Elector with Monsieur Marsin and their troops on our right, and Monsieur de Tallard with all his on our left; which last fell to my share; they had two rivulets, besides a morass before them which we were obliged to pass over in their view, and Prince Eugene was forced to take a great compass to come to the enemy, so that it was one of the clock before the battle began. It lasted with great vigour till sunset, when the enemy were obliged to retire, and by the blessing of God we obtained a complete victory.

We have cut off great numbers of them, as well in the action as in the retreat, besides upwards of twenty squadrons of the French, which I pushed into the Danube, where we saw the greater part of them perish. Monsieur Tallard, with several of his general officers being taken prisoners at the same time, and in the village of Blenheim, which the enemy had entrenched and fortified, and where they made the greatest opposition, I obliged twenty-six entire battalions, and twelve squadrons of dragoons, to surrender themselves prisoners at discretion. We took likewise all their tents standing, with their cannon and ammunition, as also a great number of standards, kettle-drums, and colours in the action, so that I reckon the greatest part of Monsieur Tallard's army is taken or destroyed.

The bravery of all our troops on this occasion cannot be

expressed, the Generals, as well as the officers and soldiers, behaving themselves with the greatest courage and resolution. The horse and dragoons were obliged to charge four or five several times. The Elector and Monsieur de Marsin were so advantageously posted, that Prince Eugene could make no impression on them, till the third attack, near seven at night, when he made a great slaughter of them. But being near a woodside, a great body of Bavarians retired into it, and the rest of that army retreated towards Lawringen, it being too late, and the troops too much tired to pursue them far.

I cannot say too much in praise of that Prince's good conduct, and the bravery of his troops on this occasion. You will please to lay this before her Majesty and his Royal Highness, to whom I send my Lord Tunbridge with the good news. I pray you likewise inform yourself, and let me know her Majesty's pleasure, as well relating to Monsieur Tallard and the other general officers, as for the disposal of near one thousand two hundred other officers, and between eight and nine thousand common soldiers, who being all made prisoners by her Majesty's troops, are entirely at her disposal: but as the charge of subsisting these officers and men must be very great, I presume her Majesty will be inclined that they be exchanged for any other prisoners that offer.

I should likewise be glad to receive her Majesty's directions for the disposal of the standards and colours, whereof I have not yet the number, but guess there cannot be less than one hundred, which is more than has been taken in any battle these many years.

You will easily believe that, in so long and vigorous an action, the English, who had so great a share in it, must have suffered as well in officers as men; but I have not the particulars.

I am, Sir,

Your most obedient,

humble servant,

Marlborough.

From the camp at Hochstet

After his great victory at Blenheim, Marlborough honoured his defeated opponent, Marshal Tallard, by inviting him to inspect the allied army. Their conversation went: Marlborough: 'I am very sorry that such a cruel misfortune should have fallen upon a soldier for whom I have the highest regard.'

Tallard: 'And I congratulate you on defeating the best soldiers in the world.'

Marlborough: 'Your lordship, I presume, excepts those who had the honour to beat them.'

Two years later, at Ramillies in Flanders, Marlborough's men again bested the French. Not, as it transpired, that all Marlborough's men were men.

'the surgeons saw my breasts, and . . . concluded I had given suck'
Private Ross

RAMILLIES
PRIVATE ROSS IS WOUNDED BY A SHELL . . .
AND DISCOVERED TO BE A WOMAN
23 May 1706

I escaped unhurt, though in the hottest of the battle, till the French were entirely defeated; when an unlucky shell from a steeple, on which, before the battle, they had planted some mortars and cannon, which played all the time of the engagement, struck the back part of my head and fractured my skull. I was carried to Meldre, or Meldert, a small town in the quarter of Louvain, two leagues south-east from that university, and five leagues north-west from Ramillies, upon a small brook which washes Tirlemont. I was here trepanned, and great care taken of me, but I did not recover in less than ten weeks. Though I suffered great torture by this wound, yet the discovery it caused of my sex, in the fixing of my dressing, by which the surgeons saw my breasts, and, by the largeness of my nipples, concluded I had given suck, was a greater grief to me. No sooner had they made this discovery, but they acquainted Brigadier Preston, that his pretty dragoon (so I was always called) was, in fact, a woman. He was very loath to believe it, and did me the honour to say, he had always looked upon me as the prettiest fellow, and the best man he had. His incredulity made him send for my brother, whom he now imagined to be my husband; when he came, the brigadier said to him, 'Dick, I am surprised at a piece of news these gentlemen tell me; they say, your brother is, in reality, a woman.' 'Sir,' said he, 'since she she is discovered, I cannot deny it; she is my wife, and I have had three children by her.' The news of this discovery spread far and near, and reaching, among others, my Lord John Hay's ear, he came to see me, as did all my former comrades. My lord would neither ask me, nor suffer any one else, any questions; but called for my husband, though first for my comrade, who had been long my bedfellow, and examined him closely. The fellow protested, as it was truth, that he never knew I was a woman, or even suspected it; 'It is well known,' continued he, 'that she had a child lain to her, and took care of it.' My lord then calling in my husband, desired him to tell the meaning of my disguise. He gave him a full and satisfactory account of our first acquaintance, marriage, and situation, with the manner of his having entered into the service, and my resolution to go in search of him; adding the particulars of our meeting, and my obstinate refusal of bedding with him. My lord seemed very well entertained with my history, and ordered that I should want for nothing and that my pay should be continued while under cure.

Cross-dressed soldiers like Mother Ross (aka Christian Cavanaugh) were rare. Phoebe Hessel joined the army as a drummer boy in circa 1720; Hannah Snell served four and a half years in the marines in the 1750s; Mary-Anne Talbot served in Flanders in the late 1700s, and it was to great surprise that Dr James Barry, inspector-general of the Army Medical Department, was found on 'his' death in 1865 to be female.

'Petticoats' usually figured in the lives of redcoats as wives (potential or actual) or prostitutes, not fellows in arms.

Some soldiers thought women in barracks or in the field were beneficial; Sir James Turner, in his classic history of warfare, *Pallas Armata*, 1683, concluded: '... women are great helpers to armies ... [they] provide, buy and dress their husbands meat when their husbands are on duty, or newly come from it, they bring in fewel for fires, and wash their linen, and in such manner of employment, a Souldier's wife may be helpful to her husband and herself.' On the other hand, James Wolfe, the future hero of Quebec, ordered his subordinates to 'discourage matrimony amongst the men as much as possible, the service suffers by the multitude of women already in the regiment'.

Wolfe's view predominated. The Married Roll for most regiments was 6 per cent until the late 19th century.

'It was as bloody a battle as has been fought either this war or the last'
CAPTAIN JOHN BLACKADER

BLACKADER AT MALPLAQUET
11 SEPTEMBER 1709

Malplaquet was the bloodiest of Marlborough's victories over the French; 'the butcher's bill' amounted to more than 36,000 killed. As with all Marlborough's best battles, he went on the offensive, backfooting the white-jacketed French until they lost balance and fell to ruin. The diary of Blackader, 26th Cameronian Regiment, uses the Old Style calendar:

29 August 1709. The enemy being now near we marched suddenly. In the afternoon they came in view, and our line of battle was formed and posted. They are in strong ground. They raised batteries and played upon us with their cannon. There was not a place in the whole line so much exposed as where our regiment and two or three more stood, and we had considerable loss. Many a cannon-ball came very near, but He gave His angels charge over me. *Thou art my shield and buckler.* This I trusted in, and repeated several times when I saw the cannon-balls coming straight towards me, as I thought; but the goodness of God let none of them touch me. This night was an unpleasant, uneasy night to our regiment, for they have wanted bread these five days and are faint. It was a cold, wet night, and we lay at our arms. I laid me down and slept sound, for God sustained me; and I am not afraid of ten thousands that set themselves against us round about.

30 August. Next morning we expected to have been saluted by break of day with their batteries, as last night; and we laid our account, if we stayed upon the same spot of ground, with having a third of our regiment killed and wounded, for the general would not allow us to draw back our men a little way behind a rising ground that covered us. But God in mercy prevented us, for the enemy had drawn off their cannon from that place and did not trouble us all the day. In the afternoon an extraordinary thing happened. The French officers and ours, as if it had been concerted between them, went out between the two camps, and conversed with one another, and called for their

acquaintances, and talked together as friends, as if there had been a cessation of arms; but it was broken off by the generals on both sides . . .

Early in the morning (the 31st) we attacked the enemy in their camp, a strong camp, and strongly intrenched by two days working. We fought, and by the mercy and goodness of God have obtained a great and glorious victory. The battle began about seven o'clock, and continued till near three in the afternoon. It was the most deliberate, solemn and well-ordered battle that ever I saw-a noble and fine disposition, and as nobly executed. Every man was at his post, and I never saw troops engage with more cheerfulness, boldness and resolution . . . Providence ordered it so, that our regiment was no farther engaged than by being cannonaded, which was indeed the most severe that ever our regiment suffered, and by which we had considerable loss. But the soldiers endured it without shrinking, very patiently, and with great courage . . . Our regiment, with some others, were honoured in particular to do some very good service, by marching up and manning a retrenchment which the enemy had left. And there we sustained our own horse, which were pushed by the French horse, and might have been of dangerous consequence had not the foot sustained them . . . The French foot did not behave themselves well. They soon quitted their retrenchments; but the horse stood more stiffly to it. I did not expect to see a cowed army fight so well. I believe the loss may be about equal on both sides. It was as bloody a battle as has been fought either this war or the last . . .

1 September. This morning I went to view the field of battle, to get a preaching from the dead, which might have been very edifying, for in all my life I have not seen the dead bodies lie so thick as they were in some places about the retrenchments, particularly at the battery where the Dutch Guards attacked. For a good way I could not go among them, lest my horse should tread on the carcasses that were lying, as it were, heaped on one another. I was also surprised to see how strong they had made their camp. They had a breast-work before them, round about like the rampart of a town, to fire over. The Dutch have suffered most in this battle of any. Their infantry is quite shattered, so that it is a dear victory. The potsherds of the earth are dashed

together, and God makes the nations a scourge to each other to work His holy ends by sweeping sinners off the face of the earth. It is a wonder to me the British escape so cheap, who are the most heaven-daring sinners in this army. But God's judgments are a great depth. He has many arrows in His quiver, and is not tied to our times and ways.

———◆———

'Here . . . was a fair trial of skill between the two Royal Regiments of Ireland'
LIEUTENANT ROBERT PARKER

MALPLAQUET
THE ROYAL IRISH REGIMENT ENGAGES IRISHMEN IN SERVICE OF THE FRENCH
11 SEPTEMBER 1709

The Irishmen Parker engaged at Malplaquet were recruited from the isle's Catholic population.

We continued marching slowly on, till we came to an opening in the wood. It was a small plain, on the opposite side of which, we perceived a Battalion of the enemy drawn up. Upon this Colonel Kane, who was then at the head of the Regiment, having drawn us up, and formed our Platoons, advanced gently towards them, with six platoons of our first fire made ready. When we had advanced within six hundred paces of them, they gave us a fire of one of their ranks; Whereupon we halted, and returned them the fire of our first six Platoons at once; and immediately made ready the six Platoons of our second fire, and advanced upon them again. They then gave us the fire of another rank, and we returned them a second fire, which made them shrink; however, they gave us the fire of a third rank after a scattering manner, and then retired into the wood in great disorder; on which we sent our third fire after them, and saw them no more. We advanced cautiously up to the ground which they had quitted, and found several of them killed and wounded; among the latter was one Lieutenant O'Sullivan, who told us the Battalion we had engaged, was the Royal Regiment of Ireland. Here, therefore, there was a fair trial of skill between the two Royal Regiments of Ireland; one in the

British, the other in the French service; for we met each other upon equal terms, and there was none else to interpose.

The advantage on our side will be easily accounted for, first from the weight of our ball; for the French Arms carry bullets of 24 to the pound; Whereas our British Firelocks carry ball of only 16 to the pound, which will make a considerable difference in the execution. Again, the manner of our firing was different from theirs; the French at that time fired all by Ranks, which can never do equal execution with our Platoon-firing, especially when six Platoons are fired together.

The British invention of platoon-firing, by which platoons of soldiers fired one after the other down the line, created an almost continuous torrent of bullets. It was a system of fire-control which would stand the red coats in good stead in countless future battles in the age of the musket.

'there was water but they would not let us have a drop'
A ROYAL DRAGOON

WAR OF THE SPANISH SUCCESSION
TAKEN PRISONER
SPAIN, NOVEMBER 1710

All of Britain's glories in the 'War of the Spanish Succession', fought to prevent the French putting their candidate on the Spanish throne, happened under Marlborough in Bavaria and Flanders; down in barren pro-France Spain itself, there was no genius to lead the British expeditionary force. Or properly equip them.

A dragoon was a mounted infantryman with a firearm (which spitted fire like a 'dragon'.)

On Wednesday the 19 of November in the year of our Lord 1710 we [were] all ordered to march with a strong party of [Spanish] Horse to guard us & indeed the [British] officers marched according to the articles [of surrender] agreed on, with their horses and their swords & their pistols, but as they never did regard the men so now we found to our cost the truth of it, for they being on horseback & we on foot they marched so fast that we were in a manner to run after them; & the regiments of Foot that was drawn up on both sides of the street, as we marched over our dead men that laid out . . . they [the Spanish] catch[ed] hold of us and took our bags & what was in them, and our cloaks. As for our clothes that was on our backs [they] was not worth the taking, and our officers kept on marching with the Horses that was to guard us & we had to march up a very high hill and there stood tents standing and one of the officers servants came & looked on us and said in Spanish language 'the flower of the world is taken today. What had your officers apiece for you?'. I heard him speak it. So when we had got up the hill they marched us along, full 7 English leagues and [we] went by villages where there was water but they would not let us have a drop and at last we came to our journey's end for that night [we got] to Guardolaharro, which is the name of the town; we had been there before, when they bare[d] arms. They used us very basely: they ran lighted straw in our faces & firebrand[s] and cursing our Queen and us, & we were forced to run to keep up with our guards; & them that could not keep up they stripped & if they had no money nor lining . . . then they would beat them & strip them naked & them that was so served was forced to take it patiently, though we would have wished it other ways.

The dragoon was later able to rejoin the British army in the peninsula, but only in time for the defeat at Brihuega on 28 November 1710.

So on Tuesday the 28 of November 1710 we had all of us orders . . . to go with our arms in order to keep the enemy from coming into the town. We presently did and we were posted at a gate of the town where our officers thought it to be the weakest of all the town's [gates], as the enemy knew, for they set the gate on fire three times, but we did put it out at fist & kept them out to the degree that could not well be expected, considering we had no cannon to defend us nor offend them, and we should have kept them out longer but now our ammunition began to be wanting that our men was forced to be careful of it, and the enemy finding this made them brisker and bolder. Thus we kept defending ourselves so well as we could but there was a stallage (in English a public house or inn) that joined to the walls of the town that our people knew not of, but the peasants or the people of the town gave the enemy notice of it and how they might come into the town so that by 3 or 4 of the clock in the afternoon great part of their army was got into the town & houses and made holes in the walls of the houses & knocked us down as fast as they could shoot. We blocked up the street that led into the market place but it was all in vain, for by this time the enemy began to march in all the streets and we had no ammunition, it being all spent, [so] that they came up within a dozen yards of our breastwork and stood and looked upon us. This was about 9 of the clock at night and General Carpenter stood at the breastwork & it was supposed a musket ball was shot from some house afar off, for it was a dead [spent] ball and shot Carpenter in the mouth and just made the blood come ... But presently there was orders for our drum major to beat a parley ... & when the parley was heard they [the enemy] came to our breast work & talked with us, for our Generals had all the writings ready & the Duke of Vandome readily signed them.

Stanhope, the British commander at Brihuega, wrote of his capitulation: 'I thought myself in conscience obliged to try and save so many brave men who had done good service to the Queen . . . if after this misfortune, I should ever be entrusted with troops, I never desire to serve with better men'.

Stalemate in the War of Spanish Succession gave breath to the pro-peace lobby at home and the martial Marlborough was dismissed his command. Britain (as the isles had become after the Act of Union, 1707) did not yet love a soldier. Even a brilliant one.

'Thomas Lobster', as the British infantryman was monikered courtesy of his red coat, fared no better than his general. Distinguished regiments were disbanded, others sent overseas to garrison Britain's ever-greater territorial possessions. Some of these regiments were left, literally, to die. The 38th Regiment spent 60 unbroken years garrisoning the West Indies.

Garrison duty in the Mediterranean was little better.

'with the harmless diversions of drinking, dancing, revelling,
whoring, gaming . . . to pass the time'
'S.H.'

DIARY OF A GARRISON SOLDIER UNDER SIEGE

GIBRALTAR, 1727–8

'The Rock' was seized from Spain during the War of the Spanish succession, but disputed by that country forever after.

March 9th. Came a deserter who reports that while our guns were firing at them an officer pulled off his hat, huzzaed and called God to damn us all, when one of our balls with unerring justice took off the miserable man's head and left him a wretched example of the Divine justice.

April 12th. A recruit who refused to work, carry arms, eat or drink was whipped for the fifth time, after which being asked by the officer he said he was now ready to do his duty.

May 7th. This morning Ensign Stubbs of Colonel Egerton's regiment retired a little out of the camp and shot himself.

June 17th. Today two corporals of the Guards boxed over a rail until both expired, but nobody can tell for what reason.

October 11th. One of Pearce's regiment went into the belfry of a very high steeple, threw himself into the street, and broke his skull to pieces.

October 16th. Will Garen, who broke his back, was hanged.

December 9th. Last night a deserter clambered up within a little of Willis's battery and was assisted by a ladder of ropes by our men. When the officers came to examine his face, they found him to have deserted out of the Royal Irish two months ago. Asking the reason of his return, he said he chose rather to be hanged than continue in the Spanish service, so is to have his choice.

January 2nd 1728. Here is nothing to do nor any news, all things being dormant and in suspense, with the harmless diversions of drinking, dancing, revelling, whoring, gaming and other innocent debaucheries to pass the time – and really, to speak my own opinion I think and believe that Sodom and

Gomorrah were not half so wicked and profane as this worthy city and garrison of Gibraltar.

More scandalous treatment awaited the redcoat. In 1739 Prime Minister Walpole declared war on Spain after a seaman, Captain Jenkins, lost an ear during a spat with Spanish customs officials.

Of the expeditionary force sent to Central America, 2,000 men lost their lives to 'Yellow Jack' (yellow fever). The survivors then laid siege to Cartagena, Colombia, in a poor facsimile of a military operation. Afterwards the wounded and the sick alike were herded together in the expedition's ships. Tobias Smollett was an assistant surgeon on the expedition:

The sick and wounded were squeezed into certain vessels, which there obtained the name of hospital ships, though methinks they scarce deserved such a creditable title, seeing few of them could boast either a surgeon, nurse or cook; and the space between the decks was so confined that the miserable patients had not room to sit upright in their beds. Their wounds . . . being neglected, contracted filth and putrefaction, and millions of maggots were hatched amidst the corruption of their sores. This inhuman disregard was imputed to the scarcity of surgeons; though it is well known, that every great ship in the fleet could have spared one at least for this duty; an expedient which could have been more than sufficient to remove this shocking inconvenience. But, perhaps, the general was too much of a gentleman to ask a favour of this kind from his fellow chief, who on the other hand, would not derogate so much from his own dignity, as to offer such assistance unasked; for I may venture to affirm, that, by this time, the Demon of Discord, with her sooty wings, had breathed her influence upon our counsels; and it might be said of these great men . . . as of Caesar and Pompey, the one could not brook a superior, and the other was impatient of an equal . . .

By the end of the so-called 'War of Jenkins' Ear' in 1742, 90 per cent of the British expeditionary force had died.

Treated well, however, the British soldier could bite off the whole head of the French army.

'and did not fire till we came within sixty paces'
ANONYMOUS OFFICER

DETTINGEN
IN THE FIRING LINE WITH THE ROYAL WELCH FUSILIERS
BAVARIA, 27 JUNE 1743

Dettingen was the last occasion on which a British king personally commanded his troops in battle. George II did not lack courage, stumping around in his redcoat amidst the shot and shell, his horse having unpatriotically bolted, but he lacked purpose. Luckily his Royal Welch Fusiliers did not. Having got up close enough to see the whites of French eyes, the Royal Welch Fusiliers thundered out musket fire as though on parade. The 'long bullets' referred to are artillery; Dettingen was fought in pursuit of the 'War of the Austrian Succession', 1740–8, another in the long cycle of wars needed to stem the spread of French influence in Europe.

Our men were eager to come to action, and did not at all like the long bullets (as they term'd them), for indeed they swept off ranks and files. However, when we came to the small ones, they held them in such contempt that they really kept the same order as at any other time . . .

Our Army gave such shouts before we were engaged, when we were about one hundred paces apart before the action began, that we hear by deserters it brought a pannick amongst them. We attacked the Regiment of Navarre, one of their prime regiments. Our people imitated their predecessors in the last war gloriously, marching in close order, as firm as a wall, and did not fire till we came within sixty paces, and still kept advancing: for, when the smoak blew off a little, instead of being amongst their living we found the dead in heaps by us; and the second fire turn'd them to the right about, and upon a long trot. We engaged two other regiments afterwards, one after the other, who stood but one fire each; and their Blue French Foot Guards made the best of their way without firing a shot.

Our Colonel fell in the first attack, shot in the mouth, and out at the neck; but there are hopes of his recovery. The Gens d'Armes are quite ruin'd who are their chief dependence, and intended to cut us to pieces without firing a shot.

Our Regiment sustained little loss, tho' much engaged; and indeed our whole army gives us great honour. Brigadier Huske, who behaved gloriously, and quite cool, was shot thro' the foot at the same time that our Colonel fell, yet continued his post. We have no more than fifty killed and wounded, and one officer besides the Colonel. What preserved us was our keeping close order, and advancing near the enemy ere we fir'd. Several that popp'd at one hundred paces lost more of their men, and did less execution for the French will stand fire at a distance, tho' 'tis plain they cannot look men in the face.

'Till we obtained this victory we wanted bread, and 'tis not to be imagined what fatigures the Army underwent by continual alarms. 'till now, I assure you, I have not been under cover above two nights in fourteen. The night after the action it rain'd without intermission, 'till eight next morning, and very violent.

To revenge his reverses at Dettingen, Louis XV of France sponsored a coup in Scotland by supporters of the deposed Stuart line – the 'Jacobites' (from Jacobus, the Latin for James). Leading them was James II's son, Charles Stuart. The banner of 'Bonnie Prince Charlie', however, was not a draw to all:

'I am too old a soldier to surrender . . . without bloody noses'
SERGEANT J. MOLLOY

THE JACOBITE RISING OF '45
SERGEANT MOLLOY REFUSES TO SURRENDER,
THE RUTHVEN REDOUBT
SCOTLAND, 30 AUGUST 1745

An NCO's report:

HON. GENERAL, – This goes to acquaint you that yesterday [29th] there appeared in the little town of Ruthven about three hundred of the enemy, and sent proposals to me to surrender the redoubt upon Condition that I should have liberty to carry off bags and baggage. My answer was, '*I am too old a soldier to surrender a garrison of such strength without bloody noses!*' They threatened to hang me and my men for refusal. I told them I would take my chance. This morning they attacked me about twelve o'clock with about one hundred and fifty men; they attacked the fore-gate and sally-port. They drew off about half an hour after three. I expect another visit this night, but I shall give them the warmest reception my weak party can afford. I shall hold out as long as possible.

I conclude, Honourable General, with great respect,

Your most humble servant,

J. Molloy, Sergt. 6th

Molloy and his twelve men beat off one attack, and only surrendered – on terms which allowed them to march to a loyalist garrison – when the Jacobites reappeared with artillery. On the intervention of General Sir John Cope, Molloy was promoted to lieutenant for 'his gallant behaviour'.

Notwithstanding the efforts of Sergeant Molloy, the Jacobite Rising of '45 was initially a deadly success, with the Highlanders reaching as far south as Derby – until it occurred to the more sage among them that they had no serious support in England. In less than a month, the Jacobites were back in Scotland with the British army hard on their tail. At Culloden Moor on 16 April 1746 the two sides engaged. For once the terrifying Highland charge failed to carry all before it: British artillery firing canister – scattershot, essentially – removed dozens of Highlanders of the front rank. Next, a British soldier recalled: 'we saw them coming towards us in great Haste and Fury. We fired at about 50 Yards distance, which made hundreds Fall . . . they still advanced, and were almost upon us before we loaded again. We immediately gave them another full fire'. The remains of the charge ended up on a spiked wall of British bayonets.

Some 1,500 rebels were killed or wounded on Culloden Moor. But the biggest casualty of the day was the Stuart cause, which was dead forever. Culloden was the last battle on British soil. Henceforth the British soldier would fight all his wars across the seas.

'Sing tow, row, row, row, row, row, row to the British grenadiers'

ANONYMOUS

THE BRITISH GRENADIER

c 1745

One of the first recorded British soldier's songs. The grenadiers were originally throwers of hollow bombs filled with gunpowder (from the Spanish *granada*, pomegranate) used to reduce fortifications, and first seen in Britain in 1677; a year later the diarist John Evelyn described them as having 'cropped crownes like Janizaries which made them look very fierce'. By the mid-eighteenth century, the grenadiers, chosen for their height and strength, had become a general storm-troop; from the 1760s onwards they wore bearskin caps.

Some talk of Alexander and some of Hercules,
Of Hector, and Lysander, and such great names as these;
But of all the world's brave heroes, there's none that can compare,
With a tow, row, row, row, row, row, row for the British Grenadiers!
* * *
Those heroes of antiquity never saw a cannon-ball,
Nor knew the force of powder to slay their foes withal,
But our brave lads do know it, and banish all their fears,
With a tow, row, row, row, row, row, row, for the British Grenadiers!
* * *
And Jove the God of Thunder, and Mars the God of War,
Great Neptune in his chariot, Apollo in his car,
And all the powers celestial, descending from their spheres,
Behold with admiration the British Grenadiers.
* * *
Then let us fill a bumper, and drink a health to those
Who carry caps and pouches, and wear the looped clothes;
May they and their commanders live happy all their years!
With a tow, row, row, row, row, row, row for the British Grenadiers!

'The British Grenadier' is not the only song about the grenadiers. 'The Grenadiers March' was adopted as the regimental march of the Grenadier Guards in 1815. It is still played at the Trooping the Colour ceremony.

'many . . . were soon suffocated'
JOHN Z. HOLWELL

THE BLACK HOLE OF CALCUTTA
20–21 JUNE 1756

The East India Company, formed in 1600, was the advance guard of Britain's colonisation of the Indian subcontinent. During the 1756 uprising against the

Company led by the traditionalist Nawab of Bengal, soldiers from the Company's Calcutta garrison were imprisoned in an 18-foot square guardroom: the 'Black Hole of Calcutta'.

My thirst grew now insupportable, and the difficulty of breathing much increased; and I had not remained in this situation, I believe, ten minutes, when I was seized with a pain in my breast, and palpitation of heart, both to the most exquisite degree. These roused and obliged me to get up again; but still the pain, palpitation, thirst, and difficulty of breathing increased. I retained my senses notwithstanding; and had the grief to see death not so near me as I hoped; but could no longer bear the pains I suffered without attempting a relief, which I knew fresh air would and could only give me. I instantly determined to push for the window opposite to me; and by an effort of double the strength I had ever before possessed, gained the third rank at it, with one hand seized a bar, and by that means gained the second, though I think there were at least six or seven ranks between me and the window.

In a few moments the pain, palpitation, and difficulty of breathing ceased; but my thirst continued intolerable. I called aloud for *Water for God's sake.* I had been concluded dead; but as soon as they found me amongst them, they still had the respect and tenderness for me, to cry out, *Give him water, give him water!* nor would one of them at the window attempt to touch it until I had drank. But from the water I had no relief; my thirst was rather increased by it; so I determined to drink no more, but patiently wait the event; and kept my mouth moist from time to time by sucking the perspiration out of my shirt sleeves, and catching the drops as they fell, like heavy rain, from my head and face; you can hardly imagine how unhappy I was if any of them escaped my mouth.

I came into the prison without coat or waistcoat; the season was too hot to bear the former, and the latter tempted the avarice of one of the guards, who robbed me of it, when we were under the Veranda. Whilst I was at this second window, I was observed by one of my miserable companions on the right of me, in the expedient of allaying my thirst by sucking my shirt-sleeve. He took the hint, and robbed me from time to time of a considerable part of my store; though after I detected him, I had even the address to begin on that sleeve first, when I thought my reservoirs were sufficiently replenished; and our mouths and noses often met in the contest. This plunderer I found afterwards was a worthy young gentleman in the service, Mr Lushington, one of the few who escaped from death, and since paid me the compliment of assuring me, he believed he owed his life to the many comfortable draughts he had from my sleeves. Before I hit upon this happy expedient, I had in an ungovernable fit of thirst, attempted drinking my urine; but it was so intensely bitter, there was no enduring a second taste, whereas no Bristol water could be more soft or pleasant than what arose from perspiration . . .

Many to the right and left sunk with the violent pressure, and were soon suffocated; for now a steam arose from the living and the dead, which affected us in all its circumstances, as if we were forcibly held by our heads over a bowl of strong volatile spirit of hartshorn, until suffocated; nor could the effluvia of the one be distinguished from the other; and frequently, when I was forced by the load upon my head and shoulders, to hold my face down, I was obliged, near as I was to the window, instantly to raise it again, to escape suffocation . . .

When the day broke . . . the suba (viceroy of Bengal), who had received an account of the havock death had made amongst us, sent one of his Jemmautdaars to enquire if the chief survived. They shewed me to him; told I had appearance of life remaining; and believed I might recover if the door was opened very soon. This answer being returned to the suba, an order came immediately for our release, it being then near six in the morning.

As the door opened inwards, and as the dead were piled up against it, and covered all the rest of the floor, it was impossible to open it by any efforts from without; it was therefore necessary that the dead should be removed by the few that were within, who were become so feeble, that the task, though it was the condition of life, was not performed without the utmost difficulty, and it was twenty minutes after the order came before the door could be opened.

About a quarter after six in the morning, the poor remains of 146 souls, being no more than three and twenty, came out of the black hole alive, but in a condition which made it very doubtful whether they would see the morning of the next day; among the living was Mrs Carey, but poor Leech was among the dead. The bodies were dragged out of the hole by the soldiers, and thrown promiscuously into the ditch of an unfinished ravelin, which was afterwards filled with earth.

The task of avenging the Black Hole was given to Robert Clive, an East India Company officer. At Plassey on 23 June 1757 Clive's East India Company force faced 50,000 soldiers led by the Nawab of Bengal; the Nawab's army included a contingent of gunners thoughtfully provided by France, then fighting Britain in the Seven Years War (1756–63). Below is Clive's report on Plassey, sent to the Company's directors:

At daybreak we discovered the Nabob's army moving towards us, consisting, as we since found, of about fifteen thousand horse and thirty-five thousand foot, with upwards of forty pieces of cannon. They approached apace, and by six began to attack with a number of heavy cannon, supported by the whole army, and continued to play on us very briskly for several hours, during which our situation was of the utmost service to us, being lodged in a large grove with good mud banks. To succeed in an attempt on their cannon was next to impossible, as they were planted in a manner round us, and at considerable distances from each other. We therefore remained quiet in our post, in expectation of a successful attack upon their camp at night.

About noon the enemy drew off their artillary, and retired to their camp . . . We immediately sent a detachment accompanied with two field-pieces, to take possession of a tank with high banks, which was advanced about three hundred yards above our grove, and from which the enemy had considerably annoyed us with some cannon managed by Frenchmen. This motion brought them out a second time; but on finding them make no great effort to dislodge us, we proceeded to take possession of one or two more eminences lying very near an angle of their camp . . . They made several attempts to bring out their cannon, but our advance field-pieces played so warmly and so well upon them that they were always drove back. Their horse exposing themselves a good deal on this occasion, many of them were killed, and among the rest four or five officers of the first distinction, by which the whole army being visibly dispirited and thrown into some confusion, we were encouraged to storm both the eminence and the angle of their camp, which were carried at the same instant, with little or no loss . . . On this a general rout ensued; and we pursued the enemy six miles, passing upwards of forty pieces of cannon they had abandoned, with an infinite number of carriages filled with baggage of all kinds. Suraj-ud-Daulah escaped on a camel, and reaching Moorshedabad early next morning, despatched away what jewels and treasure he conveniently could, and he himself followed at midnight with only two or three attendants.

It is computed there are killed of the enemy about five hundred. Our loss amounted to only twenty-two killed and fifty wounded, and those chiefly blacks.

Plassey was the turning point in the eastern career of the British. It halted French advance on the subcontinent and established the foundations of the British Empire. Clive himself was elevated to the peerage.

On the other side of the world, British troops were about to deal the French another reeling blow.

'and showed them a front . . . a thing not to be expected
from troops already twice attacked'
LIEUTENANT HUGH MONTGOMERY

AND WE SHALL SHOCK THEM
THE INFANTRY AT MINDEN
GERMANY, 1 AUGUST 1759

A hardly remembered battle of the Seven Years War, Minden saw a feat of arms never surpassed: infantrymen breaking, in succession, three lines of cavalry.

The regiments which achieved this impossible exploit were the British 12th, 20th, 23rd (Royal Welch Fusiliers), 25th, 37th and 51st regiments. Pitted against them at Minden, in a far-flung corner of north-west Germany, were the cavalry and infantry columns of Marshal Contades of France. Montgomery served with the 12th Foot.

Dear Madam, – The pursuit of the enemy, who have retired with the greatest precipitation, prevents me from giving you so exact an account of the late most glorious victory over the French army as I would, had I almost any leisure, however here goes as much as I can.

We marched from camp between 4 and 5 o'clock in the morning, about seven drew up in a valley, from thence marched about three hundred yards, when an eighteen pound ball came gently rolling up to us. Now began the most disagreeable march that I ever had in my life, for we advanced more than a quarter of a mile through a most furious fire from a most infernal battery of eighteen-pounders, which was at first upon our front, but as we proceeded, bore upon our flank, and at last upon our rear. It might be imagined, that this cannonade would render the regiments incapable of bearing the shock of unhurt troops drawn up long before on ground of their own choosing, but firmness and resolution will surmount almost any difficulty. When we got within about 100 yards of the enemy, a large body of French cavalry galloped boldly down upon us; these our men by reserving their fire until they came within thirty yards, immediately ruined, but not without receiving some injury from them, for they rode down two companies on the right of our regiment, wounded three officers, took one of them prisoner with our artillery Lieutenant, and whipped off the Tumbrells. This cost them dear for it forced many of them into our rear, on whom the men faced about and five of them did not return. These visitants being thus dismissed, without giving us a moment's time to recover the unavoidable disorder, down came upon us like lightning the glory of France in the persons of the Gens d'Armes. These we almost immediately dispersed without receiving hardly any mischief from the harmless creatures. We now discovered a large body of infantry consisting of seventeen regiments moving down directly on our flank in column, a very ugly situation; but Stewart's Regiment and ours wheeled, and showed them a front, which is a thing not to be expected from troops already twice attacked, but this must be placed to the credit of General Waldgrave and his aide-de-camp. We engaged this corps for about ten minutes, killed them a good many, and as the song says, 'the rest then ran away'.

The next who made their appearance were some Regiments of the Grenadiers of France, as fine and terrible looking fellows as I ever saw. They stood us a tug, notwithstanding we beat them off to a distance, where they galded us much, they having rifled barrels, and our muskets would not reach them. To remedy this we advanced, they took the hint, and ran away. Now we were in hopes that we had done enough for one day's work, and that they would not disturb us more, but soon after a very large body of fresh infantry, the last resource of Contades, made the final attempt on us. With them we had a long but not very brisk engagement, at last made them retire almost out of reach, when the three English regiments of the rear line came up, and gave them one fire, which sent them off for good and all. But what is wonderful to tell, we ourselves after all this success at the very same time also retired, but indeed we did not then know that victory was ours. However we rallied, but all that could now be mustered was about 13 files private with our Colonel and four other officers one of which I was so fortunate to be. With this remnant we returned again to the charge, but to our unspeakable joy no opponents could be found. It is astonishing, that this victory was gained by six English regiments of foot, without their grenadiers, unsupported by cavalry or cannon, not even their own battalion guns, in the face of a dreadful battery so near as to tear them with grape-shot, against forty battalions and thirty-six squadrons, which is directly the quantity of the enemy which fell to their share.

It is true that two Hanoverian regiments were engaged on the left of the English, but so inconsiderably as to lose only 50 men between them. On the left of the army the grenadiers, who now form a separate body, withstood a furious cannonade. Of the English there was only killed one captain and one sergeant; some Prussian dragoons were engaged and did good service. Our artillery which was stationed in different places, also behaved well, but the grand attack on which depended the fate of the day, fell to the lot of the six English regiments of foot. From this account the Prince might be accused of misconduct for trusting the issue of so great an event to so small a body, but this affair you will have soon enough explained to the disadvantage of a great man whose easy part, had it been properly acted, must have occasioned to

France one of the greatest overthrows it ever met with. The sufferings of our regiment will give you the best notion of the smartness of the action. We actually fought that day not more than 480 private and 27 officers, of the first 302 were killed and wounded, and of the latter 18. Three lieutenants were killed on the spot, the rest are only wounded, and all of them are in a good way except two. Of the officers who escaped there are only four who cannot show some marks of the enemy's good intentions, and as perhaps you may be desirous to know any little risks that I might have run, I will mention those of which I was sensible. At the beginning of the action I was almost knocked off my legs by my three right hand men, who were killed and drove against me by a cannon ball, the same ball also killed two men close to Ward, whose post was in the rear of my platoon, and in this place I will assure you that he behaved with the greatest bravery, which I suppose you will make known to his father and friends. Some time after I received from a spent ball just such a rap on my collar-bone as I have frequently from that once most dreadful weapon, your crooked-headed stick; it just swelled and grew red enough to convince the neighbours that I was not fibbing when I mentioned it. I got another of these also on one of my legs, which gave me about as much pain, as would a tap of Miss Mathews's fan. The last and greatest misfortune of all fell to the share of my poor old coat for a musket ball entered into the right skirt of it and made three holes. I had almost forgot to tell you that my spontoon was shot through a little below my hand; this disabled it, but a French one now does duty in its room. The consequences of this affair are very great, we found by the papers, that the world began to give us up, and the French had swallowed us up in their imaginations. We have now pursued them above 100 miles with the advanced armies of the hereditary prince, Wanganheim, and Urff in our front, of whose success in taking prisoners and baggage, and receiving deserters, Francis Joy will give you a better account than I can at present. They are now entrenching themselves at Cassel, and you may depend on it they will not show us their faces again during this campaign.

I have the pleasure of being able to tell you that Captain Rainey is well; he is at present in advance with the Grenadiers plundering French baggage and taking prisoners. I would venture to give him forty ducats for his share of prize money.

I have now contrary to my expectations and in spite of many interruptions wrote you a long letter, this paper I have carried this week past in my pocket for the purpose, but could not attempt it before. We marched into this camp yesterday evening, and shall quit it early in the morning. I wrote you a note just informing you that I was well the day after the battle; I hope you will receive it in due time. Be pleased to give my most affectionate duty to my uncles and aunts . . . and believe me to be

With the greatest affection,

Your very dutiful son,

Camp at Paderton   H[h] Montgomery.
9th August, 1759.

. . . The noise of the battle frightened our sutler's wife into labour the next morning. She was brought to bed of a son, and we have had him christened by the name of Ferdinand.

A British soldier, writing home from his hospital bed after Minden, hoped that 'the nation is now satisfied as there was plenty of blood for their money'. There was: of the Allies' 2,760 losses, half were British; the losses would have been less but for the prevarication of the cavalry commander Lord Sackville, who refused to bring his men to action.

Throughout the mid 18th century the British soldier performed far better than his nation had the right to expect. He was poorly paid, he was usually recruited from the poorest (and thus least healthy) layer of society, he was lashed, he was forced to spend hours pipe-claying his breeches and spatter dashes (gaiters), so beloved of George II, and he was universally despised. Dr Johnson thought the lifeguardsman as congenial a visitor as a felon. Most civilians only encountered the soldier when, in the absence of a police force, he was detailed on public order duties. Or when he was carousing off-duty. He was also convincingly outnumbered by the old enemy: the British army in 1739 stood at 18,000; the French at 133,000.

And yet, in battlefield gallantry and courage he was unsurpassable. There was more proof, if proof were needed in 1759, the *annus mirabilis* of the redcoat soldier. Having broken the French at Minden, he then bested them at Quebec. But in the doing lost a hero.

' "Now, God be praised, I will die in peace" '
CAPTAIN JOHN KNOX

THE DEATH OF GENERAL WOLFE ON THE HEIGHTS OF ABRAHAM

QUEBEC, 13 SEPTEMBER 1759

It was of James Wolfe that George II remarked, 'Mad, is he? Then I hope he will *bite* some of my other generals'. Son of a senior soldier, Wolfe received his ensign's commission in 1743, fought at Dettingen and Culloden, and was the main instigator behind the seizure of Louisburg in 1758.

Before day-break this morning we made a descent upon the north shore, about half a quarter of a mile to the eastward of Sillery; . . . we had, in this debarkation, thirty flat-bottomed boats, containing about sixteen hundred men. This was a great surprise on the enemy, who, from the natural strength of the place, did not suspect, and consequently were not prepared against, so bold an attempt . . . As fast as we landed, the boats put off for reinforcements . . . the General, with Brigadiers Monckton and Murray, were a-shore with the first division. We lost no time here, but clambered up one of the steepest precipices that can be conceived, being almost a perpendicular, and of an incredible height. As soon as we gained the summit, all was quiet, and not a shot was heard, owing to the excellent conduct of the light infantry under Colonel Howe; it was by this time clear day-light. Here we formed again . . . we then faced to the right, and marched towards the town by files, till we came to the plains of Abraham; an even piece of ground which Mr. Wolfe had made choice of, while we stood forming upon the hill. Weather showery: about six o'clock the enemy first made their appearance upon the heights, between us and the town; whereupon we halted, and wheeled to the right, thereby forming the line of battle . . . The enemy had now likewise formed the line of battle, and got some cannon to play on us, with round and canister shot; but what galled us most was a body of Indians and other marksmen they had concealed in the corn opposite to the front of our right wing . . . but Colonel Hale . . . advanced some platoons . . . which, after a few rounds, obliged these skulkers to retire. We were now ordered to lie down, and remained some time in this position. About eight o'clock we had two pieces of short brass six-pounders playing on the enemy, which threw them into some confusion ... About ten o'clock the enemy began to advance briskly in three columns, with loud shouts and recovered arms, two of them inclining to the left of our army, and the third towards our right, firing obliquely at the two extremities of our line, from the distance of one hundred and thirty, until they came within forty yards; which our troops withstood with the greatest intrepidity and firmness, still reserving their fire, and paying the strictest obedience to their Officers: this uncommon steadiness, together with the havoc which the grape-shot from our field-pieces made among them, threw them into some disorder, and was most critically maintained by a well-timed, regular and heavy discharge of our small arms, such as they could no longer oppose; hereupon they gave way, and fled with precipitation, so that, by the time the cloud of smoke was vanished, our men were again loaded, and profiting by the advantage we had over them, pursued them almost to the gates of the town, and the bridge over the little river, redoubling our fire with great eagerness, making many Officers and men prisoners. The weather cleared up, with a comfortably warm sunshine ... Our joy at this success is inexpressibly damped by the loss we sustained of one of the greatest heroes which this or any other age can boast of – General James Wolfe, who received his mortal wound as he was exerting himself at the head of the grenadiers of Louisbourg ...

After our late worthy general, of renowned memory, was carried off wounded, to the rear of the front line, he desired those who were about him to lay him down; being asked if he would have a Surgeon, he replied, 'It is needless; it is all over with me'. One of them then cried out, 'They run, see how they run'. 'Who runs?' demanded our hero, with great earnestness, like a person roused from sleep. The Officer answered, 'The enemy, Sir, Egad they give way everywhere'. Thereupon the General rejoined, 'Go one of you, my lads, to Colonel Burton; tell him to march Webb's regiment with all speed down to Charles's river, to cut off the retreat of the fugitives from the bridge'. Then, turning on his side, he added, 'Now, God be praised, I will die in peace:' and thus expired.

The fall of Quebec gave Britain control over North America.

Back in invasion-fearing Britain, the amateur part-time army had undergone one of its periodic makeovers in the Militia Act of 1757, by which each county was to raise a fixed quota of men, all over five feet two, these men to be selected by ballot. Their upkeep was to come out of rates. With the French banging on the door in 1759 it became wildly, if briefly, fashionable among young men (and not such young men) to don a red coat in the militia. The future author of the *The Decline and Fall of the Roman Empire* was one who did his bit.

⊶⊷

'my temper was insensibly soured by the society of our rustic officers'
LIEUTENANT EDWARD GIBBON

MR EDWARD GIBBON IN THE MILITIA
1760–2

When the King's order for our embodying came down, it was too late to retreat, and too soon to repent. The south battalion of the Hampshire militia was a small independent corps of four hundred and seventy-six, officers and men, commanded by Lieutenant-Colonel Sir Thomas Worsley, who, after a prolix and passionate contest, delivered us from the tyranny of the Lord Lieutenant, the Duke of Bolton. My proper station, as first captain, was at the head of my own company, and afterwards of the grenadier company; but in the absence, or even in the presence, of the two field officers, I was entrusted by my friend and my father with the effective labour of dictating the orders, and exercising the battalion . . . From Winchester, the first place of assembly (June 4, 1760), we were removed, at our own request, for the benefit of a foreign education. By the arbitrary, and often capricious orders of the War Office, the battalion successively marched to the pleasant and hospitable Blandford (June 17); to Hilsea barracks, a seat of disease and discord (September 1); to Cranbrook in the Weald of Kent (December 11); to the seacoast of Dover (December 27); to Winchester camp (June 25, 1761); to the populous and disorderly town of Devizes (October 23); to Salisbury (February 28, 1762); to our beloved Blandford a second time (March 9): and finally, to the fashionable resort of Southampton (June 2); where the colours were fixed till our final dissolution (December 23). On the beach at Dover we had exercised in sight of the Gallic shores. But the most splendid and useful scene of our life was a four months' encampment on Winchester Down, under the command of the Earl of Effingham. Our army consisted of the thirty-fourth regiment of foot and six militia corps. The consciousness of defects was stimulated by friendly emulation. We improved our time and opportunities in morning and evening field-days; and in the general reviews the South Hampshire were rather a credit than a disgrace to the line. In our subsequent quarters of the Devizes and Blandford, we advanced with a quick step in our military studies; the ballot of the ensuing summer renewed our vigour and youth; and had the militia subsisted another year, we might have contested the prize with the most perfect of our brethren.

The loss of so many busy and idle hours was not compensated by any elegant pleasure; and my temper was insensibly soured by the society of our rustic officers. In every state there exists, however, a balance of good and evil. The habits of a sedentary life were usefully broken by the duties of an active profession: in the healthful exercise of the field I hunted with a battalion, instead of a pack; and at that time I was ready, at any hour of the day or night, to fly from quarters to London, from London to quarters, on the slightest call of private or regimental business. But my principal obligation to the militia was the making me an Englishman, and a soldier . . .

Outside the heady atmosphere of imminent invasion by the perfidious French, the militia were liked and loathed in equal measure. Some regarded the militia as English citizenry in arms, a necessary counterweight to a standing army, which had been the backbone of both Cromwellian dicatorship and tyrannical continental monarchies. Others thought the militia ramshackle, a waste of time. The poets merely found the militia risible. In John Dryden's words in *Cymon and Iphigenia:*

> The country rings around with loud alarms,
> And raw in fields the rude militia swarms;
> Mouths without hands; maintained at vast expense,
> In peace a charge, in war a weak defence;
> Stout once a month they march, a blustering band,
> And ever, but in times of need, at hand.

> This was the morn when, issuing on the guard,
> Drawn up in rank and file they stood prepared
> Of seeming arms to make a short essay,
> Then hasten to be drunk, the business of the day.

And in William Cowper's *The Task Book IV*:

> 'By slow degrees, / Unapt to learn, and formed of
> stubborn stuff, / He yet by slow degrees puts off
> himself, / Grows conscious of a change, and likes
> it well: / He steps right onward, martial in his
> air . . . / But with his clumsy port the wretch has
> lost / His ignorance and harmless manners too!
>
>   *   *   *
>
> 'To swear, to game, to drink; to show at home / By
> lewdness, idleness, and sabbath-breach, / The
> great proficiency he made abroad; / To astonish
> and to grieve his gazing friends, / To break some
> maiden's and his mother's heart; / To be a pest
> where he was useful once; / Are his sole aim, and
> all his glory, now!'

The Seven Years War was brought to an end by the Treaty of Paris, 1763. British victory was absolute: France lost Canada, America east of the Mississippi, and islands in the West Indies.

There remained the small matter of paying for the war effort; at peak, in 1760, the British army had exceeded 200,000 men, around 10,000 of which had protected Great Britain's American colonies from the French. To the British government it seemed reasonable that the American colonials should pay for their own salvation. The Americans thought otherwise.

The logic of war proved inescapable.

'With grenadiers and infantry we made them to surrender'
ANONYMOUS

AMERICAN WAR OF INDEPENDENCE
BUNKER HILL: THE SOLDIER'S SONG
17 JUNE 1775

Fighting between American militiamen and the British army started up on 19 April 1775 at Lexington, Massachusetts, when a redcoat detachment was ambushed on its way to destroy a colonialist arms dump at Concord. Major W. Soutar of the Marines was there:

> We marched all Night without molestation, and about daylight in marching thro' a Village called Lexington, the Van Comp'y of the Light Troops was staggered by seeing a Flash of a Pan from a man with Arms, and soon after a Report and whistling of two Balls fired on it, on which the Light Company rushed forward and saw a dozen or eighteen Men drawn up with Arms, the Light Companies on hearing a shout from the leading Company, immediately formed, and a fire was given on their running off which killed most of them, for my part I was amazed when I heard the Shout, and being the third Com'y that led in the front, took it for granted we were surprised, not imagining in the least that we should be attacked or even molested on the March, for we had but that Instant loaded and had marched all night without being loaded.

In what the Americans termed the 'Battle' of Lexington, the redcoats fought a painful, running retreat into Boston, sniped at from every 'Bush, Stone hedge or Tree' along the way. Soutar himself was 'wounded in my leg, by a Villian behind a Stone wall who waited until he was sure of me, and then . . . off he went . . . The Ball just grazed the Bone but has not shattered it'.

Fired up on the transcendent idea of independence, the raggedy Yankee militias proved a worthy match for the red coat regulars in the War of Independence, though they rarely beat them in a pitched, fair fight. Bunker Hill was no exception.

Afterwards the red coats sang:

> It was on the seventeenth by break of day, the Yankees did surprise us,

With their strong works they had thrown up, to burn the town
and drive us;
But soon we had an order came, an order to defeat them,
Like rebels stout they stood it out and thought we ne'er could
beat them.

*   *   *

About the hour of twelve that day an order came for marching,
With three good flints and sixty rounds, each man hoped to
discharge them;
We marched down to the long wharf, where boats were ready
waiting;
With expedition we embarked, our ships kept cannonading.

*   *   *

And when our boats all filled were with officers and soldiers,
With as good troops as England had, to oppose who dare
control us?
And when our boats all fillèd were we rowed in line of battle,
Where showers of balls like hail did fly, our cannon loud did
rattle.

*   *   *

There was Cops-hill battery near Charlestown, our twenty-fours
they played,
And the three frigates in the stream, that very well behaved:
The Glasgow frigate cleared the shore, all at the time of landing,
With her grape shot and cannon balls no Yankees ne'er could
stand them.

*   *   *

And when we landed on the shore we drawed up all together,
The Yankees they all manned their works and thought we'd
ne'er come thither;
But soon they did perceive brave Howe, brave Howe, our bold
commander;
With grenadiers and infantry we made them to surrender.

*   *   *

Brave William Howe on our right wing cried, 'Boys, fight on like
thunder;
You soon will see the rebels flee with great amaze and wonder.'
Now some lay bleeding on the ground and some full fast a-
running,

O'er hills and dales and mountains high, crying, 'Zounds, brave
   Howe's a-coming.'
                         *   *   *
They began to play on our left wing where Pigot he
   commanded,
But we returned it back again with courage most undaunted;
To our grape shot and musket hot to which they were but
   strangers,
They thought to come with sword in hand but soon they found
   their danger.
                         *   *   *
And when the works we got into and put them to the flight, sir,
Some of them did hide themselves and others died with fright, sir;
And when their works we got into, without great fear or danger,
Their works we made so firm and strong the Yankees are great
   strangers.
                         *   *   *
But as for our artillery they all behaved dainty,
For while their ammunition held we gave it to them plenty;
But our conductor he got broke for his misconduct sure, sir,
The shot he sent for twelve-pound guns was made for twenty-
   four, sir.
                         *   *   *
There is some in Boston please to say, as we the field were
   taking,
We went to kill their countrymen while they their hay were
   making;
But such stout whigs I never saw, to hang them all I'd rather,
For making hay with musket pills and buckshot mixed together.
                         *   *   *
Brave Howe is so considerate as to prevent all danger,
He allows us half a pint a day, to rum we are not strangers;
Long may he live by land and sea for he's belov'd by many,
The name of Howe the Yankees dread, we see it very plainly.
                         *   *   *
And now my song is at an end, so to conclude my ditty,
It is the poor and ignorant, and only them I pity;
And as for their king, that John Hancock, and Adams, if they're
   taken,

Their heads for signs shall hang up high upon that hill called
   Bacon.

In the War of Independence the British soldier hardly lost a battle, but still lost the
war. Lord Cornwallis, the British commander, allowed himself to become trapped
between the Americans on land and a fleet – provided by the ever-interfering French
– on the sea. After the British surrender at Yorktown, the redcoats marched out to
their bands playing 'The World Turned Upside Down'.
Britain recognised America's independence in 1783.

' "... drink success to the British Arms" '
SERGEANT SAMUEL ANCELL

PORTRAIT OF A DRUNKEN SOLDIER
GIBRALTAR, 15 APRIL 1781

Ancell of the 58th Regiment served throughout the 1779–83 siege of Gibraltar by the
Spanish, in one of their periodic attempts to re-take the Rock. Ancell writes to his
brother.

I cannot, dear Brother, omit penning an entertaining conversation I had with a soldier in Irish Town yesterday. I met Jack
Careless in the street, singing with uncommon glee (notwithstanding the enemy were firing with prodigious warmth), part of
the old song,

'A soldier's life, is a merry life,
From care and trouble Free.'

He ran to me with eagerness, and presenting his bottle cry'd,
'D – m me, if I don't like fighting: I'd like to be ever tanning the
Dons: – Plenty of good liquor for carrying away – never was the
price so cheap – fine stuff – enough to make a miser quit his
gold.' 'Why, Jack,' says I, 'what have you been about?' With an
arch grin, he replied, 'That would puzzle a Heathen philosopher,

or yearly almanack-maker, to unriddle. I scarce know myself. I have been constantly on foot and watch, half-starved, and without money, facing a parcel of pitiful Spaniards. I have been fighting, wheeling, marching, and counter-marching; sometimes with a firelock, then a handspike, and now my bottle' (brandishing it in the air). 'I am so pleased with the melody of great guns, that I consider myself as a Roman General, gloriously fighting for my country's honour and liberty.' A shell that instant burst, a piece of which knocked the bottle out of his hand; with the greatest composure he replied (having first graced it with an oath), 'This is not any loss, I have found a whole cask of good luck,' and brought me to view his treasure. 'But, Jack,' says I, 'are you not thankful to God, for your preservation?' 'How do you mean?' he answered. 'Fine talking of God with a soldier, whose trade and occupation is cutting throats. Divinity and slaughter sound very well together, they jangle like a crack'd bell in the hand of a noisy crier: Our King is answerable to God for us. I fight for him. My religion consists of a firelock, open touch-hole, good flint, well rammed charge, and seventy rounds of powder and ball. This is my military creed. Come, comrade, drink success to the British Arms.'

The drinking culture of the soldiery was not confined to those on active service. Back in Britain, soldiers were habitually billeted on innkeepers; the billeted soldiers, who had two meals a day, breakfast and lunch, filled their hungry bellies in afternoons by drinking their regulation daily five free pints of beer. And then spent the 2d of pay left over from 'off reckonings' on the innkeeper's cheap gin. Hence the expression, 'drunk for a penny, dead drunk for tuppence'.

Hard drinking affected the officer class, too. Captain John Peebles of the 42nd Regiment confided to his diary in an entry almost contemporaneous with Ancell's encounter with Careless, 'dined with our light captain and got foul with claret'.

Alcohol was doubtless a factor in the ongoing epidemic of military crime which, by 1868, resulted in nearly 14 per cent of the army being court-martialled.

There was one benefit of the drinking culture. Urine from pubs, many of them frequented by soldiers, was used in the dyeing of the army's red coats. The urine collector was colloquially known as 'Piss Harry'.

—➤•◄—

*'neither adjutant, paymaster, or quarter-master could move
an inch without my assistance'*
REGIMENTAL SERGEANT-MAJOR WILLIAM COBBETT

THE NCO'S LOT

CANADA, C 1785

By the late 18th century the purchasing of commissioned ranks in the army had undergone a change; although still exchanged for money, the commission was no longer a licence for larceny. It was, instead, a passport to fashionable society. When George Wickham, the factor's scion, joined the officers' mess in Jane Austen's *Pride and Prejudice* he epitomized a social trend. By becoming an officer he became a gentleman. Naturally, the more exclusive the regiment, the higher the cost of the commission, with the Horse Guards being priciest of all.

Unfortunately, many of these 'epaulette gentry' were poor peacetime leaders of soldiers, as NCO William Cobbett discovered on enlisting in the 54th Foot in 1784.

While I was Corporal I was made clerk to the regiment. In a very short time, the whole of the business in that way fell into my hands; and, at the end of about a year, neither adjutant, paymaster, or quarter-master, could move an inch without my assistance. The accounts and letters of the paymaster went through my hands; or, rather, I was the maker of them. All the returns, reports, and other official papers were of my drawing up.

Then I became Sergeant-Major to the regiment, which brought me in close contact at every hour, with the whole of the epaulette gentry, whose profound and surprising ignorance I discovered in a twinkling. The military part of the regiment's affairs fell under my care. In early life, I contracted the blessed habit of husbanding well my time. To this more than to any other thing, I owed my very extraordinary promotion in the army. I was always ready: never did any man, or anything, wait one moment for me. Being raised from corporal to sergeant-major at once, over the heads of thirty sergeants, I naturally should have been an object of envy and hatred; but this habit of early rising really subdued these passions; because everyone felt that what I did he had never done, and never could do. Long before any other man was dressed for parade, my work for the morning was well done, and I myself was on parade walking in fine weather, for an hour perhaps. My custom was this: to get up, in summer, at daylight, and in winter at four o'clock; shave, dress, even to the putting of my sword belt over my shoulder, and having my sword lying on the table before me, ready to hang by my side. Then I ate a bit of cheese, or pork, and bread. Then I prepared my report, which was filled up as fast as the companies brought me in the materials. After this I had an hour or two to read, before the time came for any duty out of doors, unless when the regiment or part of it went out to exercise in the morning. When this was the case, and the matter was left to me, I always had it on the ground in such time as that the bayonets glistened in the rising sun, a sight which gave me delight, of which I often think, but which I should in vain endeavour to describe. If the officers were to go out, eight or ten o'clock was the hour, sweating the men in the heat of the day, breaking in upon the time for cooking their dinner, putting all things out of order and all men out of humour. When I was commander, the men had a long day of leisure before them: they could ramble into the town or into the woods; go to get raspberries, to catch birds, to catch fish, or to pursue any other recreation, and such of them as chose, and were qualified, to work at their trades. So that here, arising solely from the early habits of one very young man, were pleasant and happy days given to hundreds.

About this time, the new discipline, as it was called, was sent out to us in little books, which were to be studied by the officers of each regiment, and the rules of which were to be immediately conformed to. Though any old woman might have written such a book; though it was excessively foolish from beginning to end; still, it was to be complied with, it ordered and commanded a total change.

To make this change was left to me, while not a single officer in the regiment paid the least attention to the matter; so that, when the time came for the annual review, I had to give lectures of instruction to the officers themselves, the Colonel not excepted; and, for several of them, I had to make out, upon large cards, which they bought for the purpose, little plans of the position of the regiment, together with lists of the words of command, which they had to give in the field. There was I, at the review, upon the flank of the grenadier company, with my worsted shoulder-knot, and my great high, coarse, hairy cap; confounded in the ranks amongst other men, while those who were commanding me to move my hands or my feet, thus or thus, were, in fact, uttering words, which I had taught them; and were, in everything except mere authority, my inferiors; and ought to have been commanded by me. It was impossible for reflections of this sort not to intrude themselves; and, as I advanced in experience, I felt less and less respect for those, whom I was compelled to obey.

But I had a very delicate part to act with those gentry; for, while I despised them for their gross ignorance and their vanity, and hated them for their drunkenness and rapacity, I was fully sensible of their power. My path was full of rocks and pitfalls; and, as I never disguised my dislikes, or restrained my tongue, I should have been broken and flogged for fifty different offences, had they not been kept in awe by my inflexible sobriety, impartiality, and integrity, by the consciousness of their inferiority to me, and by the real and almost indispensable necessity of the use of my talents. They, in fact, resigned all the discipline of the regiment to me, and I very freely left them to swagger about and to get roaring drunk.

To describe the various instances of their ignorance, and the various tricks they played to diguise it from me, would fill a volume. It is the custom in regiments to give out orders every day from the officer commanding. These are written by the Adjutant, to whom the Sergeant-Major is a sort of deputy. The man whom I had to do with was a keen fellow, but wholly illiterate. The orders which he wrote most cruelly murdered our mother-tongue. But in his absence, or during a severe drunken fit, it fell to my lot to write orders. As we both wrote in the same book, he used to look at these. He saw commas, semi-colons, colons, full points, and paragraphs. The questions he used to put to me, in an obscure sort of way, in order to know why I made these divisions, and yet, at the same time, his attempts to disguise his object, have made me laugh a thousand times. He at last fell upon this device: he made me write, while he pretended to dictate! Imagine to yourself, me sitting, pen in hand, to put upon paper the precious offspring of the mind of this stupid curmudgeon! But, here, a greater difficulty than any former arose. He that could not write good grammar, could not, of course, dictate good grammar. Out would come some gross error, such as I was ashamed to see in my handwriting, I would stop; suggest another arrangement; but this I was at first obliged to do in a very indirect and delicate manner. But this course could not continue long; and he put an end to it in this way: he used to tell me his story, and leave me to put it upon paper; and this we continued to the end of our connection.

Cobbett left the army in 1791, and later became a radical MP, farmer and author. For all the accuracy of Cobbett's portrait of the late 18th century commissioned officer, that self-same officer is a paradox. Ignorant, drunken, snobbish, and brutal he may have been, but he also led his men to outfight the French on the battlefields of Europe in the twenty-year round of wars with revolutionary France. Starting with Valenciennes.

——➤◆⬥——

'I will do more yet for my King and Country's saik'
GEORGE ROBERTSON

ONE MAN'S WAR
LETTERS HOME
1793

Robertson of the Royal Artillery took part in the joint British–Hanoverian drive against the French in the Netherlands; he participated in the storming of 'Valencine' [Valenciennes].

Woolwich, February 26, 1793

Dear Mother
I have just received orders for Germeny under the command of the Duke of York, with 2,200 foot guards. We expect to embark tomorrow to go with His Royal Highness as a Bodyguard of British Heroes. We are to lead the Dutch Prushen and Hanover Troops into the field, as there is none equal to the British Army. We are chosen troops sent by His Majesty to show an example to the other Troops, to go in front, & lead the combined army against the French which consists of 150,000 able fighten men. You may judge if we shall have anything to dow. I had the pleasure to conquer the French last war; but God knows how it will be this

war. I cannot expect to escape the Bullets of my enemies much longer, as non has ever entred my flesh as yet. To be plain with you and not dishearten you, I don't expect to come off so cleare as I did last war. But it is death or honour. I exspeck to be a Gentleman or a Cripel. But you shall never see me destress you. If I cannot help you, I never shall destress you.

Dear Mother, I take my family with me. Where I go, they must go. If I leave them, I should have no luck. My wife and two children is in good health, & in good spirits, fear not for us. I hope God will be on our side.

Valencine, August 1, 1793

I received your kind letter and am happy to find you are yet in the land of the Living and well. Dear Mother and Townsmen, I have great news for you. On the night of the 23rd, our British Troops stormed the Outworks of Valencine, and took them; killed and wounded 500 French; our lose about ten only. The Elements was like on fire with Bomb shell. Never did my eyes behold the like before; and on the 26th, we heard a horn blow in the Town for a parley, and a flag of Truce to come upon Terms, which was agreed on; on these terms, that the British Troops shall have possession of the Town & Garrison and no other. On the 1st day of August, we enter the Town with two 6-pounders and a silk Flag at the head of the British Grenadiers. This is over. Thank God. The number killed in that time in the town is 6,000, and a number of Women and Children. The British Artillery manned a Battery of eight 12-pounders which hurt them more than all the firing troops. I commanded one of those Guns one day on the Battry, when a 24-pound shot went thro' one of my men's shoulders & brock my Gun wheel. The blood and flesh of the man was all over my Cloas. The pipol in the Camp thought we was all gone. Mother, you cannot think how happy my wife and children was to see me return safe to my Tent. Every time I went to the Battery, I took leave of my wife & family. We staid 24 hours at a time; and when we returned, it was the same as new life to us both . . .

I will do more yet for my King and Country's saik. My country shall never be stained by me. After things is settled hear, we exspect to march for Dunkirk, to besiege that Town & Garrison.

Then we shall winter, and rest till the Spring; and then I hope for Parris. Keep a good heart at home; we will conquer our enemies, and bring them down. May the British flag ever flourish over the world . . .

God bless you, Dear Mother, adu, adu, God bless you. I hope my Townsmen will drink sucksess to George Robertson.

Your ever loving Son,
Geo. Robertson

━━━◆◆◆━━━

'the skin of my eyes and face was drawn so tight . . .
I could not possibly shut my eyes'
PRIVATE JOHN SHIPP

A REDCOAT, A FIGHT AND A HAIR-DO
A BOY SOLDIER'S INTRODUCTION TO THE ARMY
1797

Shipp, an orphan, had wanted to be a soldier since seeing his first recruiting band: 'It was all about Gentleman soldiers, merry life, muskets rattling, cannon roaring, drums beating, colours flying, regiments charging and shouts of victory! Victory!' He enlisted in the 22nd Regiment of Foot in 1797, aged thirteen, although he had tried to enlist earlier.

On the following morning I was taken to a barber's, and deprived of my curly brown locks. My hair curled beautifully, but in a minute my poor little head was nearly bald, except a small patch behind, which was reserved for a future operation. I was then paraded to the tailor's shop, and deprived of my new clothes – coat, leathers, and hat – for which I received, in exchange, red jacket, red waistcoat, red pantaloons, and red foraging-cap. The change, or metamorphosis, was so complete, that I could hardly imagine it to be the same dapper little fellow. I was exceedingly tall for a boy of ten years of age; but, notwithstanding this, my clothes were much too large, my sleeves were two or three inches over my hands, or rather longer than my fingers; and the whole hung on me, to use a well-known expression, like a purser's shirt on a hand-spike. My pride was humbled, my spirits drooped, and I followed the drum-major, hanging my head like a felon going to the place of execution. I cut such a queer figure, that all who met me turned round and stared at me. At last, I mustered up courage enough to ask one little chap what he was staring at, when he replied, 'Ask my eye, Johnny Raw;' at the same time adding his extended fingers and thumb to the length of his nose. Passing some drummers on their way to practicc, I got finely roasted. 'Twig the raw-skin!' – 'Smoke his pantaloons!' – 'Them there trousers is what I calls a knowing cut!' – 'Look at the sign of the Red Man!' &c., &c. Under this kind of file-firing I reached my barrack, where I was doomed to undergo the same routine of quizzing, till at length I got nettled, and told one of the boys, if he did not let me alone, I should take the liberty of giving him a good threshing. This 'pluck', as they termed it, silenced my tormentors, and I was permitted, for a time, to remain unmolested.

Only for a time; Shipp was shortly picked on by the barrack-room bully, and the ensuing fight went to six rounds before Shipp emerged the winner; 'This my first victory established that I was neither a coward nor to be coaxed with impunity. Eulogiums were showered down upon me, and the shouting and uproar were beyond description'. Shipp's first morning in the army continued:

After this I went into town, to purchase a few requisites, such as a powder-bag, puff, soap, candles, grease &c.; and, having procured what I stood in need of, I returned to my barrack, where I underwent the operation of having my hair tied for the first time, to the no small amusement of all the boys assembled. A large piece of candle-grease was applied, first to the sides of my head, then to the hind long hair; after this, the same kind of operation was performed with nasty stinking soap – sometimes the man who was dressing me applying his knuckles, instead of the soap, to the delight of the surrounding boys, who were bursting their sides with laughter, to see the tears roll down my cheeks. When this operation was over, I had to go through one of a more serious nature. A large pad, or bag filled with sand, was poked into the back of my head, round which the hair was gathered tight, and the whole tied round with a leather thong. When I was dressed for parade, I could scarcely get my eyelids to perform their office; the skin of my eyes and face was drawn so tight by the plug that was stuck in the back of my head, that I could not possibly shut my eyes; and to this, an enormous high stock was poked under my chin; so that, altogether, I felt as stiff as if I had swallowed a ramrod, or a sergeant's halberd. Shortly after I was thus equipped, dinner was served; but my poor jaws refused to act on the offensive, and when I made an attempt to eat, my pad behind went up and down like a sledge-hammer.

The 'queue' was phased out in 1808.

Shipp went on to have an original army career; at the age of 15 he was sentenced to 999 lashes for desertion, but this was cancelled by a humane CO. Shipp was then promoted from the ranks – rare enough in itself – not once but twice. And twice sold his commission.

'The Sultan was . . . interred . . . with the compliments due to his exalted rank'
ANONYMOUS OFFICER

THE TAKING OF SERINGAPATAM
INDIA, 1799

Seringapatam was the seat of Tipoo Sultan, ruler of Mysore, whose anti-British brutality was boundless; he murdered captured redcoats by driving nails into their skulls. Nonetheless, after his death in the siege of Seringapatam, in a display of British decency or, perhaps, whimsy, he was buried with full military honours.

We arrived here on the 4th of April, 1799, since which time, the siege has continued with uninterrupted success on our part, although not without the loss of blood. The few first days after we came we were employed in collecting the necessary materials, and after that, there were daily skirmishes, taking his outposts, &c. so that our breaching batteries did not open till near the latter end of the month. The breach being at length practicable, on the 4th of May, being exactly one month from the day of our arrival, it was determined to storm; and at three o'clock in the morning, the flank companies of every corps in the field, besides two or three European regiments, complete, moved down to the trenches, where we sat in anxious expectation of the signal to begin, till near one o'clock, during which time our batteries kept up an incessant firing. About that time, the storming party, under the command of General Baird, began to move on, covered by the constant fire from our batteries, and suffering a very galling one of grape from the fort. The enemy soon abandoned the ramparts after our brave countrymen reached them; in about half an hour, the fire from the fort had ceased entirely, and the British flag was displayed in various parts of it.

Soon after the storm 300 grenadiers rushed into the place, and were about to plunder it, when they were called off. Those inside immediately shut the gates, and the 33rd Regiment and a Native Corps drew up in front; we then learnt that the Sultan with his wives, sons, treasure, &c., were all in the palace. Soon after Major Allan came up with a flag of truce from General Baird, and after explaining to those who were in the balcony, that no violence should be offered, desired them to call the Sultan; they replied that he was wounded; that they did not know whether he was in the palace or not, but they would go and look for him.

After much delay it was suspected that this was only a pretence to give him time to make his escape; upon which the General ordered a 6 pounder to be brought in front of the gate, and told them, that, if the Sultan did not immediately make his appearance, he would burst it open. They then said that he was not in the palace, but that his sons would come out immediately; we waited some time longer, but as they did not come Major Allan, carrying the flag of truce, and accompanied by two other officers, went in. They returned in about half an hour with the two young princes, who, though they did not seem depressed by their situation, yet appeared at the same time to feel it. Being asked what servants should attend them to the camp, they replied, that they had no right to order; and when the General told them they had only to name the people who should accompany them, they said, that in the morning they could have called for many, but now, they feared, there were very few remaining! General Baird gave them in charge to Major Agnew, who conveyed them in palanquins, to head-quarters.

As it was now near sun-set, everyone was anxious to secure the Sultan, if possible.

After much inquiry, they found a person who seemed to be a

man of consequence; he said that Tipoo had been killed in endeavouring to escape; he was immediately seized, and told that his life would answer for it if he did not immediately shew the place.

He accordingly led the way, and we followed, to a kind of gateway leading to a bridge across the ditch – there, in a place about 4 feet wide and 12 feet long, were upwards of 70 dead bodies lying, and in the midst of them appeared the Sultan's palanquin; immediate search was made for his body, but it was upwards of an hour before he was discovered. He had received a shot in his arm at the time of the storm, for he was himself on the ramparts; after this, in endeavouring to make his escape, he was met by a party of Europeans, who wounded him in the side with a bayonet; he had also received a shot through the temple, which put an end to his existence.

The body was recognised by some of his palanquin boys, who were but slightly wounded; it was still warm when we discovered it.

He appeared to be rather above the middle size, stout and well made; his head was shaved close; he seemed to be between 40 and 50, and rather corpulent.

His dress was very plain. The Sultan was next day interred in the Lal Bag, on the left of his father, (his mother being on the right) with the compliments due to his exalted rank.

The commander of the Seringapatam campaign was a 29-year-old colonel called Arthur Wellesley.

The campaign in India was shadow fighting; the Indian potentates were encouraged and financed by revolutionary France as a means of indirectly attacking Albion. In a few years Wellesley would return to Europe to fight the French directly in the Napoleonic Wars, 1803–15, and find his destiny as the Duke of Wellington. The Iron Duke.

'The number of women allowed by the Government to embark . . .
are six for every hundred men'

Anonymous

RULES FOR SOLDIERS' WIVES

1801

Extract from the regulations of the 95th Rifle Corps, stationed at Shorncliffe, Kent.

The marriage of soldiers being a matter of benefit to a regiment, of comfort to themselves, or of misery to both exactly in proportion as it is under good or bad regulations, this article has been much considered.

The number of women allowed by Government to embark on service are six for every hundred men, inclusive of all Non-Commissioned Officers' wives.

This number is ample and indeed more than sufficient for a light corps, as every officer and soldier who have ever seen service must admit. It should never be exceeded on any pretext whatever, because the doing so is humanity of the falsest kind. Women who have more than two children can also never be of the number to embark except in extraordinary cases, because that is a still greater act of inhumanity.

The Rifle Corps shall be a home of comfort to those who are entitled to feel its benefits, but shall not be a source, as is too often the case, of multiplying misery and prostitution among those who should be under every good soldier's peculiar care and protection.

Before the mode is pointed out of employment and comfortable livelihood to those women who do remain, all women of immoral or drunken character, or who refuse to work for the men, are warned that they will not be permitted to remain ever to disgrace the Corps; but their friends will be written to or they must be received into some poor house or situation where they can earn their bread. To help the married women all regimental needlework and washing was to be done by them. The Colonel requests that the officers will never give their linen to wash out of the regiment, and also that they will distribute it nearly equally among the sergeants' wives.

The Quartermaster will never give any needlework out of the regiment which can be done in it, and officers are requested to do the same; the women are also recommended to look for needlework in the neighbourhood of wherever the regiment may be, and the officers to give them any aid in their power to procure the same.

Whenever a soldier's wife requires some pecuniary aid for illness, her husband will apply to the surgeon, who will represent it to the Commanding Officer, when such assistance as the Charity Fund can afford will be given her. The children of the regiment will be paid every attention to; the Commanding Officers of Companies will consider them, as well as the women, under their care, will attend to their being well and cleanly clothed, and to the regular attendance at the school of all those who can go there.'

Wives who followed their husbands overseas were selected by ballot; on campaign they marched, or rode donkeys, ahead of their husbands to prepare meals and bivouacs. If their husband was killed, his comrades would offer condolence – and a hand in marriage, partly out of charity, partly out of practical and lustful self-interest. Usually, the widow accepted. Sometimes, though, widows were inconsolable. Benjamin Harris offered his hand 'on the first opportunity' to Mrs Joseph Cochan, after her husband had been killed beside him in the Peninsula in 1808, but she had had too great a shock to think of marrying another soldier; 'she therefore thanked me for my good feeling towards her, but declined my offer, and left us soon afterwards . . .'

If anything, wives left behind in Britain suffered more than those who went on campaign, for they endured not only separation but poverty. There was no married allowance.

But then the life of the woman on the 'Married Roll' was always grim. From 1792 onwards, soldiers were billeted in barracks instead of inns, corners of which were given to married couples and their families. Such a corner was described by a 'lady correspondent' to Charles Dickens' magazine Household Words: 'At the end of this room, near the windows, was the narrow space allotted to the sergeant – a married man. Two iron bedsteads lashed together, formed the family couch. Four iron rods, fastened at the corners, supported a cord on which some curtains looped up.' This curtain is all that separated the sergeant's wife, aged nineteen, from the men; she had given birth in that very barrack room, behind the curtain, nine months before.

Not until the end of the Crimean War in 1855 did the lot of the soldier's wife improve.

➔•◆•←

'I never saw a man's back so horrible to look on'
PRIVATE ALEXANDER ALEXANDER

A FLOGGING
CHATHAM, 1801

Almost every morning there were some absent without leave, and the flogging was of course threatened in a more terrific manner. This threat of flogging was no idle matter in our eyes; there being scarce a day in which we did not see one or more of the soldiers get from three to seven hundred lashes. We never could see any crime these poor fellows had committed to merit such cruelty. We heard their crimes read to us indeed, as we were all forced to be present, such as unsoldierlike conduct, (this was a common crime, laid to our charge at drill every day a hundred times,) or insolence to bombardier 'A' or lance-corporal 'B' on duty. For petty misdemeanors, such as these, I saw the men every day punished with a severity I had never beheld exercised on the slaves in Carriacou. At this time, and indeed for years after, I have actually trembled at the threat of a lance-bombardier; and not myself only, but the stoutest and oldest soldier did the same; for so severe was the discipline, that if he had only malice enough to make the charge, a flogging was certain to follow.

The first man I saw punished my heart was like to burst. It was with difficulty I could restrain my tears, as the thought broke upon me of what I had brought myself to. Indeed, my spirits sunk from that day, and all hopes of bettering my condition in life fled forever. I had hitherto only seen the pomp of war – the gloss and glitter of the army; now I was introduced into the arcana of its origination, and under the direct influence of its stern economy. I felt how much I had been deceived.

Another circumstance I must not omit before I leave Chatham; it made a great impression on me and all the troops. A poor fellow of the 9th regiment, said to be a farmer's son in Suffolk, had the misfortune to be found asleep on his post. General Sir J.

Moore had the command of the Chatham division at the time; he was a severe disciplinarian. The soldier was tried by a court-martial, and sentenced to be flogged; all the troops were paraded to witness the punishment. It was a very stormy morning; the frost, which had continued for some days, gave way during the night, and the wind and sleet drove most pitiously: it was a severe punishment to stand clothed looking on, how much more so to be stripped to the waist, and tied up to the halberts. The soldier was a fine-looking lad, and bore an excellent character in his regiment; his officers were much interested in his behalf, and made great intercession for him to the General. But all their pleading was in vain, the General remained inflexible and made a very long speech after the punishment, in which he reflected in very severe terms on the conduct of the officers and non-commissioned officers present, observing, that if they did their duty as strictly as they had any regard for their men, they ought never to report them to him, for he would pardon no man when found guilty. The poor fellow got two hundred and twenty-nine lashes, but they were uncommonly severe. I saw the drum-major strike a drummer to the ground for not using his strength sufficiently. General Sir John Moore was present all the time. At length, the surgeon interfered, the poor fellow's back was black as the darkest mahogany, and dreadfully swelled. The cats being too thick, they did not cut, which made the punishment more severe. He was instantly taken down and carried to the hospital, where he died in eight days afterwards, his back having mortified. It was the cold I think that killed him; for I have often seen seven hundred lashes inflicted, but I never saw a man's back so horrible to look upon.

Flogging was by no means the only military punishment of the Georgian era; chastisements spanned simple detention to death by hanging, breaking upon the wheel, or shooting. The cruelly sophisticated whirligig was a wooden spinning cage in which the incarcerated offender became sick with giddiness. Running the gauntlet involved the bare backed prisoner proceeding between two rows of soldiers, who struck him as he passed; in riding the wooden horse an offender sat on a sharp-edged frame, frequently with weights attached to his feet to have his genitals crushed.

Gradually the more barbaric corporal punishments were phased out; the longest-lasting of them, flogging, was abolished in 1881. One of the principal campaigners against flogging was ex-Regimental Sergeant-Major Cobbett, who was imprisoned for two years for his opposition to the punishment.

'I would have given a good round sum . . . to have been in any situation rather than the one in which I now found myself'
PRIVATE BENJAMIN HARRIS

STERN DUTY
PRIVATE HARRIS IS DETAILED FOR A FIRING SQUAD
WINCHESTER, 1802

Whilst lying at Winchester (where we remained three months), young as I was in the profession, I was picked out, amongst others, to perform a piece of duty that, for many years afterwards, remained deeply impressed upon my mind, and gave me the first impression of the stern duties of a soldier's life. A private of the 70th Regiment had deserted from that corps, and afterwards enlisted in several other regiments; indeed, I was told at the time (although I cannot answer for so great a number) that sixteen different times he had received the bounty and then stolen off. Being, however, caught at last, he was brought to trial at Portsmouth, and sentenced by general court-martial to be shot.

The 66th received a route to Portsmouth to be present on the occasion, and, as the execution would be a good hint to us young 'uns, there were four lads picked out of our corps to assist in this piece of duty, myself being one of the number chosen.

Besides these men, four soldiers from three other regiments were ordered on the firing-party, making sixteen in all. The place of execution was Portsdown Hill, near Hilsea Barracks, and the different regiments assembled must have composed a force of about fifteen thousand men, having been assembled from the Isle of Wight, from Chichester, Gosport, and other places. The sight was very imposing, and appeared to make a deep impression on all there. As for myself, I felt that I would have given a good round sum (had I possessed it) to have been in any situation rather than the one in which I now found myself; and when I looked into the faces of my companions I saw, by the pallor and anxiety depicted in each countenance, the reflection of my own feelings. When all was ready, we were moved to the front, and the culprit was brought out. He made a short speech to the parade, acknowledging the justice of his sentence, and that drinking and evil company had brought the punishment upon him.

He behaved himself firmly and well, and did not seem to flinch. After being blindfolded, he was desired to kneel down behind a coffin, which was placed on the ground, and the drum-major of the Hilsea depot, giving us an expressive glance, we immediately commenced loading.

This was done in the deepest silence, and, the next moment, we were primed and ready. There was then a dreadful pause for a few moments, and the drum-major, again looking towards us, gave the signal before agreed upon (a flourish of his cane), and we levelled and fired. We had been previously strictly enjoined to be steady, and take good aim, and the poor fellow, pierced by several balls, fell heavily upon his back; and as he lay, with his arms pinioned to his sides, I observed that his hands waved for a few moments, like the fins of a fish when in the agonies of death. The drum-major also observed the movement, and, making another signal, four of our party immediately stepped up to the prostrate body, and placing the muzzles of their pieces to the head, fired, and put him out of his misery. The different regiments then fell back by companies, and the word being given to march past in slow time, when each company came in line with the body, the word was given to 'mark time', and then 'eyes left', in order that we might all observe the terrible example. We then moved onwards, and marched from the ground to our different quarters. The 66th stopped that night about three miles from Portsdown Hill, and in the morning we returned to Winchester.

'soldiers, their wives and children, all lying together in a state
of the most deadful sea-sickness'
SERGEANT JOHN SHIPP

CONVOY TO INDIA

1803

Shipp and his regiment were ordered to India to fight the Mahratta Confederacy, one of the most substantial remaining native powers. Conditions aboard the leaky, over-crowded troop ships used by the War Office were unfailingly foul; many a soldier considered the sea passage to foreign parts the worst part of service.

I was dreadfully wet and cold, and my teeth chattered most woefully; so I made towards the gun-deck, some portion of which was allotted for the soldiers. There the heat was suffocating, and the stench intolerable. The scene in the orlop-deck was truly distressing: soldiers, their wives and children, all lying together in a state of the most dreadful sea-sickness, groaning in concert, and calling for a drop of water to cool their parched tongues. I screwed myself up behind a butt, and soon fell into that stupor which sea-sickness will create. In this state I continued until morning; and, when I awoke, I found that the hurricane had returned with redoubled fury, and that we were standing towards land. The captain came a-head to look out, and, after some consideration, he at last told the officer to stand out to sea. The following morning was ushered in by the sun's bright beams diffusing their lustre on the dejected features of frightened and helpless mortals. The dark clouds of sad despair were in mercy driven from our minds, and the bright beams of munificent love from above took their place. The before downcast eye was seen to sparkle with delight, and the haggard cheek of despondency resumed its wonted serenity . . .

Some three weeks after this we were again visited by a most dreadful storm, that far exceeded the former one, and from which we suffered much external injury, our main top-mast, and other smaller masts, being carried away. But the interior of our poor bark exhibited a scene of far greater desolation. We were then far from land, and a pestilential disease was raging among us in all its terrific forms. Nought could be seen but the pallid cheek of disease, or the sunken eye of despair. The sea-gulls soared over the ship, and huge sharks hovered around, watching for their prey. These creatures are sure indications of ships having some pestilential disease on board, and they have been known to follow a vessel so circumstanced to the most distant climes – to countries far from their native element. To add to our distresses, some ten barrels of ship's paint, or colour, got loose from their lashings, and rolled from side to side, and from head to stern, carrying everything before them by their enormous weight. From our inability to stop them in their destructive progress, they one and all were staved in, and the gun deck soon became one mass of colours, in which lay the dead and the dying, both white and black.

It would be difficult for the reader to picture to himself a set of men more deplorably situated than we now were; but our distresses were not yet at their height: for, as though our miseries still required aggravation, the scurvy broke out among us in a most frightful manner. Scarcely a single individual on board escaped this melancholy disorder, and the swollen legs, the gums protruding beyond the lips, attested the malignancy of the visitation. The dying were burying the dead, and the features of all on board wore the garb of mourning.

Every assistance and attention that humanity or generosity could dictate, was freely and liberally bestowed by the officers on board, who cheerfully gave up their fresh meat and many other comforts, for the benefit of the distressed: but the pestilence baffled the aid of medicine and the skill of the medical attendants. My poor legs were as big as drums; my gums swollen to an enormous size; my tongue too big for my mouth; and all I could eat was raw potatoes and vinegar. But my kind and affectionate officers sometimes brought me some tea and coffee, at which the languid eye would brighten, and the tear of gratitude would intuitively fall, in spite of my efforts to repress what was thought unmanly. Our spirits were so subdued by suffering, and our frames so much reduced and emaciated, that I have seen poor men weep bitterly, they knew not why. Thus passed the time; men dying in dozens, and, ere their blood was cold, hurled into the briny deep, there to become a prey to sharks. It was a dreadful sight to see the bodies of our comrades the bone of disputation with these voracious natives of the dreary deep; and the reflection that

The Mahratta Confederacy was smashed at Assaye in 1803; two years later the Grand Moghul of India accepted British protection. India was now effectively a British possession.

'I was very mistaken about the money lasting'
WILLIAM LAWRENCE

WILLIAM LAWRENCE GOES FOR A SOLDIER
1804

Britain was in dire need of soldiers in 1804, for it was already plunged deep into what contemporaries would call the Great War, and what later generations would call the Napoleonic Wars. Britain was under threat of invasion. Napoleon had 500,000 men under arms; the British raised 230,000 for the regular army. Nearly 40 per cent of these were volunteers siphoned off from the militia; some were existing regulars; and some, like William Lawrence, a farm boy seeking escape from the rural round, were new recruits:

Dorchester was only eight miles from my parents' house, but I never seriously thought of going to them. Unable to make up my mind what to do, or where to go, I ambled through the town watching the preparations for the fair, which was to take place the next day. I wandered into the stable-yard of one of the principal inns and was brought to my senses when a voice sang out: 'Hey you! What do you want?'

It was the ostler. I told him I was hungry but had no money, and was in search of employment. He said if I brushed about a bit and helped him rub down the horses, he would find me plenty to eat. I did so and, sure enough, he brought me a lump of bread and beef, enough for two or three meals. I ate as much as I wanted. Afterwards I felt tired. I made up a bed with some straw and, putting the remainder of my meal into my handkerchief to serve as a pillow, I lay down. The ostler had given me a rug and this I pulled over me. I slept soundly all night.

In the morning I did some more work in the stable, then walked out into the street with my new friend. We saw some soldiers and I said I wanted to be a soldier too. The ostler knew where he could enlist me and took me straight to the rendezvous which was a public-house. Inside was a sergeant of artillery, who gave him two guineas for bringing me and myself five for coming. My measurements were taken – which caused a lot of amusement – and I was put into an old soldier's coat. With three or four yards of ribbon hanging from my cap, I paraded around town with the other recruits, entering almost every public-house, treating someone or other.

In the very first inn sat a Briantspuddle farmer, a man I knew well. He exclaimed in surprise at seeing me. I begged him not to tell my father and mother where I was, and how he had seen me, and hurried out. Then later in the day I encountered my father's next-door neighbour. He recognized me immediately. I offered him the price of a gallon of ale not to say anything to my parents. He took the money and promised he wouldn't. How I spent the rest of the night can better be imagined than described, but the next morning, I had to be sworn in at the Town Hall. I was on my way there with an officer when who should meet us but my father and mother. As soon as the neighbour had got home, he had gone and told them what I was up to. They told the officer I was an apprentice, and he gave me up to them without any trouble, but he asked me what had become of the bounty of five guineas. Discovering that I had only seventeen shillings and sixpence left, he kindly relieved me of even that. My parents marched me off home, and my father went to see a magistrate to find out what he should do about me. The magistrate advised him to take me back to Dorchester to be tried at the next sitting. This my father did and I was severely reprimanded by the bench. They gave me the choice of serving my time as an apprentice or going to prison. Of course, I chose the former, so they gave me a letter to give to Henry Bush [his employer].

When I got downstairs, the officer was there. He said that if my master was unwilling to take me back, he would enlist me again. He asked if I had any money. I didn't, so he gave me a shilling and wished me well.

My father sent me off from Dorchester immediately, giving me strict orders to get back to Studland as quickly as I could. I received no blessing, or anything else so, with a heavy heart, I set off. I hadn't gone far when I was overtaken by a dairy cart. The dairy-man offered me a lift and I accepted. He asked where I was going. I told him some of my story and showed him the letter, getting him to open it so that I could find out what was inside. He said my master would not be able to hurt me, that it was safe to go back to Studland. That was cheering, but I didn't intend to go back anyway.

I rode with the man as far as he went, then continued on foot to a village called Winfrith. Being hungry I went into a public-house and ordered some bread and cheese. A soldier was there and the sight of him revived my spirit, and my longing to be like him. I got into conversation with him and discovered that he was on furlough, bound for Bridport. I said I wanted to be a soldier too. Straight away he said that he could enlist me in the 40th Regiment of Foot which gave 16 guineas bounty. It sounded a great deal of money. I thought that if I got hold of it I would not want for money for a long time, so I accepted his proposal without hesitation.

We headed for Bridport but, afraid of finding myself in Dorchester again, I tried to persuade the soldier to go around it. He wouldn't, but we slipped through at night, safely reaching Winterborne, where we put up.

Next morning we got the coach to Bridport and when we arrived, the coachman surprised me by remarking that it was only yesterday that my father had got me out of the artillery! He meant well but, of course, the soldier then asked me if I was an apprentice and I had no choice but to admit I was. He promptly made me get down. He took me across some fields to his home and there kept me quietly for three days.

As the barracks of the 40th Regiment were in Taunton, Somersetshire, it was there we thought it best to go. We went to see the colonel and the soldier told him that I was a recruit. The colonel asked me what trade I was in.

'I'm a labourer,' I replied.

'Labourers make the best soldiers,' he said and offered me a bounty of 2½ guineas, which was considerably less than the sixteen we had been expecting so we decided to try the Marines. Their recruiting sergeant promised us 16 guineas bounty when I arrived at their Plymouth headquarters but this did not suit my conductor because, after paying the coach expenses, there would have been nothing left over for him. He asked me what I intended to do, advising me to go back to my master, and forget about the expense he had gone to for me. But I had destroyed the letter so I told him I preferred the 40th Regiment. We went back to the colonel, he gave my companion 2 guineas, and I was sent into barracks.

Next day I received my clothes, and about a week later was sworn in before a magistrate, receiving my bounty at the same time. I was very mistaken about the money lasting.

Shortly afterwards orders came for the regiment to march to Winchester. There we remained for about a month. I had begun to drill twice a day I soon learnt the foot drill and was then put on musketry drill.

After Winchester, we moved to Portsmouth. We were there a week before being ordered into barracks at Bexhill in Sussex. Our 1st Battalion was there and, in order to make it 1,000 strong, a number of men were drafted into it from our Battalion – the 2nd. I was one of them. Soon orders came for us to go to Portsmouth; we were about to embark on foreign service.

———⇒•◆•——

'This was the first blood I had ever seen shed in battle'
A PRIVATE OF THE 71ST

FIRST ACTION
MONTEVIDEO
1806

The anonymous private of the 71st was a member of the disastrous expedition sent to South America to harm the empire of Napoleon's ally, Spain.

This was the first blood I had ever seen shed in battle; the first time the cannon had roared in my hearing charged with death. I was not yet seventeen years of age, and had not been six months from home. My limbs bending under me with fatigue, in a sultry clime, the musket and accoutrements that I was forced to carry were insupportably oppressive. Still I bore all with invincible patience. During the action, the thought of death never once crossed my mind. After the firing commenced, a still sensation stole over my whole frame, a firm determined torpor, bordering on insensibility. I heard an old soldier answer, to a youth like myself who inquired what he should do during the battle, 'Do your duty.'

Montevideo was taken, but the Spanish repelled the British at Buenos Aires (due to the incompetence of Lieutenant-General John Whitelocke) and gleefully decorated Buenos Aires cathedral with the British colours.

By the summer of 1807, courtesy of his stunning victories over Russia, Prussia, and Austria, Napoleon was master of mainland Europe. Save, that is, for the troublesome Iberian peninsula, where Portugal refused to implement the Continental System (a blockade of British ports, for all its grandiose title) and Spain was dragging its feet in the matter. Never the diplomat, Napoleon invaded Iberia and set his brother Joseph on the Spanish throne. The Spanish broke into a nationalist revolt – and requested the aid of their former enemy, Britain.

The aid arrived on 1 August 1808. At Mondego Bay, Portugal, the first troops of Britain's expeditionary force to Iberia struggled ashore through the surf. The Peninsular War had begun.

Barely a fortnight later, Sir Arthur Wellesley's expeditioners were in action at Rolica, where they shrugged aside an inferior French force. Tougher measures against the British were clearly needed, so the French general Junot headed out with 13,000 men to intercept Wellesley at Vimeiro on 21 August. Unfortunately for Junot, Wellesley had – in what would become his trademark – chosen an elevated position and bade the enemy come to him. They did, for two and a half furious hours. When the sounds of battle ceased the British had lost 720 men; the beaten and bowed French had lost 2000.

Plenty of pickings, then, for the magpie-like British soldier.

'I . . . was quickly rewarded for my labour by finding a yellow silk purse'
RIFLEMAN BENJAMIN HARRIS

THE PENINSULAR WAR
PLUNDERING A DEAD FRENCH SOLDIER
AFTER THE BATTLE OF VIMEIRO
21 AUGUST 1808

Harris transferred from the 66th Foot to the 95th Rifles, after encountering one of their recruiting bands in Ireland; they looked so stylish in their green jackets he joined at once. Recruiters and recuits then journeyed to England, 'three sheets to the wind' all the way. The Rifles were equipped with the Baker rifle instead of the standard British Army smooth-bore musket, 'Brown Bess'.

After the battle I strolled about the field in order to see if there was anything to be found worth picking up amongst the dead. The first thing I saw was a three-pronged silver fork, which, as it lay by itself, had most likely been dropped by some person who had been on the look-out before me. A little further on I saw a French soldier sitting against a small rise in the ground or bank. He was wounded in the throat, and appeared very faint, the bosom of his coat being saturated with the blood which had flowed down. By his side lay his cap, and close to that was a bundle containing a quantity of gold and silver crosses, which I concluded he had plundered from some convent or church. He looked the picture of a sacrilegious thief, dying hopelessly, and overtaken by Divine wrath. I kicked over his cap, which was also full of plunder, but I declined taking anything from him. I felt fearful of incurring the wrath of Heaven for the like offence, so I left him, and passed on. A little further off lay an officer of the 50th regiment. I knew him by sight, and recognized him as he lay. He was quite dead, and lying on his back. He had been plundered, and his clothes were torn open. Three bullet-holes were close together in the pit of his stomach: beside him lay an empty pocket-book, and his epaulette had been pulled from his shoulder.

I had moved on but a few paces when I recollected that perhaps the officer's shoes might serve me, my own being considerably the worse for wear, so I returned again, went back, pulled one of his shoes off, and knelt down on one knee to try it on. It was not much better than my own; however, I determined on the exchange, and proceeded to take off its fellow. As I did so I was startled by the sharp report of a firelock, and, at the same moment, a bullet whistled close by my head. Instantly starting up, I turned, and looked in the direction whence the shot had come. There was no person near me in this part of the field. The dead and the dying lay thickly all around; but nothing else could I see. I looked to the priming of my rifle, and again turned to the dead officer of the 50th. It was evident that some plundering scoundrel had taken a shot at me, and the fact of his doing so proclaimed him one of the enemy. To distinguish him amongst the bodies strewn about was impossible; perhaps he might himself be one of the wounded. Hardly had I effected the exchange, put on the dead officer's shoes, and resumed my rifle, when another shot took place, and a second ball whistled past me. This time I was ready, and turning quickly, I saw my man: he was just about to squat down behind a small mound, about twenty paces from me. I took a haphazard shot at him, and instantly knocked him over. I immediately ran up to him; he had fallen on his face, and I heaved him over on his back, bestrode his body, and drew my sword-bayonet. There was, however, no occasion for the precaution as he was even then in the agonies of death.

It was a relief to me to find I had not been mistaken. He was a French light-infantry man, and I therefore took it quite in the way of business – he had attempted my life, and lost his own. It was the fortune of war; so, stooping down, with my sword I cut the green string that sustained his calibash, and took a hearty pull to quench my thirst.

After I had shot the French light-infantry man, and quenched my thirst from his calibash, finding he was quite dead, I proceeded to search him. Whilst I turned him about in the endeavour at finding the booty I felt pretty certain he had gathered from the slain, an officer of the 60th approached, and accosted me.

'What! looking for money, my lad,' said he, 'eh?'

'I am, sir,' I answered; 'but I cannot discover where this fellow has hid his hoard.'

'You knocked him over, my man,' he said, 'in good style, and deserve something for the shot. Here,' he continued, stooping down and feeling in the lining of the Frenchman's coat, 'this is the place where these rascals generally carry their coin. Rip up the lining of his coat, and then search in his stock. I know them better than you seem to do.'

Thanking the officer for his courtesy, I proceeded to cut open the lining of his jacket with my sword-bayonet, and was quickly rewarded for my labour by finding a yellow silk purse, wrapped up in an old black silk handkerchief. The purse contained several doubloons, three or four napoleons, and a few dollars. Whilst I was counting the money, the value of which, except the dollars, I did not then know, I heard the bugle of the Rifles sound out the assembly, so I touched my cap to the officer, and returned towards them.

The men were standing at ease, with the officers in front. As I approached them, Major Travers, who was in command of the four companies, called me to him.

'What have you got there, sir?' he said. 'Show me.'

I handed him the purse, expecting a reprimand for my pains. He, however, only laughed as he examined it, and, turning, showed it to his brother officers.

'You did that well, Harris,' he said, 'and I am sorry the purse is not better filled. Fall in.' In saying this, he handed me back the purse, and I joined my company. Soon afterwards, the roll being called, we were all ordered to lie down and gain a little rest after our day's work.

'the last we ever saw of poor Sitdown and his wife . . .
perishing in each other's arms in the snow'
RIFLEMAN BENJAMIN HARRIS

SUFFERING, DESPAIR, AND IRON DISCIPLINE
SCENES FROM THE THE RETREAT TO VIGO, THE PENINSULA
JANUARY 1809

On hearing the news that Napoleon and 80,000 men were marching upon them, the British expeditionary army of Sir John Moore was obliged to beat a desperate winter retreat through the mountains of northern Spain to the ports of Corunna and Vigo.

Being constantly in rear of the main body, the scenes of distress and misery I witnessed were dreadful to contemplate, particularly amongst the women and children, who were lagging and falling behind, their husbands and fathers being in the main body in our front. We now came to the edge of a deep ravine, the descent so steep and precipitous, that it was impossible to keep our feet in getting down, and we were sometimes obliged to sit and slide along on our backs; whilst before us rose a ridge of mountains quite as steep and difficult of ascent. There was, however, no pause in our exertion, but, slinging our rifles round our necks, down the hill we went; whilst mules with the baggage on their backs, wearied and urged beyond their strength, were seen rolling from top to bottom, many of them breaking their necks with the fall, and the baggage crushed, smashed, and abandoned.

I remember, as I descended this hill, remarking the extra-ordinary sight afforded by the thousands of our red-coats, who were creeping like snails, and toiling up the ascent before us, their muskets slung round their necks, and clambering with both hands as they hauled themselves up. As soon as we ourselves had gained the ascent we were halted for a few minutes, in order to give us breath for another effort, and then onwards we moved again.

The enemy, I should think, were at this time frequently close upon our trail; and I thought at times I heard their trumpets come down the wind as we marched. Towards the dusk of the evening of this day I remember passing a man and woman lying clasped in each other's arms, and dying in the snow. I knew them both; but it was impossible to help them. They belonged to the Rifles, and were man and wife. The man's name was Joseph Sitdown. During this retreat, as he had not been in good health previously, himself and wife had been allowed to get on in the best way they could in the front. They had, however, now given in, and the last we ever saw of poor Sitdown and his wife was on that night lying perishing in each other's arms in the snow.

The Craufurd mentioned below was Major-General Robert Craufurd (1764–1812), commander of the Light Brigade in the Peninsula, and known universally as 'Black Bob' for his moods. He was killed during the siege of Ciudad Rodrigo.

I do not think I ever admired any man who wore the British uniform more than I did General Craufurd.

I could fill a book with descriptions of him; for I frequently had my eye upon him in the hurry of action. It was gratifying to me, too, to think he did not altogether think ill of me, since he has often addressed me kindly when, from adverse circumstances, you might have thought that he had scarcely spirits to cheer up the men under him. The Rifles liked him, but they also feared him; for he could be terrible when insubordination showed itself in the ranks. 'You think, because you are Riflemen, you may do whatever you think proper,' said he one day to the miserable and savage-looking crew around him in the retreat to Coruña; 'but I'll teach you the difference before I have done with you.' I remember one evening, during the retreat, he detected two men straying away from the main body: it was in the early stage of that disastrous flight, and Craufurd knew well that he must do his utmost to keep the division together. He halted the brigade with a voice of thunder, ordered a drum-head court-martial on the instant, and they were sentenced to a hundred a-piece. Whilst this hasty trial was taking place, Craufurd, dismounting from his horse, stood in the midst, looking stern and angry as a worried bulldog. He did not like retreating at all, that man.

The three men nearest him, as he stood, were Jagger, Dan Howans, and myself. All were worn, dejected, and savage, though nothing to what we were after a few days more of the retreat. The whole brigade were in a grumbling and discontented mood; and Craufurd, doubtless, felt ill-pleased with the aspect of affairs altogether.

'D – n his eyes!' muttered Howans, 'he had much better try to get us something to eat and drink than harass us in this way.'

No sooner had Howans disburdened his conscience of this growl, than Craufurd, who had overheard it, turning sharply round, seized the rifle out of Jagger's hand, and felled him to the earth with the butt-end.

'It was not I who spoke,' said Jagger, getting up, and shaking his head. 'You shouldn't knock me about.'

'I heard you, sir,' said Craufurd; 'and I will bring you also to a court-martial.'

'I am the man who spoke,' said Howans. 'Ben Jagger never said a word.'

'Very well,' returned Craufurd, 'then I'll try you, sir.'

And, accordingly, when the other affair was disposed of, Howans' case came on. By the time the three men were tried, it was too dark to inflict the punishment. Howans, however, had got the complement of three hundred promised to him; so Craufurd gave the word to the brigade to move on. He marched all that night on foot; and when the morning dawned, I remember that, like the rest of us, his hair, beard, and eyebrows were covered with the frost as if he had grown white with age. We were, indeed, all of us in the same condition. Scarcely had I time to notice the appearance of morning before the general once more called a halt – we were then on the hills. Ordering a square to be formed, he spoke to the brigade, as well as I can remember, in these words, after having ordered the three before-named men of the 95th to be brought into the square:

'Although,' said he, 'I should obtain the goodwill neither of the officers nor the men of the brigade here by so doing, I am resolved to punish these three men, according to the sentence awarded, even though the French are at our heels. Begin with Daniel Howans.'

This was indeed no time to be lax in discipline, and the general knew it. The men, as I said, were, some of them, becoming careless and ruffianly in their demeanour; whilst others again I saw with the tears falling down their cheeks from the agony of their bleeding feet, and many were ill with dysentery from the effects of the bad food they had got hold of and devoured on the road. Our knapsacks, too, were a bitter enemy on this prolonged march. Many a man died, I am convinced, who would have borne up well to the end of the retreat but for the infernal load we carried on our backs. My own knapsack was my bitterest enemy; I felt it press me to the earth almost at times, and more than once felt as if I should die under its deadly embrace. The knapsacks, in my opinion, should have been abandoned at the very commencement of the retrograde movement, as it would have been better to have lost them altogether, if, by such loss, we could have saved the poor fellows who, as it was, died strapped to them on the road.

There was some difficulty in finding a place to tie Howans up, as the light brigade carried no halberts. However, they led him to a slender ash tree which grew near at hand.

'Don't trouble yourselves about tying *me* up,' said Howans, folding his arms; 'I'll take my punishment like a man!'

He did so without a murmur, receiving the whole three hundred. His wife, who was present with us, I remember, was a strong, hardy Irishwoman. When it was over, she stepped up and covered Howans with his grey great-coat. The general then gave the word to move on. I rather think he knew the enemy was too near to punish the other two delinquents just then; so we proceeded out of the cornfield in which we had been halted, and toiled away upon the hills once more, Howans' wife carrying the jacket, knapsack, and pouch, which the lacerated state of the man's back would not permit him to bear.

It could not have been, I should think, more than an hour after the punishment had been inflicted upon Howans, when the general again gave the word for the brigade to halt, and once more formed them into a square. We had begun to suppose that he intended to allow the other two delinquents to escape under the present difficulties and hardships of the retreat. He was not, however, one of the forgetful sort, when the discipline of the army under him made severity necessary.

'Bring out the two other men of the 95th,' said he, 'who were tried last night.' . . .

Many who read this, especially in these peaceful times, may suppose this was a cruel and unnecessary severity under the dreadful and harassing circumstances of that retreat; but I, who was there, and was, besides, a common soldier of the very regiment to which these men belonged, say *it was quite necessary.* No man but one formed to stuff like General Craufurd could have saved the brigade from perishing altogether; and, if he flogged two, he saved hundreds from death by his management. I detest the sight of the lash; but I am convinced the British army can never go on without it.

It was perhaps a couple of days after this had taken place that we came to a river. It was tolerably wide, but not very deep, which was just as well for us; for, had it been deep as the dark regions, we must have somehow or other got through. The avenger was behind us, and Craufurd was along with us, and the two together kept us moving, whatever was in the road. Accordingly into the stream went the light brigade, and Craufurd, as busy as a shepherd with his flock, riding in and out of the water to keep his wearied band from being drowned as they crossed over. Presently he spied an officer who, to save himself from being wet through, I suppose, and wearing a damp pair of breeches for the remainder of the day, had mounted on the back of one of his men. The sight of such a piece of effeminacy was enough to raise the choler of the general, and in a very short time he was plunging and splashing through the water after them both.

'Put him down, sir! put him down! I desire you to put that officer down instantly!' And the soldier in an instant, I dare say nothing loth, dropping his burden like a hot potato into the stream, continued his progress through. 'Return back, sir,' said Craufurd to the officer, 'and go through the water like the others. I will not allow my officers to ride upon the men's backs through the rivers: all must take their share alike here.'

Wearied as we were, this affair caused all who saw it to shout almost with laughter, and was never forgotten by those who survived the retreat.

Later Harris fell out of the march, and was left struggling to make his own way to the coast.

After progressing some miles, I came up with a cluster of poor devils who were still alive, but apparently, both men and women, unable to proceed. They were sitting huddled together in the road, their heads drooping forward, and apparently patiently awaiting their end.

Soon after passing these unfortunates, I overtook a party who were being urged forward under charge of an officer of the 42nd Highlanders. He was pushing them along pretty much as a drover would keep together a tired flock of sheep. They presented a curious example of a retreating force. Many of them had thrown away their weapons, and were linked together arm in arm, in order to support each other, like a party of drunkards. They were, I saw, composed of various regiments; many were bare-headed, and without shoes; and some with their heads tied up in old rags and fragments of handkerchiefs. . .

Slowly and dejectedly crawled our army along. Their spirit of endurance was now considerably worn out, and judging from my own sensations, I felt confident that if the sea was much further from us, we must be content to come to a halt at last without gaining it. I felt something like the approach of death as I proceeded – a sort of horror, mixed up with my sense of illness – a reeling I have never experienced before or since. Still I held on; but with all my efforts, the main body again left me behind. Had the enemy's cavalry come up at this time I think they would have had little else to do but ride us down without striking a blow.

It is, however, indeed astonishing how man clings to life. I am certain that had I lain down at this period, I should have found my last billet on the spot I sank upon. Suddenly I heard a shout in front, which was prolonged in a sort of hubbub. Even the stragglers whom I saw dotting the road in front of me seemed to have caught at something like hope; and as the poor fellows now reached the top of a hill we were ascending, I heard an occasional exclamation of joy – the first note of the sort I had heard for many days. When I reached the top of the hill the thing spoke for itself. There, far away in our front, the English shipping lay in sight.

Its view had indeed acted like a restorative to our force, and the men, at the prospect of a termination to the march, had plucked up spirit for a last effort. Fellows who, like myself, seemed to have hardly strength in their legs to creep up the ascent seemed now to have picked up a fresh pair to get down with. Such is hope to us poor mortals!

There was, I recollect, a man of the name of Bell, of the Rifles, who had been during this day holding a sort of creeping race with me – we had passed and repassed each other, as our strength served. Bell was rather a discontented fellow at the best of times; but during this retreat he had given full scope to his ill-temper, cursing the hour he was born, and wishing his mother had strangled him when he came into the world, in order to have saved him from his present toil. He had not now spoken for some time, and the sight of the English shipping had apparently a very beneficial effect upon him. He burst into tears as he stood and looked at it.

'Harris,' he said, 'if it pleases God to let me reach those ships, I swear never to utter a bad or discontented word again.'

As we proceeded down the hill we now met with the first symptoms of good feeling from the inhabitants it was our fortune to experience during our retreat. A number of old women stood on either side of the road, and occasionally handed us fragments of bread as we passed them. It was on this day, and whilst I looked anxiously upon the English shipping in the distance, that I first began to find my eyesight failing, and it appeared to me that I was fast growing blind. The thought was alarming; and I made desperate efforts to get on. Bell, however, won the race this time. He was a very athletic and strong-built fellow, and left me far behind, so that I believe at that time I was the very last of the retreating force that reached the beach, though doubtless many stragglers came dropping up after the ships had sailed, and were left behind.

As it was, when I did manage to gain the sea-shore, it was only by the aid of my rifle that I could stand, and my eyes were now so dim and heavy that with difficulty I made out a boat which seemed the last that had put off.

Fearful of being left half blind in the lurch, I took off my cap, and placed it on the muzzle of my rifle as a signal, for I was totally unable to call out. Luckily, Lieutenant Cox, who was aboard the boat, saw me, and ordered the men to return, and, making one more effort, I walked into the water, and a sailor stretching his body over the gunwale, seized me as if I had been an infant, and hauled me on board. His words were characteristic of the English sailor, I thought.

'Hollo there, you lazy lubber!' he said, as he grasped hold of me, 'who the h – ll do you think is to stay humbugging all day for such a fellow as you?'

Five thousand British troops died on the retreat to Vigo and Corunna. At the latter port, even as embarkation was taking place, the tattered redcoats fought a spirited battle against the French advance on 16 January 1809. Captain Charles Napier of the 50th Regiment led a counter-attack, only to be ambushed and find himself alone and fighting for his life amongst French troops:

> They struck me with their muskets, clubbed and bruised me much, whereupon, seeing no help near, and being overpowered by numbers, and in great pain from my wounded leg, I called out '*Je me rend*', remembering the expression correctly from an old story of a fat officer whose name being James called out '*Jemmy round*'. Finding they had no disposition to spare me, I kept hold of the musket, vigorously defending myself with the body of the little Italian who had first wounded me; but I soon grew faint, or rather tired. At that moment a tall dark man came up, seized the end of the musket with his left hand, whirled his brass-hilted sabre round, and struck me a powerful blow on the head, which was bare, for my cocked hat had fallen off. Expecting the blow would finish me, I had stooped my head in hopes it might fall on my back, or at least on the thickest part of the head, and not on the left temple. So far I succeeded, for it fell exactly on the top, cutting me to the bone but not through it. Fire sparkled from my eyes. I fell on my knees, blinded but not quite losing my senses, and holding still on to the musket. Recovering in a moment I saw a florid, handsome young French drummer holding the arm of the dark Italian, who was in the act of repeating the blow. Quarter was then given; but they tore my pantaloons in tearing my watch and purse from my pocket and a little locket of hair which hung round my neck. But while this went on two of them were wounded, and the drummer, Guilbert, ordered the dark man who had sabred me to take me to the rear.

The commander of British forces at Corunna, Sir John Moore, was less lucky. He was killed in action and interred in the city ramparts. The episode was made immortal in Charles Wolfe's famous poem, 'The Burial of Sir John Moore After Corunna':

> Not a drum was heard, not a funeral note,
> As his corpse to the rampart we hurried;
> Not a soldier discharged his farewell shot
> O'er the grave where our hero we buried.

> We buried him darkly at dead of night,
> The sods with our bayonets turning,
> By the struggling moonbeam's misty light
> And the lanthorn dimly burning . . .

The individual fates of Moore and Napier aside, 27,000 British troops were evacuated home from Vigo and Corunna. It was a foreshadowing of the deliverance from Dunkirk in 1940.

Then, in April in 1809, Wellesley went back to Iberia. After a stunning victory at Oporto, Wellington (as Wellesley was now titled, courtesy of the barony rewarding Oporto) became overstretched and the Peninsular War went into reverse as the British were driven back on Lisbon.

It wasn't only in the Peninsula that the British were suffering failure: an amphibious expedition to the Dutch island of Walcheren became a haunting byword for disaster.

—◆—

'an awful visitation came suddenly upon us'
RIFLEMAN BENJAMIN HARRIS

THE EXPEDITION TO WALCHEREN
HOLLAND, AUGUST 1809

The objective of the Walcheren expedition was to seize the islands in the Scheldt as the precursor for the taking of Antwerp, employed by Napoleon as 'a pistol pointed at the heart of England'.

Stuck fast on the malarial island of Walcheren, no fewer than 4,000 – a tenth – of General Lord Chatham's troops died of fever.

. . . A fair wind soon carried us off Flushing, where one part of the expedition disembarked; the other made for South Beveland, among which latter I myself was. The five companies of Rifles immediately occupied a very pretty village, with rows of trees on either side of its principal streets, where we had plenty of leisure to listen to the cannonading going on amongst the companies we had left at Flushing. The appearance of the country (such as it was) was extremely pleasant, and for a few days the men enjoyed themselves much.

But at the expiration of (I think) less time than a week, an awful visitation came suddenly upon us. The first I observed of it was one day as I sat in my billet, when I beheld whole parties of our Riflemen in the street shaking with a sort of ague, to such a degree that they could hardly walk; strong and fine young men who had been but a short time in the service seemed suddenly reduced in strength to infants, unable to stand upright – so great a shaking had seized upon their whole bodies from head to heel. The company I belonged to was quartered in a barn, and I quickly perceived that hardly a man there had stomach for the bread that was served out to him, or even to taste his grog, although each man had an allowance of half-a-pint of gin per day. In fact I should say that about three weeks from the day we landed, I and two others were the only individuals who could stand upon our legs. They lay groaning in rows in the barn, amongst the heaps of lumpy black bread they were unable to eat.

This awful spectacle considerably alarmed the officers, who were also many of them attacked. The naval doctors came on shore to assist the regimental surgeons, who, indeed, had more upon their hands than they could manage; Dr. Ridgeway of the Rifles, and his assistant, having nearly five hundred patients prostrate at the same moment. In short, except myself and three or four others, the whole concern was completely floored.

Under these circumstances, which considerably confounded the doctors, orders were issued (since all hopes of getting the men upon their legs seemed gone) to embark them as fast as possible, which was accordingly done with some little difficulty. The poor fellows made every effort to get on board; those who were a trifle better than others crawled to the boats; many supported each other; and many were carried helpless as infants. . . . On shipboard the aspect of affairs did not mend; the men beginning to die so fast that they committed ten or twelve to the deep in one day. It was rather extraordinary that myself, and Brooks, and a man named Bowley, who had all three been at Corunna, were at this moment unattacked by the disease, and notwithstanding the awful appearance of the pest-ship we were in, I myself had little fear of it, I thought myself so hardened that it could not touch me. It happened, however, that I stood sentinel (men being scarce) over the hatchway, and Brooks, who was always a jolly and jeering companion (even in the very jaws of death) came past me, and offered me a lump of pudding, it being pudding-day on board. At that moment I felt struck with a deadly faintness, shaking all over like an aspen, and my teeth chattering in my head so that I could hardly hold my rifle. Brooks looked at me for a moment with the pudding in his hand, which he saw I could not take, 'Hullo', he said, 'why Harris, old boy, you are not going to begin are you?' I felt unable to answer him, but only muttered out as I tumbled, 'For God's sake get me relieved, Brooks!' . . . In fact I was now sprawling upon the forecastle, amongst many others, in a miserable state, our knapsacks and our great-coats over us . . . and thus we arrived at Dover . . . The Warwickshire Militia were at this time quartered at Dover. They came to assist in disembarking us, and were obliged to lift many of us out of the boats like sacks of flour. If any of those militiamen remain alive, they will not easily forget that piece of duty; for I never beheld men more moved than they were at our helpless state.

Some 240,000 British soldiers perished during the Revolutionary and Napoleonic Wars with France, 1793–1815, 85 per cent of them from disease.

'Our party formed up ready to charge down the street'
LIEUTENANT WILLIAM TOMKINSON

THE PENINSULAR WAR
DIARY OF A CAVALRY OFFICER
9TH OCTOBER 1810

Tomkinson was gazetted to a cornetcy in the 16th Light Dragoons in 1807; the 16th were archetypal light cavalry and performed, as well as eye-catching battlefield charges, skirmishing, patrol and piquet duties in the peninsula. It was dangerous work, for both men and horses. During five and a half years of peninsular campaigning one dragoon regiment was recorded as having lost 1,564 horses in action; there is no reason to suppose that the 16th were any less demanding on their mounts.

Oct. 9th.

It rained nearly incessantly from the time we yesterday left Rio Mayor. We lay down in the middle of the road, it raining nearly the whole night. The enemy did not move till late this day. Nearly the whole way from the Quinta de Toro to Alquentre, the country is open with ravines and bogs running at right angles to the road.

Captain Cocks' squadron was on piquet behind me, and Captain Linsingen's two miles in our front. At 2 p.m. they attacked Captain Linsingen with two regiments of cavalry; they were aware that we had nothing up to support the piquet, and it was their intention to take it. In his rear he had a bit of very bad road to pass, and charged two or three times their advance on the road, to secure his retreat. In these charges he lost nineteen men taken, and several wounded, he himself cut in the arm in different parts, though not severely. They drove him in on our squadron, which was formed behind the bridge nearest the Quinta, and seeing it was his intention to pass, pressed him hard in hopes of taking more of his men. We just allowed the Hussars to pass and then charged, driving them back over the bridge. Farther we could not go, as on getting in the open ground the enemy had people on each of our flanks. We then retired, expecting the Hussars would have been ready to have covered us, as we did them. They could not form in the time, having been so scattered, and on our retiring, the enemy followed in very good style close at our heels; we again charged them, and drove them on the bridge. Again we retired close to the bridge immediately below the Quinta de Toro, and passed the defile over the bridge, forming on the plain beyond, with the remainder of the bridgade. In both the charges we took some prisoners, but could only get one away. We lost one man of Captain Belli's troop killed, with four horses from the squadron. The regiment with which we were engaged was the 3rd Hussars, and I never saw their cavalry behave so well.

In retiring the second time I caught my bradoon rein in the appointments of a French Hussar who was dismounted lying on the ground, and cut it just as they were about to make me prisoner. My horse's head was held down to the ground, being caught in his appointments; they were not five yards from me when I cut it. I spurred my horse two or three times in hopes he would break it; this he did not, and I was fortunate in catching the rein fair the first cut, and going through it. I will take care not to go into action with a loose bradoon rein.

On the ground near Quinta de Toro, Sir Stapleton intended to check the enemy, there being only one pass up to it by the bridge and causeway on the main road. This he did for some time with the guns firing a few shots at their cavalry; but their infantry coming up, and getting through the bog up the bank near where we were formed, he was obliged to retire. Had this not been the case, an order which he received from Lord Wellington would have brought us back at night. Our squadron was so much knocked up from the two days' duty, that we were sent to the rear, the horses scarcely able to get along . . .

On arriving at our bivouac, I saw some Portuguese officers and soldiers in a shed at the back of the wine vault. I gave the alarm that the French were expected, when they turned out in an instant, marched away, and I put myself and horses into the place. My old dragoon (Robinson) had got me a turkey out of a house he passed on the march. We had plucked it coming along, and on my return from seeing the men I found him holding it in the flame of the fire, by legs and wings at a time. He had no wood at hand, and broke up and burnt some cane-bottomed chairs, for the purpose of making a fire, which the Portuguese had brought from an adjacent Quinta to sit upon. I rather reproached him, and the only answer I got was that I should find the turkey very good; we soon finished it.

The rain continued, and from the dreadful night and bad camp the regiment was in a sad state. We got under cover in Carrigada, and at 12 noon there arrived an order for us to retire within the infantry. We marched to Povoa, passing the right of our position at Alhandra. One squadron, the left centre, remained piquet outside the lines. It rained incessantly the whole day; and thus, for the first time since we left Rio Mayor, was there an opportunity of getting on dry clothes.

Wellington expressly forbade plundering the natives in the peninsula, but Tomkinson's servant, like many other peninsula soldiers, ignored the injunction; the official method of obtaining provisions from the Spanish was to exchange money or a promissory receipt for goods taken.

Such additions to rations were necessary; for officers and men alike the daily ration on campaign was 1 lb of meat, 1 lb of biscuit (or 1½ lbs of rice or bread) and 1 pint of wine (or ⅓ pint of spirit). The meat was brewed up on a Flanders Iron Kettle, one for every 10 infantrymen, to make – invariably – a thin broth called skilly. The army biscuit was so hard that, stored in a breast pocket, it was known to turn French musket balls.

Soon after Tomkinson's turkey dinner the British retired behind the Lines of Torres Vedras, the fortifications Wellington had presciently built around Lisbon. Marshal Massena of France battered up against them, but was unable to breach them. Luckless, Massena abandoned his invasion of Portugal. Though no one yet knew it, the Peninsular War had reached its turning point.

'We fought them till we were hardly a Regiment'
LIEUTENANT G. CROMPTON

ALBUERA
THE FRENCH ATTACK, THE PENINSULA, MORNING
16 MAY 1811

At 'Bloody Albuera' Sir William Beresford's road-block of 32,000 Allied troops was assaulted by Marshal Nicholas Soult, marching to the relief of Badajoz.

Beresford's force contained just 7000 British, most of the remainder being semi-trained Spanish and Portuguese troops, Soult, by contrast, marched with 20,000 infantry and 4000 cavalry, all veterans. By the rules of war, the French should have won at Albuera; but for neither the first nor the last time the rules broke on the British soldier's discipline, Brown Bess and bayonet.

'Die hard, 57th, die hard!' shouted Lieutenant-Colonel William Inglis – his chest ripped open by grapeshot – to his men as the French engaged. They did. So did the remainder of the British force on the slopes of Albuera hamlet.

A few lines, my dearest Mother, I, in haste sit down and write, to say, that under the protection of Almighty God, I have escaped unhurt in one of the severest actions that ever was contested between France and England; to describe the Horrors that were witnessed on the ever memorable 16th of May would be impossible, but as the part the unfortunate 1st Brigade of the 2 Division took on that day might be a little interesting to you, I will relate it as far as I am able.

I think it was about 10 o'clock a.m. when the French menaced an attack on our left; we immediately moved to support it. It proved, however, to be a feint, and the Right of the Line was destined to be the spot (Oh, never to be effaced from my mind) where Britons were to be repulsed; 3 solid columns attacked our regiment alone. We fought them till we were hardly a Regiment. The Commanding Officer was shot dead, and the two Officers carrying the Colours close by my side received their mortal wounds. In this shattered state, our Brigade moved forward to charge. Madness alone would dictate such a thing, and at that critical period Cavalry appeared in our rear. It was then that our men began to waver, and for the first time (and God knows I hope the last) I saw the backs of English soldiers turned upon French. Our Regiment once rallied, but to what avail! we were independent of Infantry: out-numbered with Cavalry. I was taken prisoner, but re-taken by the Spanish Cavalry.

Oh, what a day was that. The worst of the story I have not related. Our Colours were taken. I told you before the 2 Ensigns were shot under them; 2 Sergeants shared the same fate. A Lieutenant seized a Musket to defend them, and he was shot to the heart; what could be done against Cavalry?

Adieu, my Dear Mother, for the present. Give my most affectionate and kindest love to my Father, Annie, William and all at home, and believe me to be your most affectionate Son.

[Signed] G. Crompton,

A miserable Lt. of the unfortunate 66th Regt.

P.S. – The Fuziler Brigade afterwards came on, also the other Brigades in the Division with some Spaniards and Portuguese beat back the French and gained a complete Victory.

After Albuera, Soult moaned to Napoleon: 'The British were completely beaten and the day was mine, but they did not know it and would not run'.

" 'We'll do this business with the cold iron' "
LIEUTENANT WILLIAM GRATTAN

STORMING THE BREACHES
AT CIUDAD RODRIGO
THE PENINSULA
19 JANUARY 1812

After ten days of battering forced two breaches in the walls of the French-held fortress of Ciudad Rodrigo, British redcoats were ordered to storm the town. Among them was William Grattan of the Connaught Rangers:

It was now five o'clock in the afternoon, and darkness was approaching fast, yet no order had arrived intimating that we were to take a part in the contest about to be decided. We were in this state of suspense when our attention was attracted by the sound of music; we all stood up, and pressed forward to a ridge, a little in our front, and which separated us from the cause of our movement, but it would be impossible for me to convey an adequate idea of our feelings when we beheld the 43rd Regiment, preceded by their band, going to storm the left breach; they were in the highest spirits, but without the slightest appearance of levity in their demeanour – on the contrary, there was a cast of determined severity thrown over their countenances that expressed in legible characters that they knew the sort of service they were about to perform, and had made up their minds to the issue. They had no knapsacks – their firelocks were slung over their shoulders – their shirt-collars were open, and there was an indescribable *something* about them that at one and the same moment impressed the lookers-on with admiration and awe. In passing us, each officer and soldier stepped out of the ranks for an instant, as he recognised a friend, to press his hand – many for the last time; yet, notwithstanding this animating scene, there was no shouting or huzzaing, no boisterous bravadoing, no unbecoming language; in short, every one seemed to be impressed with the seriousness of the affair entrusted to his charge, and any interchange of words was to this effect: 'Well, lads, mind what you're about tonight'; or, 'We'll meet in the town by and by'; and other little familiar phrases, all expressive of confidence. The regiment at length passed us, and we stood gazing after it as long as the rear platoon continued in sight: the music grew fainter every moment, until at last it died away altogether; they had no drums, and there was a melting sweetness in the sounds that touched the heart.

The first syllable uttered after this scene was, 'And are we to be left behind?' The interrogatory was scarcely put, when the word 'Stand to your arms!' answered it. The order was promptly obeyed, and a breathless silence prevailed when our commanding officer, in a few words, announced to us that Lord Wellington had directed our division to carry the grand breach. The soldiers listened to the communication with silent earnestness, and immediately began to disencumber themselves of their knapsacks, which were placed in order by companies and a guard set over them. Each man then began to arrange himself for the combat in such manner as his fancy or the moment would admit of – some by lowering their cartridge-boxes, others by turning theirs to the front in order that they might the more conveniently make use of them; others unclasping their stocks or opening their shirt-collars, and others oiling their bayonets; and more taking leave of their wives and children. This last was an affecting sight, but not so much so as might be expected, because the women, from long habit, were accustomed to scenes of danger, and the order for their husbands to march against the enemy was in their eyes tantamount to a victory; and as the soldier seldom returned without plunder of some sort, the painful suspense which his absence caused was made up by the gaiety which his return was certain to be productive of; or if, unfortunately, he happened to fall, his place was sure to be supplied by some one of the company to which he belonged, so that the women of our army had little cause of alarm on this head. The worst that could happen to them was the chance of being in a state of widowhood for a week.

It was by this time half-past six o'clock, the evening was piercingly cold, and the frost was crisp on the grass; there was a keenness in the air that braced our nerves at least as high as *concert pitch*. We stood quietly to our arms, and told our companies off by files, sections, and sub-divisions; the sergeants called over the rolls – not a man was absent.

It appears it was the wish of General Mackinnon to confer a

mark of distinction upon the 88th Regiment, and as it was one of the last acts of his life, I shall mention it. He sent for Major Thompson, who commanded the battalion, and told him it was his wish to have the forlorn hope of the grand breach led on by a subaltern of the 88th Regiment, adding at the same time that, in the event of his surviving, he should be recommended for a company. The Major acknowledged this mark of the General's favour, and left him folding up some letters he had been writing to his friends in England – this was about twenty minutes before the attack of the breaches. Major Thompson, having called his officers together, briefly told them the wishes of their General; he was about to proceed, when Lieutenant William Mackie (*then senior Lieutenant*) immediately stepped forward, and dropping his sword said, 'Major Thompson, I am ready for that service.' For once in his life poor old Thompson was affected – Mackie was his own townsman, they had fought together for many years, and when he took hold of his hand and pronounced the words, 'God bless you, my boy,' his eye filled, his lip quivered, and there was a faltering in his voice which was evidently perceptible to himself, for he instantly resumed his former composure, drew himself up, and gave the word, 'Gentlemen, fall in,' and at this moment Generals Picton and Mackinnon, accompanied by their respective staffs, made their appearance amongst us.

Long harangues are not necessary to British soldiers, and on this occasion but few words were made use of. Picton said something animating to the different regiments as he passed them, and those of my readers who recollect his deliberate and strong utterance will say with me, that his mode of speaking was indeed very impressive. The address to each was nearly the same, but that delivered by him to the 88th was so characteristic of the General, and so applicable to the men he spoke to, that I shall give it word for word; it was this:-

'Rangers of Connaught! it is not my intention to expend any powder this evening. We'll do this business with the cold iron.'

I before said the soldiers were silent – so they were, but the man who could be silent after such an address . . . had better have stayed at home. It may be asked what did they do? Why, what would they do, or would any one do, but give the loudest hurrah he was able.

The burst of enthusiasm caused by Picton's address to the Connaught Rangers had scarcely ceased, when the signalgun announced that the attack was to commence. Generals Picton and Mackinnon dismounted from their horses, and placing themselves at the head of the right brigade, the troops rapidly entered the trenches by sections right in front; the storming party under the command of Major Russell Manners of the 74th heading it, while the forlorn hope, commanded by Lieutenant William Mackie of the 88th, and composed of twenty volunteers from the Connaught Rangers, led the van, followed closely by the 45th, 88th, and 74th British, and the 9th and 21st Portuguese; the 77th and 83rd British, belonging to the left brigade, brought up the rear and completed the dispositions.

While these arrangements were effecting opposite the grand breach, the 5th and 94th, belonging to the left brigade of the 3rd Division, were directed to clear the ramparts and Fausse Braye wall, and the 2nd Regiment of Portuguese Caçadores, commanded by an Irish colonel of the name of O'Toole, was to escalade the curtain to the left of the lesser breach, which was attacked by the Light Division under the command of General Robert Craufurd.

It wanted ten minutes to seven o'clock when these dispositions were completed; the moon occasionally, as the clouds which overcast it passed away, shed a faint ray of light upon the battlements of the fortress, and presented to our view the glittering of the enemy's bayonets as their soldiers stood arrayed upon the ramparts and breach, awaiting our attack; yet, nevertheless, their batteries were silent, and might warrant the supposition to an unobservant spectator that the defence would be but feeble.

The two divisions got clear of the covered way at the same moment, and each advanced to the attack of their respective points with the utmost regularity. The obstacles which presented themselves to both were nearly the same, but every difficulty, no matter how great, merged into insignificance when placed in the scale of the prize about to be contested. The soldiers were full of ardour, but altogether devoid of that blustering and bravadoing which is truly unworthy of men at such a moment; and it would be difficult to convey an adequate idea of the enthusiastic bravery which animated the troops. A cloud that had for some time before obscured the moon, which was at its full, disappeared altogether, and the countenances of the soldiers were for the first time, since Picton addressed them, visible – they presented a material change. In place of that joyous animation which his fervid and impressive address called forth, a look of severity, bordering on ferocity, had taken its place; and although ferocity is by no means one of the characteristics of the British soldier, there was, most unquestionably, a savage expression in the faces of the men that I had never before witnessed. Such is the difference between the storm of a breach and the fighting a pitched battle.

Once clear of the covered way, and fairly on the plain that separated it from the fortress, the enemy had a full view of all that was passing; their batteries, charged to the muzzle with case-shot, opened a murderous fire upon the columns as they advanced, but nothing could shake the intrepid bravery of the troops. The Light Division soon descended the ditch and gained, although not without a serious struggle, the top of the narrow and difficult breach allotted to them; their gallant General, Robert Craufurd, fell at the head of the 43rd, and his second in command, General Vandeleur, was severely wounded, but there were not wanting others to supply their place; yet these losses, trying as they were to the feelings of the soldiers, in no way damped their ardour, and the brave Light Division carried the left breach at the point of the bayonet. Once established upon the ramparts, they made all the dispositions necessary to ensure their own conquest, as also to render every assistance in their power to the 3rd Division in their attack. They cleared the rampart which separated the lesser from the grand breach, and relieved Picton's division from any anxiety it might have as to its safety on its left flank.

The right brigade, consisting of the 45th, 88th, and 74th, forming the van of the 3rd Division, upon reaching the ditch, to its astonishment, found Major Ridge and Colonel Campbell at the head of the 5th and 94th mounting the Fausse Braye wall. These two regiments, after having performed their task of silencing the fire of the French troops upon the ramparts, with a noble emulation resolved to precede their comrades in the attack of the grand breach. Both parties greeted each other with a cheer, only to be understood by those who have been placed in a similar situation; yet the enemy were in no way daunted by the shout raised by our soldiers – they crowded the breach, and defended it with a bravery that would have made any but troops accustomed to conquer, waver. But the 'fighting division' were not the men to be easily turned from their purpose; the breach was speedily mounted, yet, nevertheless, a serious affray took place ere it was gained. A considerable mass of infantry crowned its summit, while in the rear and at each side were stationed men, so placed that they could render every assistance to their comrades at the breach without any great risk to themselves; besides this, two guns of heavy calibre, separated from the breach by a ditch of considerable depth and width, enfiladed it, and as soon as the French infantry were forced from the summit, these guns opened their fire on our troops.

The head of the column had scarcely gained the top, when a discharge of grape cleared the ranks of the three leading battalions, and caused a momentary wavering; at the same instant a frightful explosion near the gun to the left of the breach, which shook the bastion to its foundation, completed the disorder. Mackinnon, at the head of his brigade, was blown into the air. His aide-de-camp, Lieutenant Beresford of the 88th, shared the same fate, and every man on the breach at the moment of the explosion perished. This was unavoidable, because those of the advance, being either killed or wounded, were necessarily flung back upon the troops that followed close upon their footsteps, and there was not a sufficient space for the men who were ready to sustain those placed *hors de combat* to rally. For an instant all was confusion; the blaze of light caused by the explosion resembled a huge meteor, and presented to our sight the havoc which the enemy's fire had caused in our ranks; while from afar the astonished Spaniard viewed for an instant, with horror and dismay, the soldiers of the two nations grappling with each other on the top of the rugged breach which trembled beneath their feet, while the fire of the French artillery played upon our columns with irresistible fury, sweeping from the spot the living and the dead. Amongst the latter was Captain Robert Hardyman and Lieutenant Pearse of the 45th, and many more whose names I cannot recollect. Others were so stunned by the shock, or wounded by the stones which were hurled forth by the explosion, that they were insensible to their situation; of this number I was one, for being close to the magazine when it blew up, I was quite overpowered, and I owed my life to the Sergeant-Major of my regiment, Thorp, who saved me from being trampled to death by our soldiers in their advance, ere I could recover strength sufficient to move forward or protect myself.

The French, animated by this accidental success, hastened once more to the breach which they had abandoned, but the leading regiments of Picton's division, which had been disorganised for the moment by the explosion, rallied, and soon regained its summit, when another discharge from the two flank guns swept away the foremost of those battalions.

There was at this time but one officer alive upon the breach (Major Thomson, of the 74th, acting engineer); he called out to those next to him to seize the gun to the left, which had been so fatal to his companions – but this was a desperate service. The gun was completely cut off from the breach by a deep trench, and soldiers, encumbered with their firelocks, could not pass it in sufficient time to anticipate the next discharge – yet to deliberate was certain death. The French cannoniers, five in number, stood to, and served their gun with as much *sang froid* as if on a parade, and the light which their torches threw forth showed to our men the peril they would have to encounter if they dared to attack a gun so defended; but this was of no avail. Men going to storm a breach generally make up their minds that there is no great probability of their ever returning from it to tell their adventures to their friends; and whether they die at the bottom or top of it, or at the muzzle, or upon the breech of a cannon, is to them pretty nearly the same!

The first who reached the top, after the last discharge, were three of the 88th. Sergeant Pat Brazil – the brave Brazil of the Grenadier company, who saved his captain's life at Busaco – called out to his two companions, Swan and Kelly, to unscrew their bayonets and follow him; the three men passed the trench in a moment, and engaged the French cannoniers hand to hand; a terrific but short combat was the consequence. Swan was the first, and was met by the two gunners on the right of the gun, but, no way daunted, he engaged them, and plunged his bayonet into the breast of one; he was about to repeat the blow upon the other, but before he could disentangle the weapon from his bleeding adversary, the second Frenchman closed upon him, and by a *coup de sabre* severed his left arm from his body a little above the elbow; he fell from the shock, and was on the eve of being massacred, when Kelly, after having scrambled under the gun, rushed onward to succour his comrade. He bayoneted two Frenchmen on the spot, and at this instant Brazil came up; three of the five gunners lay lifeless, while Swan, resting against an ammunition chest, was bleeding to death. It was now equal numbers, two against two, but Brazil in his over-anxiety to engage was near losing his life at the onset; in making a lunge at the man next to him, his foot slipped upon the bloody platform, and he fell forward against his antagonist, but as both rolled under the gun, Brazil felt the socket of his bayonet strike hard against the buttons of the French-man's coat. The remaining gunner, in attempting to escape under the carriage from Kelly, was killed by some soldiers of the 5th, who just now reached the top of the breach, and seeing the serious dispute at the gun, pressed forward to the assistance of the three men of the Connaught Rangers.

While this was taking place on the left, the head of the column remounted the breach, and regardless of the cries of their wounded companions, whom they indiscriminately trampled to death, pressed forward in one irregular but heroic mass, and putting every man to death who opposed their progress, forced the enemy from the ramparts at the bayonet's point. Yet the garrison still rallied, and defended the several streets with the most unflinching bravery; nor was it until the musketry of the Light Division was heard in the direction of the Plaza Mayor, that they gave up the contest! but from this moment all regular resistance ceased, and they fled in disorder to the Citadel.

Three months later Wellington's men stormed the fortress of Badajoz, where 5,000 of them died, most in a space of just 100 yards square. Once inside the town, British troops ran amok in scenes of outrage greater even than those at Ciudad Rodrigo. 'The whole of the soldiers', Wellington's medical officer, James McGrigor, reported, 'appeared to be in a state of mad drunkenness. In every street, and in every corner we met them forcing their way like furies into houses . . . In passing some houses which they had entered we heard the shrieks of females, and sometimes the groans of those they were no doubt butchering . . .' It was 29 hours before the troops were brought under control. A year later San Sebastian was sacked in an orgy of indiscipline, just as Ciudad Rodrigo and Badajoz had been before it.

The 'scum of the earth' opined Wellington, about his men.

If Wellington disliked his redcoats' morals, he had no great opinion of their bodies either, complaining in October 1812 that his soldiers 'become sickly as soon as they are obliged to make a march'. As remedy, Wellington ordered three route marches a week. The medicine worked, even more spectacularly than the Duke might have dared hope; in the summer of the following year, the army tramped 600 miles through Spain in five weeks until it neared Vittoria, where it trounced the French in battle on 21 June 1813. An anonymous soldier of the 71st recalled the engagement:

We halted, and drew up in column. Orders were given to brush out our locks, oil them, and examine our flints. We being in the rear, these were soon followed by orders to open out from the centre, to allow the 71st to advance.

Forward we moved up the hill. The firing was now very heavy. Our rear had not engaged, before word came for the doctor to assist Colonel Cadogan, who was wounded. Immediately we charged up the hill, the piper playing, 'Hey Johny Cope.' The French had possession of the top, but we soon forced them back, and drew up in column on the height, sending out four companies to our left to skirmish. The remainder moved on to the opposite height. As we advanced, driving them before us, a French officer, a pretty fellow, was pricking and forcing his men to stand. They heeded him not – he was very harsh. 'Down with him!' cried one near me; and down he fell, pierced by more than one ball.

Scarce were we upon the height, when a heavy column dressed in great-coats, with white covers on their hats, exactly resembling the Spanish, gave us a volley, which put us to the right about at double-quick time down the hill, the French close behind, through the whins. The four companies got the word, the French were on them. They likewise thought them Spaniards, until they got a volley, that killed or wounded almost every one of them. We retired to the height, covered by the 50th, who gave the pursuing column a volley which checked their speed. We moved up the remains of our shattered regiment to the height. Being in great want of ammunition, we were again served with sixty rounds a man, and kept up our fire for some time, until the bugle sounded to cease firing.

We lay on the height for some time. Our drought was excessive; there was no water upon the height, save one small spring, which was rendered useless. One of our men, in the heat of the action, called out he would have a drink, let the world go as it would. He stooped to drink; a ball pierced his head; he fell with it in the well, which was discoloured with brains and blood. Thirsty as we were, we could not taste it.

At this time the Major had the command, our second Colonel being wounded. There were not 300 of us on the height able to do duty, out of above 1,000 who drew rations in the morning. The cries of the wounded were most heart-rending.

The French, on the opposite height, were getting under arms; we could give no assistance, as the enemy appeared to be six to one of us. Our orders were to maintain the height while there was a man of us. The word was given to shoulder arms. The French, at the same moment, got under arms. The engagement began in the plains. The French were amazed, and soon put to the right about, through Vittoria. We followed, as quick as our weary limbs would carry us. Our legs were full of thorns, and our feet bruised upon the roots of trees. Coming to a bean field at the bottom of the heights, immediately the column was broke, and every man filled his haversack.

It wasn't only beans that brought the chase to a halt. Thousands of powder-stained redcoats energetically plundered the French baggage-train. 'The soldiers of the army', wrote Wellington to Earl Bathurst, 'have got about a million sterling in money' and were 'totally knocked up' from looting.

Discipline restored, the British then drove the remnants of the 'Army of Portugal', 'Army of the Centre' and 'Army of the South' out of Spain and halfway up France. It wasn't entirely easy, of course. On the river Nivelle, Wellington had to storm Soult's positions, and in the doing lost 3,700 men. Among the wounded that day was Robert Blakeney of the 28th Foot.

'But my personal advance was momentary; being struck by a shot'
LIEUTENANT ROBERT BLAKENEY

NIVELLE
WOUNDED
10 NOVEMBER 1813

Arriving immediately under the fort I perceived the enemy regularly drawn up behind trees cut down to the height of about five feet, the branches pointing forward, forming an abattis. I immediately turned about, and after receiving an appropriate salute retraced my steps with redoubled speed. I seized the king's colour carried by Ensign Montgomery, which I immediately halted; and called for the regimental Colour Ensign, McPherson, who answered, 'Here am I.' Having halted both colours in front of the foremost men, I prevented any from going forward. By these means we shortly presented a tolerably good front, and gave the men a few moments' breathing time. The whole operation did not take above ten minutes; but the men coming up every instant, each minute strengthened the front. At this exciting moment my gallant comrades, Lieutenants Vincent and L'Estrange, who stood by my side, remarked that if I did not allow the regiment to advance, the 61st Regiment would arrive at the redoubt as soon as we should. I immediately placed my cap on the point of my sword and passing to the front of the colours gave the word, 'Quick march. Charge!' We all rushed forward, excited by the old British cheer. But my personal advance was momentary; being struck by a shot which shattered both bones of my left leg, I came down. Vincent instantly asked what was the matter. I told him that my leg was broken, and that was all. I asked him to put the limb into a straight position, and to place me against a tree which stood close by; in this position I asked for my cap and sword, which had been struck from my hand in the fall; and then I cheered on the regiment as they gallantly charged into the redoubt.

The fort being carried, the regiment pursued the enemy down the opposite side of the hill, whilst I remained behind idly to look around me. The scene was beautifully romantic and heroically sublime. Groups of cavalry were seen judiciously, although apparently without regularity, dotted along the sides of every hill, watching an opportunity of falling on the discomfited foe. Our troops gallantly bore on over an unbroken series of intrenchments, thickly crowded with bayonets and kept lively by incessant fire. The awful passing events lay beneath my view; nor was there aught to interrupt my observation save a few bodily twitches, the pangs of prostrated ambition, and the shot and shells which burst close, or nearly cut the ground from under me.

Immediately after the redoubt was taken, under which I fell, another fort on our right, not yet attacked, turned some of its guns against the one just captured; and their shot and shell ploughing the ground all around me nearly suffocated me with dust and rubbish. Those who were not very severely wounded scrambled their way down the hill; but I might as well have attempted to carry a millstone as to drag my shattered leg after me. I therefore remained among the dead and dying, who were not few. My situation was not enviable. After some hours Assistant-Surgeon Simpson of the regiment appeared. I then got what is termed a field dressing; but unfortunately there were no leg splints; and so arm splints were substituted. Through this makeshift I suffered most severely during my descent. Some of the band coming up, I was put into a blanket and carried down the hill; but as we proceeded down this almost perpendicular descent, the blanket contracted from my weight in the middle, and then owing to the want of the proper long splints the foot drooped beyond the blanket's edge; it is almost impossible to imagine the torture which I suffered. Having gained the base of the hill towards dark, a cottage was fortunately discovered and into this I was carried.

Up to the noon of this day I congratulated myself on my good fortune in having served in the first and last battle fought in Spain, and proudly contemplated marching victoriously through France. I recalled too with pleasure and as if it were a propitious omen, that on this day five years ago I first trod Spanish ground. On November 16th, 1808, we marched into Fuentes de Oñoro, under the command of Sir John Moore. Then I was strong hale and joyous, with the glorious prospects of war favourably presented to view; but the afternoon of this, the fifth anniversary, proved a sad reverse. On this day I was carried out of Spain, borne in a blanket, broken in body and depressed in mind, with all my brilliant prospects like myself fallen to the ground. Such is glorious war.

After the field dressing Simpson departed in search of other wounded persons; and on his report of my wound two or three other medical officers sought me, fortunately in vain, that they might remove the limb. On the fourth day I was conveyed to a place where a hospital was established; but the inflammation of the leg was then so great (it was as big as my body) that no amputation could be attempted. A dressing took place which was long and painful, for I had bled so profusely while in the cottage that a cement hard as iron was formed round the limb, and before my removal it was absolutely necessary to cut me out of the bed on which I lay. After a considerable time passed in steeping with tepid water, the piece of mattress and sheet which I carried away from the cottage were removed; and now began the more painful operation of setting the leg. Staff-Surgeon Mathews and Assistant-Surgeon Graham, 31st Regiment, were the operators. Graham seized me by the knee and Mathews by the foot. They proposed that four soldiers should hold me during the operation; to this I objected, saying with a kind of boast that I was always master of my nerves. They now twisted and turned and extended my leg, aiming along it like a spirit level. The torture was dreadful; but though I ground my teeth and the big drops of burning perspiration rapidly chased each other, still I remained firm, and stifled every rising groan. After all was concluded I politely thanked Mathews, carelessly remarking that it was quite a pleasure to get wounded to be so comfortably dressed. This was mock heroism, for at the moment I trembled as if just taken from the rack.

'The Americans were highly elated at having beaten the British'
SERGEANT JOHN SPENCER COOPER

THE WAR OF 1812
THE BATTLE OF NEW ORLEANS
8 JANUARY 1815

The causes of the War of 1812 lay in the desire of the United States to poach British possessions in North America whilst Britain was occupied in the life-or-death struggle with Napoleon. The War began well, with the repelling of an US attack on Canada, even the occupation of Washington, but ended in a damp, ignominious squib. Sergeant John Spencer Cooper of the 7th Royal Fusiliers was among those lucky enough to survive the debacle at New Orleans.

After landing, we marched towards New Orleans, each man carrying a cannon ball in his haversack, as we had no baggage animals. Now two balls would have been more easily carried than one, because they would have poised each other.

'Tis said 'Delays are dangerous.' So we proved it. The troops that had preceded us had been on shore about three weeks; but not being strong enough to meet the enemy, they had not advanced far from the sea.

As the fleet could not approach within about forty miles of the position, all the artillery, ammunition, and provisions, etc., had to be brought to us in boats. While all went on so tardily, the Americans were cutting trenches, mounting cannon, etc., across a narrow plain, which had the mighty Mississippi on the right, and a marshy dense wood on the left. A frigate also was posted on the river in such a situation that it could rake the whole line. Batteries were also planted on the right or farther bank of the river.

The force which the Americans had to defend this narrow front was said to be about 14,000. A deep wide ditch, in front of high breastworks, ran along the whole line of defence. Our whole force for attacking this formidable work, did not exceed 7,000 including several hundred sailors sent from the fleet.

The front of our position was perfectly flat, on which three small guns were planted; but these were of little use, being only six pounders.

On the day before the battle, I, with three or four more, was selected to join my old comrades in the Light Company, from which I had been transferred when made sergeant; but the captain would not let me go back. This probably saved my life, for the Light Company, with a company of the 43rd, and one of the 85th, stormed the right redoubt next day, and would have established themselves there, had they been supported.

The same evening, hearing that we were to storm the enemy's works in the morning, several of us went to the colonel's tent, and reminded him that we should have been discharged at Portsmouth and sent home, according to orders from the Duke of York, then Commander-in-Chief. He said it could not be helped. This did not satisfy us, so we hurried to Head Quarters, to speak to Sir Edward Pakenham, but he was out viewing the enemy's defences.

Early in the morning of January 8th, 1815, we were assembled within cannon shot of the American entrenchments, as the reserve or second line. This was certainly a grand mistake, for the troops in front were composed of two black West India regiments, and other corps that had not been employed in sieges, etc., as we had in Spain.

Just as the day was breaking, a rocket whizzed aloft. All stood ready for the assault. At the word 'Forward!' the two lines approached the ditch under a murderous discharge of musketry; but crossing the ditch and scaling the parapet were found impossible without ladders. These had been prepared, but the regiment that should have carried them left them behind, and thereby caused, in a few minutes, a dreadful loss of men and officers; while the enemy suffered little, being ensconced behind the parapet. The front line now fell into great confusion, and retreated behind us, leaving numerous killed and wounded. We then advanced to within musket shot; but the balls flew so thickly that we were ordered to lie down to avoid the shower.

In the meantime our Light Company, and the two companies before mentioned, had gained a footing on the right of the American works; but having no support at hand, the enemy returned in force, and drove them into the ditch, where they were exposed to a plunging fire from above, and a flank fire from the frigate. One of the officers in the ditch vented his spleen at the enemy above by throwing stones. At last, the companies bolted from the ditch and ran off stoopingly in different directions. One of them, named Henry Axhorn, a smart young fellow, received a ball above his hip, which ran up his body, and stuck near his eye. It was extracted in a hospital at New Orleans. He joined us again after the peace, much altered in shape, and not fit for further service. Our Light Company went into this action sixty-four strong, and returned sixteen – having lost forty-eight.

That part of our force which was despatched to storm the enemy's works on the other side of the river, pushed off when the rocket was fired; but being few in number, they effected nothing of importance.

The Americans were highly elated at having beaten the Britishers, and I believe they boast of it to this day. But all things considered, they had little reason. Let us recapitulate – they were in number about 14,000, behind strong breastworks, and a deep ditch; a frigate protected their right flank, a wood and morass their left. Cannon were plentiful all along their front.

Our force numbered about 7,000 including perhaps 1,000 sailors. We had no works, no ditch and only three small guns. Shelter we had none, for the ground in front of the enemy's works for about a mile was as flat as a bowling green.

Of the 1,200 that should have crossed the river, no more than three or four hundred could be supplied with boats. But the chief cause of our failure was the want of ladders, which a certain regiment should have carried, but did not. Had Wellington been there, the Americans would have had less to boast of.

Tragically, peace had already been concluded before New Orleans was fought; the news had not reached the combatants down in Louisiana.

British losses at New Orleans were 2,000 killed, wounded or captured; American losses were eight dead.

Sergeant Cooper would have been consoled to know that Wellington was present to command the British in the greatest battle of the age. Waterloo.

———◆———

'I am sure I am to fall'
A SOLDIER OF THE 71ST

WATERLOO
ON THE MORNING OF BATTLE A COMRADE FORESEES HIS DEATH
BELGIUM, 18 JUNE 1815

Forced to abdicate in 1814 by his marshals, Napoleon came back from exile the following year for a last grasp at imperial glory: 'The Hundred Days'. Immediately, he went on the offensive against the only Allied armies in the field, Wellington's mixed force and Blucher's Prussians. After a draw at Quatre-Bras and a win at Ligny, a cockily confident Napoleon moved on to Waterloo. There he was awaited by Wellington, who had positioned his 68,000-strong force along a line of hills, with advance posts at the farms of La Haye Sainte and Hougoumont. Napoleon commanded 72,000 men.

Two hours after daybreak General Hill came down, taking away the left subdivision of the 10th company to cover his recognisance. Shortly afterwards we got half an allowance of liquor, which was the most welcome thing I ever received. I was so stiff and sore from the rain I could not move with freedom for some time. A little afterwards, the weather clearing up, we began to clean our arms and prepare for action. The whole of the opposite heights were covered by the enemy.

A young lad who had joined but a short time before said to me, while we were cleaning: 'Tom, you are an old soldier and have escaped often, and have every chance to escape this time also. I am sure I am to fall.' 'Nonsense, be not gloomy.' 'I am certain,' he said. 'All I ask is that you will tell my parents when you get home that I ask God's pardon for the evil I have done and the grief I have given them. Be sure to tell I died praying for their blessing and pardon.' I grew dull myself, but gave him all the heart I could. He only shook his head. I could say nothing to alter his belief.

The artillery had been tearing away since daybreak in different parts of the line. About twelve o'clock we received orders to fall in for attack. We then marched up to our position, where we lay on the face of a brae, covering a brigade of guns. We were so overcome by the fatigue of the two days' march that, scarce had we lain down, until many of us fell asleep. I slept sound for some time while the cannonballs, plunging in amongst us, killed a great many. I was suddenly awakened. A ball struck the ground a little below me, turned me heels-over-head, broke my musket in pieces and killed a lad at my side. I was stunned and confused and knew not whether I was wounded or not. I felt a numbness in my arm for some time.

We lay thus, about an hour and a half, under a dreadful fire, which cost us about 60 men, while we had never fired a shot. The young man I lately spoke of lost his legs by a shot at this time. They were cut very close; he soon bled to death. 'Tom,' he said, 'remember your charge: my mother wept sore when my brother died in her arms. Do not tell her how I died; if she saw me thus, it would break her heart. Farewell, God bless my parents!' He said no more, his lips quivered and he ceased to breathe.

———⊷•⊶———

'We still stood in line. The carnage was frightful'
ENSIGN EDMUND WHEATLEY

WATERLOO
THE VIEW OF AN INFANTRY ENSIGN
18 JUNE 1815

A Londoner, Wheatley joined 5th Line Battalion of the King's German Legion, the largest of the foreign corps in the British army and an easy route to a commission for a native without wealth or influence.

About ten o'clock, the order came to clean out the muskets and fresh load them. Half an allowance of rum was then issued, and we descended into the plain, and took our position in solid Squares. When this was arranged as per order, we were ordered to remain in our position but, if we like, to lay down, which the battalion did [as well as] the officers in the rere.

I took this opportunity of surveying our situation. It was singular to perceive the shoals of Cavalry and artillery suddenly in our rere all arranged in excellent order as if by a magic wand. The whole of the horse Guards stood behind us. For my part I thought they were at Knightsbridge barracks or prancing on St James's Street.

A Ball whizzed in the air. Up we started simultaneously. I looked at my watch. It was just eleven o'clock, Sunday ... morning. In five minutes a stunning noise took place and a shocking havock commenced.

One could almost feel the undulation of the air from the multitude of cannon shot. The first man who fell was five files on my left. With the utmost distortion of feature he lay on his side and shrivelling up every muscle of the body he twirled his elbow round and round in acute agony, then dropped lifeless, dying as it's called a death of glory, heaving his last breath on the field of fame. *Dieu m'engarde!*

A black consolidated body was soon seen approaching and we distinguished by sudden flashes of light from the sun's rays, the iron-cased cavalry of the enemy. Shouts of 'Stand firm!' 'Stand fast!' were heard from the little squares around and very quickly these gigantic fellows were upon us.

No words can convey the sensation we felt on seeing these heavy-armed bodies advancing at full gallop against us, flourishing their sabres in the air, striking their armour with the handles, the sun gleaming on the steel. The long horse hair, dishevelled by the wind, bore an appearance confounding the senses to an astonishing disorder. But we dashed them back as coolly as the sturdy rock repels the ocean's foam. The sharp-toothed bayonet bit many an adventurous fool, and on all sides we presented our bristly points like the peevish porcupines assailed by clamorous dogs.

The horse Guards then came up and drove them back; and although the sight is shocking 'tis beautiful to see the skirmish of Cavalry.

The French made repeated attacks of this kind. But we stood firm as the ground we stood on, and two long hours were employed in these successive attacks.

About two o'clock the cavalry ceased annoying and the warfare took a new turn. In order to destroy our squares, the enemy filled the air with shells, howitzers and bombs, so that every five or six minutes, the whole Battalion lay on its face then sprang up again when the danger was over.

The Prince of Orange gallop'd by, screaming out like a new born infant, 'Form into line! Form into line!' And we obeyed.

About this time the battle grew faint and a mutual cannonade with musketry amused us for one and a half hours, during which time I walked up and down chatting and joking with the young officers who had not until then smelt powder.

An ammunition cart blew up near us, smashing men and horses. I took a calm survey of the field around and felt shocked at the sight of broken armour, lifeless bodies, murdered horses, shattered wheels, caps, helmets, swords, muskets, pistols, still and silent. Here and there a frightened horse would rush across the plain trampling on the dying and the dead. Three or four poor wounded animals standing on three legs, the other dangling before them. We killed several of these unfortunate beasts and it would have been an equal Charity to have perform'd the same operation on the wriggling, feverish, mortally lacerated soldiers as they rolled on the ground.

About four o'clock the battle was renewed with uncommon ardour. We still stood in line. The carnage was frightful. The balls which missed us mowed down the Dutch behind us, and swept away many of the closely embattled Cavalry behind them.

I saw a cannon ball take away a Colonel of the Nassau Regiment so cleanly that the horse never moved from under him. While I was busy in keeping the men firm in their ranks, closing up the vacuities as the balls swept off the men, inspecting the fallen to detect deception or subterfuge, a regiment of Cuirassiers darted like a thunderbolt among us. At the instant a squadron of horse Guards dashed up to our rescue. In the confusion of the moment I made for the Colors to defend them. And we succeeded with infinite difficulty in rallying the men again.

I parried with great good fortune a back stroke from a horseman as he flew by me and Captain Sander had a deep slice from the same fellow on the head the instant after.

The battalion once more formed into a solid square, in which we remained the whole afternoon.

I felt the ardor of the fight increase very much within me, from the uncommon fury of the engagement.

Just then I fired a slain soldier's musket until my shoulder was nearly jellied and my mouth was begrimed with gunpowder to such a degree that I champed the gritty composition unknowingly.

Nothing could equal the splendor and terror of the scene. Charge after charge succeeded in constant succession. The clashing of swords, the clattering of musketry, the hissing of balls, and shouts and clamours produced a sound, jarring and confounding the senses, as if hell and the Devil were in evil contention.

About this time I saw the Duke of Wellington running from a charge of Cavalry towards the Horse-Guards, waving his hat to beckon them to the encounter.

All our artillery in front fell into the French power, the bombardiers skulking under the carriages. But five minutes put them again into our hands and the men creeping out applied the match and sent confusion and dismay into the retreating enemy.

Several times were these charges renewed and as often defeated. Charge met charge and all was pellmell. The rays of the sun glittered on the clashing swords as the two opposing bodies closed in fearful combat and our balls clattered on the shining breastplates like a hail shower.

As I stood in the square I looked down, I recollect, to take a pinch of snuff and thought of the old ballad, which I had seen somewhere, of the aged Nurse who describes the glorious battles of Marlborough to the child. After each relation of valor and victory, the infant says:

> 'Ten thousand slain you say and more?
> What did they kill each other for?'
> 'Indeed I cannot tell,' said she,
> 'But 'twas a famous victory.'

The field was now thickened with heaps of bodies and shattered instruments. Carcases of men and beasts lay promiscuously entwined. Aide-de-Camps scoured across with inconceivable velocity. All was hurry and indefatigable exertion. The small squares on our right kept up incessant firings and the fight was as obstinate as at the commencement.

The Duke of Wellington passed us twice, slowly and coolly.

No advantage as yet was discernible on either side. The French

Cavalry were less annoying. Their brave, repeated assaults had cost them very dear.

About six o'clock a passe-parole ran down the line – not to be disheartened, as the Prussians were coming up to our left, which news we received with loud cheers. And on looking to the left I perceived at some distance a dark swarm moving out of a thick wood. In twenty minutes a fresh cannonading began as if in rere of the French and the battle raged with increased vehemence.

A French Regiment of Infantry before us opposite the Farm house called the holy hedge (La Haye Sainte) advanced considerably just then and poured a destructive fire into our Battalion.

Colonel Ompteda ordered us instantly into line to charge, with a strong injunction to 'walk' forward, until he gave the word. When within sixty yards he cried 'Charge', we ran forward huzzaing. The trumpet sounded and no one but a soldier can describe the thrill one instantly feels in such an awful moment. At the bugle sound the French stood until we just reached them. I ran by Colonel Ompteda who cried out, 'That's right, Wheatley!'

I found myself in contact with a French officer but ere we could decide, he fell by an unknown hand. I then ran at a drummer, but he leaped over a ditch through a hedge in which he stuck fast. I heard a cry of, 'The Cavalry! The Cavalry!' But so eager was I that I did not mind it at the moment, and when on the eve of dragging the Frenchman back (his iron-bound hat having saved him from a Cut) I recollect no more. On recovering my senses, I look'd up and found myself, bareheaded, in a clay ditch with a violent head-ache. Close by me lay Colonel Ompteda on his back, his head stretched back with his mouth open; and a hole in his throat. A Frenchman's arm across my leg.

So confused was I that I did not remember I was on the field of Battle at the moment. Lifting up a little, I look'd over the edge of the ditch and saw the backs of a French Regiment and all the day's employment instantly suggested itself to my mind. Suddenly I distinguished some voices and heard one say '*En voici! En voici!*'

I lay down as dead, retaining my breath, and fancied I was shot in the back of my head. Presently a fellow cries, '*Voici un autre b.*' And a tug at my epaulette bespoke his commission. A thought struck me – he would turn me round to rifle my pockets. So starting up, I leaped up the ditch; but a swimming seized me and I was half on the ground when the fellow thrust his hand in my collar, grinning, '*Ou vas tu, chien?*' I begged of him to let me pick up my cap and he dragged me into the house.

An hour later, at around 7 p.m., Napoleon called up the Garde Impériale to adminster the knock-out blow to Wellington's centre. As the Garde Impériale advanced, a previously concealed British Guards brigade arose from the cornfield and poured musket fire into the French from 50 yards. 'Whether it was from the sudden and unexpected appearance of a Corps so near them . . . or the tremendous heavy fire we threw in to them,' wrote Captain Powell of the First Foot Guards later, '*La Garde*, who had never before failed in an attack suddenly stopped'. And then turned and fled.

'Sauve qui peut' went up the cry from the French army. Save yourself who can. The British had won 'the nearest run thing'.

'*The wounded crawling along the rows of dead was a horrible spectacle . . .*'
A SOLDIER OF THE 71ST

WATERLOO
AFTER BATTLE
18–19 JUNE 1815

The battlefield of Waterloo was littered with around 50,000 casualties. The Napoleonic Wars, with their close-range musket firing and heavy artillery bombardments, were perhaps the most deadly ever fought by the British soldier; even in winning he could expect to lose 15 per cent of his comrades.

We . . . lay down under the canopy of heaven, hungry and wearied to death. We had been oppressed, all day, by the weight of our blankets and great coats, which were drenched with rain, and lay upon our shoulders like logs of wood.

Scarce was my body stretched upon the ground, when sleep closed my eyes. Next morning, when I awoke, I was quite stupid. The whole night my mind had been harassed by dreams. I was fighting and charging, re-acting the scenes of the day, which were strangely jumbled with the scenes I had been in before. I rose up and looked around, and began to recollect. The events of the

18th came before me, one by one; still they were confused, the whole appearing as an unpleasant dream. My comrades began to awake and talk of it; then the events were embodied as realities. Many an action had I been in, wherein the individual exertions of our regiment had been much greater, and our fighting more severe; but never had I been where the fighting was so dreadful, and the noise so great. When I looked over the field of battle, it was covered and heaped in many places; figures moving up and down upon it. The wounded crawling along the rows of dead was a horrible spectacle; yet I looked on with less concern, I must say, at the moment, that I have felt at an accident, when in quarters. I have been sad at the burial of a comrade who died of sickness in the hospital, and followed him almost in tears: yet I have seen, after a battle, fifty men put into the same trench, and comrades amongst them, almost with indifference. I looked over the field of Waterloo as a matter of course – a matter of small concern.

In the morning we got half an allowance of liquor; and remained here until mid-day, under arms; then received orders to cook. When cooking was over, we marched on towards France.

Captain Cavalié Mercer, commander G Troop, Royal Horse Artillery, also slept on the field that night of the 18th June, but somewhat fitfully. At midnight he got up to 'contemplate a battle-field by the pale moonlight':

Oh, it was a thrilling sensation thus to stand in the silent hour of the night and contemplate that field – all day long the theatre of noise and strife, now so calm and still – the actors prostrate on the bloody soil, their pale wan faces upturned to the moon's cold beams, which caps and breast-plates, and a thousand other things, reflected back in brilliant pencils of light from as many different points! Here and there some poor wretch, sitting up amidst the countless dead, busied himself in endeavours to stanch the flowing stream with which his life was fast ebbing away. Many whom I saw so employed that night were, when morning dawned, lying stiff and tranquil as those who had departed earlier. From time to time a figure would half raise itself from the ground, and then, with a despairing groan, fall back again. Others, slowly and painfully rising, stronger, or having less deadly hurt, would stagger away with uncertain steps across the field in search of succour.

There was little succour; for the 30,000 injured men there were some 500 Allied and French doctors to tend them.

And the reward for the British soldier who survived Waterloo? To be dismissed from the service. With the outbreak of peace the army was massively reduced in strength:

———◆◆◆———

'I wish I was a soldier again'
A SOLDIER OF THE 71ST

A DISCHARGED SOLDIER'S FAREWELL TO HIS FAMILY
EDINBURGH, MAY 1818

Edinburgh, May 1818

Dear John,

These three months I can find nothing to do. I am a burden on Jeanie and her husband. I wish I was a soldier again. I cannot even get labouring work. God will bless those, I hope, who have been good to me. I have seen my folly. I would be useful, but can get nothing to do. My mother is at her rest, – God receive her soul! – I will go to South America. Maria de Parides will put me in a way to do for myself, and be a burden to no one. Or, I shall go to Spain, and live in Boho. – I will go to Buenos Ayres. – Farewell! John, this is all I have to leave you. It is yours: do with it as you think proper. If I succeed in the South, I will return and lay my bones besides my parents: if not, I will never come back.

It wasn't only fit rankers who were turned out from the army to beg, or subsist in the aftermath of Waterloo. Officers were sent home on half pay. Meanwhile, invalid Sergeant Jackson of the Coldstream Guards, who had lost a leg in 1814, appeared before the commissioners of the Royal Hospital at Chelsea. They, after giving him a once over, opined: ' "Oh, he is a young man, able to get his living". No questions asked of me', wrote Jackson, 'but at sight I was knocked off with the pitiful reward of a shilling a day'.

Jackson, having no more use for his scarlet coat, sold it for thirty shillings. Those soldiers who carried on wearing the redcoat in the army found themselves in a new world. At home, with the creation of the Metropolitan Police Force in 1826, soldiers were gradually relieved of unpopular civil duties, such as the infamous quashing of the 'riot' by reformers at Peterloo in 1819; abroad, France – save for the passing, unfounded scare – was no longer the enemy. The 'native' was. Under Queen Victoria, who succeeded to the throne in 1837, the British turned outwards to carry the Empire into the Dutch East Indies, Ceylon, Egypt, South Africa and other far corners.

Only in the rarest instances was this Empire built by soldiers; it was built by missionaries and traders. The soldier's job was to keep the map pink when the natives or emerging powers objected. Which, almost inevitably, they did. And so it was that Queen Victoria's reign saw 'Tommy Atkins', as the redcoat was now nicknamed, fight a string of little wars in foreign lands.

To join the British army in the early 19th century was to see the world. The global tour of John Clarke, 17th Foot, was by no means unusual.

Clarke's first campaign with the 17th Foot was in Tasmania, where he 'put the natives down' and captured a bush ranger named Jenkins. Then, in 1839, he was off to Afghanistan, fighting to place the British-backed Emir on the throne. He saw among other sights 'two men blown from a cannon' on the orders of the emir, and one of his own comrades blown up by lighting his pipe whilst sitting on an ammunition box. Clarke took part in the assault on Ghuznee, but mostly he did long marches, sometimes more than 20 miles a day, on short rations (¼lb of meat, ¼ flour a day), and 'never saw a bit of tea, or sugar, or coffee all the eighteen months we were out'. Colour-Sergeant Clarke continued his military service with 'three years in misery' in Aden, where he 'got scurvy very badly and had to take lime juice and pickled limes'.

Clarke's last posting was Ireland, where he was discharged after twenty-three years and three months' service in 1852.

Private John Ryder, 32nd Regiment, served Queen and country for just four years, but it was enough time to take him to Ireland and to India:

➤●◄

'One man went out of his mind, and ran through the jungle'
PRIVATE JOHN RYDER

ONE MAN'S SIKH WAR
DEATH MARCH, CLOSE-COMBAT AND RETURNING HOME UNKNOWN
INDIA, 1849

John Ryder fought in the Sikh Wars, which lasted 1845–9. Like the rest of his comrades in the 32nd Foot, Ryder found marching in the alien subcontinental terrain as hellish as fighting the martially minded Sikhs of the Punjab:

We struck camp at 12 o'clock, p.m. To give a proper description of this day, is more than I can do. The wind blew a perfect hurricane and the sand rose in clouds, cutting our faces and eyes dreadfully, and completely darkening the air. The country all round was a barren desert.

Officers and men became frantic for want of water, and our guides informed us that we must go six miles further before we could get any more; those who had flasks filled them. Mine did not hold more than half-a-pint. I could have sold it for any money before we got far on the way. The wind blew fearfully, and the sand rose in clouds; so that we could not see one another. My company was on the advance guard, and we lost the regiment on the plains. The sand rose in such clouds that we could not see them, and the wind blew so strong that they could not hear our bugle sound 'the close'. Our officers rode in all directions in search of them; at length, they succeeded. The storm abated for a short time, but soon commenced again, and the sand rose in such clouds, and the wind was so hot, that the men fell by numbers. The want of water was past everything – the best and strongest men were beaten up – the cry of 'water, water,' 'well, well,' was heard on every side. Men were in the greatest agonies. I found my drop of water of more value than gold; but how I stood it more than the rest I do not know. I carried a bit of ginger in my mouth always – perhaps it was that. Although I was ill, very ill, and wished I was dead, yet God was good and merciful to me, and I pulled through.

We came to a well and a few Indian huts at 4 o'clock. All became disorder; men rushed out of the ranks like madmen, and all the officers could do to keep order was useless. I and two others got into the huts, and the natives gave us all the water they had; so we did pretty well. We halted here about three quarters of an hour, when the wind dropped to a calm. We saw a large, black, dismal-looking cloud rising to our right – for it was now daylight. In a short time after, a gentle breeze sprang up, and ruffled the sand as it came slowly along. We all expected it was going to rain; but alas! alas! we were mistaken, – the breeze began to be stronger and of a cool kind, which made us shudder – though not a cold shudder; something seemed to be awful about it.

The wind now got to the east, and began to blow stronger; and the men fell sick by numbers. I felt very bad. It was a sickly kind of a feel. There the men lay, groaning in the greatest of agony. The doctors and apothecaries were all bustle, bleeding the men as they lay upon the sand, until pools of black blood were spread all over the ground. It was a most shocking sight to behold. There they were, – some dead, and some dying. The dead were as follows: – one captain, one sergeant and four privates. One man shot himself, to put an end to his troubles; thus making a total of seven dead, and very near half the regiment sick. Luckily, the wind changed to the south-west, and the sickness abated. Those who were not so very bad revived all at once.

Our poor colonel was nearly distracted, not knowing what to do for the best. The wind by this time was blowing as bad as it did when we first started, and the sand rose in masses. One part of the regiment lost the other in the storm; but the officers rode all round, and the bugles sounding 'the close', we got together again.

We pitched our camp about six o'clock, with those tents at least which had arrived; for some of the tents and baggage did not come until late in the day; they got lost in the sandstorm. Two of our camp followers had fallen dead. Our colonel went all over the ground to see that his men were as comfortable as they could be. The wind dropped in the evening. We paraded at six o'clock, to bury our dead; they were sown up in their beds, and put altogether into a pit which was made for that purpose. The captain was put in a few boards, knocked up together, and buried by their side. We fired three volleys of blank cartridge over them. The colonel read the funeral service. The only thing that marked the spot was a few trees near an Indian village.

During the time we were burying them, a thunderstorm rose. The sky was one complete sheet of fire, and the peals of thunder were dreadful, as if the heavens were coming down. The whole of the men looked pale, sad, and downcast. The doctor told the colonel that he must halt the next day, as it was impossible to move the whole of the sick. One man went out of his mind, and ran through the jungle, and was not captured until a few days after.

Having endured such miseries, then went the British soldier into battle. Among other actions, Ryder participated in the famous storm of Gujerat on 21–22 February 1849.

As we now stood formed for battle, awaiting further orders to advance, I took a survey of the country all round us. It was a level plain, well cultivated, the corn a little above knee high, with here and there a fresh piece of ploughed ground ... The city of Goojerat was visible about four miles in our front. This was the enemy's headquarters and the centre of his position, from which he had a good view, and so could watch all our movements.

It was about six o'clock, a.m., when the line advanced, covered by skirmishers, who soon became engaged with the enemy. They retired as we came up out of most of their advanced villages. Our line kept good order as if on a common parade. The artillery was now ordered forward and a most fearful cannonading commenced such as had never been heard before; the whole artillery of both armies now being in full play upon each other. We were ordered to lie down so that the enemy's shot might pass over us; and over us they did pass, tearing up the ground all round us until it looked as though it had been fresh ploughed, and we were covered with earth, though not many were killed ...

The artillery had been in play for about two hours when the enemy's guns began to slacken ... The infantry was now ordered to advance; and as we went forward we could see the enemy forming their line to receive us. They commenced firing at a long range of musketry. We advanced and did not discharge a shot till within 150 yards or less, when we opened such a murderous and well-directed fire that they fell by hundreds. They, on their part, kept up a good fire but it was badly directed; as most of their balls went over our heads. With levelled bayonets we charged; but they could not stand the shock of cold steel. They gave way in all directions ...

On we rushed, bearing all down before us, charging and cheering. We took every gun we came up to, but their artillery fought desperately: they stood and defended their guns to the last. They threw their arms around them, kissed them and died. Others would spit at us, when the bayonet went through their bodies ...

Everything was carried before us, and the dead and dying lay strewed all over the ground in heaps. In some places might be seen men lying in whole ranks, as they fell; and in more than one place I saw artillerymen and horses one upon another, as they had been shot down by whole batteries at the time their guns were dismounted. The carriages lay broken and scattered in all directions. The enemy as they retreated made daring attempts to stand at the villages; but they were stormed, and very few escaped, for they were all either shot or bayonetted. The left of our line suffered the most, the villages lying the thickest in their front. However, nothing could daunt the courage of the British soldiers, nor resist the shock of the levelled bayonets. We drove them before us in disorder through their camp, which was pitched round Goojerat. We captured all their tents and camp equipage, with all their stores and magazines, and nearly all their artillery.

On his return to England in 1850, the sun tanned Ryder found that no one recognised him, not even his own family:

At night I went home to Twyford, and, on arriving there, I went to Mr. Goodman's, the public-house near to my father's; for I thought it would be better than going in home at once, and putting them about, as they did not in the least expect me. I had sent for my father, by an old neighbour, to meet me at the public house. On my going in I called for some drink. In the house were two of my old companions; one was the very next door neighbour, and was of the same age as myself. We had been at school together, and play-fellows: but they neither of them knew me. The landlord who brought me the ale had known me from a child, but did not appear to have the slightest recollection of me then. He passed the time of day, and the remarks on the weather, and so did my two companions. They eyed me all over, and wondered who I was. While I was in talk, my father came in. He looked round, but did not see any one whom he knew, who wanted him. He sat down, and I called to him, and said, 'Come, old man, will you have a glass of drink?' He looked very hard at me, and came. I handed him a glass, when he wished my good health and drank. The old man had altered much since I had last seen him: he stooped much, and his hair was quite grey. He set the glass down, and was going away, when I said, 'You had better have another'. He stood, and I handed him another. He drank it, and thanked me, and was going away, when I said, 'Well then, father, so you do not know me.' He was quite overcome. He knew me then. The house was now all surprised. My companions also knew me then, and this caused no small stir in the village. The news soon flew. My mother heard it, and came to see; when she came in she looked round, but did not know me, though I was sitting beside my father. After she had looked round, and did not (as she supposed) see me, she appeared very confused, and said, 'Some one said my boy had come, but I did not believe it.' I handed her a glass of ale, and told her to drink, and not think of such things; and she was going away quite contented, till I called her back, and said, 'Do you not see him?' but she did not know me then, until I said, 'Mother, *you* ought to know me'. The poor old woman then knew me, and would have fallen to the floor, if she had not been caught. She was some time before she overgot it.

Ryder had romantically wished to join the army from childhood, although his father, a veteran of the Waterloo campaign, had sought to dissuade him. Most men, though, joined the early Victorian army for mundane reasons:

———◆◆◆———

'*1. Indigent. . . . 80 in 120*'
SERGEANT J. MACMULLEN

REASONS FOR ENLISTMENT IN THE ARMY
1840s

From *Camp and Barrack Room: or, the British Army as it is, 1846* by an ex-staff sergeant of the 13th Infantry.

1. Indigent. – Embracing labourers and mechanics out of employ, who merely seek for support .... 80 in 120.
2. Indigent. – Respectable persons induced by misfortune or imprudence .... 2,, 120.
3. Idle. – Who consider a soldier's life an easy one ..16 ,, 120.
4. Bad characters. – Who fall back upon the army as a last resource ....8 ,, 120.
5. Criminals. – Who seek to escape from the consequence of their offences ....1 ,, 120.
6. Perverse sons. – Who seek to grieve their parents ..2 ,, 120.

7.   Discontented and restless ....8 „ 120.
8.   Ambitious ....1 „ 120.
9.   Others ....2 „ 120.

MacMullen's estimate of the proportion of 'blackguards' (criminals and bad characters) in the Victorian army as 9 in 120 was slightly higher than that of the Royal Commission on Corporal Punishment in 1853, which put the number of truly bad elements at 10–20 per regiment of 500.

———➤•◆•———

'Discipline was maintained to the last'
CORPORAL JOHN O'NEIL

THE SINKING OF HM TROOPSHIP *BIRKENHEAD*
OFF THE COAST OF SOUTH-WEST AFRICA
26 FEBRUARY 1852

The *Birkenhead* was carrying reinforcements, together with their families, to the Kaffir War. There were about 638 souls on board:

The drafts on board included 100 of the Argyll and Sutherlands and an officer of ours, Major Wright.

I and my escort had only been on board half an hour when the vessel struck on a rock between Simon's Bay and Port Elizabeth, somewhere near Danger Point. She struck a mile and a quarter from shore. It is fair to suppose the disaster was caused by reckless navigation, because outside the breakers the sea was as smooth, almost, as this floor; there was scarcely a ripple on the surface of the water. It was a strange scene when she struck. The Captain of the ship, ah! I recollect well the last words he uttered. He rushed down below and told the sailors to man the boats. 'Lower your boats, men,' said he, 'we are all lost!' I never saw him again. Major Wright gave the order, 'All hands fall in on deck,' and we fell in, every man. He told off so many soldiers, and so many sailors to each boat, to get them out and save the women and children. I forget how many boats there were, but every boat available was got over the side. No man was allowed to leave the ranks till the boats were pushed off. Major Wright threatened to shoot any man who stepped towards the boats, but no one thought of doing it. Any rush would have swamped the boats for certain. Discipline was maintained till the last. The ship went down twenty minutes after striking. It was a terrible time, but we stood on. We all expected to die, but the women and children were got safely off. Not one of them was drowned, thank God! They and their escort comprised the greater part of the 179 who were saved. The water rose as the ship was sinking. Before we left her we were up to our necks in water on the top deck. Just before the end came Major Wright addressed us. 'You men who cannot swim,' said he, 'stick to some wreckage – whatever you can lay hands on. As for you who can swim, I can give you no advice. As you see, there are sharks about, and I cannot advise you how to avoid them,' which of course he could not. There was many a quiet hand-shake and silent goodbye. Few of us hoped to live through it. The breakers between us and the shore were awful. At last the ship sank. There was a lurch and a plunge, and all was over. I found myself in the water and struck out for shore. I had next to nothing on in the way of clothing. It was a fight for life. We were not above a mile and a quarter from land, as far as my eye served me; but that is plenty far enough when there are breakers and sharks! The breakers were so big. Luckily I knew how to swim breakers, or I should not be here now. Any one not knowing how to would have been drowned, as sure as fate! They would smother him. With proper management a breaker will sometimes sweep you in for hundreds of yards. The backwash was the worst. I stuck to it, and got ashore at last, escaping the sharks. I saw nothing of the rest, or of the ship's boats. All the trouble was not over when I got ashore. I had to walk sixteen miles stark naked under a blazing sun before I met any one or obtained any assistance. I shall never forget Major Wright. If it had not been for him all hands would have been lost, women and children and all. You may know that he was afterwards granted an annuity of £100, and he deserved it. I believe there was a lot of treasure on board the *Birkenhead* when she foundered. The military chest was on board for the troops – so we were led to understand. I think it is true, because for some time afterwards we were paid with Mexican dollars. They never recovered anything from the wreck.

So impressed was the Prussian army by the bravery of the British troops on the *Birkenhead* that accounts of their valour were read out to every one of its regiments. The *Birkenhead* was only the most famous of sea disasters involving British troops in the 19th century. In 1816 the transport *Seahorse* was lost off Ireland; in 1847 a fire broke out on the *Sarah Sands*, bound for India, and the crew abandoned ship. The soldiers left behind spent 14 hours putting out the conflagration, and somehow managed to bring the limping, sinking ship to safety.

'That Men Should All Tie Up Their Wives and
Chain Up All Their Daughters'
ANONYMOUS

SCARLET FEVER
THE LURE OF A MAN IN UNIFORM
CHOBHAM CAMP
SURREY, 1852

In Summer 1852, 18,000 soldiers were brought together in a mass exercise at Chobham Camp, Surrey, one of the few times in the Victorian period that troops trained outside their regiment. So many soldiers gathered together provoked a moral panic that local girls would be encouraged into 'loose' ways; the redcoats did nothing to allay such fears. They sang:

Come all you lads and lasses gay, whose age is under fifty,
Clap a bayonet in your belt and toddle off so thrifty;
And all old maids and bachelors and married women, right slap,
In merry June strike up the tune, 'Good morning to your
   nightcap'.

* * *

Chorus
This glorious sight on Chobham Heath fills all the world with
   wonder,
Where ladies tramp and soldiers camp and cannons roar like
   thunder.

* * *

A party to the queen did go, and there they serious told her
That every girl had left her home and bolted with the soldiers;
A proclamation she sent out to reach Virginia Water,

That men should all tie up their wives and chain up all their
    daughters.

        *   *   *

Or else, our gracious queen did say, her generals had told her,
The country would be over-run with lots of little soldiers,
Born with knapsacks on their backs, with sash and sword so
    clever,
And on their pretty little heads a blooming cap and feather.

        *   *   *

You married men, mark what I pen, this camping must be bested;
Lock all your wives and daughters up and chain them to the
    bedstead
For if to Chobham they do go o'er hedges, stiles and ditches,
From camping they'll be coming home in soldier's coat and
    breeches.

        *   *   *

I met a lady eighty-five, a-going on a rum way,
She sung and whistled 'Jack's alive' and 'Seventeen come
    Sunday';
When all the girls of —— town like flocks of bees did crowd her,
Then 'Off she goes', 'Gee up, gee wo', like cannon balls and
    powder.

        *   *   *

There's bakers' wives and butchers' wives and snobs as fierce as
    monkeys,
There's fifes and flutes and soldiers' boots and farmers' wives on
    donkeys;
There's powder, shot, and ginger pop, and England's queen –
    behold her–
And thirty thousand pretty girls encamping with the soldiers.

        *   *   *

When Chobham Camp is at an end and soldiers off do hurry,
There will not be a female left in Hampshire or in Surrey,
Or in any part of Berkshire, 'cause the queen said they had told
    her
They were afraid the pretty maids would run away with the soldiers.

'Scarlet fever' was the term coined for the seductive quality of an army redcoat.
The Victorian soldier believed that his hirsuteness – with its association with

Samson's virility – was also a magnet for women. Not that he had much choice in the matter of facial hair. In 1838, only a year after her accession, Queen Victoria ordered that all mounted men were to be moustachioed. By the 1850s moustaches and whiskers were *de rigueur* throughout the service.

Two years after the great camp at Chobham, Britain found herself at crossed bayonets with Russia, her first premier-league enemy since Waterloo.

At the top of the army, Major-General Sir Harry Smith proclaimed to the men of the 93rd Sutherland Highlanders: 'Soldiers have nothing to do with the causes of quarrels, their duty is to fight; but in this instance you have a noble cause to fight for, the protection of the weak by the strong . . .' Or, more banally, the defence of Turkey from Russia.

Sir Harry was not alone in his estimate of the Crimean War as a noble cause. Further down the ranks of the army, Gunner Whitehead versed: 'Grim war does summon me hence/And I deem it my duty to fight/Tis a honour to stand in proud England's defence/When once she is proved in the right.'

Dispatched on a wave of 'just war' fever, British – and French – troops landed in the Crimea in October 1854 to body-blow 'Johnny Rooskie' by seizing Sevastopol. Not for the last time in the Crimea, someone blundered. Instead of a short, sharp storming the Allies found themselves engaged in a long siege campaign – in winter, and with no proper rations or equipment.

Private Parsons arrived at the Balaclava front in November:

Then began our experience of the soldier's life whilst on campaign. The weeding out of the weaklings commencing in real earnest – in our tent alone we were reduced from 19 down to eight in the first three months – and this, not by the hand of the enemy, but by those companions of active service – exhaustion and disease – for it was no unusual sight in the morning to see the dead bodies of two or three men taken out from the tents, the men having passed away during the night, owing to the ravages of exhaustion or dysentery, and no wonder at this, when the food we had to live upon is taken into consideration, for raw beef and pork were delicacies at this time, occasionally washed down with coffee – the coffee being previously prepared by us by being put into a piece of old biscuit bag and pounded. Chocolate also used to be sent out to us, this reaching us made up in shape something like a big flat cheese. This chocolate we found would burn, so breaking it into pieces and piling stone around, we then would set fire to it, place our canteen on the top and then wait for something warm; this being the only way we succeeded in doing so for the first few months.

My impression of the first sights of our men before Sebastopol I shall never forget, their appearance being appalling. The men were unshaven, unkempt, dirty-looking, ragged, and filthy; and as I saw them wading about up to the knees in mud and 'slurry', I could not discern whether they were British, Turks, or Russians, until speech disclosed that they were British; but soon we were as bad as they.

The rifle with which we had to defend ourselves was not like the modern magazine rifle, but the old-fasioned 'Brown Bess' with round bullet, the charge having to be rammed home in the rifle with the ramrod. Many a night when our duty and need for the rifle came, it was found impossible to use it, the ramrod being frozen to the rifle and quite immovable, the bayonet and butt end of the rifle having then to be brought into use.

There were attempts, by such saints in nurse's uniform as Florence Nightingale and Mary Seacole, to mitigate the appalling conditions of the servicemen, but to minor effect. Microbes and deprivation would massacre 17,225 British troops in the Crimea – four times as many as would die from bullet, bayonet and shell.

'that ride of horrors'
PRIVATE JAMES WIGHTMAN

THE CHARGE OF THE LIGHT BRIGADE
BALAKLAVA, 11.10 A.M., 25 OCTOBER 1854

It was a morning which began and ended in glory. When a surprise Russian attack ground through the Turkish redoubts before Balaklava, all that was left between the Russian cavalry and Balaklava itself were the 93rd Highlanders, a battery of artillery and some plucky, rallied Turks. As the Russian cavalry streamed on towards the Highlanders, 'Remember', said Sir Colin Campbell, 'there is no retreat from here. You must die where you stand'. The Highlanders did not budge an inch; watching from a nearby hilltop, William Howard Russell of *The Times* turned the clash into a legend: 'The Russians . . . in one grand line dashed at the Highlanders. The ground flies between their horses' feet; gathering speed at every stride, they dash on towards that thin red streak tipped with steel'.

His coined phrase, altered slightly, became the legendary thin red line.

The Russians pitted against the Highlanders retreated. Meanwhile, the main body of Russian cavalry, 2,000 strong, descended towards the Heavy Brigade, who were disadvanted in numbers (being 600 strong) and on the lower ground. Despite this, the brigade commander, General Scarlett, charged the enemy – uphill. The Russians, fascinated, were almost rooted to the spot – until Scarlett and his men arrived plumb in their centre. Russell was still watching from his hill top: 'There was a clash of steel and a light play of sword blades in the air, and then the Greys and the redcoats disappear in the midst of the shaken and quivering columns . . . It was a terrible moment. 'God help them! They are lost!' was the exclamation of more than one man, and the thought of many'. Luckily, reinforcements arrived and the Russians were driven off.

Up to this point of the battle, the Light Brigade remained motionless, unused. But their time had now come. Wightman rode with the 17th Lancers.

After the Heavies' charge the Light Brigade was moved a little way 'left back' and then forward, down into the middle of the upper part of the outer valley, and fronting straight down it, the Heavies remaining a little in advance to the right about the crest of the Causeway Ridge. We stood halted in those positions for about three quarters of an hour, Lord Cardigan in front of his brigade, Lord Lucan on our right front about midway between the two brigades. I may here describe the composition of the first line of the Light Brigade and my own particular place therein. On the right were the 18th Light Dragoons (now Hussars) in the centre of the 17th Lancers, on the left the 11th Hussars, which latter regiment before the charge began was ordered back in support, so that during the charge the first line consisted only of the 13th Light Dragoons and the 17th Lancers. All three regiments were but of two squadrons each; the formation of course was two deep. I belonged to the right troop of the 1st (the right) squadron of the 17th Lancers; my squadron leader being Captain (now General) R. White, my troop leader Captain Morgan, now Lord Tredegar. On the extreme right of the front rank of the squadron rode Private John Lee, a grand old soldier who had long served in India and whose time was nearly up; I was next to him, and on my left was my comrade Peter Marsh.

As we stood halted here, Captain Nolan, of the 15th Hussars, whom we knew as an aid-de-camp of the head-quarter staff, suddenly galloped out to the front through the interval between us and the 13th, and called out to Captain Morris, who was directly in my front, 'Where is Lord Lucan?' 'There,' replied Morris, pointing – 'there, on the right front!' Then he added, 'What is it to be, Nolan? – are we going to charge?' Nolan was off already in Lord Lucan's direction, but as he galloped away he shouted to Morris over his shoulder, 'You will see! you will see!' Just then we had some amusement, Private John Vey, who was the regimental butcher, had been slaughtering down at Balaclava, came up at a gallop on a troop horse of a Heavy who had been killed, and whom Vey had stripped of his belt and arms and accoutred himself with them over his white canvas smock frock, which, as well as his canvas trousers tucked into his boots, were covered with blood-stains. His shirt-sleeves were rolled up above his elbows, and his face, arms, and hands were smeared with blood, so that as he formed up on Lee's right shouting – he had some drink in him – that 'he'd be d – d if he was going to be left behind his regiment and so lose the fun,' he was indeed a gruesome yet laughable figure. Mr. Chadwick, the adjutant, ordered him to rein back and join his own troop in the 2nd squadron and I saw no more of him, but afterwards knew that he rode the charge, had his horse shot, but came back unwounded, and was given the distinguished conduct medal.

I cannot call to mind seeing Lord Lucan come to the front of the Light Brigade and speak with Lord Cardigan, although of course I know now that he did so. But I distinctly remember that Nolan returned to the Brigade and his having a mere momentary talk with Cardigan, at the close of which he drew his sword with a flourish, as if greatly excited. The blood came into his face – I seem to see him now; and then he fell back a little way into Cardigan's left rear, somewhat in front of and to the right of Captain Morris, who had taken post in front of his own left squadron. And I remember as if it were but yesterday Cardigan's figure and attitude, as he faced the brigade and in his strong hoarse voice gave the momentous word of command, 'The brigade will advance! First squadron of 17th Lancers direct!' Calm as on parade – calmer indeed by far than his wont on parade – stately, square and erect, master of himself, his brigade, and his nobler charge, Cardigan looked the ideal cavalry leader, with his stern firm face, and his quite soldierly bearing. His long military seat was perfection on the thoroughbred chestnut 'Ronald' with the 'white-stockings' on the near hind and fore, which my father, his old riding-master, had broken for him. He was in the full uniform of his old corps, the 11th Hussars, and he wore the pelisse, not slung, but put on like a patrol jacket, its front one blaze of gold lace. His drawn sword was in his hand at the slope, and never saw I man fitter to wield the weapon.

As I have said, he gave the word of command, and then turning his head toward his trumpeter, Britten of the Lancers, he quietly said 'Sound the Advance!' and wheeled his horse, facing the dark mass at the farther end of the valley, which we knew to be the enemy. The trumpeter sounded the 'Walk'; after a few horse-lengths came the 'Trot'. I did not hear the 'Gallop' but it was sounded. Neither voice nor trumpet, so far as I know, ordered the 'charge'; Britten was a dead man in a few strides after he had sounded the 'Gallop'. We had ridden barely two hundred yards and were still at the trot, when poor Nolan's fate came to him. I did not see him cross Cardigan's front, but I did see the shell explode, of which a fragment struck him. From his raised sword-hand dropped the sword, but the arm remained erect. Kinglake writes that 'what had once been Nolan maintained the strong military seat until the erect form dropped out of the saddle;' but this was not so. The sword-arm indeed remained upraised and rigid, but all the other limbs so curled in on the contorted trunk as by a spasm, that we wondered how for the moment the huddled form kept the saddle. It was the sudden convulsive twitch of the bridle hand inward on the chest, that caused the charge to wheel rearward so abruptly. The weird shriek and the awful face as rider and horse disappeared haunt me now to this day, the first horror of that ride of horrors.

As the line at the trumpet sound broke from the trot into the gallop, Lord Cardigan, almost directly behind whom I rode, turned his head leftward toward Captain Morris and shouted hoarsely, 'Steady, steady, Captain Morris!' The injunction was no doubt pointed specially at the latter, because he, commanding the regiment one of the squadrons of which had been named to direct, was held in a manner responsible to the brigade commander for both the pace and direction of the whole line.

Later, when we were in the midst of our torture, and, mad to be out of it and have our revenge, were forcing the pace, I heard again, high above the turmoil and din, Cardigan's sonorous command, 'Steady, steady, the 17th Lancers!' and observed him check with voice and outstretched sword Captain White, my squadron leader, as he shot forward abreast of the stern disciplined chief leading the brigade. But, resolute man though he was, the time had come when neither the commands nor the example of Cardigan availed to restrain the pace of his brigade; and when to maintain his position in advance, indeed, if he were to escape being ridden down, he had to let his charger out from the gallop to the charge. For hell had opened upon us from front and either flank, and it kept open upon us during the minutes – they seemed hours – which passed while we traversed the mile and a quarter at the end of which was the enemy. The broken and fast-thinning ranks raised rugged peals of wild fierce cheering that only swelled the louder as the shot and shell from the battery tore gaps through us, and the enfilading musketry fire from the Infantry in both flanks brought down horses and men. Yet in this stress it was fine to see how strong was the bond of discipline and obedience. 'Close in! Close in!' was the constant command of the squadron and troop officers as the casualties made gaps in the ragged line, but the order was scarcely needed, for of their own instance and, as it seemed, mechanically, men and horses alike sought to regain the touch.

We had not broke into the charging pace when poor old John Lee, my right-hand man on the flank of the regiment, was all but smashed by a shell; he gave my arm a twitch, as with a strange smile on his worn old face he quietly said, 'Domino! chum,' and fell out of the saddle. His old grey mare kept alongside of me for some distance, treading on and tearing out her entrails as she galloped, till at length she dropped with a strange shriek. I have mentioned that my comrade, Peter Marsh, was my left-hand man; next beyond him was Private Dudley. The explosion of a shell had swept down four or five men on Dudley's left, and I heard him ask Marsh if he had noticed 'what a hole that b——shell had made' on his left front. 'Hold your foul-mouthed tongue,' answered Peter, 'swearing like a blackguard, when you may be knocked into eternity next minute!' Just then I got a musket-bullet through my right knee, and another in the shin, and my horse had three bullet wounds in the neck. Man and horse were bleeding so fast that Marsh begged me to fall out; but I would not, pointing out that in a few minutes we must be into them, and so I sent my spurs well home, and faced it out with my comrades. It was about this time that Sergeant Talbot had his head clean carried off by a round shot, yet for about thirty yards further the headless body kept the saddle, the lance at the charge firmly gripped under the right arm. My narrative may seem barren of incidents of the charge but amid the crash of shells and the whistle of bullets, the cheers and the dying cries of comrades, the sense of personal danger, the pain of wounds, and the consuming passion to reach an enemy, he must be an exceptional man who is cool enough and curious enough to be looking serenely about him for what painters call 'local colour'. I had a good deal of 'local colour' myself, but it was running down the leg of my overalls from my wounded knee.

Well, we were nearly out of it at last, and close on those cursed guns. Cardigan was still straight in front of me, steady as a church, but now his sword was in the air; he turned in his saddle for an instant, and shouted his final command, 'Steady! steady! Close in!' Immediately afterwards there crashed into us a regular volley from the Russian cannon. I saw Captain White go down and Cardigan disappear into the smoke. A moment more and I was within it myself. A shell burst right over my head with a hellish crash that all but stunned me. Immediately after I felt my horse under me take a tremendous leap into the air. What he jumped I never saw or knew; the smoke was so thick I could not see my arm's length around me. Through the dense veil I heard noises of fighting and slaughter, but saw no obstacle, no adversary, no gun or gunner, and, in short, was through and beyond the Russian battery before I knew for certain that I had reached it.

I then found that none of my comrades were close to me. There was no longer any semblance of a line. No man of the Lancers was on my right, a group was a little way on my left. Lord Cardigan must have increased his distance during or after passing through the battery, for I now saw him some way ahead, alone in the midst of a knot of Cossacks. At this moment Lieutenant Maxse, his Lordship's aid-de-camp, came back out of the tussle, and crossed my front as I was riding forward. I saw that he was badly wounded; and he called to me, 'For God's sake, Lancer, don't ride over me! See where Lord Cardigan is,' pointing to him, 'rally on him!' I was hurrying on to support the brigade commander, when a Cossack came at me and sent his lance into my right thigh. I went for him, but he bolted; I overtook him, drove my lance into his back and unhorsed him just in front of two Russian guns which were in possession of Sergeant-Majors Lincoln and Smith, of the 18th Light Dragoons, and other men of the Brigade. When pursuing the Cossack I noticed Colonel Mayow deal very cleverly with a big Russian cavalry officer. He tipped off his shako with the point of his sword, and then laid his head right open with the old cut seven. The chase of my Cossack had diverted me from rallying on Lord Cardigan; he was now nowhere to be seen, nor did I ever again set eyes on the chief who had led us down the valley so grandly. The handful with the guns, to which I momentarily attached myself, were presently outnumbered and over-powered, the two sergeant-majors being taken prisoners, having been dismounted. I then rode towards Private Samuel Parkes, of the 4th Light Dragoons, who, supporting with one arm the wounded Trumpet-Major (Crawford) of his regiment, was with the other cutting and slashing at the enemies surrounding them. I struck in to aid the gallant fellow, who was not overpowered until his sword was shot away, when he and the trumpet-major were taken prisoners, and it was with difficulty I was able to cut my way out. Presently there joined me two other men, Mustard, of my own corps, and Fletcher, of the 4th Light Dragoons. We were now through and on the further side of a considerable body of the Russian cavalry, and so near the bottom of the valley that we could well discern the Tcherbaya river. But we were all three wearied and weakened by loss of blood; our horses wounded in many places; there were enemies all about us, and we thought it was about time to be getting back. I remember reading in the regimental library of an officer who said to his commander 'We have done enough for honour,' that was our humble opinion too, and we turned our horses' heads. We forced our way through ring after ring of enemies, fell in with my comrade Peter Marsh, and rode rearward, breaking through party after party of Cossacks, until we heard the familiar voice of Corporal Morley, of our regiment, a great, rough, bellowing Nottingham man. He had lost his lance hat, and his long hair was flying out in the wind as he roared, 'Coom ere! coom ere! Fall in, lads, fall in!' Well, with shouts and oaths he had collected some twenty troopers of various regiments. We fell in with the handful this man of the hour had rallied to him, and there joined us also under his leader-ship Sergeant Major Ranson and Private John Penn, of the 17th. Penn, a tough old warrior who had served with the 3rd Light in the Sikh war, had killed a Russian officer, dismounted, and with great deliberation accoutred himself with the belt and sword of the defunct, in which he made a great show. A body of Russian Hussars blocked our way. Morley, roaring Nottingham oaths by way of encouragement, led us straight at them, and we went through and out at the other side as if they had been made of tinsel paper. As we rode up the valley, pursued by some Hussars and Cossacks, my horse was wounded by a bullet in the shoulder, and I had hard work to put the poor beast along. Presently we were abreast of the Infantry who had blazed into our right as we went down; and we had to take their fire again, this time on our left. Their firing was very impartial; their own Hussars and Cossacks following close on us suffered from it as well as we. Not many of Corporal Morley's party got back. My horse was shot dead, riddled with bullets. One bullet struck me on the forehead, another passed through the top of my shoulder; while struggling out from under my horse a Cossack standing over me stabbed me with his lance once in the neck near the jugular, again above the collar-bone, several times in the back and once under the short rib; and when, having regained my feet, I was trying to draw my sword, he sent his lance through the palm of my hand. I believe he would have succeeded in killing me, clumsy as he was, if I had not blinded him for the moment with a handful of sand. Fletcher at the same time lost his horse, and, it seems, was wounded. We were very roughly used. The Cossacks at first hauled us along by the tails of our coatees and our haversacks. When we got on foot they drove their lance-butts into our backs to stir us on. With my shattered knee and the other bullet wound on the shin of the same leg, I could barely limp, and good old Fletcher said 'Get on my back, chum!' I did so, and then found that he had been shot through the back of the head. When I told him of this, his only answer was, 'Oh, never mind that, it's not much, I don't think.' But it was that much that he died of the wound a few days later; and here he was a doomed man himself, making light of a mortal wound, and carrying a chance comrade of another regiment on his back. I can write this, but I could not tell of it in speech, because I know I should play the woman.

'C'est magnifique, mais ce n'est pas la guerre', murmured the observing French general Bosquet as the Light Brigade rode towards the battery.

Of the 666 troopers who took part in the Charge, 156 were reported killed and missing, and 122 wounded.

'Someone had blundered', again. In all probability, the Light Brigade should have charged the captured British guns to the side of the valley, not the Russian battery at its mouth. A mistake. And yet the perfect illustration of the British Victorian soldier's unquestioning sense of duty and valour. 'Theirs not to reason why, Theirs but to do and die', as Tennyson famously expressed it in his poem, The Charge of the Light Brigade.

There were six Victoria Crosses 'for valour in the presence of the enemy' awarded to the Light Brigade for actions during the Charge, the citations for which read:

Victoria Cross citation
Private Samuel Parkes, 4th Light Dragoons

His horse having been shot, he went to the aid of Trumpeter Crawford, who was dismounted and disarmed, and placed himself between the trumpeter and two Cossacks, and drove them away with his sword. They were attacked by a further six Russians, whom Parkes kept at bay until he was deprived of his sword.

Victoria Cross citation
Lieutenant Alexander Dunn, 11th Hussars

For having saved the life of Sergeant Bentley, 11th Hussars, by cutting down two or three Russian lancers who were attacking him from the rear, and afterwards cutting down a Russian hussar, who was attacking Private Levett, 11th Hussars.

Victoria Cross citation
Sergeant John Berryman, 17th Lancers
His horse being shot under him, he stopped on the field with a wounded officer, Captain Webb, amidst a shower of shot and shell, although repeatedly told by that officer to consult his own safety and leave him, but he refused to do so, and on Sergeant John Farrell coming by, with his assistance carried Captain Webb out of range of the guns.

Victoria Cross citation
Sergeant John Farrell, 17th Lancers
For having remained amidst a shower of shot and shell with Captain Webb, who was severely wounded and whom he and Sergeant Berryman had carried as far as the pain of his wounds would allow, until a stretcher was procured, when he assisted Berryman to carry that officer off the field.

Victoria Cross citation
Corporal Joseph Malone, 13th Light Dragoons
For having stopped under a very heavy fire to take charge of Captain Webb, 17th Lancers, until others arrived to assist him in removing that officer, who was mortally wounded. Malone performed this act of bravery while returning on foot from the charge, in which his horse had been shot.

Victoria Cross citation
Sergeant Charles Wooden, 17th Lancers
For being instrumental, together with Doctor James Mouat, in saving the life of Captain Morris of the 17th Lancers, by proceeding under a heavy fire to his assistance when he was lying very dangerously wounded in an exposed position.

'I was armed with a Brown Bess . . . I could not touch the barrel it was so hot'
ANONYMOUS MARINE

THE SOLDIER'S BATTLE
INKERMAN
5 NOVEMBER 1854

Inkerman was the 'soldier's battle' of the Crimean War. In the drizzling misty morning of 5 November, the Russians launched a surprise attack, more than 50,000-strong, on the British positions on Mount Inkerman. Such was the weather that the scant 8,000 British troops could not be deployed – they were simply shoved into the maws of the battle whenever and wherever Russian columns appeared out of the fog. This account of Inkerman is by a 'blue-jacket' of the Royal Marines Light Infantry.

On Sunday morning, just before daybreak, we were startled by a scattering fire of musketry, which, before we had time to fall in, became a prolonged roar, and the well-planned surprise of the Russians burst into our camp; our outlying picquets, who were being relieved at the time, and luckily being thus double, disputed the ground bravely, as they were driven in by the immense masses of the enemy. This gave us time to shake ourselves together a bit; the guards away on our right were not so fortunate, being nearest to the enemy, they had to strike their bell tents to make room to fight on.

The din of artillery now added to the uproar, accompanied by the continued yelling of the Russian army, that could be heard at Balaklava, six miles off. We found out after they were all supplied with Dutch courage in the shape of a drink, something like the arrack in India, maddening stuff; and thus began our Sunday's work. Very soon an aide-de-camp came galloping up to us with the order to advance at once to a small rising ground where General Codrington was. Here we halted for a few minutes lying down, as the round shot came hopping over us; there was no wonder at the Lancashire recruits' exclamation: 'Naw gi'e o'er, gi'e o'er, throwing them lumps of iron about, somebody'll be getting hurt.' During this short halt I said my prayers more devoutly than I ever did before or since.

Whilst sheltering from the storm of shot and shell in rear of this mound of earth a sergeant of the Royal Artillery in charge of two guns was ordered out to the front, but came galloping in again very quick, shouting to the general, 'It's no use, sir, I will only lose the horses.' 'Very well,' said General Codrington, 'go round and join your battery.' When his Aide, Colonel Yeo, came galloping in on his grey horse, saying, 'They will never hold it, sir, they are ten to one; better send the Marines out.' We marched out accordingly, our appearance in the open being greeted by a tempest of shot and shell from a six-gun battery, and some five hundred yards in our front.

I was one of eight told off to two stretchers; we had two killed instantly, our drummer having his drum shot away from his arm, and a piece of his trousers from the back part of the legs without getting a scratch; our lot was now in extended order advancing towards the edge of a steep ravine which separated us from the Russians. I got rather confused wandering about with the stretcher in the rear, and, not liking the job, I called to a comrade, 'Come on, Harry, let us join the mob.' The last I saw of the stretcher was one fellow dragging it after him. . . . As our position was the extreme left, it was a particularly warm quarter, the guns from the Russian shipping in the harbour on our left making a cross fire of artillery. We got what cover we could as we replied to the tempest of bullets that came across that ravine. We saw the plumes of an English battery bobbing above the brushwood on our right, where they unlimbered and opened fire on the six guns in our front, which very soon rid us of their presence. I heard one hurrah on our side, which came from the 88th Connaught Rangers in one of their mad charges against the masses opposed to them. They were very strong in the field, having seven companies engaged. They suffered heavily that day, maintaining one portion of the character that Wellington gave the Regiment in the Peninsula, viz., 'You are the greatest ruffians and the best soldiers that I have.'

It was getting about nine o'clock when the mist cleared off, and we found our great coats an encumbrance. We had stopped the 'yelling' of the Russians, for they were falling fast and thick before the deadly 'Minie' rifles. I was armed with a Brown Bess, which was now getting clogged, so that I had to hammer my ramrod down with a stone; it kicked dreadfully, and I could not touch the barrel, it was so hot. Towards noon I found myself close to a rifleman whose coolness struck me. He was seated on the ground with his cap by his side loading and firing with the greatest deliberation, laying his ramrod on the ground beside him to save time. Noticing me, he observed casually as he wiped his face, 'It's rather warm,' meaning the weather. I replied, 'I think it's rather hot, myself,' thinking of the fight.

Towards the afternoon the Russians at length began to retire, sullenly, and at their leisure, leaving the field of battle strewn with six thousand killed alone.

Whilst still waiting orders to return to camp, we witnessed a fight between a rifleman and a Russian. The former was bringing the latter in a prisoner. The rifleman was a strapping young fellow about 5 ft. 10 in., but the Russian was a giant, and refusing to give up his sword, they had a scuffle for it, the Russian throwing his adversary away from him as though he were a child, every time he attempted to take it. We could easily have shot the Russian, but an officer of the Rifles shouted, 'Let them fight it out, I'll back my man wins.' The young rifleman changed his tactics, and began to give it to the Russian with his fists, when he had it all his own way, and the Muscovite – who was quite at sea in this mode – was fain to surrender.

Shortly after we marched back to camp, but before we left the field I and another had a narrow escape. A shell from the shipping buried itself in the earth between us. We thought it a round shot; when it exploded I felt the heat of it on my face. The fragments nearly all went upwards, but one of them struck my companion lightly on the arm. When we got in we had the inevitable roll-call; our two companies went into camp 112 strong, our loss in killed and wounded amounting to thirty-eight. We had a captain shot through the jaw.

'It was too deep in mud in the trenches to walk about.'
SERGEANT JOHN HOPKINS

WINTER IN THE TRENCHES
BEFORE SEBASTOPOL

1854

Hopkins, of the Grenadier Company, 97th Regiment, writes home during the siege of Sebastopol, the fortified harbour of the Russian Black Sea Fleet, which commenced on 27th September 1854.

Camp before Sebastopol
Christmas Day, 1854

My Dear Brother,

I am almost too vexed to write to you; for since I came from England I have had but two letters from you, and I think I have wrote about a dozen to you; but something tells me you are not to blame, so I am not vexed at all; but I hope this will find you in good health, in which I am sorry to say it does not leave me, for since I came to the Crimea I have been ill. I was attacked with diarrhoea almost as soon as I landed here. I continued to do my duty til I was a mere skeleton. We have trench duty, which, to a sick man, was indeed trying. I did not like to give in till forced to do so by weakness. The trenches are full three miles from our camp, and we have had continual rain every day. In going to the trenches we have to cross two ravines, which, in wet weather, are complete rivers. About three weeks ago I was for what is called the advanced works, in the day. It is situated about 200 yards from the Russian lines – a very dangerous post. We crossed the ravines; it was more than knee deep in water. It rained heavily all day, till about 4 o'clock in the evening. It was too deep in mud in the trenches to walk about. We had, therefore, to stand in the wet, with stones under our feet, leaning against the breastwork. I tried to amuse myself, firing at every moving object I could see in the Russian lines; but as evening came, I was beat up. I was not able to stand or walk; but, my dear Bob, I had many kind friends, and, amongst them is an officer. He joined our company in Pentelouis; his name is Mr Dawes, a native of Bolton. He has shown a decided liking for me since he first knew me. Upon the day in question he was on duty with me; in the morning he gave me his arm to help me along. In the evening, I told him it would be midnight before I got to camp; he took my rifle from me, slung it on his back, and told me to do my best. The rain was succeeded by a heavy fog. I lost my way home, and it was midnight before I got to camp. I was wet through. I had eaten nothing for 24 hours; all I took was my grog, a gill of rum. I laid down in my tent and the next morning was carried to hospital, more dead than alive. Every officer in the regiment came to see me, for on coming here I was as strong a man as stood in the regiment, and now I was like a child; the once stout and firm limbs were gone; my big broad face was completely hid in the hair which grows on it, for I have not shaved this six months, to speak the truth. I was a fright. I was in hospital only four days; the diarrhoea was gone, and weakness only remained. The doctors and all about me showed me the greatest kindness. I was discharged from hospital, but was to do no duty till strong. The officer, Mr Dawes, took me to his tent; he supplied me with every luxury that a well-filled purse could supply, and told me to make free with anything that was in his tent. We are served out with coffee in its green state, and we have to roast and grind it, that is, to pound it in a bag between two mallets. When done, it is bad. The officer, therefore, gave me what tea I could use, a glass of whiskey punch twice per day, cheese, rice, fresh bread, and, if I could get anything for money, he would give me his purse to satisfy myself. My dear brother, what would I not face by the side of such an officer? Would I shrink from death? Perish the idea! I am now recovering fast, and should this arm recover its former strength before the attack on Sebastopol, should he want its aid, how freely shall it be extended towards him. I had many presents from other officers, and soon, my dear Bob, shall the light and merry song of happy Jack be heard in camp again. My dear brother, the duty is very hard; we are in the trenches every other night; sometimes two or three nights after one another. I have exchanged many shots with the Russians, though I have not been exactly in an engagement, and scarcely a day passes but we have someone wounded. The day I mentioned before, we had one shot dead and three wounded. At night we find sentries in advance of those works. I was on one night, very moonlight. All the sentries have a wall to cover them; but forgetting myself, I walked from my cover, when about a dozen of what they call needle-balls whizzed past my ear. I soon returned to my cover, nor left it again until relieved. In rear of those works we have what they call the Cow Horn Battery, also a Lancaster Battery, in fact we have batteries surrounding this part of the town; and if you were to walk from our camp to Balaclava you would think there were English and French troops enough to eat Sebastopol if it were pudding. On this most remarkable of all pudding-eating days, there is little of it here; but I hope you did not forget my health in brown stout, for I drank yours in muddy water, for it was all I could get, and little of that, for I have not washed my shirt since I came here, and never had my clothes off except for an hour during the day, for a rather disgusting purpose, which you may easily guess, when I have been more than a month with my clothes on; but it is common here even with officers. The reason we do not attack Sebastopol is, we are making a battery to destroy shipping which, when finished, I think will be the signal for attack. My dear Bob, I have no more paper, and to obtain more I should have to walk seven miles and pay 6d for a sheet and envelope, and 6d is what I have not seen since my arrival here. I enclose a note for James. We have lost half the draft they sent us, also a great number of old hands. Give my kind love to all at home. Wishing soon to hear from you, I remain my dear brother, yours ever, with my usual prayer of God bless you all.

'Obtaining a pick and spade I buried him alone.'
PRIVATE PARSONS

PRIVATE PARSONS
FINDS HIS BROTHER'S BODY
ON THE BATTLEFIELD
SEBASTOPOL, 8 JUNE 1855

One night in particular I remember, and that was the night we took the quarries. That night we had a hard tussle and lost a lot of our poor fellows, the enemy turning out in very strong force. But eventually we drove them back and succeeded in taking the quarries, although both sides lost heavily. In this attack I had a brother killed, belonging to the 7th Royal Fusiliers. I knew he was in the engagement, and after it was over made enquiry and finding no trace of him, next day – the flag of truce being hoisted – I went out amongst the dead to search for the body, in this being successful. Obtaining a pick and spade I buried him alone, the other bodies being placed in heaps. I had another brother belonging to the marines, also engaged in this action, but he fortunately escaped. It is after the battle when the field is strewn with the dead and wounded, that the full horror of war makes itself felt; a horror which words but feebly express, and entirely fail to describe, were you bold enough to attempt to describe such scenes; but the soldier has no place for fine feeling, and at the call of duty he must do or die, and leave the sentiment for others.

If Parsons had wanted a chaplain to perform the burial service for his brother he would have struggled to find one. Few had been sent out to the Crimea. In extremis, the more religious soldiers arranged their own services and prayer meetings. Captain Hedley Vicars of the 97th wrote to his sister: 'I have not seen a clergyman or a missionary yet. How I should enjoy meeting one who would talk to the men simply about the Cross of Christ! The Holy Ghost always blesses such preaching. We have meetings in my tent for Scripture-reading as often as we can get together, and delightful sessions they are'.

<hr>

'I have not been able to get much of a trophy'.
SERGEANT JOHN HOPKINS

SERGEANT HOPKINS
WRITES HOME AFTER THE FALL OF SEBASTOPOL
16 SEPTEMBER 1855

Sebastopol finally fell to an Allied storm on 8 September 1855

Camp before Sebastopol
16 September 1855

My Dear Brother
Most likely before this reaches you you have heard both of the downfall of Sebastopol and of my safety, as I wrote to mother two days after the action, and I desired her to send the letter to you

after reading it; but I merely stated in that that I had come off all right, so I dare say a few particulars will be welcome. Our regiment has suffered very much. You must know it was one of those regiments that had never been engaged since it was re-organised in 1822; but still it was a regiment that was always praised for appearance, steadiness, and cleanliness by all generals who ever saw us; and as we always thought ourselves second to none, we were determined, if ever an opportunity occurred, to prove it. On the morning of the 8th we paraded, as we thought to see if we were ready – that is, with two days rations, &c. we thought it was only a parade; but alas, my dear brother, it was the last for many. Volunteers for the first storming, or ladder party, were ordered to the front. I need not to tell you, I suppose, that I was amongst the those. So well was the secret kept, we knew not of the attack till then. We were marched to the trenches, and our party occupied a sap leading in an oblique direction from our advanced trench to the Russian battery known as Redan. The regiment was to storm along with the 3rd, 90th and 41st, all of which occupied the advanced trench. In fact all the army was in position by nine o'clock; nor did the enemy appear to know or suspect anything extra; I suppose he thought we should not have the audacity to attack his strongholds in the noonday. But no sooner had the sun reached the meridian than the tricoloured flag of France appeared over the Mamelon, and with a cheer the French began to pour into the mightly Malakoff, an overwhelming force taking the Russians completely by surprise; and in less time than I have taken to relate it the eagle was planted on the parapet which was the signal for our attack. Its appearance was enough. The word 'Forward' was indeed given, but not needed. But the attack of the French had put the Russians on the alert, and no sooner did we show ourselves than they began to pour on us their deadly charges of grape; in fact it was a complete storm. However, we carried our ladders in spite of all, and planted them in the ditch, which was about 14 feet deep on our side; but on the Russian side it could not be less than 20, as it ran up to the parapet. The side was composed of a sandy sort of substance, and it was with difficulty we could keep our feet, even when we had gained it; but soon we made an entrance, and then came the work. For a considerable time it was bayonet work on both sides and the Russians being more than treble our number, it was for a time doubtful which side would carry it. At last, with a cheer and a rush we made them give way; and then came a battle of musketry. In this they had the advantage, for the works of the Redan afforded them every shelter, and the force from the Malakhoff joining those in the Redan, likewise troops from the town, made it impossible for us to keep it. We were not supported as we ought to have been, or we should not have lost so many. We kept our ground, and as we were first in we were the last to leave, and when we did we had not half the number of the 97th left uninjured. But now to myself. As I was a volunteer I kept my place amongst the foremost, and on leaving the battery I turned round on the parapet, with the butt of a broken firelock, my only weapon having had it smashed in my hand, the blood of a slight wound in the forehead trickling down my face. I did my best, but I got knocked off my position, backwards, and fell stunned into the ditch, and it was miracle how I escaped falling upon a dozen of our bayonets, belonging to men who had got in, and for want of a good spirit could not get out; but, however, I got out, and without the aid of a scaling ladder, after two hours' hard fighting against a superior force. Shortly after we gained the trench. The conduct of the regiment was the admiration of everyone, particularly the general of the division and his staff. It is impossible for me to convey to you my feeling upon being ordered home – I mean to camp – to find we had lost the flower of the regiment. As for myself, I was not much hurt, though I have not been able to do any duty since . . . I have had the pleasure of being in town since it was taken, but found it the ruins of a once grand city. I have not been able to get much of a trophy, through not being able to move about for a few days after its downfall; but anyhow the trophy I am anxious to bring you is my own head, and I have not the least doubt that will please you best. In Sebastopol there was a large bell, that often brought us in fancy to the days of childhood. Now, the shipping was an eyesore – the bell was an eyesore. Some time ago, whilst in the trenches, I wrote some lines on this bell, which I send you, though I do not think them finished, as the downfall of Sebastopol interrupted it. However, I have got a piece of the said bell, which was brought down by a shot from our battery. I could get firelocks and swords, but if we took the field I could not carry them.

THE SEBASTOPOL BELL

When night's cloudy mantle around us is spread,
And the bright silver moon its radiance shed
We have watched, we have wept for comrades that fell
Whilst listening to the sound of the Sebastopol bell;

And often with limbs all benumb'd with the cold,
And fainting with hunger the moments have told,
Whilst thinking each sound was our own death knell,
As 'twas borne on the breeze from Sebastopol bell.
Again, when the rain in torrents did pour,
And darkness hid us from each rampart and tower,
We have heard from our foe a fearful yell,
Mingling strangely with the sounds of Sebastopol bell.
The column after column of Russians advance,
But are met by the warriors of England and France;
Whilst the honour of their homes makes each bosom swell,
As they fight mid the sounds of Sebastopol bell.
Then back to the batteries the Russians fly,
And leave their wounded men to die;
And whilst their rage they try to quell,
There's a dismal sound from Sebastopol bell.
But the winter it passed and summer came,
And still the bell tolled on the same,
As Russians swore they would dearly sell,
The spot where tolled that dismal bell.
But on we toiled, with pick and spade,
And miles of sap and trenches made;
Through rock, ravine and mossy dell,
We slowly neared Sebastopol bell.

My dear brother, if you like you may finish this; but give me love
to all at home. God bless you.

Another early visitor to the fallen city was the enterprising Fanny Duberly, wife of the
paymaster of the 8th Royal Irish Hussars. Crimea was the last war in which British
soldiers' wives would campaign alongside their husbands.

The Russians had little more stomach for the war after Sebastopol's fall, and by March of the next year peace was concluded.

Britain went mad with euphoria. Pubs (the Sebastopol Arms) and girls (Alma) were named after Crimea's battles. But the pride was intermingled with anger. The faults of the Crimean campaign, poor organization and poor conditions, had been brought home telegraphically by William Howard Russell of *The Times*. The public pushed for, and got, a reform of the army: its running henceforth came under one office of government, the Secretary of State for War, not seventeen; the Army Medical Service was overhauled; proper instructional camps were set up, at Aldershot, Colchester, and Curragh; also established were a small arms factory, an army clothing factory, a school of musketry and a school of gunnery. A programme of building works finally provided separate accomodation for married soldiers and their families.

As for Tommy Atkins himself, he was soon back in action. Again in a far-flung place.

'many were run through with the bayonet'
PRIVATE CHARLES WICKINS

INDIAN MUTINY
THE RELIEF OF THE RESIDENCY ... AND THE INGRATITUDE OF THE RESCUED WOMEN
LUCKNOW, 16–22 NOVEMBER 1857

Rumours that the British army used cartridges smeared with pig and cow fat (thus simultaneously insulting Muslims and Hindus) in its new Enfield rifles induced native soldiers of the Bengal Army to refuse their use on 10 May 1857. Within three weeks this protest had grown into the 'Devil's Wind' – the Indian Mutiny – and had engulfed the entire Ganges basin. There were fewer than 40,000 troops to control 40,000,000 Indians. In Delhi one British officer of a Sepoy regiment found himself running for his life:

> I persuaded the Sepoys to let me take the regimental colour, and I took it outside, but on calling for my groom I found he had bolted with my horse. You can imagine my horror at this. I went back into the Quarter Guard and replaced the colour, but on coming out a trooper dismounted and took deliberate shot at me, but, missing his aim I walked up to him and blew his brains out. Another man was then taking aim at me, when he was bayoneted by a Sepoy of my company. The firing then became general, and

I was compelled to run the gauntlet across the parade ground, and escaped unhurt miraculously, three bullets having passed through my hat and one through the skirt of my coat. having gone as far as my weak state of health would permit, and being exhausted, I took refuge in a garden under some bushes.

Among the towns besieged by the mutineers were Lucknow and Cawnpore; at the latter 1,000 civilians and soldiers held out under pitiless sun, incessant cannon fire, cholera and starvation for three weeks, before being offered safe passage by mutineer leader, Nana Sahib. Treacherously, Sahib then murdered the surrendering survivors. Only four Britons got away from Cawnpore alive.

Lieutenant Richard Barter, adjutant of the 75th Foot ('the Stirlingshire Regiment, good men and true'), was among the British relief force that reached Cawnpore too late:

The inside of the house was of course bare of furniture and there was no matting or carpet on the floor, but instead blood, thick clotted blood looking like Russia leather, with which the walls also for three or four feet from the ground were spattered, and in some places smeared as if a great spout of it had gushed out on them, while here and there were marks where the murderers had dried their bloody hands by rubbing them against the walls in which were also deep sword cuts, as if some poor victim had dodged aside from the blow. There were also several pencil inscriptions, noting the date of arrival there, and memoranda of deaths of friends or relatives, or short prayers for help. Bonnets, slippers, hats, stays and various other articles of female clothing, with tresses and plaits of hair were scattered about with fragments of books, most, if not all of them Bibles and prayer books. Some of the bonnets and hats were hanging from the beams in the back verandah, which as well as the back yard was covered thick with clotted blood. All the way to the well was marked by a regular track along which the bodies had been dragged and the thorny bushes had entangled in them scraps of clothing and long hairs. One of the large trees to the left of this track going to the well had evidently had children's brains dashed out against its trunk, for it was covered thick with blood and children's hair matted into the coarse bark, and an eye, glazed and withered could be plainly made out pasted into the trunk. A few paces on and you stood by the well itself, now the receptacle of all these poor mangled bodies. It looked old and going fast to decay for the bricks and mortar had given way and crumbled in many places round the low edge. I think it must have been dry or very nearly so. After peering into it for some time until the eyes had become accustomed to the gloom, you could see members of human bodies, legs and arms sticking up browned and withered like those of a mummy. But there was no putrid smell or anything of that kind that I could perceive. Those dead arms of our murdered country people seemed to be making a mute appeal to us from the darkness below; far more eloquent than words they called to Heaven for vengeance on the ruthless perpetrators of untold atrocities, and many a vow was registered over that well never to spare should they be met with hand to hand in the approaching struggle for the Relief of Lucknow . . .

After Cawnpore, the British soldier was in a rare mood of murderous revenge. Ringleaders of the mutiny were blasted from the mouths of cannon; in combat the sepoys were shown no quarter. The Indian Mutiny was a war of the bayonet more than the bullet. Even seasoned troops found themselves in hand-to-hand fighting for the first time, among them Private Charles Wickins, 9th Regiment, who took part in Lucknow's relief:

We knew that we were to advance at 6 a.m. but long before this we had formed up and were awaiting orders to move off at 5.80. Sir Colin and his staff rode by the column. Sir Colin called for the officers of the various corps. He told them that the enemy was to be attacked that morning and that the men could be sparing of their ammunition, thereby intimating that the bayonet would be used as much as possible. Sir Colin said that the officers and men would have an opportunity of distinguishing themselves before noon. He then gave the word to advance.

We crossed the river and were soon in a very narrow, intricate and circuitous lane with houses on either side, through which it was very difficult to pass. At length we arrived at an opening in the lane on the south west side of Secunder Bagh. The enemy opened a brisk fire upon us from a little loophole or two a little past the opening and we were ordered to rest our rifles against the wall of a mud building. We were then ordered to man two large ropes attached to an eight-inch howitzer, which we immediately drew up a steep embankment under a very heavy fire, but thanks be to God not a man of us was hurt.

The guns were soon in position and were ranging away in first-rate style. A breach was soon made on the south side. A few horses were killed and a few artillery men wounded, when we got the word to storm the place and in two minutes the building which was one hundred and twenty yards square was surrounded. The 93rd lost a good many men, and the detachments under command of a Major Barnston also lost a few killed and wounded. But the awful retribution that this day fell upon the sepoys, 16th November, exceeded the expectations of all engaged that morning. For in the Secunder Bagh was upwards of two thousand of the enemy; these two thousand and upwards met with all sorts of deaths; some were killed by the explosion of our shells, others were killed by the shot from our cannon and our Enfields, others met with these deaths – by jumping off the tops of the walls and breaking their necks, some were cut down by the sword; others were burnt alive and many were run through with the bayonet. Not a man escaped to tell the tale.

The following few days were occupied in bringing such of the guns that were serviceable out of the old palace and in bursting upwards of two hundred guns of native manufacture and also in making a covered way, whereby the women and children might be brought out in safety. The whole of the men available were engaged day and night in making this covered way for the ladies and need I say that they ran great danger. For the enemy had got the range of more than one or two places, where there was no covering whatever from the enemy's shot, which we had got pretty well acquainted with and to which we paid but little attention however. We soon had a trench thrown up, that protected us from imminent peril. Tent walls, or more properly speaking tent canauts, were brought out and so arranged that the enemy could not see anything that was going on. Everything was carried out in a style that totally deceived the enemy. Engineers and sappers were employed in running a mine which was to blow up the Kaiser Bagh and all that were in it. The Naval Brigade had a mortar battery playing on and into the new place. The heavy guns were likewise employed in making a breach in the western side of the palace walls. But all this time our army was employed in making every preparation for retiring from Lucknow. The guns and treasure, which amounted to 23 lacs of rupees or two hundred and thirty thousand pounds, were safely brought out of the Residency and taken to the Dilkoosha Park.

The Ladies, women and children were all brought out in safety without a single casualty. And now let us see what were the thanks we got from the ladies for all that we had done for their safety and for their personal comfort. We, the relieving force, were called all sorts of foul names – dirty, ill-looking fellows, not in any way to be compared to the clean, respectable and ever-obliging sepoy. The reader will scarcely believe that in 1857 there were at Lucknow Englishwomen who actually refused help to a poor fellowcountry-man to a drop of water. Yea, I assure you it is a fact, these Englishwomen, who had been rescued from a fate too horrible to think of and had been protected during their imprisonment with the beleaguered garrison of Lucknow by the ever-brave and generous English soldier! And so protecting them he had met with his death wound and now he is unable to rise from his cot. He calls on his countrywomen for a drop of water, either to quench his parched lips or otherwise to wash his wounds. But what must have been the consternation of the poor dying soldier to have these women reply to him in words to this effect? Pointing to the well they said, 'There is the well, my man, and you can get the water yourself.' And this to a dying man! And all likewards this man had his death wound through rendering some assistance to his ungrateful countrywomen.

'the other put his musket close to my body'
LIEUTENANT FREDERICK ROBERTS

INDIAN MUTINY
LIEUTENANT ROBERTS SURVIVES
A POINT-BLANK SHOOTING
2 JANUARY 1858

The future field marshal witnesses, at rather too close quarters, 'a flash in the pan'; he rode with the 5th Punjab Cavalry.

The ground sloped gradually upwards towards Khudaganj, and the regiments moving up to attack made a fine picture. The 93rd followed the impulsive 53rd, while Greathead's brigade took a line to the left; and as they neared the village the rebels hastily limbered up their guns and retired. This was an opportunity for mounted troops such as does not often occur; it was instantly seized by Hope Grant, who rode to the cavalry drawn up behind some sandhills and gave the word of command, 'Threes left, trot, march.' The words had hardly left his lips before we had started in pursuit of the enemy, by this time half a mile ahead, the 9th Lancers leading the way, followed by Younghusband's, Gough's and Probyn's squadrons. When within 300 yards of the fugitives, the 'charge' was sounded, and in a few seconds we were in their midst. A regular mêlée ensued, a number of the rebels were killed, and seven guns captured in less than as many minutes. The general now formed the cavalry into a long line, and placing himself at the head of his own regiment (the 9th Lancers), followed up the flying foe. I rode a little to his left with Younghusband's squadron.

On the line thundered, overtaking groups of the enemy, who every now and then turned and fired into us before they could be cut down, or knelt to receive us on their bayonets before discharging their muskets. The chase continued for nearly five miles, until daylight began to fail and we appeared to have got to the end of the fighting, when the order was given to wheel to the right and form up on the road. Before, however, this movement could be carried out, we overtook a batch of mutineers, who faced about and fired into the squadron at close quarters. I saw

Younghusband fall, but I could not go to his assistance as at that moment one of his sowars was in dire peril from a sepoy who was attacking him with his fixed bayonet, and had I not helped the man and disposed of his opponent, he must have been killed. The next moment I descried in the distance two sepoys making off with a standard, which I determined must be captured, so I rode after the rebels and overtook them; while wrenching the staff out of the hands of one of them, whom I cut down, the other put his musket close to my body and fired, fortunately for me it missed fire and I carried off the standard. For those two acts I was awarded the Victoria Cross.

By now the Mutiny was in its last throe.

So too was Brown Bess; the Mutiny was the last campaign in which the .75 inch flintlock musket was used by British troops.

——— ❧ ———

'I was enticed into drinking a drop too much'
EDWIN MOLE

EDWIN MOLE
TAKES THE QUEEN'S SHILLING
LONDON, JUNE 1863

Mole was a disgruntled teenage hotel employee when he encountered Gibbs, recruiting sergeant of the 14th Hussars:

When the theatre was over, Sergeant Gibbs said he had a spare bed in his quarters, and I might as well use it. So we returned to Charles Street, where drinks were called for, and what with one thing and what with another, I was enticed into taking a drop too much, and never rightly remember what happened that night or how I got to bed.

Next morning, when I awoke, my head was very lumpy. The first thing I saw was Sergeant Gibbs, sitting up in bed, smoking.

'Hello!' he cried. 'You've woke up, have you? Could you do with a drop of beer?'

'No beer for me,' I answered, 'but I'd like some tea or coffee.'

'Coffee you shall have and that directly, for you'll have to go before the doctor this morning, and as it's rather late I think you had better get up at once.'

'What have I to go before the doctor for?'

'Why, because you 'listed last night, of course; and there's the medical to pass. You're a soldier now. If you feel in your pocket you'll find the bob, and if you want any luck you'd better come down-stairs and break it, for that's the custom and according to the Articles of War.'

This information staggered me, for I had no recollection of taking any shilling. Thinking Sergeant Gibbs was only joking, I said: 'Don't talk silly. If I had 'listed last night I should have remembered it.'

'Not by the way you looked when you went to bed,' he replied. 'Why, you drank me and Hudson blind, toasting your new regiment; and it was as much as we could do to carry you upstairs and sling you on to your cot. But just look in your pocket.'

I had my trousers on, and I slipped my hand into my pocket and pulled out what was there. All my money, I found, was gone, except a few coppers and –

'The Queen's Shilling,' put in Sergeant Gibbs, with a knowing nod of his head, as I picked out a solitary one and held it in front of me, between finger and thumb.

It was just the same as any other shilling – yet I could not help looking at it with a bit of awe, and wondering if I had gone and 'prenticed myself to twelve years' soldiering for this little bit of silver.

'Come on, my tulip, buck about,' cried the sergeant, breaking into my reflections; 'you've done it now and Parliament itself can't undo it.'

'*And then the fun began*'
Private Robert Blatchford

FIRST DRILL
c 1870

Blatchford served with the Royal Bombay Fusiliers.

It was very cold when we turned out for our first recruits' drill at six o'clock one morning. We . . . were new men in our scarlet serge jackets, blue serge trousers, glengarry caps, and regulation boots. We were handed over first of all to a corporal, who took us to the gymnasium. Here we put on canvas shoes and belts, and hung up our caps and tunics. Then a short, red-headed, crabby gymnastic sergeant came and looked us over; after which a corporal formed us into fours and led us on a run of one thousand yards round a field. This over, we went to dumb-bells and parallel bars, and very funny were some of the attempts made by the raw boys who had never seen a gymnasium before. Those over, we re-dressed, and with aching limbs and rather dizzy heads ran back to breakfast.

And then the fun began. We were marched out on to the gravel parade and left to the tender mercies of the drill-instructors . . . First came a Cockney corporal, a most caustic little beast, who pushed and pulled us into something like a line, finding a fresh insult for each in turn. Then came a coarse growl from the rear. 'Don't dress the scarecrows, Corporal Oliver. I'll damn soon lick the lubbers into shape', and forth stepped one of the quaintest figures my eyes have ever beheld.

Sergeant Hallowell was one of the drill-sergeants transferred from the Guards. He was a tall man, over six feet high, and of a spare and angular figure. His chest was so outrageously padded that it gave him the appearance of a pouter pidgeon. He had high shoulders and long legs. He had a comic face, with a red nose, bushy eyebrows, and a rusty, bristly moustache. His expression, at once fierce and comic, reminded one irresistibly of a Jack-in-the-box or Punch. In the deepest, harshest bass voice that ever spoke, and with his cheek bulged out by a quid of tobacco, this remarkable warrior at once began to address us.

First of all he stalked up very close to the line and glared down at us as though he thought of drawing our teeth. Then he growled in a sepulchral manner: 'You miserable devils; you *miserable* devils'. Having paid over this compliment, he walked slowly backwards for some twenty yards, halted, gave his quid a wrench, and roared out: 'You – miserable – *devils*'. And we stood motionless, and with an uncomfortable feeling that we deserved the description thoroughly. 'Now,' said the sergeant, putting his shoulders back, and glancing his whimsical eye along the line, 'pay attention to me. You are raw recruits; raw and green. I'm here to dress you and drill you, and frizzle you and grill you, and pepper you and salt you till you're done to a turn; and by whiskers I shall *do* it. Don't grin at me, that man with the muffin face. I'll soon sweat the smiles off you. And look to your front, you poor, unsaved sinners, and learn wisdom.'

Here the sergeant made a rush at a man near the flank and roared out, 'What's your name?' 'Firwood, sir.' 'Don't "sir" me; call me sergeant. What's your father?' 'A tailor, sergeant.' 'A tailor! If he doesn't make better coats than soldiers he ought to be hanged for a botch. Go to centre, Firwood, and grow, and trust God, Firwood, and turn out your toes, you – *miserable* – devil.'

The sergeant stepped backwards again. 'Now,' he went on, 'when I say "Eyes front" look straight to your front, or as straight as you can, and forget your past sins and listen to me. I shall make men of you. I shall be your father and your mother and your Uncle Tom from Devizes, and you'll live to bless me in the coming years – if I don't murder you in the process. Eyes *front*.'

As the drills went on our Uncle Tom from Devizes taught us to march, and turn, and stand at ease, and wheel, and halt, and mark time; and all these branches of the martial art were made more or less delightful by his mordant humour. 'Now, men, a steady double. Don't run, you rascals, don't run; the police ain't after you again. Mark time! Now, then, Cowley, don't get your knees up to your chin; you're not on the treadmill *now*' . . .

They kept us as recruits pretty busy. We were at drill, or school, or gymnasium from six in the morning to six in the evening, if we had the luck not to be at club-drill from six to seven. And then we were at liberty to clean our arms and accoutrements or scrub tables. But we were young, and the air was good. And the gymnastics, the drilling, and the regular hours and plain food began to tell. In a few weeks we were straight and smart, and stood and moved lightly. In the bronzed, alert, upright young soldiers no one could have recognised the mob of assorted ragamuffins who had tramped in the dust from Cowes . . .

The routine of our new life varied little from day to day. It began with a rather dismal bugle call at about 5.45. This call was 'the rouse', but it was known to us as 'the donkey'. It was the 'quarter' for Réveillé. The rouse was to wake us, the Réveillé meant turn out. But we turned out before Réveillé, for the 79th Highlanders lay in the same barracks, and between our two calls it was the jovial custom to march a brace of pipers up and down the lines and charm our ears with 'Hey, Johnny Cope'. I am one of the few southrons who like the bagpipes. My English and Irish comrades used to get up to swear.

After 'Johnny Cope' came the Réveillé. First of all, the buglers, massed on the square, sounded the call. Then the drums beat 'the points of war'. Then the drums and fifes played a kind of reel, called 'Old Mother Grey-Goose'. Then our corporal began to shout, and we carried our beds and bedding outside, laid them on the ground, and ran to the wash house. At half-past six we were dressed and marching to the gymnasium. Breakfast was at a quarter to eight. It consisted of a pound of dry bread and a pint of coffee. The coffee came from the cookhouse in large cans, and was served in white delt basins on deal tables innocent of tablecloths.

Dinner was at one o'clock. It consisted of beef or mutton and potatoes. There was not much dinner. But I found that to leave the table feeling unsatisfied means being free for work and free from drowsiness . . . Tea – Well, we had a pint of slop in a basin and half a pound of dry bread.

Supper could be had if one went to the canteen and paid for it. On the whole, rather a meagre diet for growing lads who spent the whole day working in the open air. But I am bound to acknowledge that we throve on it.

Ascetic though barracks life was in the late Victorian period, it was a better lodging than anything the British soldier had known hitherto.

Before the Crimean War soldiers in barracks had a third of the living space given to convicts in prison, and no lavatories or washing facilities (a large wooden tub was used as the night urinal; the smell in the closely packed barrack room, of urine, sweat and smoke made more than one visitor vomit on entry); after the Crimean War, the 1857 Royal Commission into the Sanitary Condition of the Army recommended a minimum of 600 cubic feet per man, and the addition of 'ablution rooms' to the barracks – the wash-house Blatchford runs to after reveille. Blatchford was not only enjoying conditions superior to those of his redcoat predecessors, he was enjoying a billet superior to most in civilian street.

The 1870s were good times for the British army, thanks to the enlightened rule of Liberal Secretary of State for War, Edward Cardwell. In 1870 Cardwell introduced short service (enlistment for twelve years, six of them with the reserve); in 1871 the purchase of commissions was banned; in 1872 regiments were organised into linked battalions, whereby one battalion trained recruits at the home depot for the manpower needs of the battalion abroad. Which were great: Queen Victoria's little imperial wars were almost ceaseless.

'At about ten-thirty the Zulus were seen coming over the hills in thousands'
LIEUTENANT HORACE SMITH-DORRIEN

'FIX BAYONETS AND DIE LIKE BRITISH SOLDIERS DO!'
ISANDHLWANA, ZULULAND, MORNING
22 JANUARY 1879

22 January 1879 was the graveyard of the Victorian British Army. In the late morning 20,000 Zulus attacked Lord Chelmsford's invading army at Isandhlwana Hill – and destroyed it. Of 2,000 men only 55 escaped the slaughter – among them Lieutenant Horace Smith-Dorrien, 95th Regiment, later to become Commander 2nd Army, BEF, 1914–15.

The last order to British troops at Isandhlwana, who were largely from the 24th Foot, was 'Fix bayonets and die like British soldiers do!' They did. And they did.

Since I wrote the first part of my letter a dreadful disaster has happened to us. It seems to me a pure miracle that I am alive to tell you about it. On the 21st January an order came to me, then stationed at Rorke's Drift, to go out to advanced camp [Isandhlwana] to escort a convoy of twenty-five waggons from there to Rorke's Drift and bring them back loaded with supplies.

Accordingly I slept in camp. At about three a.m. on the morning of the 22nd the General sent for me and told me not to take the waggons, but to convey a dispatch to Colonel Durnford, who was at Rorke's Drift, with about 500 mounted black fellows, as a battle was expected. He (Colonel Durnford) accordingly started off with his men to join the camp. I did not return with him, but came out an hour afterwards by myself.

When I arrived in camp, I found the greater part of the column gone out with the General [Lord Chelmsford] to meet the Zulu force, so that there was really only a caretaking force left in the camp – viz., five companies of the 1st Battalion of the 24th, two guns, about 600 Native Contingent, and a few servants looking after the tents; the Army Hospital Corps (thirteen men), and the sick in the hospital tents. The first Zulu force appeared about six o'clock in the morning. Two companies of the 24th were sent out after them. The Zulus seemed to retire, and there was firing kept up at long ranges. At about ten-thirty the Zulus were seen coming over the hills in thousands. They were in most perfect order, and seemed to be in about twenty rows of skirmishers one behind the other. They were in a semi-circle round our two flanks and in front of us and must have covered several miles of ground. Nobody knows how many there were of them, but the general idea is at least 20,000.

Well, to cut the account short, in half an hour they were right up to the camp. I was out with the front companies of the 24th handing them spare ammunition. Bullets were flying all over the place, but I never seemed to notice them. The Zulus nearly all had firearms of some kind and lots of ammunition. Before we knew where we were they came right into the camp, assegaiing everybody right and left. Everybody then who had a horse turned to fly. The enemy were going at a kind of very fast half walk and half-run. On looking round we saw that we were completely surrounded and the road to Rorke's Drift was cut off. The place where they seemed thinnest was where we all made for. Everybody went pell-mell over ground covered with huge boulders and rocks until we got to a deep spruit or gulley. How the horses got over I have no idea. I was riding a broken-kneed old crock which did not belong to me, and which I expected to go on its head every minute. We had to go bang through them at the spruit. Lots of our men were killed there. I had lots of marvellous escapes, and was firing away at them with my revolver as I galloped along. The ground there down to the river was so broken that the Zulus went as fast as the horses, and kept killing all the way. There were very few white men; they were nearly all mounted blacks of ours flying. This lasted till we came to a kind of precipice down to the River Buffalo.

I jumped off and led my horse down. There was a poor fellow of the mounted infantry (a private) struck through the arm, who said as I passed that if I could bind up his arm and stop the bleeding he would be all right. I accordingly took out my handkerchief and tied up his arm. Just as I had done it, Major Smith of the Artillery came down by me wounded, saying, 'For God's sake get on, man, the Zulus are on the top of us.' I had done all I could for the wounded man and so turned to jump on my horse. Just as I was doing so the horse went with a bound to the bottom of the precipice, being struck with an assegai. I gave up all hope, as the Zulus were all round me, finishing off the wounded, the man I had helped and Major Smith among the number. However, with the strong hope that everybody clings to that some accident would turn up, I rushed off on foot and plunged into the river, which was little better than a roaring torrent.

I was being carried down the stream at a tremendous pace, when a loose horse came by me and I got hold of his tail and he landed me safely on the other bank; but I was too tired to stick to him and get on his back. I got up again and rushed on and was several times knocked over by our mounted blacks, who would not get out of my way, then up a tremendous hill with my wet clothes and boots full of water. About twenty Zulus got over the water and followed us up the hill, but I am thankful to say they had not their firearms. Crossing the river, however, the Zulus on the opposite side kept firing at us as we went up the hill and killed several of the blacks round me. I was the only white man to be seen until I came to one who had been kicked by his horse and could not mount. I put him on his horse and lent him my knife. He said he would catch me a horse. Directly he was up he went clean away. A few Zulus followed us for about three miles across the river, but they had no guns and I had a revolver, which I kept letting them know. Also the mounted blacks stopped a little and kept firing at them. They did not come in close, and finally stopped altogether.

Well, to cut it short, I struggled into Helpmakaar, about twenty miles off, at nightfall, to find a few men who had escaped, about ten or twenty, with others who had been entrenched in a waggon laager [a defensive circle of wagons]. We sat up all night, momentarily expecting attack. The next day there was a dense fog all day, nearly as bad as night, and we could not make out what had happened to everybody. I was dead beat of course, but on the 24th I struggled down to Rorke's Drift, my former headquarters, which had been so gallantly defended for a whole night against the Zulus by a single company, to find that the General and remainder of the column had arrived all right. I am there now in a laager. We keep a tremendous look-out, and sit up all night expecting attack. It has been raining for the last three hours, and did so all last night. We have not a single thing left. The men have no coats or anything, all being taken by the Zulus. We shall have another dreadful night of it tonight, I expect, lying on the wet ground. I have just had to drop this for a minute for one of our numerous alarms. I have no time for more now. What we are to do for transport I have not the faintest idea, the Zulus having captured 107 waggons and about 2,000 oxen, mules, horses, etc. However, we must begin to work again to get fresh transport together. I thank God I am alive and well, having a few bruises. God bless you.

P.S. We are expecting pestilence to break out here, to add to our enemies, what with the rain and the air tainted with dead bodies, as there were about 350 Zulus killed here and some are buried in the ruins.

If the morning of 22 January 1879 was the British Victorian army's cemetery, the afternoon was its glory.

*'Time after time the Zulus gripped the muzzle and
tried to tear the rifle from my grasp'*
PRIVATE HENRY HOOK

THE STAND AT RORKE'S DRIFT
ZULULAND
22–23 JANUARY 1879

The slaughter of Islandhlwana over, a Zulu impi comprising the Uthulwana, uDloko and inDyluyengwe regiments hurried on to 'wash its spears' at the British hospital and garrison ten miles away at Rorke's Drift. Facing the 4,000 Zulus were a mere eight British officers and 131 NCOs and men, of whom 36 were sick. Henry Hook, a cook, was among the 11 soldiers awarded the Victoria Cross for valour that long afternoon in Zululand.

Just before half past four we heard firing behind the conical hill at the back of the drift, called Oskarsberg Hill, and suddenly about five or six hundred Zulus swept around, coming for us at a run. Instantly the natives – Kaffirs who had been very useful in making the barricade of waggons, mealie-bags and biscuit boxes around the camp – bolted towards Helpmakaar, and what was worse their officer and a European sergeant went with them. To see them deserting like that was too much for some of us, and we fired after them. The sergeant was struck and killed. Half-a-dozen of us were stationed in the hospital, with orders to hold it and guard the sick. The ends of the building were of stone, the side walls of ordinary bricks, and the inside walls or partitions of sundried bricks of mud. These shoddy inside bricks proved our salvation, as you will see. It was a queer little one-storeyed building, which it is almost impossible to describe; but we were pinned like rats in a hole, because all the doorways except one had been barricaded with mealie-bags and we had done the same with the windows. The interior was divided by means of partition walls into which were fitted some very slight doors. The patients' beds were simple rough affairs of boards, raised only about half a foot above the floor. To talk of hospitals and beds gives the idea of a big building, but as a matter of fact this hospital was a mere little shed or bungalow, divided up into rooms so small that you could hardly swing a bayonet in them. There were about nine men who could not move, but altogether there were about thirty. Most of these, however could not help to defend themselves.

As soon as our Kaffirs bolted, it was seen that the fort as we had first made it was too big to be held, so Lieutenant Chard instantly reduced the space by having a row of biscuit-boxes drawn across the middle, about four feet high. This was our inner entrenchment, and proved very valuable. The Zulus came on at a wild rush, and although many of them were shot down they got to within about fifty yards of our south wall of mealie-bags and biscuit boxes and waggons. They were caught between two fires, that from the hospital and that from the storehouse, and were checked; but they gained the shelter of the cookhouse and ovens, and gave us many heavy volleys. During the fight they took advantage of every bit of cover there was, anthills, a tract of bush that we had not had time to clear away, a garden or sort of orchard which was near us, and a ledge of rock and some caves (on the Oskarsberg) which were only about a hundred yards away. They neglected nothing, and while they went on firing, large bodies kept hurling themselves against our slender breastworks.

But it was the hospital they assaulted most fiercely. I had charge with a man that we called Old King Cole of a small room with only one patient in it. Cole kept with me for some time after the fight began, then he said he was not going to stay. He went outside and was instantly killed by the Zulus, so that I was left alone with the patient, a native whose leg was broken and who kept crying out, 'Take my bandage off, so that I can come.' But it was impossible to do anything except fight, and I blazed away as hard as I could. By this time I was the only defender of my room. Poor Old King Cole was lying dead outside and the helpless patient was crying and groaning near me. The Zulus were swarming around us, and there was an extraordinary rattle as the bullets struck the biscuit boxes, and queer thuds as they plumped into the bags of mealies. Then there was the whizz and rip of the assegais, of which I had experience during the Kaffir Campaign of 1877–8. We had plenty of ammunition, but we were told to save it and so we took careful aim at every shot, and hardly a cartridge was wasted. Private Dunbar, shot no fewer than nine Zulus, one of them being a Chief.

From the very first the enemy tried to rush the hospital, and at last they managed to set fire to the thick grass which formed the roof. This put us in a terrible plight, because it meant that we were either to be massacred or burned alive, or get out of the building.

All this time the Zulus were trying to get into the room. Their assegais kept whizzing towards us, and one struck me in front of the helmet. We were wearing the white tropical helmets then. But the helmet tilted back under the blow and made the spear lose its power, so that I escaped with a scalp wound which did not trouble me much then, although it has often caused me illness since. Only one man at a time could get in at the door. A big Zulu sprang forward and seized my rifle, but I tore it free and, slipping a cartridge in, I shot him point-blank. Time after time the Zulus gripped the muzzle and tried to tear the rifle from my grasp, and time after time I wrenched it back, because I had a better grip than they had. All this time Williams was getting the sick through the hole into the next room, all except one, a soldier of the 24th named Conley, who could not move because of a broken leg. Watching for my chance I dashed from the doorway, and grabbing Conley I pulled him after me through the hole. His leg got broken again, but there was no help for it. As soon as we left the room the Zulus burst in with furious cries of disappointment and rage.

Now there was a repetition of the work of holding the doorway, except that I had to stand by a hole instead of a door, while Williams picked away at the far wall to make an opening for escape into the next room. There was more desperate and almost hopeless fighting, as it seemed, but most of the poor fellows were got through the hole.

. . . All this time, of course, the storehouse was being valiantly defended by the rest of the garrison. When we got into the inner fort, I took my post at a place where two men had been shot. While I was there another man was shot in the neck, I think by a bullet which came through the space between two biscuit boxes that were not quite close together. This was at about six o'clock in the evening, nearly two hours after the opening shot of the battle had been fired. Every now and then the Zulus would make a rush for it and get in. We had to charge them out. By this time it was dark, and the hospital was all in flames, but this gave us a splendid light to fight by. I believe it was this light that saved us. We could see them coming, and they could not rush us and take us by surprise from any point. They could not get at us, and so they went away and had ten or fifteen minutes of a war-dance. This roused them up again, and their excitement was so intense that the ground fairly seemed to shake. Then, when they were goaded to the highest pitch, they would hurl themselves at us again. We could sometimes, by the light of the flames, keep them well in sight, so well that we could take aim and fire coolly. When we could do this they never advanced as far as the barricade, because we shot them down as they ran in on us. But every now and then one or two managed to crawl in and climb over the top of the sacks. They were bayoneted off.

All this time the sick and wounded were crying for water. We had the water-cart full of water, but it was just by the deserted hospital, and we could not hope to get at it until the day broke, when the Zulus might begin to lose heart and to stop their mad rushes. But we could not bear the cries any longer, and three or four of us jumped over the boxes and ran and fetched some water in.

The long night passed and the day broke. Then we looked around us to see what had happened, and there was not a living soul who was not thankful to find that the Zulus had had enough of it and were disappearing over the hill to the south-west.

—————✶•✶—————

'*All night long we could hear the native tom-toms beating*'
PRIVATE HARRY ETHERINGTON

BROKEN SQUARE
AT ABU KLEA
SUDAN, 17 JANUARY 1885

Private Etherington, of the Royal Sussex Regiment, was part of the flying column dispatched to relieve Colonel Gordon, surrounded in Khartoum by the Islamic nationalist army of Muhammed Ahmad, al-Mahdi ('the chosen one').

On January 16th we approached Abu Klea Wells, which are situated in a defile between some low hills. We brought up for dinner three miles off in the desert, and sent forward a party of Hussars to see if the wells were occupied. As they did not return,

General Stewart ordered an advance, when all at once there were shouts of 'Dismount! Undo ammunition!' and we saw the Hussars riding back for their lives, and announcing that the Mahdists were thousands strong at the wells.

We were at once formed into a three-sided square, with the camels in the middle; one man being told off to look after six camels. Then we began to advance over the broken ground. About two miles from the wells it became dusk, and just as the sun was setting on the skyline, we saw the gleam of hundreds of native spears on the brow of a low hill. Some sharp shooting followed, but we were too far off to do any good, and in a few minutes it was dark.

Then commenced a night of terror. We formed a zereba of bushes and crouched behind it; many a man prayed that night who was not in the habit of doing so, I can assure you. You see it is one thing to face a foe in the field, and quite another to lie awake at night expecting to be killed every minute. All the while the Mahdists kept up a desultory firing – for they had two thousand Remingtons, captured from Hicks Pacha – and we lost several men and a number of camels.

All night long we could hear the native tom-toms beating, and every moment we expected a charge. I was told off for outpost duty, which was not very pleasant under the circumstances, but we did not go more than a hundred yards from the column. My regiment was in the rear, the heavy Camel corps being in front. Colonel Burnaby came round to us all, and said, 'Don't strike a light, and don't fire on any account, or you will show the enemy where you are; wait till you see the white of their eyes, and then bayonet them.'

By this time we were almost maddened with thirst, for our supply of water was nearly exhausted and we had only a pint per man left. Hence it was absolutely necessary that we should capture the wells before we went any farther.

The next morning we had one of those glorious sunrises that are only seen in the tropics. At eight o'clock we again formed square, for the Mahdists were beginning to descend from the hills. We sent out skirmishers to attack them, and Lieutenant de Lisle was shot while we were forming square.

The enemy then formed in three columns of five thousand

men each, with riflemen on each side, the rest being armed with
spears, and all thoroughly well disciplined.

We were only two deep in square till within fifty yards of the
enemy, when our skirmishers retired, and we opened square to let
them in. At that moment the Mahdists charged, but were
repulsed. A second charge failed, but at the third they succeeded
in breaking one corner of the square, and then the position
became very serious indeed. Probably their success was due to the
fact that our men at that corner were not used to the bayonet but
to the sword. Anyhow, the Soudanese broke a British square, and
that is something to their credit

Our seven-pounders were thus left outside, and Colonel
Burnaby rushed out of the square to recapture them. He fought
like a hero, but was thrust in the throat by a Mahdist spearman
and killed We dragged him back to the square, but it was too late.

It was at this point that Gunner Smith won the only Victoria
Cross of the campaign. When the square was broken, Major
Guthrie stuck to the guns, and fought till he fell wounded. Then
Gunner Smith rushed to the rescue. He had lost his rifle, but he
caught up a gun spike, beat off the Soudanese, and dragged the
Major back into the square.

When the square was re-formed a lot of the Mahdists were
inside, but you may be sure that none of them lived to get out
again. One odd incident happened inside the square. We were
carrying a number of chests of bullion for Gordon, and these
were knocked open in mistake for ammunition, so that the
ground was literally strewn with sovereigns.

At last the Gatling guns were got into action, and that
practically ended the battle. The Soudanese were simply mown
down. Their bodies flew up into the air like grass from a lawn-
mower. But their pluck was astonishing. I saw some of the natives
dash up to the Gatling guns, and thrust their arms down the
muzzles, trying to extract the bullets which were destroying their
comrades! Of course, they were simply blown to atoms.

The battle lasted off and on from eight in the morning till five
in the afternoon, when the Soudanese finally fled. We did not
pursue them, but with a ringing cheer we dashed to the wells, for
we had drunk nothing all day, and were nearly maddened with
thirst. Altogether sixty-five of our men were killed, and a hundred

and eighty wounded, while about two thousand natives lay dead upon the sand.

Gordon in Khartoum withstood siege for ten months; Harry Etherington's relief column arrived in Khartoum 48 hours too late to save him.

In death Gordon became a Victorian icon, and the public clamoured for revenge. It would come. Eventually

—⇒•◆•⇐—

'I might fairly claim I had worked out the Queen's shilling'
Ex-Sergeant–Major E. Mole

A FAREWELL TO ARMS
27 July 1888

On the 27th July, 1888, I passed out of the profession into civilian life, feeling I might fairly claim I had worked out the Queen's shilling.

With the record of a sergeant's and sergeant-major's rank for seventeen years; with a discharge bearing against the word character the description 'very good'; with a good-conduct medal on my breast, a pension of upwards of forty pounds a year to draw, and a balance of several hundred pounds in the savings bank, in perfect health and strength, and indeed feeling fit to do another quarter of a century of soldiering, I left the army. And I thought that day, and think still, that had I my life in front of me instead of behind, I would start again, just as I did when I was a lad of eighteen, and desire nothing better than to live those happy twenty five years over again in the ranks of the Old 14th as a King's Hussar.

Pay had gone up over the course of Mole's career, so that by 1888 the private soldier had a clear 1s a day after 'off reckonings'. Good conduct pay was also available. A sober-minded soldier like Mole therefore was able to save up a nest-egg over the course of his army career.

The more feckless soldiery still lapsed into poverty on discharge; the old begging soldier was a common sight until the 1920s.

And feckless soldiers there were aplenty:

—⇒•◆•⇐—

'men are continually returning . . . in every conceivable condition'
ANONYMOUS PRIVATE

BARRACK-ROOM BLUES
ALDERSHOT, C 1892

The writer served with the 2nd Battalion, Royal East Kent Regiment ('the Buffs').

The time that I cared for least of all was the evening between 7 p.m. & 9.30 p.m. between these hours men are continually returning to their barrack rooms in every conceivable condition & the utter callousness and shamelessness of the conversation until order was demanded for the roll-call made me long for the morning & work as a grateful relief: picture if you can a large room with about 15 beds 18 inches apart in the centre the tables with plates & basins upon them & perhaps the bread and butter for the next days consumption. On & in the beds are the men, some vomiting, some lying full-dressed on the beds in a semi-drunken stupor occasionally muttering curses, others smoking & some snoring, try & picture this & you will have some slight idea of the misery endured by a steady young man in the army in hundreds of barrack rooms in the country . . .

Outside the barracks [at Aldershot] were dozens of those unfortunate women always to be found in a garrison town. I found that to be able to boast of a frequent connection with these poor women was considered to be a most manly thing by a great many of the men & in fact the conversation in my own barrack room at night would have astonished anyone chancing to hear it by its absolutely immoral nature. Now & then an Army Scripture Reader would come round the rooms and distribute a few tracts & we marched to church once a week, with these exceptions everyone followed his own sweet will as far as Military discipline would permit without any moral or spiritual influence whatsoever . . .

'Unfortunate women' were a major cause of the epidemic of venereal disease which gripped the Victorian army. Officers as well as men. One prostitute's ditty ran:

The next I met a cornet was
In a regiment of dragoons

I gave him what he didn't like
And stole his silver spoons.

Not all the prostitutes in garrison towns worked outside the camp; one moral reform group in the 19th century found a soldier's wife catering for ten of his comrades per night in the barracks.

Troops in India, where the army ran regimental brothels ('lal bazaars'), were particularly prone to catching 'what he didn't like', despite medical inspection of the occupants. Some units had more than 40 per cent of their men infected by VD. However, the incidence of VD in the British army was on the decline by the end of the 19th century simply because the proportion of rankers allowed to marry was doubled to 12 per cent.

Redcoat drunkeness, meanwhile, not only offended the more sober of soldiers, it was a major cause of the low esteem in which the Victorians held the soldier. Even so, the redcoat's war-winning ways were beginning to produce more public affection for him. Rudyard Kipling perfectly caught the the Victorian ambivalence to 'Tommy Atkins' in poetry:

'But it's "Savior of 'is country" when the guns begin to shoot'
RUDYARD KIPLING

TOMMY
1892

'Tommy Atkins', as a term to describe the British soldier, derived from its use in a War Office publication of 1815; the 'widow' mentioned in the poem is Queen Victoria herself.

Oh it's Tommy this an' Tommy that, an' 'Tommy go away',
But it's 'Thank you, Mr. Atkins' when the band begins to play.
Then it's 'Tommy this, an' Tommy that, an' Tommy 'ows yer
    soul?'
But its 'Thin red line of 'eroes' when the drums begin to roll.
       * * *
We aren't no thin red 'eroes, nor we aren't no blackguards too,
But simple men in barricks most remarkable like you,
An' if sometimes our conduck isn't all your fancy paints,
Why, simple men in barricks don't grow into plaster saints.

* * *

For it's 'Tommy this an' Tommy that' an' 'Chuck him out, the
    brute!'
But it's 'Saviour of 'is country' when the guns begin to shoot.
An' it's Tommy this, an' Tommy that an' anything you please,
An' Tommy ain't a blooming fool – you bet that Tommy sees!

' 'I have been away now over 6 years, & I have seen some
different sights during that time'
FRED

ONE MAN'S WAR
A LETTER HOME TO MOTHER, PESHAWAR
INDIA, 31 OCTOBER 1897

The writer served with the Somerset Light Infantry.

Peshawar
31/10/[18]97

Dear Mother,

Just a few lines to let you know that I am alive & well. You will see
by my address that I am back in Peshawar. I have seen some hard
& trying times since I passed through here on the 8th of August
last. I will just give you a slight account, we got orders to march to
Shabkadar & relieve the fort there, which was surrounded by 8000
of the Mohmand tribes, we got there on the night of the 6th &
drove the enemy from the fort, but slept with all our equipment
on & rifles with bayonets fixed all night. Next morning we got up
before it was light & marched towards the hills, two miles distant.
We had got within half a mile of the hills, when they swarmed
down on us there, seemed to be no end of them, & there was only
1200 of us Cavalry & Artillery all told, at any rate the Artillery
came into Action, & they sent our two Companies [of the
Somerset Light Infantry] to guard the left flank. We were firing at
some of the Enemy at 800 yards, when suddenly a perfect hail of
bullets came over from our left and rear about 100 yards away, so
we had to alter our position. Just then Major Lumb got shot
through the neck & Serjeant White got killed & we had to take 4

men back wounded, then we had to fight for all our worth, we could hear nothing only the continual roar of Rifles & Big Guns going off. The fight lasted I should think about 5 hours, then General Elles came & made us take up a position on a high bank & whilst we were doing that the Enemy pressed us, & we lost some more men, two men got left behind somehow I dont know how it happened, nobody missed them till the roll was called at night when they didn't answer their names. They sent the Cavalry over the battle field again & found them cut & quartered, they did not know how to separate them, they had to put them in one blanket and sew them up, we buried them and all the remainder that night under the fort walls, with every thing on just as they fell, not a prayer book in the fort. The General spoke a few words to us, he said that our comrades had died fighting for our Queen & Country & hoped that we all would do our duty in the future as we had done it that day. We spent a miserable night, as the fort is very small, & we could hear the groans of the wounded & men with fever & Sunstroke were lying all over the place we couldn't sleep, although we were tired out, we were too hungry. We couldn't get nothing to eat, & we got nothing for two days only what the Native soldiers gave us. Our Regt came in next day from Peshawar to Reinforce us, & they were deeply cut up when they heard how the Enemy had served those two men of ours. We stopped at Shabkadar for a long time when there was an Expedition formed to go into their Country & punish them. Our Regt was in the 1st Brigade. No Europeans had been in this Country before, so they did not know much about it, the first march was very hard & very hot, no water to be got anywhere. The next march much easier, we marched several days then we met General B. Blood's Troops, they had come from a different direction. The Enemy fired into us all that night, they tried to rush our camp but we met them with steady volleys & soon drove them away. We blowed all their towers & forts up and burned their villages & took away their wheat & grain, everywhere we went. At last we got to Badmanni Pass & we wanted to get over this pass to get to Hadda Mullah's City & Mosque. The Enemey held this pass in force so we had to camp this side of it that night, but they would not let us sleep as they fired all night at us. Next morning the General left two regts to guard the baggage, then we started for the pass, we opened out for attack & after about 6 hours sharp fighting, the pass was won, we held the pass till all our transport was over then we camped for the night on the other side, thoroughly done up. The enemy would not let us sleep though, they fired into us from the hills all around all the night. We got to Jarobi next day it was a place perched on a great mountain, Afghanistan was the other side, so our General thought he would be crossing the boundary if he sent flanking parties out, so he only attacked in front, left the flanks exposed. We reached the place & blowed it up & burned every thing we could, & came back again the enemy followed us and it took us 4 hours to do 4 miles. We lost a lot of men that day. Hadda Mulla fled to Afghanistan so that ended the Expedition, & we marched back to Peshawar, & now half the Regiment is sick with Malarial fever & Ague. We was for the Tirah Campaign but the Regt is too sick for it. Us signallers expect to go soon, I hope we do as I dont like Peshawar, I will tell you more news another time. Remember me to my Father tell him that I am allright & am pleased he has got a good job. I hope he will have a job for me when I come home, I have been away now over 6 years, & I have seen some different sights during that time. I shall be glad to settle down quietly when I get the chance now. Give my love to Laura. I shall have something to tell her when I come home. If you see Will Remember me to him & anybody that Knows me. I have received your letters allright I got one in the Mohmand Country, & I was pleased to hear from you up there. I hope you are enjoying good health, & got into better circumstances than you have been. Space is short, so you must accept my best love from your loving.

Son Fred.   WRITE SOON
WRITE SOON

In another part of the Empire on which the sun never set, the British were about to take a long-awaited revenge.

'. . . a long dancing row of lances couched ready for the charge'
LIEUTENANT WINSTON CHURCHILL

OMDURMAN
THE 21ST LANCERS CHARGE THE DERVISHES
2 SEPTEMBER 1898

Thirteen years after the death of General Gordon at the hands of the Mahdi, the British were back in Sudan with a punitive long-range expedition led by Sirdar ('Commander-in-Chief') Horatio Kitchener. After defeating the Mahdists at Atbara, the British met them again under the walls of Khartoum at Omdurman.

Lieutenant Churchill later served in the First World War; he was prime minister of Britain during the Second World War.

I propose to describe exactly what happened to me: what I saw and what I felt. I recalled it to my mind so frequently after the event that the impression is as clear and vivid as it was a quarter of a century ago. The troop I commanded was, when we wheeled into line, the second from the right of the regiment. I was riding a handy, sure-footed, grey Arab polo pony. Before we wheeled and began to gallop, the officers had been marching with drawn swords. On account of my shoulder I had always decided that if I were involved in hand-to-hand fighting, I must use a pistol and not a sword. I had purchased in London a Mauser automatic pistol, then the newest and the latest design. I had practised carefully with this during our march and journey up the river. This then was the weapon with which I determined to fight. I had first of all to return my sword into its scabbard, which is not the easiest thing to do at a gallop. I had then to draw my pistol from its wooden holster and bring it to full cock. This dual operation took an appreciable time, and until it was finished, apart from a few glances to my left to see what effect the fire was producing, I did not look up at the general scene.

Then I saw immediately before me, and now only half the length of a polo ground away, the row of crouching blue figures firing frantically, wreathed in white smoke. On my right and left my neighbouring troop leaders made a good line. Immediately behind was a long dancing row of lances couched for the charge. We were going at a fast but steady gallop. There was too much trampling and rifle fire to hear any bullets. After this glance to the right and left and at my troop, I looked again towards the enemy. The scene appeared to be suddenly transformed. The blue-black men were still firing, but behind them there now came into view a depression like a shallow sunken road. This was crowded and crammed with men rising up from the ground where they had hidden. Bright flags appeared as if by magic, and I saw arriving from nowhere Emirs on horseback among and around the mass of the enemy. The Dervishes appeared to be ten or twelve deep at the thickest, a great grey mass gleaming with steel, filling the dry watercourse. In the same twinkling of an eye I saw also that our right overlapped their left, that my troop would just strike the edge of their array, and that the troop on my right would charge into air. My subaltern comrade on the right, Wormald of the 7th Hussars, could see the situation too; and we both increased our speed to the very fastest gallop and curved inwards like the horns of the moon. One really had not time to be frightened or to think of anything else but these particular necessary actions which I have described. They completely occupied mind and senses.

The collision was now very near. I saw immediately before me, not ten yards away, the two blue men who lay in my path. They were perhaps a couple of yards apart. I rode at the interval between them. They both fired. I passed through the smoke conscious that I was unhurt. The trooper immediately behind me was killed at this place and at this moment, whether by these shots or not I do not know. I checked my pony as the ground began to fall away beneath his feet. The clever animal dropped like a cat four or five feet down on to the sandy bed of the watercourse, and in this sandy bed I found myself surrounded by what seemed to be dozens of men. They were not thickly-packed enough at this point for me to experience any actual collision with them. Whereas Grenfell's troop next but one on my left was brought to a complete standstill and suffered very heavy losses, we seemed to push our way through as one has sometimes seen mounted policemen break up a crowd. In less time than it takes to relate, my pony had scrambled up the other side of the ditch. I looked round.

Once again I was on the hard, crisp desert, my horse at a trot. I had sensation of fear. I felt myself absolutely alone. I thought these riflemen would hit me and the rest devour me like wolves. What a fool I was to loiter like this in the midst of the enemy! I crouched over the saddle, spurred my horse into a gallop and drew clear of the *mêlée*. Two or three hundred yards away I found my troop all ready faced about and partly formed up.

The other three troops of the squadron were re-forming close by. Suddenly in the midst of the troop up sprung a Dervish. How he got there I do not know. He must have leaped out of some scrub or hole. All the troopers turned upon him thrusting with their lances: but he darted to and fro causing for the moment a frantic commotion. Wounded several times, he staggered towards me raising his spear. I shot him at less than a yard. He fell on the sand, and lay there dead. How easy to kill a man! But I did not worry about it. I found I had fired the whole magazine of my Mauser pistol, so I put in a new clip of ten cartridges before thinking of anything else.

I was still prepossessed with the idea that we had inflicted great slaughter on the enemy and had scarcely suffered at all ourselves. Three or four men were missing from my troop. Six men and nine or ten horses were bleeding from spear thrusts or sword cuts. We all expected to be ordered immediately to charge back again. The men were ready, though they all looked serious. Several asked to be allowed to throw away their lances and draw their swords. I asked my second sergeant if he had enjoyed himself. His answer was 'Well, I don't exactly say I enjoyed it, Sir; but I think I'll get more used to it next time.'

There would be few 'next times'; the ride of the 21st Lancers at Omdurman was one of the last occasions when British cavalry would charge out across a battlefield. Twenty thousand dervishes were killed and wounded at Omdurman but relatively few of them by Churchill and his fellow horse-soldiers; the devastation was done by a whirlwind of British artillery, machine-gun and rifle fire. It was to these arms, not the medieval lance and sabre, that the future belonged.

———————◆◆◆———————

'Mallow was staggering on a bit . . . without his head'
PRIVATE THOMAS HUMPHREYS

BOER WAR
SPION KOP
19–24 JANUARY 1900

Nearly all the myriad wars of Victoria's latter reign were fought against numerous but poorly armed 'natives'. In the Boer War of 1899 to 1902 the British Army got its own taste of modern warfare.

Initially, the war went all the way of the Boers, who surrounded the British garrisons at Mafeking, Ladysmith and Kimberley. Although rustics without manufacturing, the Boers of South Africa had used their mineral riches to buy in state-of-the-art arms. The resultant volumes of rifle, machine-gun and shell fire the Boers were able to pour down on the British were unlike anything the Tommies had ever endured. Even an old hand like Private Thomas Humphreys of the Middlesex Regiment.

At least the Tommies on the Kop were no longer wearing the sights-friendly 'red rag'; the Boer War was the first major campaign in which khaki was worn.

We toiled upward, slowly, in the sweltering heat, almost cursing the very weapons on which we had to rely for our existence. We had left our great-coats at the foot of the hill. We were free of the weight of them, but many a man, when the bitter night came, who was lying helpless on the barren heights, would have given almost life itself for the despised covering which he had looked upon as a burden.

I do not exaggerate when I say that, on reaching the plateau, as we did at last, we were in the thick of a very hell of fire – not rifle-fire, but the infinitely more merciless and destructive shell-fire. It was terrible to see the havoc which had been wrought already; pitiful to notice the dead, and unendurable to look upon the wounded. It was marvellous that human beings could live at all; yet the valiant men of Lancashire were holding grimly on, despite what looked like certain death. As soon as I could get to work with my Lee-Metford I began to fire. Wherever I saw a sign of man in the distance I let a bullet go. For the most part, I am sure, the ammunition was wasted; but in many shots some are sure to be effective. You can empty a magazine swiftly, and each man had eighty rounds; besides, fresh supplies came up, and the pouches were refilled, emptied, and refilled again.

I believe that during the day I myself fired at least two hundred rounds. Other men did the same, so that, although the band of soldiers on the plateau was small, yet the total number of rounds of ammunition used was very large.

I should not like to calculate the weight of the shot and shell which swept the plateau, nor how many came each minute. Not everyone did mischief; if that had happened there would not have been a living soul on Spion Kop. Rifle bullets are terrible things as wound creators, bayonets are worse; but neither of them can be named in the same breath as a shell wound. This is too awful yet most of the injury on Spion Kop was caused by shell.

It was a bitter, merciless battle. Men on both sides fought to kill, and so to win. It was the only way. May I be evermore spared from looking on such a scene, and sharing in such a struggle.

Tragedies occurred on every hand, and on every hand, too, were seen such deeds of heroism as you sometimes think and dream of, but never expect to witness; and such endurance and tenacity as you can get only from men who are stubbornly and heroically led.

We had got used to shell fire by that time; but not to such a withering cannonade as we were forced to face on Spion Kop. Hot, sweating, tired, mad with thirst, we gained the plateau, and set out to hold it. Water was wanted, but it was not to be had, and so, with parched mouths, we went on firing.

If you can get very near your enemy and use the bayonet, there is at any rate some satisfaction; but there we were, mere targets, scarcely seeing a Boer, although at times they got so near us, under cover, that I do not think more than fifty yards separated the two forces. Nor could we get at our food, although within easy reach were Irish stew rations – one for every two men. They were 'iron' or emergency rations; but we left them where they were. They were not worth shell fire just then. If it comes to that, we were in a big enough stew ourselves, without falling back on the Maconochie productions.

The bursting shells made a veritable hell of the plateau. It was miraculous that men could live in such a fire, and that troops could hold the ground they had won, especially with such sights to look upon as they saw on every hand.

Torn by the shot and shell earlier in the morning, the Lancashire Fusiliers had suffered terribly. My own battalion was baptised in blood as soon as it reinforced the north countrymen.

Captain Muriel, one of our company officers, stopped for a moment to give a wounded man a cigarette. He was shot through the cheek while doing it. Undaunted he held on to his post, and led his company until he was struck by a bullet. This time he fell and did not rise, for the bullet had gone through his brain.

Very near me was my own sergeant – Murphy. I heard one of the awful sounds which told of somebody being struck by a shell, then a cry of 'My God'!

I looked at the spot where I had seen the sergeant standing, and saw that the shell had torn both his legs away. What was left of him was lying on the ground, where he bled to death.

More pitiless still was another shell, which came and killed four men in a cluster. They literally seemed, when I saw them, as if they were on fire, and their clothes smouldered. Corporal Cakebread was amongst them.

In front of me also was a man of the Lancaster Regiment named Mallow. We were all mixed up by that time, irrespective of regiments. We clustered and huddled as best we could. There was no ceremony about it – we simply and solely wished to get as well out of the way of the shells as possible.

A pom-pom screeched past me. I looked and saw a ghastly sight. Mallow was staggering on a bit, just two or three steps, without his head, for the pom-pom had carried it away.

It was death, or worse, to be in the open, and an almost certain fate befel the man who, being under shelter, dared to show even so much as his head. Shell or bullet would account for him. I saw a man of the Durham Light Infantry peep round the corner of a little kopje where he was sheltering. Instantly a pom-pom smashed his head against the side, and he fell to the ground.

Even the dead were struck or riddled as they lay, and it was not possible for the wounded to escape.

I saw two Natal refugees, as we called them, carrying off a wounded Engineer – those splendid Sappers who did such fine work in making trenches – on a stretcher. Both of them were struck, and became as helpless as the burden they were bearing.

It was all terrible beyond expression, yet we held on. We had been sent off with the order of 'No surrender!' and we were doing our utmost to obey. And in that attempt we had one of the finest and most thrilling examples that ever fell to the lot of British troops in action.

General Woodgate had fallen – I saw him borne away to the dressing hospital – and his place had been taken by Colonel Thorneycroft. Men were wavering – of some it could be said that they were missing, which meant that the enemy had got them. Ammunition had been shot away or could not be obtained.

It had taken us three hours of incessant toiling to reach the plateau and to get within the zone of shell fire. The pluck had vanished from a mere handful of soldiers – three dozen or so – and they had gone so far towards caving in that they had thrown their rifles down and were making their way towards the spot where the enemy was to give themselves up.

The Boers were coming on to take the fruits of what they thought would be their victory and the capture of the hill.

It was a moment of the gravest, sternest peril. If these men surrendered, who was to say that the day would be ours, and that Spion Kop, won at such a dreadful sacrifice, would be kept?

Suddenly a man of gigantic stature, himself wounded, hurried after the handful who were giving themselves up.

The men in khaki were on the very point of putting themselves into the hands of the Boers, who were armed, and waving white flags or rags.

The big man rushed to the front and roared to the leader of the enemy, telling him to take his men back with him and go to – 'I'll have no surrenders here!' he shouted. Then he added: 'Follow me, men!'

They obeyed, and he led them back to where the good old Pothooks were lying, and put heart of grace into the lot of them and us.

That was Colonel Thorneycroft. He was a valiant leader, and where you get a British officer like that you have men who don't surrender while there is a chance at all of life and victory.

Throughout the whole of that appalling afternoon we went on

fighting. I settled down to it in the most dogged manner. I was caked and choked with dust and parched with thirst, and I was hungry; but food didn't count at such a time. I only wanted something to drink – and there was no water or other liquid to be had.

I had been marvellously, miraculously fortunate. Men had been killed and maimed all around me, yet so far I had escaped without a scratch. I began to think that it would be my luck to get away from Spion Kop with a sound skin.

So certain was I that I was safe that I turned to a comrade and said laughingly: 'We're lucky to be here all the time without being plugged. It's nearly dark, and as soon as the "Cease fire" sounds we shall be able to celebrate our escape from a jolly hot hole. Besides, they'll send reinforcements.' Reinforcements never came, as a matter of fact; but I needn't dwell on that. They couldn't get where they were wanted.

You see, amongst other things, a shell had come and struck the ground at the very feet of four of us, yet we had escaped without a scratch. It could not have been a shrapnel, because it never burst; I daresay it was a common shell in which the fuse would not act. There had been some wonderful escapes, too, amongst them that of Sergeant Phillips, who was struck by a bullet which buried itself in his report-book. Another man had been hit on the nose by a bullet – which, luckily for him, was a spent one. He picked the bullet out and made a joke about it.

The day was waning and the swift night was coming on.

I was thankfully looking forward to the ending of the firing, till the day at any rate, when I felt a queer, dull thud on my left leg.

I looked to see what had happened, and sank to the ground, for a fifteen-pound shell had taken off the leg completely, trousers, puttie, sock, and boot. I never saw it; I don't know where it was carried – and I didn't wish to learn. The same shell took off the leg of another man of my regiment called Pasby and smashed his other foot.

I was perfectly conscious. I knew what had happened; but, believe me, I did not feel any real pain. There was only a strange numbness, and the horror of knowing that the dreadful thing had happened.

I dragged myself away from my comrades and crawled instinctively to a place of shelter, just as a wounded animal would have done. I got into a little place of refuge which was made by a couple of small kopjes – a sort of crevice. As I reached it another shell dropped at the very side of me.

For nearly an hour, as far as I can tell, I lay in my hiding-place, craving for water, hoping for help. I knew that unless I could be quickly taken into hospital I should die of exhaustion and loss of blood. The wonder is that I lived at all; yet at last, when it was dark, a surgeon and a sergeant came, and their arrival was at the very moment when another shell buried itself in the hard ground. It was only shells that seemed to have the power of penetrating the rocky face of Spion Kop.

'Are you all right?' shouted the doctor to the sergeant.

'Yes, sir,' the sergeant told him.

'Then you're a lucky man,' replied the doctor. 'It seems to me that these poor, wounded fellows are drawing all the rest of the fire on them.'

The doctor stopped the bleeding with a tourniquet, and I watched him do it, strangely fascinated. Then they made an ambulance for me – a couple of rifles and slings, and two of my own comrades began to carry me down the Kop.

They were utterly worn out and exhausted and the task was too much for them. They turned to an officer who was leading away what was left of the Scottish Rifles, and he ordered a dozen of his men to take charge of me in turn.

'Put me down, and let me die, for God's sake!' I begged them piteously, for it was terrible now to be carried and jolted down the rocks. Every movement was a torture to me; but they held on with their task, and at last my own two comrades again took charge of me.

I became unconscious at last, not because of my pain, but owing to the spirits with which they supplied me on that awful downward journey. I remember, however, being outside the operating tent, waiting in a pitiful crowd for my turn to come. After that I knew nothing till next day, and then I found that it was all over and that my leg was represented by a stump.

That was the end for the time being to something like ten days of the most terrible hardships you can imagine; but the finish did not come even then. I made the close acquaintance of a Scotch cart and a bullock waggon; I knew what it was to have to lie almost unattended on a stretcher, because fighting was still going on, and the army which had been victorious was being drawn away by its leader. Once only in seven days was I dressed, and that was when I was sent to Mori River with the wounded.

I had the personal attention of some of the ablest surgeons in the world – Sir Frederick Treves, Sir William McCormack, and Sir William Stokes; and the devoted care of a nurse who was afterwards in attendance on the King himself. At one time I was rigged up in a suit of pyjamas which a kind lady had sent out for the use of sick and wounded troops.

There are funny incidents even in such dreadful times as those. I had lost my left leg; another man had parted with his right foot. Each of us was in need of a boot, and the authorities, who have no sentiment, divided a pair between us. I took the left and the other man got its brother. The country saved something on the deal.

I knew as I was being carried down the rugged, merciless face of Spion Kop that we were not going to hold what we had won, for the order to retire had been given.

The defeat at Spion Kop was a sledge hammer blow to the cheerful, insolent confidence of Victorian Britain. Football fans in Liverpool, in ironic acknowledgement, named the high terraced end of the local stadium 'the Kop'.

Spion Kop, at least, stirred the British government into action. Out to South Africa were dispatched Lord 'Bob' Roberts and Lord Kitchener, who lifted the sieges of Mafeking, Ladysmith and Kimberley and occupied the Boer towns of Bloemfontein, Johannesburg and Pretoria.

Still the Boers would not give up. Mounted on their ponies and clutching their vicious Mauser rifles (with smokeless powder, which made their firing difficult to spot), Boer 'commandos' fought a two-year-long guerrilla war.

'I realised in a flash that I had no chance'
GUNNER OSMAN F. GREEN

BOER WAR
GUNNER GREEN IS CAPTURED BY BOER COMMANDOS
FEBRUARY 1901

Green, a gunner with the Royal Horse Artillery Mounted Rifles, writes to his parents
in England.

[In the field] *February 1901*

I have a rather unpleasant experience to relate ... We were
acting as advance party and chased the Boers 6 or 7 miles as
hard as we could go. But, on getting orders that the main body
of the force was retiring, we became the rearguard. Immediately
the Boers came back in force and tried to cut us off from the
main body as we were holding a small hill. My horse had shown
signs of being 'done up' and I was told by my sergeant to try
to get along to the main body whilst they were holding the hill.
I got my horse about a mile further when he refused to go a
step further. There I was between the rear guard and the
main body. I began to see I was going to be in a queer position
as the rearguard was withdrawing with the Boers hot on their
heels. I had just managed to get my horse started again. I was
leading it along when the boys came galloping past as hard
as they could go about 30 yards to my right. My Battery being
furthest away on my right. The Boers were about 800 yards
away and commenced firing at me. Things were desperate now
so I made no more ado and took my rifle and shot my horse
dead and, picking up my cloak, I made a run for it on foot. I had
gone about 200 yards or so when I heard a shout behind me of
'Hands up!'. When I looked round a group of Boers were not
50 yards away. One had halted his horse and was covering me
with his rifle whilst the others galloped around me. I realised in
a flash that I had no chance, so I threw down my rifle and put up
my hands.

Well there I was, a prisoner, and feeling anything but happy.
One Boer took my rifle and bandolier whilst the others made me

run in front of them until we got out of range of our rearguard, who were firing on them.

After getting over the rise they made me take off everything but my helmet and drawers. However after they had talked for a while one old Boer made one of the young men give me back my shirt, which he did very reluctantly. They also gave me an old pair of boots made from cow hide. Then one of the Boers took me to a kaffir kraal a few 100 yards away. After stopping for a couple of minutes he took me across an open space to another kraal where their Commandant was. Our rearguard had evidently been watching that kraal from a distance and directly the Boer and I commenced walking across they poured such a terrible fire at us that God only knows how I escaped. The bullets passed so close to my face and body that I could feel the rush of air they caused. It was like a small hail of lead, and bullets seemed to rip up the ground for yards around . . . I have never experienced anything like it before and hope I shan't again. I seemed to have a charm over me. I expected a bullet every second but am thankful God spared me for I got across without a scratch. I was taken before the Commandant and was questioned by my guard who could speak English. I could give them no information as I told them I was only a 'Tommy' and that I did not know anything about the size of the force, and that ordinary soldiers were not told anything about such things. They simply got orders and had to follow them out. They told me I could go. Then the Boer, who had been my guard, took me [out] . . .

I asked him to see me over the skyline as I was unarmed and there were parties of young Boers who might easily put me out. He pointed me the way to Frankfort and told me to follow the telegraph wires. So I left him and made my way as best I could.

The heat was terrible and my saliva dried up until my tongue seemed nearly too big for my mouth. I went off the track to a pool I came across and got an old tin can full of water after having had a good drink. I carried the tin full of water and kept dipping in a piece I had torn off my pants to moisten my tongue with, to stop it sticking to the roof of my mouth. I found gun wheel tracks and followed these until I reached the outskirts of Frankfort, after walking about 14 miles. I found the Battery camped outside Frankfort where I arrived at 5pm, properly footsore and done up.

Action and capture by the enemy were not Green's only worries in South Africa. For much of his campaign he was on 'half rations, which consists of two biscuits a day, half a pint of coffee without sugar or milk, and half a pint of tea. We get plenty of meat though as we have captured cattle and sheep. But too much meat is not good in this hot climate'.

'No glitter – no excitement'
LIEUTENANT DAVID MILLER

'JUST BULLET AND DIRT'
THE INFANTRYMAN'S WAR IN SOUTH AFRICA
5 AUGUST 1901

Miller writes to his mother.

5 August 1901

There is so little to describe. The infantry soldier sees nothing except the men on either side of them and the enemy in front. He hears the crackle of the enemy's fire somewhere – he does not know where – and he hears the whit! whit! of the bullets, and every now and then he knows vaguely some one near him is hit – he feels the smell of the powder (cordite) and the hot oily smell of the rifle. He fires at the range given, and at the given direction, and every now and then he hears 'Advance!' and he gets up and goes on and wonders why he is not hit as he stands up. That is all. Then the bullets cease to come and the action is over . . . He marches to the chosen camping ground and perhaps goes on picket – very tired and dirty – and he does it all again next day. That is the infantry soldier's battle – very nasty – very tiring – very greasy – very hungry – very thirsty – everything very beastly. No glitter – no excitement – no nothing. Just bullet and dirt.

'The Lesson'. Thus did Kipling appositely entitle a poem about the Boer War. By the outbreak of peace in May 1902 the British had lost 5,774 troops killed in action; the Boers had lost 4,000.

If the lesson had been learned the hard way, it had been a valuable one: the need for good shooting and flexible tactics.

The British soldier, though he did not know it, was better prepared than his European rivals for the deluge that would descend in just 12 years' time.

'the full flood of "England" swept him on from thought to thought'
Sub-Lieutenant Rupert Brooke

THE DECLARATION OF WAR
THOUGHTS OF A SOLDIER POET
August 1914

With the German invasion of neutral Belgium on 4 August 1914 all hope of British non-intervention in the First World War ended. On that day, at 10.45 in the morning, Britain declared war on Germany.

Some say the Declaration of War threw us into a primitive abyss of hatred and the lust for blood. Others declare that we behaved very well. I do not know. I only know the thoughts that flowed through the mind of a friend of mine when he heard the news. My friend – I shall make no endeavour to excuse him – is a normal, even ordinary man, wholly English, twenty-four years old, active and given to music. By a chance he was ignorant of the events of the world during the last days of July. He was camping with some friends in a remote part of Cornwall, and had gone on, with a companion, for a four-days' sail. So it wasn't till they beached her again that they heard. A youth ran down to them with a telegram: 'We're at war with Germany. We've joined France and Russia.'

My friend ate and drank, and then climbed a hill of gorse, and sat alone, looking at the sea. His mind was full of confused images, and the sense of strain. In answer to the word 'Germany', a train of vague thoughts dragged across his brain. The pompous, middle-class vulgarity of the building of Berlin; the wide and restful beauty of Munich; the taste of beer; innumerable quiet, glittering *cafés*; the *Ring*; the swish of evening air in the face, as one *skis* down past the pines; a certain angle of the eyes in the face; long nights of drinking, and singing, and laughter; the admirable beauty of German wives and mothers; certain friends; some tunes; the quiet length of evening over the Starnberger-See. Between him and the Cornish sea he saw quite clearly an April morning on a lake south of Berlin, the grey water slipping past his little boat, and a peasant-woman, suddenly revealed against apple-blossom, hanging up blue and scarlet garments to dry in the sun. Children played about her; and she sang as she worked . . .

A cloud over the sun woke him to consciousness of his own thoughts; and he found, with perplexity, that they were contin-ually recurring in two periods of his life, the days after the death of his mother, and the time of his first deep estrangement from one he loved. After a bit he understood this. Now, as then, his mind had been completely divided into two parts: the upper running about aimlessly from one half-relevant thought to an-other, the lower unconscious half labouring with some profound and unknowable change. This feeling of ignorant helplessness linked him with those past crises. His consciousness was like the light scurry of waves at full tide, when the deeper waters are pausing and gathering and turning home. Something was growing in his heart, and he couldn't tell what. But as he thought 'England and Germany', the word 'England' seemed to flash like a line of foam. With a sudden tightening of his heart, he realized that there might be a raid on the English coast. He didn't imagine any possibility of it *succeeding*, but only of enemies and warfare on English soil. The idea sickened him. He was immensely surprised to perceive that the actual earth of England held for him a quality which he found in A –, and in a friend's honour, and scarcely anywhere else, a quality which, if he'd ever been sentimental enough to use the word, he'd have called 'holiness'. His astonishment grew as the full flood of 'England' swept him on from thought to thought. He felt the triumphant helplessness of a lover. Grey, uneven little fields, and small, ancient hedges rushed before him, wild flowers, elms and beeches, gentleness, sedate houses of red brick, proudly unassuming, a countryside of rambling hills and friendly copses. He seemed to be raised high, looking down on a landscape compounded of the western view from the Cotswolds, and the Weald, and the high land in Wiltshire, and the Midlands seen from the hills above Princes Risborough. And all this to the accompaniment of tunes heard long ago, an intolerable number of them being hymns. There was, in his mind, a confused multitude of faces, to most of which he could not put a name. At one moment he was on an Atlantic

liner, sick for home, making Plymouth at nightfall; and at
another, diving into a little rocky pool through which the Teign
flows, north of Bovey; and again, waking, stiff with dew, to see the
dawn come up over the Royston plain. And continually he
seemed to see the set of a mouth which he knew for his mother's,
and A – 's face, and, inexplicably, the face of an old man he had
once passed in a Warwickshire village. To his great disgust, the
most commonplace sentiments found utterance in him. At the
same time he was extraordinarily happy . . .

Brooke himself died on 23 April 1915 of blood poisoning whilst serving with the
Royal Naval Division on the Gallipoli expedition.

On 7 August, three days after the declaration of war, Lord Kitchener made a 'Call to
Arms', complete with a poster which finger-pointed: 'Your country needs YOU!' Tens
of thousands of joyous young – and not so young – British men, their faces flushed
with patriotism, volunteered for duty. Some 761,0000 of them enlisted over the next
eight weeks, many joining alongside friends in units which would become known as
Pals Battalions. Later, they would die together in the self-same Pals Battalions.

———— · · · ————

'I was outraged to read of the Germans' cynical violation of Belgian neutrality'
ROBERT GRAVES, NORMAN DEMUTH, FRANK RICHARDS

JOINING UP
AUGUST 1914

I had just finished with Charterhouse and gone up to Harlech,
when England declared war on Germany. A day or two later I
decided to enlist. In the first place, though the papers predicted
only a very short war – over by Christmas at the outside – I hoped
that it might last long enough to delay my going to Oxford in
October, which I dreaded. Nor did I work out the possibilities of
getting actively engaged in the fighting, expecting garrison
service at home, while the regular forces were away. In the second
place, I was outraged to read of the Germans' cynical violation of
Belgian neutrality. Though I discounted perhaps twenty per cent
of the atrocity details as wartime exaggeration, that was not, of
course, sufficient.

* * *

As well as being given white feathers, there was another method
of approach. You would see a girl come towards you with a
delightful smile all over her face and you would think to yourself,
'My word this is somebody who knows me.' When she got to about
five or six paces from you she would suddenly freeze up and walk
past you with a look of utter contempt and scorn as if she could
have spat. That was far more hurtful than a white feather – it
made you curl up completely and there was no replying because
she had walked on.

However, I was given a white feather when I was sixteen, just
after I had left school. I was looking in a shop window and
I suddenly felt somebody press something into my hand and I
found it was a woman giving me a white feather. I was so
astonished I did not know what to do about it. But I had been
trying to persuade the doctors and recruiting officers that I was
nineteen and I thought, well, this must give me some added
bounce because I must look the part, and so I went round to the
recruiting offices with renewed zeal.

* * *

On the fourth of August, 1914, I was at Blaina, Monmouthshire,
having a drink in the Castle Hotel with a few of my cronies, all old
soldiers and the majority of them reservists. One had took us
around South Africa; there wasn't a Boer left in South Africa by
the time he had finished his yarn. Next I took them around India
and Burmah, and there wasn't a Pathan or Dacoit left in the world
by the time I had finished mine. Now another was taking us
through North China in the Boxer Rising of 1900; and he had
already got hundreds of Chinks hanging on the gas brackets when
someone happened to come in with a piece of news. He said that
war had broken out with Germany and that the Sergeant of Police
was hanging a notice up by the post office, calling all reservists to
the Colours. This caused a bit of excitement and language, but it
was too late in the evening for any of us to proceed to our depots
so we kept on drinking and yarning until stop-tap. By that time we
were getting a little top-heavy . . .

Richards, a reservist with twelve years' service in the regular army, was the authentic
voice of the professional Tommy. Sanguine, unsentimental.

In Aldershot, while the country was engulfed in flag-waving hysteria, the regulars sang as they marched:

> Send out the Army and the Navy,
> Send out the rank and file.
> (Have a banana!)
> Send out the brave Territorials,
> They'll face the danger with a smile.
> (I don't think!)
> Send out the boys of the girls' brigade,
> They will keep old England free,
> Send out my mother, my sister and my brother,
> But for Gawd's sake don't send me!

But the army did send them. The 120,000-strong British Expeditionary Force was rushed into battle at Mons in Belgium, to meet six field-grey divisions of the German army. Sat in his palace, the Kaiser thought the puny BEF 'contemptible': his troops in the fields around Mons, however, were astonished at the rapid – and accurate – rifle-fire of the Tommy and his Lee-Enfield. (Some Tommies achieved in 'mad minute' training a rate of one round per two seconds with a high accuracy.) One Irishman fighting in the BEF at Mons recalled: 'For us the battle took the form of well-ordered rapid rifle-fire at close range . . . they [the Germans] crumpled up – mown down as quickly as I tell it – [this] gave us a great sense of power and pleasure. It was all so easy.'

The BEF of 1914 was perhaps the best-trained force ever put into the field by the British.

Even so, after blunting the German advance, the BEF was ordered to retreat alongside the French:

'All day long we marched'
CORPORAL BERNARD DENORE

WESTERN FRONT
THE RETREAT FROM MONS
23 AUGUST – 5 SEPTEMBER 1914

The retreat from Mons lasted until 5 September. During that time Corporal Bernard Denmore, 1st Royal Berkshire Regiment, marched 251 miles. The fatigue of the troops caused mass hallucinations, most famously the 'Angel of Mons'.

August 23rd

We had been marching since 2.30 a.m. and about 11.15 a.m. an order was passed down for 'A' Company (my company) to deploy to the right and dig in on the south bank of a railway cutting.

We deployed and started digging in, but as the soil was mostly chalk, we were able to make only shallow holes. While we were digging the German artillery opened fire. The range was perfect, about six shells at a time bursting in line directly over our heads. All of us except the company commander fell flat on our faces, frightened, and surprised; but after a while we got up, and looked over the rough parapet we had thrown up; and could not see much. One or two men had been wounded, and one was killed.

There was a town about one mile away on our left front, and a lot of movement was going on round about it; and there was a small village called Binche on our right, where there was a lot of heavy firing going on – rifle and artillery.

We saw the Germans attack on our left in great masses, but they were beaten back by the Coldstream Guards.

A squadron of German cavalry crossed our front about 800 yards distant, and we opened fire on them. We hit a few and the fact that we were doing something definite improved our *moral* immensely, and took away a lot of our nervousness.

The artillery fire from the Germans was very heavy, but was dropping behind us on a British battery. The company officer, who had stayed in the open all the time, had taken a couple of men to help get the wounded away from the battery behind us. He returned about 6.30 p.m., when the firing had died down a bit, and told us the battery had been blown to bits.

I was then sent with four men on outpost to a signal box at a level crossing, and found it was being used as a clearing station for wounded. After dark more wounded were brought in from of the 9th Battery R.F.A. (the battery that was cut up). One man was in a very bad way, and kept shrieking out for somebody to bring a razor and cut his throat, and two others died almost immediately.

I was going to move a bundle of hay when someone called out,

'Look out, chum. There's a bloke in there.' I saw a leg completely severed from its body, and suddenly felt very sick and tired.

The German rifle-fire started again and an artillery-man to whom I was talking was shot dead. I was sick then.

Nothing much happened during the night, except that one man spent the time kissing a string of rosary beads, and another swore practically the whole night.

August 25th

We started off about 5 a.m., still retiring, and so far we had had no food since Sunday the 23rd. All day long we marched, and although a lot of firing was going on, we did none of it. About 6.30 p.m. we got to a place called Maroilles, and my platoon spent the night guarding a bridge over a stream. The Germans attacked about 9 p.m. and kept it up all night, but didn't get into Maroilles. About forty-five of the company were killed or wounded, including the company officer. A voice had called out in English, 'Has anybody got a map?' and when our C.O. stood up with his map, a German walked up, and shot him with a revolver. The German was killed by a bayonet stab from a private . . .

August 27th

. . . A lot of our men threw away their overcoats while we were on the road to-day, but I kept mine.

The marching was getting quite disorderly; numbers of men from other regiments were mixed up with us.

We reached St Quentin, a nice town, just before dark, but marched straight through, and dug ourselves in on some high ground, with a battery of artillery in line with us. Although we saw plenty of movement in the town the Germans didn't attack us, neither did we fire on them. During the night a man near me quite suddenly started squealing like a pig, and then jumped out of the trench, ran straight down the hill towards the town, and shot himself through the foot. He was brought in by some artillery-men . . .

August 31st

Again we were rearguard, but did little fighting. We marched instead, staggering about the road like a crowd of gipsies. Some of the fellows had puttees wrapped round their feet instead of boots; others had soft shoes they had picked up somewhere; others walked in their socks, with their feet all bleeding. My own boots would have disgraced a tramp, but I was too frightened to take them off, and look at my feet. Yet they marched until they dropped, and then somehow got up and marched again.

One man (Ginger Gilmore) found a mouth-organ, and, despite the fact that his feet were bound in blood-soaked rags, he staggered along at the head of the company playing tunes all day. Mostly he played 'The Irish Emigrant', which is a good marching tune. He reminded me of Captain Oates.

An officer asked me if I wanted a turn on his horse, but I looked at the fellow on it, and said, 'No thanks.'

The marching was getting on everyone's nerves, but, as I went I kept saying to myself, 'If you can, force your heart and nerve and sinew.' Just that, over and over again.

That night we spent the time looking for an Uhlan regiment, but didn't get in touch with them, and every time we stopped we fell asleep; in fact we slept while we were marching, and consequently kept falling over . . .

September 3rd

The first four or five hours we did without a single halt or rest, as we had to cross a bridge over the Aisne before the R.E.'s blew it up. It was the most terrible march I have ever done. Men were falling down like ninepins. They would fall flat on their faces on the road, while the rest of us staggered round them, as we couldn't lift our feet high enough to step over them, and, as for picking them up, that was impossible, as to bend meant to fall. What happened to them, God only knows. An aeroplane was following us most of the time dropping iron darts; we fired at it a couple of times, but soon lost the strength required for that. About 9 a.m. we halted by a river, and immediately two fellows threw themselves into it. Nobody, from sheer fatigue, was able to save them, although one sergeant made an attempt, and was nearly drowned himself. I, like a fool, took my boots off, and found my feet were covered with blood. I could find no sores or cuts, so I thought I must have sweated blood.

As I couldn't get my boots on again I cut the sides away, and when we started marching again, my feet hurt like hell.

We marched till about 3 p.m. – nothing else, just march, march, march. I kept repeating my line, 'If you can, force, etc.' Why, I didn't know. A sergeant irritated everyone who could hear him by continually shouting out: 'Stick it, lads. We're making history.'

The Colonel offered me a ride on his horse, but I refused, and then wished I hadn't, as anything was preferable to the continuous marching.

We got right back that afternoon among the refugees again. They were even worse off than we were, or, at least, they looked it. We gave the kids our biscuits and 'bully', hoping that would help them a little; but they looked so dazed and tired there did not seem to be much hope for them.

At 8 p.m. we bivouacked in a field and slept till dawn. Ye gods! what a relief.

The retreat stopped at the Marne, when the BEF did an about turn, and halted the German juggernaut. 'We have lost the war. It will go on for a long time but it is already lost', noted the Kaiser. He was right.

As if in proof, even the massive German offensive at Ypres, Belgium, between 20 October and 24 November, floundered on the thin khaki line of the BEF – which was getting thinner every day through death and wounds.

'I looked down and discovered that my right foot was missing'
SERGEANT J.F. BELL

SERGEANT BELL
LOSES HIS FOOT
YPRES, 29 OCTOBER 1914

Bell served with the 2nd Gordon Highlanders.

I passed a message to Lieutenant Brook, informing him our numbers were so reduced that if attacked we could not hold the trench, and received back word that he had just been killed. (The V.C. was posthumously awarded him.) A message was then sent to me to retire and join a platoon entrenched near us. I gave instructions to the few men (eight I think) to retire along the communication trench, and I would join them at the head of it, and lead them to our new position. I slipped over the rear of the trench, to cut across and meet the lads as they emerged from the communication trench, but had only gone about six yards when I received what in the regiment was called the 'dull thud'. I thought I had been violently knocked on the head, but, feeling I was not running properly, I looked down and discovered that my right foot was missing. Somehow, I stood watching men running along the communication trench. My power of speech had left me, so I could speak to none of them, then I swooned into the trench. No one had seen me being wounded, but one of the men, 'Pipe' Adams, on missing me, returned to look for me.

On seeing me lying quite helpless, he prepared to lift and carry me out of the trench. I told him I was too heavy, that it was too dangerous, and that in time our regiment would retake all the ground lost, when I would be safe. When I think of the War comradeship, of unaffected and unknown bravery, I think of 'Pipe' Adams (killed later) telling me, 'Christ, Jerry [my nickname], I could not leave you here.' However, confident that our people would return, I persuaded him to go. I then put a field dressing and a shirt from my pack over my stump and lay down to wait further developments. In this trench there would be about sixty badly wounded British soldiers (mostly Gordons) of all ranks. The soldier nearest me was a sergeant of the Grenadiers who was severely wounded in both arms and both legs. I noticed a watch quite close to me; on looking at it I found the time was 9 a.m.

I must have dropped into a kind of stupor, and I woke suddenly with the noise of great shouting. I thought it was our fellows returned to their old position, imagined I heard voices I knew, also that of my company officer, Captain Burnett, shouting, 'Where are you, Sergeant Bell?' I tried to rise, failed, but kept shouting, 'Here I am, in this trench, sir.' Judge my surprise when two German infantrymen jumped into the trench. One of them got quite excited, raised his rifle, levelled at and within a yard of me, but the other knocked his mate's rifle up and asked me when and where I was wounded. I asked them to try and do something for the wounded Grenadier, but they seemed in great haste as they jumped out of the trench. It was then twelve noon . . .

The Germans had taken a lot of ground, were busily consolidating their new position, and all morning (the 30th) groups of them and individuals kept looking into the trench.

Two German officers slowly and quietly walked along the trench, and when they saw me still alive they appeared greatly surprised. Each of them spoke to me in English, enquiring how long I had been lying there. They informed me that there were fifty-seven of my comrades dead in the trench, and that I was one of three still alive. One of them promised to send someone to pick me up, but I had doubts about him doing so. However, about an hour later, four German private soldiers arrived, bringing a waterproof sheet to carry me off. They gave me a drink of cold coffee, and when I pointed out the Grenadier, one of them went back into the trench and gave the Grenadier a drink and made him comfortable before rejoining us. One of the Germans could speak English, and in his deep-spoken voice said, 'Ah! Scotlander, you lucky man. Get out of this damned war. It last long time. What we fight for? Ah! German Army and English Navy, both damned nuisance.' They carried me with great care to a barn about half a mile away that was being used as a dressing station. All the way from the trench to the barn I saw British dead, mostly Highlanders – Black Watch, Camerons, and Gordons – and as they lay there in their uniforms, I thought how young and lonely they looked.

After Ypres, the fighting on the Western Front settled into stalemate, as the combatant sides dug defensive entrenchments, which soon stretched from the Channel to Switzerland as each tried to outflank the other.

Trench warfare had arrived. In the ensuing four years the combatants would hurl shells and bullets by the million across the wire-strewn yards of No Man's Land which divided them, the numerical inferiority of the Kaiser's army offset by the simple fact that it held the higher ground.

⸺◈⸺

'*It is* the *best fun*'
CAPTAIN THE HON JULIAN GRENFELL

A HAPPY WARRIOR
FLANDERS
3 NOVEMBER 1914

Who is the happy Warrior? Who is he
That every Man in arms should wish to be.
William Wordsworth, *Character of the Happy Warrior*, 1806

Grenfell, 1st Royal Dragoons, soldier and poet, writes to his parents:

Flanders
November 3rd, 1914

. . . I have not washed for a week, or had my boots off for a fortnight . . . It is all *the* best fun. I have never felt so well, or so happy, or enjoyed anything so much. It just suits my stolid health, and stolid nerves, and barbaric disposition. The fighting-excitement vitalizes everything, every sight and word and action. One loves one's fellow man so much more when one is bent on killing him. And picnicing in the open day and night (we never see a roof now) is the real method of existence.

There are loads of straw to bed-down on, and one sleeps like a log, and wakes up with the dew on one's face . . . The Germans shell the trenches with shrapnel all day and all night: and the Reserves and ground in the rear with Jack Johnsons, which at last one gets to love as old friends. You hear them coming for miles, and everyone imitates the noise; then they burst with a plump, and make a great hole in the ground, doing no damage unless they happen to fall into your trench or on to your hat. They burst pretty nearly straight upwards. One landed within ten yards of me the other day, and only knocked me over and my horse. We both got up and looked at each other and laughed . . .

We took a German Officer and some men prisoners in a wood the other day. One felt hatred for them as one thought of our dead; and as the officer came by me, I scowled at him, and the men were cursing him. The officer looked me in the face and saluted me as he passed; and I have never seen a man look so proud and resolute and smart and confident, in his hour of bitterness. It made me feel terribly ashamed of myself . . .

Grenfell died of wounds on 27 May 1915, at the age of 27. The letters below are from his brother, Lieutenant The Hon Gerald Grenfell, to their mother:

France
May 25th, 1915

DARLING, – Just one word of blessing and good hope. I know how strong you have been and will be. How can we feel anything but serenity about our darling Julian, whether the trumpets sound for him on this side or the other.

Your B.

Flanders
June 1st, 1915

DARLING, – The more I think of darling Julian, the more I seem to realise the nothingness of death. He has just passed on, outsoared the shadow of our night, 'here where men sit and hear each other groan,' and how could one pass on better than in the full tide of strength and glory and fearlessness. So that there is no interruption even in the work which God has for him. Our grief for him can only be grief for ourselves.

Very, very best love, from BILLY.

Gerald Grenfell was killed in action on 30 July 1915, aged 25.

'Our dugouts have caved in'
PRIVATE EDWARD ROE

TRENCH LIFE
MUD AND LICE
BELGIUM, 20 NOVEMBER 1914

Roe, an Irishman, enlisted in the East Lancashire Regiment in 1909. His battalion arrived at Ploegsteert Wood ('Plugstreet' as it was soon rechristened by the Tommies) in October 1914:

On 20 November the weather broke in earnest; it did not stop raining for a month. The first week's rain turned our trenches into canals. Bale out all day and all night was the order. We are provided with scoops. They are large ladles and are fitted onto a wooden handle about six feet in length. Holes are dug at irregular intervals in the trench. The water drains into those. You set to work with your scoop and empty the water over the parapet. It percolates through the earth in time and finds its way back into the holes in the trench floor; those holes are called sump holes. The object of a six-foot handle is to enable you to throw the water over the parapet without running the risk of getting shot through the hand or arm. I have seen men deliberately hold their hands over the trench parapet, when baling out, with the object of getting wounded. Of course their heads were kept well down. Quite a number get wounded in this manner.

Our dugouts have caved in. You lie down in the water for a couple of hours at night. You must fold yourself up as neatly as possible; if you stretch your legs out they get trodden upon by all who pass up and down the trench. Drip, drip, drip on your ground sheet, that damned rain, will it ever cease? Every ten minutes you have to scratch various parts of your body with dirty clay stained hands. The infernal lice are marching all over your body by platoons.

I felt an infinitive longing to be out of it, out of this useless slaughter, misery and tragedy. I feel that way that I would sign peace on almost any terms.

Parties of men are engaged day and night, filling sand bags in order to repair the parapets and trench walls which are constantly falling in owing to continuous rain and undermined by too many dug outs. The 'Jerries' over the way are just as bad, if not worse, as they are nearer to the River Lys than we are. A good many men are losing their lives through sheer carelessness. Before they will use the communication trenches, which are halfull of water, they dash over the top in the open. They invariably get killed or wounded. If you use a communication trench you are liable to get drowned; if you don't use it you may get shot, so you have to choose between the two.

The mud never went away. Nor did the *podiculus vestimenti*, the body louse. A lighted cigarette or a heated bayonet was used to burn them from the seams of clothes. On arrival at the front Private Henry Gregory, 19th Machine Gun Company, found men 'killing them [the lice] between their nails'. When Gregory expressed astonishment, he was informed 'You'll soon be as lousy as we are.' And he was. 'Each day brought a new batch; as fast as you killed them, others took their place'.

'the most extraordinary Christmas in the trenches you could possibly imagine'
CAPTAIN SIR EDWARD WESTROW HULSE

WESTERN FRONT
THE CHRISTMAS TRUCE
1914

28/12/14

My Dearest Mother, Just returned to billets again, after the most extraordinary Christmas in the trenches you could possibly imagine. Words fail me completely in trying to describe it, but here goes!

On the 23rd we took over the trenches in the ordinary manner, relieving the Grenadiers, and during the 24th the usual firing took place, and sniping was pretty brisk. We stood to arms as usual at 6.30 a.m. on the 25th, and I noticed that there was not much shooting; this gradually died down, and by 8 a.m. there was no shooting at all, except for a few shots on our left (Border Regt.). At 8.30 a.m. I was looking out, and saw four Germans leave their trenches and come towards us; I told two of my men to go and meet them, unarmed (as the Germans were unarmed), and to see that they did not pass the half-way line. We were 350–400 yards apart, at this point. My fellows were not very keen, not knowing what was up, so I went out alone, and met Barry, one of our ensigns, also coming out from another part of the line. By the time we got to them, they were ¾ of the way over, and much too near our barbed wire, so I moved them back. They were three private soldiers and a stretcher-bearer, and their spokesman started off by saying that he thought it only right to come over and wish us a happy Christmas, and trusted us implicitly to keep the truce. He came from Suffolk where he had left his best girl and a 3½ h.p. motor-bike! He told me that he could not get a letter to the girl, and wanted to send one through me. I made him write out a postcard in front of me, in English, and I sent it off that night. I told him that she probably would not be a bit keen to see him again. We then entered on a long discussion on every sort of thing. I was dressed in an old stocking-cap and a man's overcoat, and they took me for a corporal, a thing which I did not discourage, as I had an eye to going as near their lines as possible . . . I asked them what orders they had from their officers as to coming over to us, and they said *none*; they had just come over out of goodwill.

They protested that they had no feeling of enmity towards us at all, but that everything lay with their authorities, and that being soldiers they had to obey. I believe that they were speaking the truth when they said this, and that they never wished to fire a shot again. They said that unless directly ordered, they were not going to shoot again until we did . . . We talked about the ghastly wounds made by rifle bullets, and we both agreed that neither of us used dum-dum bullets, and that the wounds are solely inflicted by the high-velocity bullet with the sharp nose, at short range. We both agreed that it would be far better if we used the old South African round-nosed bullet, which makes a clean hole . . .

They think that our Press is to blame in working up feeling against them by publishing false 'atrocity reports'. I told them of various sweet little cases which I have seen for myself, and they told me of English prisoners whom they have seen with soft-nosed bullets, and lead bullets with notches cut in the nose; we had a heated, and at the same time, good-natured argument, and ended by hinting to each other that the other was lying!

I kept it up for half an hour, and then escorted them back as far as their barbed wire, having a jolly good look round all the time, and picking up various little bits of information which I had not had an opportunity of doing under fire! I left instructions with them that if any of them came out later they must not come over the halfway line, and appointed a ditch as the meeting place. We parted after an exchange of Albany cigarettes and German cigars, and I went straight to H.-qrs. to report.

On my return at 10 a.m. I was surprised to hear a hell of a din going on, and not a single man left in my trenches; they were completely denuded (against my orders), and nothing lived! I heard strains of 'Tipperary' floating down the breeze, swiftly followed by a tremendous burst of 'Deutschland über Alles', and as I got to my own Coy. H.-qrs. dug-out, I saw, to my amazement, not only a crowd of about 150 British and Germans at the half-way house which I had appointed opposite my lines, but six or seven such crowds, all the way down our lines, extending towards the 8th Division on our right. I bustled out and asked if there were any German officers in my crowd, and the noise died down (as this time I was myself in my own cap and badges of rank).

I found two, but had to talk to them through an interpreter, as they could neither talk English nor French ... I explained to them that strict orders must be maintained as to meeting half-way, and everyone unarmed; and we both agreed not to fire until the other did, thereby creating a complete deadlock and armistice (if strictly observed) ...

Meanwhile Scots and Huns were fraternizing in the most genuine possible manner. Every sort of souvenir was exchanged, addresses given and received, photos of families shown, etc. One of our fellows offered a German a cigarette; the German said, 'Virginian?' Our fellow said, 'Aye, straight-cut', the German said, 'No thanks, I only smoke Turkish!' (Sort of 10s. a 100 me!) It gave us all a good laugh. A German N.C.O. with the Iron Cross, gained, he told me, for conspicuous skill in sniping – started his fellows off on some marching tune. When they had done I set the note for '*The Boys of Bonnie Scotland, where the heather and the bluebells grow*', and so we went on singing everything from '*Good King Wenceslaus*' down to the ordinary Tommies' song, and ended up with '*Auld Lang Syne*', which we all, English, Scots, Irish, Prussian, Wurtembergers, etc., joined in. It was absolutely astounding, and if I had seen it on a cinematograph film I should have sworn that it was faked! . . .

From foul rain and wet, the weather had cleared up the night before to a sharp frost, and it was a perfect day, everything white, and the silence seemed extra-ordinary, after the usual din. From all sides birds seemed to arrive, and we hardly ever see a bird generally. Later in the day I fed about 50 sparrows outside my dug-out, which shows how complete the silence and quiet was.

I must say that I was very much impressed with the whole scene, and also, as everyone else, astoundingly relieved by the quiet, and by being able to walk about freely. It is the first time, day or night, that we have heard no guns, or rifle-firing, since I left Havre and convalescence! Just after we had finished '*Auld Lang Syne*' an old hare started up, and seeing so many of us about in an unwonted spot, did not know which way to go. I gave one loud 'View Holloa', and one and all, British and Germans, rushed about giving chase, slipping up on the frozen plough, falling about, and after a hot two minutes we killed in the open, a German and one of our fellows falling together heavily upon the completely baffled hare. Shortly afterwards we saw four more hares, and killed one again; both were good heavy weight and had evidently been out between the two rows of trenches for the last two months, well-fed on the cabbage patches, etc., many of which are untouched on the 'no-man's land.' The enemy kept one and we kept the other. It was now 11.30 a.m. and at this moment George Paynter arrived on the scene, with a hearty 'Well, my lads, a Merry Christmas to you! This is d–d comic, isn't it?' . . . George told them that he thought it only right that we should show that we could desist from hostilities on a day which was so important in both countries; and he then said, 'Well, my boys, I've brought you over something to celebrate this funny show with,' and he produced from his pocket a large bottle of rum (not ration rum, but the proper stuff). One large shout went up, and the nasty little spokesman uncorked it, and in a heavy unceremonious manner, drank our healths, in the name of his 'camaraden', the bottle was then passed on and polished off before you could say knife . . .

During the afternoon the same extraordinary scene was enacted between the lines, and one of the enemy told me that he was longing to get back to London: I assured him that 'So was I'. He said that he was sick of the war, and I told him that when the truce was ended, any of his friends would be welcome in our trenches, and would be well-received, fed, and given a free passage to the Isle of Man! Another coursing meeting took place, with no result, and at 4.30 p.m. we agreed to keep in our respective trenches, and told them that the truce was ended. They persisted, however, in saying that they were not going to fire, and as George had told us not to, unless they did, we prepared for a quiet night, but warned all sentries to be doubly on the alert.

During the day both sides had taken the opportunity of bringing up piles of wood, straw, etc., which is generally only brought up with difficulty under fire. We improved our dugouts, roofed in new ones, and got a lot of very useful work done towards increasing our comfort. Directly it was dark, I got the whole of my Coy, on to improving and re-making our barbed-wire entanglements, all along my front, and had my scouts out in front of the working parties, to prevent any surprise; but not a shot was fired, and we finished off a real good obstacle unmolested.

On my left was the bit of ground over which we attacked on the 18th, and here the lines are only from 85 to 100 yards apart.

The Border Regiment were occupying this section on Christmas Day, and Giles Loder, our Adjutant, went down there with a party that morning on hearing of the friendly demonstrations in front of my Coy., to see if he could come to an agreement about our dead, who were still lying out between the trenches. The trenches are so close at this point, that of course each side had to be far stricter. Well, he found an extremely pleasant and superior stamp of German officer, who arranged to bring all our dead to the half-way line. We took them over there, and buried 29 exactly half-way between the two lines. Giles collected all personal effects, pay-books and identity discs, but was stopped by the Germans when he told some men to bring in the rifles; all rifles lying on their side of the half-way line they kept carefully!

They apparently treated our prisoners well, and did all they could for our wounded. This officer kept on pointing to our dead and saying, '*Les Braves, c'est bien dommage.*' . . .

When George heard of it he went down to that section and talked to the nice officer and gave him a scarf. That same evening a German orderly came to the half-way line, and brought a pair of warm woolly gloves as a present in return for George.

The same night the Borderers and we were engaged in putting up big trestle obstacles, with barbed wire all over them, and connecting them, and at this same point (namely, where we were only 85 yards apart) the Germans came out and sat on their parapet, and watched us doing it, although we had informed them that the truce was ended . . . Well, all was quiet, as I said, that night; and next morning, while I was having breakfast, one of my N.C.O's came and reported that the enemy were again coming over to talk. I had given full instructions and none of my men were allowed out of the trenches to talk to the enemy. I had also told the N.C.O. of an advanced post which I have up a ditch, to go out with two men, *unarmed*; if any of the enemy came over, to see that they did not cross the half-way line, and to engage them in pleasant conversation. So I went out, and found the same lot as the day before; they told me again that they had no intention of firing, and wished the truce to continue. I had instructions not to fire till the enemy did; I told them; and so the same comic form of temporary truce continued on the 26th, and again at 4.30 p.m. I informed them that the truce was at an end. We had sent them over some plum-puddings, and they thanked us heartily for them and retired again, the only difference being that instead of all my men being out in the 'no-man's zone', one N.C.O. and two men only were allowed out, and the enemy therefore sent fewer.

Again both sides had been improving their comfort during the day, and again at night I continued on my barbed wire and finished it right off. We retired for the night all quiet and were rudely awakened at 11 p.m. A H.-qr. orderly burst into my dug-out, and handed me a message. It stated that a deserter had come into the 8th Division lines, and stated that the whole German line was going to attack at 12.15 midnight, and that we were to stand to arms immediately, and that reinforcements were being hurried up from billets in rear. I thought, at the time, that it was a d–d good joke on the part of the German deserter to deprive us of our sleep, and so it turned out to be. I stood my Coy, to arms, made a few extra dispositions, gave out all instructions, and at 11.20 p.m. George arrived . . . Suddenly *our* guns all along the line opened a heavy fire, and all the enemy did was to reply with 9 shell (heavy howitzers), *not one of which exploded,* just on my left. Never a rifle shot was fired by either side (except right away down in the 8th Division), and at 2.30 a.m. we turned in half the men to sleep, and kept half awake on sentry.

Apparently this deserter had also reported that strong German reinforcements had been brought up, and named a place just in rear of their lines, where, he said, two regiments were in billets, that had just been brought up. Our guns were informed, and plastered the place well when they opened fire (as I mentioned). The long and the short of it was that absolutely *nixt* happened, and after a sleepless night I turned in at 4.30 a.m., and was woken again at 6.30, when we always stand to arms before daylight. I was just going to have another sleep at 8 a.m. when I found that the enemy were again coming over to talk to us (Dec. 27th). I watched my N.C.O. and two men go out from the advanced post to meet, and hearing shouts of laughter from the little party when they met, I again went out myself.

They asked me what we were up to during the night, and told me that they had stood to arms all night and thought we were going to attack them when they heard our heavy shelling; also that our guns had done a lot of damage and knocked out a lot of their men in billets. I told them a deserter of theirs had come over to us, and that they had only him to thank for any damage done, and that we, after a sleepless night, were not best pleased with him either! They assured me that they had heard nothing of an attack, and I fully believed them, as it is inconceivable that they would have allowed us to put up the formidable obstacles (which we had on the two previous nights) if they had contemplated an offensive movement.

Anyhow, if it had ever existed, the plan had miscarried, as no attack was developed on any part of our line, and here were these fellows still protesting that there was a truce, although I told them that it had ceased the evening before. So I kept the same arrangement, namely, that my N.C.O. and two men should meet them half-way, and strict orders were given that no other man was to leave the lines ... I admit that the whole thing beat me absolutely. In the evening we were relieved by the Grenadiers, quite openly (not crawling about on all fours, as usual), and we handed on our instructions to the Grenadiers in case the enemy still wished to pay visits! . . .

The respective high commands banned further Yuletide fraternizations. Some local ones did break out, nonetheless.

Captain Hulse, Scots Guards, was killed in action in March 1915.

By the end of 1914, back in 'Blighty', 1,186,337 men had enlisted for Kitchener's volunteer 'New Army'. It would not be enough; the death-roll of mass, industrial warfare was beyond the expectation of almost everybody, save Kitchener himself. The British alone lost 89,000 officers and men in the battles of 1914. The old regular army was all but wiped out. Troops sang:

> If you want the old battalion,
> I know where they are, I know where they are,
> If you want the old battalion,
> I know where they are,
> They're hanging on the old barbed wire.
> I've seen 'em, I've seen 'em,
> Hanging on the old barbed wire . . .

———⟶◆⟵———

'The boys were certainly relaxing!'
LANCE-CORPORAL GEORGE ASHURST

TROOPS ON FURLOUGH
SUEZ, JANUARY 1915

With deadlock on the Western Front, the British planned a diversionary attack on Turkey, at Gallipoli. Ashurst, Lancashire Fusiliers, was among those sent on furlough prior to the Gallipoli landings. 'Fattening before the kill', the troops called it.

The town itself was full of Tommies. I think the whole of my battalion was in Suez that night, and of course the Aussies were splashing their money about. The hotels and the gardens in front, and the restaurants, were chock-full of dining and wining Tommies. Others were staggering about the streets, shouting and singing. The boys were certainly relaxing! Every kind of wine and liquor could be bought by the bottle, and the native shops did a roaring trade in silks and brooches, which the boys bought to send home as souvenirs to mothers, wives and sweethearts. There was a picture palace there too, owned by a Frenchman who, during our stay in Suez, arranged concerts and boxing and wrestling matches in his hall for the pleasure of the troops.

The natives did not seem to like the intrusion into their town and sat smoking their hookahs and scowling at us as we passed by. They certainly had no love for us and were not to be trusted. One or two of our boys who visited the town never returned to camp and were never seen again. These dirty, scowling fellows were certainly responsible for their disappearance. Our command must have thought so too, for they issued the order that every man going to town must wear belt and bayonet. During the boys' drinking orgies many of these natives were left bleeding and unconscious for their unfriendly attitude. Often drinking houses were turned into a shambles, arguments arose, tempers flared up, tables were overturned and bottles began to fly through the air alongside whirling belts, while drunken men lurched into the street, cursing and bleeding.

One evening as I sat with a chum having a drink in one of these 'pubs' and listening to a native who, standing on an empty cask, was doing his best to entertain us with a song, half a dozen drink-sodden Aussies lurched into the place. One of them, glaring at the native, bawled out, 'Shut that hole, you dirty nigger', and, drawing a revolver from his belt, shot at the unfortunate black. The poor fellow dropped from the cask bleeding at the shoulder. The proprietor ran to him to help, uttering curses in his native tongue; immediately an English Tommy remonstrated with the Aussie. Then the fun started. The place was very soon in darkness and I and my chum made a mad dive for the door. As we reached the safety of the street we could hear the crash of chairs and tables and the smashing of glasses and bottles mingled with the curses and oaths of drunken, fighting men . . .

After getting a skinful of drink the boys usually made their way back to camp via the railway sidings on one side of the town. Here by these railway sidings was the black spot of Suez, a bunch of houses the boys called the 'Rag'. Here lived the 'Bohemian ladies' of Suez. Girls of all nationalities lived here, their names and country printed on boards above the door. Dressed in their prettiest and flimsiest dresses they waited for Tommy. Black girls were there also, smiling and showing their pearly white teeth: these girls, of course, were the favourites of the Indian troops. Brown-skinned Arab girls, smothered in cheap rings, bracelets and beads, were also there, sitting, sipping coffee and smoking cigarettes. The houses were furnished only with a chair or two, a table, and a bed, the walls being adorned with an indecent picture or two.

The scenes at the 'Rag' in the evenings were almost unbelievable. Drunken Tommies danced with almost naked girls, no curtains or blinds were drawn to the windows, and every action of these soulless women and their drunken companions could be plainly seen. And so the immoral life went on and the half-crowns of Tommy kept accumulating in the locked iron box beside the bed, until the military police, promptly on the stroke of nine, cleared the whole place, Tommy returning to camp and the female vultures to count their ill-gotten money.

Returning to camp by the legitimate route was always very amusing. One could ride back to camp on a donkey's back for sixpence, and it was great fun to see the boys, absolutely too drunk to walk back to camp, being carried on the old donkey's back, first sliding off one side, and then the other, the old native who owned the donkey doing his best to keep Tommy mounted, and very often getting cursed for his trouble. Then on arrival at the camp no fare would be forthcoming until he had dug up some officer to help him get his sixpence.

Lance-Corporal George Ashurst was an honest recorder of his battalion's after-duty habits. On transfer to the Western Front, he and his colleagues were habitués of estaminets in Armentières where:

Drink flowed freely . . . and as the music and singing went on the boys danced with mademoiselles in the flimsiest of dresses, or flirted with them at the tables, using the most vulgar of expressions. All the evening Tommies could be seen either going to or coming from the girls' rooms upstairs, queues actually forming on the stairs leading to the rooms.

To no great surprise VD became rampant; the army recorded 416,891 hospital admissions for VD during the period 1914–18.

<hr>

'I'd never seen a dead man before . . .'
PRIVATE LEONARD THOMPSON

A SUFFOLK FARMBOY
AT GALLIPOLI
TURKEY, JUNE 1915

British and Allied troops began landing at Gallipoli, at the entrance to the Dardanelles, on 25 April 1915. The invasion ran into trouble at the outset. Major Shaw, 29th Division, recalled:

About 100 yards from the beach the enemy opened fire, and bullets came thick all around . . . As soon as I felt the boat touch, I dashed over the side into three feet of water and rushed for the barbed wire entanglements on the beach; it must have been only three feet high or so, because I got over it amidst a perfect storm of lead . . . I then found Maunsell and only two men had followed me . . . I looked back. There was one soldier between me and the wire, and a whole line in a row on the edge of the sands. The sea behind was absolutely crimson . . . I then perceived they were all hit.

Although the British and Anzacs (Australian and New Zealand Army Corps) established a bridgehead on the rocky, sun-beaten peninsula, Turko-German defences were too strong to allow an advance inland. Ironically, the Gallipoli campaign, intended to break the stalemate on the Western Front, itself fell into trench warfare. And, as with the Western Front, sniping in Gallipoli was a major hazard. 'Spent a rotten night of it', recorded Private Horace Bruckshaw, Royal Marine Light Infantry, in his diary on 9 May. 'This place is simply infested with snipers'.

Things only went from worse to worse in Gallipoli. Leonard Thompson, a former ploughboy, remembers the peninsula in June 1915:

We arrived at the Dardanelles and saw the guns flashing and heard the rifle fire. They heaved our ship, the *River Clyde*, right up to the shore. They had cut a hole in it and made a little pier, so we were able to walk straight off and on to the beach. We all sat there – on the Hellespont! – waiting for it to get light. The first things we saw were big wrecked Turkish guns, the second a big marquee. It didn't make me think of the military but of the village fêtes. Other people must have thought like this because I remember how we all rushed up to it, like boys getting into a circus, and then found it all laced up. We unlaced it and rushed in. It was full of corpses. Dead Englishmen, lines and lines of them, and with their eyes wide open. We all stopped talking. I'd never seen a dead man before and here I was looking at two or three hundred of them. It was our first fear. Nobody had mentioned this. I was very shocked. I thought of Suffolk and it seemed a happy place for the first time.

Later that day we marched through open country and came to within a mile and half of the front line. It was incredible. We were there – at the war! The place we had reached was called 'dead ground' because it was where the enemy couldn't see you. We lay in little square holes, myself next to James Sears from the village. He was about thirty and married. That evening we wandered about on the dead ground and asked about friends of ours who had arrived a month or so ago. 'How is Ernie Taylor?' – 'Ernie? – he's gone.' 'Have you seen Albert Paternoster?' – 'Albert? – he's gone.' We learned that if 300 had 'gone' but 700 were left, then this wasn't too bad. We then knew how unimportant our names were.

I was on sentry that night. A chap named Scott told me that I must only put my head up for a second but that in this time I must see as much as I could. Every third man along the trench was a sentry. The next night we had to move on to the third line of trenches and we heard that the Gurkhas were going over and that we had to support their rear. But when we got to the communication trench we found it so full of dead men that we could hardly move. Their faces were quite black and you couldn't tell Turk from English. There was the most terrible stink and for a while there was nothing but the living being sick on to the dead. I did sentry again that night. It was one – two – sentry, one – two

– sentry all along the trench, as before. I knew the next sentry up quite well. I remembered him in Suffolk singing to his horses as he ploughed. Now he fell back with a great scream and a look of surprise – dead. It is quick, anyway, I thought. On June 4th we went over the top. We took the Turks' trench and held it. It was called Hill 13. The next day we were relieved and told to rest for three hours, but it wasn't more than half an hour before the relieving regiment came running back. The Turks had returned and recaptured their trench. On June 6th my favourite officer was killed and no end of us butchered, but we managed to get hold of Hill 13 again. We found a great muddle, carnage and men without rifles shouting '*Allah! Allah!*', which is God's name in the Turkish language. Of the sixty men I had started out to war from Harwich with, there were only three left.

We set to work to bury people. We pushed them into the sides of the trench but bits of them kept getting uncovered and sticking out, like people in a badly made bed. Hands were the worst; they would escape from the sand, pointing, begging – even waving! There was one which we all shook when we passed, saying, 'Good morning', in a posh voice. Everybody did it. The bottom of the trench was springy like a mattress because of all the bodies underneath. At night, when the stench was worse, we tied crêpe round our mouths and noses. This crêpe had been given to us because it was supposed to prevent us being gassed. The flies entered the trenches at night and lined them completely with a density which was like moving cloth. We killed millions by slapping our spades along the trench walls but the next night it would be just as bad. We were all lousy and we couldn't stop shitting because we had caught dysentery. We wept, not because we were frightened but because we were so dirty.

'Always you are both in my thoughts . . .'
SERGEANT B.J. FIELDER

LOVE LETTER HOME TO A WIFE

ALEXANDRIA, 21 JULY 1915

RND Base, Alexandria, Egypt
21 July 1915

. . . I think I may be able to keep here a few weeks yet, anyhow I've got hopes of staying until the Dardanelles job [Gallipoli landings] is over . . . You ask me when the war is going to be over. Well, I will just tell you, only keep it secret. *In October.* You say we don't seem to be getting on very well out here; My Word if you only knew what a job we've got before us, just try to imagine a hill called Achi Baba, just fancy yourself at the bottom of a big hill with trenches and trenches piled on top of one another, made of concrete with thousands of Turks and machine-guns, five of these trenches we took one morning one after the other, but before we got to the first trench we left a good many of our chums behind, but it's no good stopping and the faster you can run the better chance you have of getting through the rain of bullets, and our boys went mad.

I have thought just lately what a lot of savages war turns us into, we see the most horrible sights of bloodshed and simply laugh at it. It seems to be nothing but blood, blood everywhere you go and on everything you touch, and you are walking amongst dead bodies all day and all night, human life seems to be of no value at all – you are joking with a chap one minute and the next minute you go to the back of the trench to do a job for yourself and then you see a little mound of earth with a little rough wooden cross on it with the name of the man you had been joking with a short time before. My dear Scrumps, I don't know whether I'm right in telling you this, because you worry so but I would not mention it only for the reason that I don't think I shall have any more of it, but I certainly *do* thank the One Above and you for your prayers at night together with our Boy for keeping me safe throughout it all.

Always you are both in my thoughts, I think of you both in that little kitchen by yourselves and know that you are thinking of me and wondering perhaps if you will ever see me come back again, every night at nine o'clock out here which is seven o'clock in England, I think that it is the Boy's bedtime and I always can picture him kneeling in his cot saying his prayers after Mummy. But 'Cheer up', my Scrumps, this will all end soon and we shall be together again and carry on the old life once more.

My dear Scrumps, I wonder if the Boy still thinks of the gun I promised to bring him home, I got hold of two Turks' guns to bring home and after keeping them for about two weeks, I got wounded and then of course I lost them as I did everything else. I might also say that the Deal Battalion have all lost their bags again, they were coming from the ship in a barge and a Turk shell hit the barge, so they sank to the bottom of the Dardanelles. The Naval Division is pretty well cut up, especially the Marines, they can only make 3 btns out of 4 even after the last lot came out from England. I think there is some move on to withdraw the Marines and Naval Division from the Dardanelles also the other troops which were in the first part of the fighting as they are in a bad state and I expect we'll get a quiet job as garrison for some place. I expect by this time you have got General Hamilton's report of the fighting here, my dear Scrumps I think I will wind up now as I've just looked at the watch and its a quarter to eleven. I've been writing ever since nine o'clock, so Night Night and God Bless you . . .

After sustaining 180,000 casualties the Allied expeditionary force was evacuated from Anzac and Sulva beaches at Gallipoli on 18–19 December 1915. It was a masterly withdrawal of 84,000 men (plus assorted animals and guns), done with only a handful of casualties, right under the Turkish and German noses. The military correspondent of the *Vossische Zeitung* wrote in admiration: 'As long as wars last this evacuation of Sulva and Anzac will stand before the eyes of all strategists as a hitherto unattained masterpiece . . .'

Sergeant Fielder, Royal Marines Light Infantry, survived the Gallipoli campaign only to be killed in action on 29 October 1916 on the Western Front.

'Cuinchy bred rats. They . . . fed on the plentiful corpses'.
SECOND-LIEUTENANT ROBERT GRAVES

RATS, SUICIDES, PATROLS AND FACTORING RISK
THE SUBALTERN'S WAR, LAVENTIE SECTOR, WESTERN FRONT
JULY 1915

By mid 1915 the men of the 'New Army', the volunteers who had answered Kitchener's call, were arriving on the battlefield. Among them was Second Lieutenant Robert Graves, who served with both the Welch Regiment and the Royal Welch Fusiliers.

Later, in the disillusioned 1920s, it became fashionable to dismiss the Great War's officer class as 'donkeys' leading 'lions' but most junior officers in the conflict led from the front. Courageously so. Even in the Royal Welch Fusiliers, one of the outstanding regiments of the British army in the Great War, it oftentimes took an officer's example to make the men stand or 'go over the top'.

Small wonder, then, that the life expectancy of a subaltern on the Western Front was six weeks before he was killed or wounded.

The first trenches we went into on arrival were the Cuinchy brick-stacks. My company held the canal-bank frontage, a few hundred yards to the left of where I had been with the Welsh Regiment at the end of May. The Germans opposite wanted to be sociable. They sent messages over to us in undetonated rifle-grenades. One of these was evidently addressed to the Irish battalion we had relieved:

We all German korporals wish you English korporals a good day and invite you to a good German dinner tonight with beer (ale) and cakes. Your little dog ran over to us and we keep it safe; it became no food with you so it run to us. Answer in the same way, if you please.

Another grenade contained a copy of the *Neueste Nachrichten*, a German Army newspaper printed at Lille, giving sensational details of Russian defeats around Warsaw, with immense captures of prisoners and guns. But what interested us far more was a full account in another column of the destruction of a German submarine by British armed trawlers; no details of the sinking of

German submarines had been allowed to appear in any English papers. The battalion cared as little about the successes or reverses of our Allies as about the origins of the war. It never allowed itself to have any political feelings about the Germans. A professional soldier's duty was simply to fight whomever the King ordered him to fight. With the King as colonel-in-chief of the regiment it became even simpler. The Christmas 1914 fraternization, in which the battalion was among the first to participate, had had the same professional simplicity: no emotional hiatus, this, but a common-place of military tradition – an exchange of courtesies between officers of opposing armies.

Cuinchy bred rats. They came up from the canal, fed on the plentiful corpses, and multiplied exceedingly. While I stayed here with the Welsh, a new officer joined the company and, in token of welcome, was given a dug-out containing a spring-bed. When he turned in that night, he heard a scuffling, shone his torch on the bed, and found two rats on his blanket tussling for the possession of a severed hand. This story circulated as a great joke.

The colonel called for a patrol to visit the side of the tow-path, where we had heard suspicious sounds on the previous night, and see whether they came from a working-party. I volunteered to go at dark. But that night the moon shone so bright and full that it dazzled the eyes. Between us and the Germans lay a flat stretch of about two hundred yards, broken only by shell craters and an occasional patch of coarse grass. I was not with my own company, but lent to 'B', which had two officers away on leave. Childe-Freeman, the company-commander, asked: 'You're not going out on patrol tonight, Graves, are you? It's almost as bright as day.'

'All the more reason for going,' I answered. 'They won't be expecting me. Will you please keep everything as usual? Let the men fire an occasional rifle, and send up a flare every half-hour. If I go carefully, the Germans won't see me.'

While we were having supper, I nervously knocked over a cup of tea, and after that a plate. Freeman said: 'Look here, I'll phone through to battalion and tell them it's too bright for your patrol.' But I knew that, if he did, Buzz Off would accuse me of cold feet.

So one Sergeant Williams and I put on our crawlers, and went out by way of a mine-crater at the side of the tow-path. We had no need to stare that night. We could see only too clearly. Our plan was to wait for an opportunity to move quickly, to stop dead and trust to luck, then move on quickly again. We planned our rushes from shell-hole to shell-hole, the opportunities being provided by artillery or machine-gun fire, which would distract the sentries. Many of the craters contained the corpses of men who had been wounded and crept in there to die. Some were skeletons, picked clean by the rats.

We got to within thirty yards of a big German working-party, who were digging a trench ahead of their front line. Between them and us we counted a covering party of ten men lying on the grass in their greatcoats. We had gone far enough. A German lay on his back about twelve yards off, humming a tune. It was the 'Merry Widow' waltz. The sergeant, from behind me, pressed my foot with his hand and showed me the revolver he was carrying. He raised his eyebrows inquiringly. I signalled 'no'. We turned to go back; finding it hard not to move too quickly. We had got about half-way, when a German machine-gun opened traversing fire along the top of our trenches. We immediately jumped to our feet; the bullets were brushing the grass, so to stand up was safer. We walked the rest of the way home, but moving irregularly to distract the aim of the covering party if they saw us. Back in the trench, I rang up brigade artillery, and asked for as much shrapnel as they could spare, fifty yards short of where the German front trench touched the tow-path; I knew that one of the night-lines of the battery supporting us was trained near enough to this point. A minute and a quarter later the shells started coming over. Hearing the clash of downed tools and distant shouts and cries, we reckoned the probable casualties.

The next morning, at stand-to, Buzz Off came up to me: 'I hear you were on patrol last night?'

'Yes, sir.'

He asked for particulars. When I told him about the covering party, he cursed me for not 'scuppering them with that revolver of yours.' As he turned away, he snorted: 'Cold feet!'

* * *

I jumped up on the fire-step beside the sentry and cautiously raised my head, staring over the parapet. I could see nothing except the wooden pickets supporting our protecting barbed-wire entanglements, and a dark patch or two of bushes beyond. The darkness seemed to move and shake about as I looked at it; the bushes started travelling, singly at first, then both together. The pickets did the same. I was glad of the sentry beside me; he gave his name as Beaumont. 'They're quiet tonight, sir,' he said. 'A relief going on; I think so, surely.'

I spent the rest of my watch in acquainting myself with the geography of the trench-section, finding how easy it was to get lost among culs-de-sac and disused alleys. Twice I overshot the company frontage and wandered among the Munster Fusiliers on the left. Once I tripped and fell with a splash into deep mud. My watch ended when the first signs of dawn showed. I passed the word along the line for the company to stand-to-arms. The N.C.O.s whispered hoarsely into the dug-outs: 'Stand-to, stand-to,' and out the men tumbled with their rifles in their hands. Going towards company headquarters to wake the officers I saw a man lying on his face in a machine-gun shelter. I stopped and said: 'Stand-to, there!' I flashed my torch on him and saw that one of his feet was bare.

The machine-gunner beside him said: 'No good talking to him, sir.'

I asked: 'What's wrong? Why has he taken his boot and sock off?'

'Look for yourself, sir!'

I shook the sleeper by the arm and noticed suddenly the hole in the back of his head. He had taken off the boot and sock to pull the trigger of his rifle with one toe; the muzzle was in his mouth.

'Why did he do it?' I asked.

'He went through the last push, sir, and that sent him a bit queer; on top of that he got bad news from Limerick about his girl and another chap.'

* * *

Like everyone else, I had a carefully worked out formula for taking risks. In principle, we would all take any risk, even the certainty of death, to save life or to maintain an important position. To take life we would run, say, a one-in-five risk, particularly if there was some wider object than merely reducing the enemy's man-power; for instance, picking off a well-known sniper, or getting fire ascendancy in trenches where the lines came dangerously close. I only once refrained from shooting a German I saw, and that was at Cuinchy, some three weeks after this. While sniping from a knoll in the support line, where we had a concealed loop-hole, I saw a German, perhaps seven hundred yards away, through my telescopic sights. He was taking a bath in the German third line. I disliked the idea of shooting a naked man, so I handed the rifle to the sergeant with me. 'Here, take this. You're a better shot than I am.' He got him; but I had not stayed to watch.

About saving the lives of enemy wounded there was disagreement; the convention varied with the division. Some divisions, like the Canadians and a division of Lowland territorials, who claimed that they had atrocities to avenge, would not only avoid taking risks to rescue enemy wounded, but go out of their way to finish them off. The Royal Welsh were gentle-manly: perhaps a one-in-twenty risk to get a wounded German to safety would be considered justifiable. An important factor in calculating risks was our own physical condition. When exhausted and wanting to get quickly from one point in the trenches to another without collapse, we would sometimes take a short cut over the top, if the enemy were not nearer than four or five hundred yards. In a hurry, we would take a one-in-two-hundred risk, when dead tired, a one-in-fifty risk. In battalions where morale was low, one-in-fifty risks were often taken in laziness or despair. The Munsters of the First Division were said by the Welsh to 'waste men wicked' by not keeping properly under cover while in the reserve lines. The Royal Welsh never allowed wastage of this sort. At no time in the war did any of us believe that hostilities could possibly continue more than another nine months or a year, so it seemed almost worth while taking care; there might even be a chance of lasting until the end absolutely unhurt.

Graves had better luck than most subalterns; he lasted at the front for a year, until the battle of the Somme in 1916.

If the first batches of New Army officers were ex-public school boys like Graves, by mid-war the majority of newly commissioned officers had previously served in the ranks. Of the 230,000 new commissions granted during the First World War, some 108,000 were for ex-rankers.

The Royal Welch Fusiliers were blessed with men who could wield the pen as well as the sword. In addition to Graves, fellow Royal Welch Fusiliers Siegfried Sassoon and Alan Jones became poets, while James Dunn and Frank Richards both wrote major memoirs of the conflict, *The War The Infantry Knew* and *Old Soldiers Never Die* respectively.

⟶⋆◉⋆⟵

'I saw a blinding flash in front of me and a great column of flame and earth rose into the sky'
SECOND LIEUTENANT GRAHAM GREENWELL

SHELLED
WESTERN FRONT
19 OCTOBER 1915

Greenwell writes home. He served with the Oxfordshire and Buckinghamshire Light Infantry.

October 19th, 1915
[Hebuterne Trenches]

Thank God, in two or three hours' time I shall have left these trenches for billets.

Since I wrote to you yesterday we have had a ghastly time. The German bombardment, for so it became after lunch, grew extremely violent; they were using some of their largest shells, which shook the earth and sent splinters flying hundreds of yards away.

At 4.30 p.m. a white faced officer, one of our subalterns, came up to my trench from somewhere behind and told me that the front line trenches were completely wrecked: the officer in charge buried and killed in the signallers' dug-out, all the telephone wires were cut, and that I, in fact, was virtually the front line. This news was certainly depressing and I gave up Conny for lost as he had gone up there a few minutes before.

About a quarter of an hour later the Colonel came up, called me out and ordered me to take my Platoon down to the front line as quickly as possible, as it had been reported that the German front line and saps were full of men; they might be in our trench now for all he knew. I hastily turned them out and rushed down the communication trench with only about two men at my heels, hearing appalling explosions ahead of me.

The trench was blocked in one place by a stretcher with a wounded or dead signaller on it, and this delayed us until I got him removed. Finally, when I reached the front trench the most terrible scene of destruction confronted me; it was impossible to see the old trench line. Then Conny came running up very dishevelled and shouted to me to take my men down one of the front trenches at once and stand to, ready to be attacked. As it was impossible to get to this trench except overland – the communication trench being filled in – it was a nasty job. The Huns had turned on to the spot which we had to pass their most appalling of all engines – the meinenwerfer or mine-thrower. As I was about to go across I saw a blinding flash in front of me and a great column of flame and earth rose into the sky: the concussion hurled me backwards into a deep German dug-out. I felt shaken to pieces: it was a most horrible feeling of being absolutely dazed and helpless just at the wrong moment. A corporal who was with me pulled me up and we went back to get the rest of my men up, as they were straggling behind and getting lost in the confusion. As we were waiting about a few minutes later Conny saved our lives by yelling out 'Look out for the meinenwerfer!' He had just heard the faint sound of its discharge. There was a rush backwards and everyone flung themselves face downwards under any sort of protection that offered. There was another terrific explosion and we were covered with filthy smoke and falling mud and earth. However, after this I ran the gauntlet and got safe into the trench, which I found quite intact, thank Heaven, though it was cut off at the end. It was now mercifully too dark for the shelling to continue, so we had the meinenwerfer instead. About three fell in it, all of which, by some extraordinary chance, did no damage to life. I felt most frightfully shaken and pretty rotten, but after about half an hour it passed off.

Two other Platoons had by this time reinforced the front line; the enemy had ceased every kind of fire and there was dead quiet. We posted sentries all the way along and the rest had to work like niggers to try to rebuild the trenches before daylight – luckily we got plenty of sand-bags. A large party of R.E.s came up and a few

Gloucesters. The men worked splendidly. We were on duty all night without a stop, building up to the front line, renewing the wire in front, and clearing the entrances to the trench so that we could get out when it became light.

The wreckage was awful, dug-outs completely smashed in and everything pitched up all over the shop. It is a miracle how few the casualties were. Captain Treble, who was taking charge of our Platoon in the front line, as we had an officer away, was killed sitting by the telephone in the signallers' dug-out. The shell scored a direct hit on it and his head was smashed in by the timbers. The signaller was, I think, mortally wounded and one bomber broke down. There were no other casualties.

During the worst part of the show I saw a young subaltern of the Seaforths, the battalion on our right, who had actually come round to have a look. They had had it as badly as we had, but had only three casualties. He seemed pretty cool and was wearing a squash hat – a Homburg. We fraternised over the wreckage and voted the Huns rotten beasts.

Twenty minutes later.

I thought this letter would end abruptly at 'beasts.' For just after I had written that word I heard to my horror one of those awful explosions which made yesterday so hideous, followed by two or three others. They were again firing, away to the right this time. I telephoned back to Conny to ask him where the shells were actually falling, and he said that it was a good way over to the right on the next Division. It turns out that they were not the heavy guns as I had thought, but only that formidable melnenwerfer firing from the German front trench. Our heavy guns then put shells into their front trench with wonderful accuracy; the ground shook, huge clouds of yellow smoke arose and some of the fragments flew back to our trench. Since then we have had peace; it looks like raining and I pray that it will pour. We have only another two hours here and then freedom.

The row these things make is incredible and I can hear nothing but the low whistle of heavy shells; every puff of the wind startles me and I feel as nervous as a cat. It is the sitting still throughout a solid day listening the whole time to shells and wondering if the next will be on the dug-out or not which is so unnerving. I cannot understand what sort of men they are who can stand three or four days of continued bombardment. Of course, at the end the ones who are alive are absolutely demoralised.

Death from shell-fire came in a number of whimsical ways. Aside from the annihilation caused by a direct hit, the blast of high-explosive shells produced an oxygen vacuum that caused death by suffocation. Reactions to shell-fire varied, as Private Frank Richards in the Royal Welch Fusiliers observed:

Some men were perfect philosophers under heavy shell-fire, whilst others used to go through severe torture and would cower down, holding their heads in their hands, moaning and trembling. For myself I wasn't worrying so much if a shell pitched clean among us: we would never know anything about it. It was the large flying pieces of a shell bursting a few yards off that I didn't like: they could take arms and legs off or, worse still, rip our bellies open and still leave us living. We would know something about *them* all right.

Arthur Osburn witnessed the damage done to a group of cavalrymen at Aisne by a shell. One terribly wounded man begged his brother, serving in the same unit, to put him out of his agony: '"Shoot me. Tom! Oh! Shoot me! For the love of God! Shoot me, will you! WILL YOU!" he began to scream piteously'. Morphine failed to dull the man's pain, so Osburn chloroformed him.

Some shells plainly had their victim's number on them. Captain Rowland Feilding of the Coldstream Guards asked for Sergeant-Major McGrath to be sent out from home; within a half an hour of his arrival in the fire trench McGrath was dead from a mortar blast.

The British 'dish' steel helmet, introduced in 1916, was intended to protect the head and neck from shrapnel blast. For bellies, arms and legs there was nothing. Seventy per cent of troops killed on the Western Front were the victims of shell or mortar fire.

❖

'I'd rather stay in England/In merry, merry England/
And fuck my bloody life away'
ANONYMOUS

SOLDIERS' SONGS
1915–16

I like to hear the news from the Dardanelles,
I like to hear the whistle of the Allyman's shells.
I like to hear the rifle-fire,
I like to see the blinking Allymans retire.
I like to hear the click-click of the pick and spade,
(the French they are no bon.)
Look out, look out, the gas clouds are coming:
Go get your respirator on.

* * *

I don't want to be a soldier,
I don't want to go to war.
I'd rather stay at home
Around the streets to roam
And live on the earnings of a fucking lady-typist.
I don't want a bayonet in my belly,
I don't want my bollocks shot away,
I'd rather stay in England,
In merry, merry England,
And fuck my bloody life away.

The war saw a loosening of conventional behaviour; few young men wanted to die virgin soldiers, and not a few 'dizzy' girls on the home front wanted to display their patriotism by sleeping with them. 'Khaki fever', the newspapers called it. Volunteer policewomen patrolled garrison towns seeking to keep troops and girls apart, and invariably failed to do so.

Staying in England and 'fucking my bloody life away', however, ceased to be an option for young men in 1916. With voluntary recruitment failing to provide enough troops to satisfy the maws of death on the Western Front, on 27 January 1916 the Military Services Act was passed by parliament. This conscripted all able-bodied men from the ages of 18–41 for the army, unless they were in reserved occupations. It was done reluctantly, for the British had long held that conscription was incompatible with liberty.

Meanwhile, the 1914–15 volunteers of the New Army trained enthusiastically for the front. Second-Lieutenant Donald Hankey, 1st Royal Warwickshire Regiment, penned this portrait of the New Army:

'The New Army', 'Kitchener's Army', we go by many names. The older sergeants – men who have served in regular battalions – sometimes call us 'Kitchener's Mob' and swear that to take us to war would be another 'Massacre of the Innocents' . . . We are a mixed lot – a triumph of democracy, like the Tubes [London Underground]. Some of us have fifty years to our credit and only own to thirty; others are sixteen and claim to be eighteen. Some of us have enlisted for glory, some for fun, and a few for fear of starvation. Some of us began by being stout . . . others were weedy and are filling out . . . for the most part we are aggressively cheerful, and were never fitter in our lives . . . We sing as we march. Such songs we sing! . . . We shall sing

Where's yer girl?

Ain't yer got none?

as we march into battle.

Battle! Battle! Murder and sudden death! How incredibly remote all that seems! We don't believe in it really. It is just a great game we are learning . . . Anyway we are Kitchener's Army, and we are quite sure it will be alright. Just send us to Flanders, and see if it ain't. We are Kitchener's Army, and we don't care if it snows ink.

Donald Sankey was killed in action on the Somme.

Even when confronted with the reality of trench warfare, the men of the New Army rarely lost their optimism or their sense of duty:

⇒•⇐

'It's all one long blaze of glory'
Captain Bill Bland

LAST POST
France, 18 February 1916

Bill Bland, a former lecturer, served in France with the 7th Manchester Pals.

18 February 1916

Darling, I can't bear you to be unhappy about me. Don't be grey and old, darling. Think of the cause, the cause. It is England, England, England, always and all the time. The individual counts as nothing, the common cause everything. Have faith, my dear. If only you will have faith in the ultimate victory of the good, the true and the beautiful, you will not be unhappy even if I never return to you. Dear, if one's number is up, one will go under. I am here, and I shall either survive or not survive. In the meantime, I have never been truly happier.

P.S. Hardship be damned! It's all one long blaze of glory.

Bland was killed in action on the first day of the battle of the Somme, 1 July 1916.

'Has your boy a mechanical turn of mind? . . . Then buy him a flammenwerfer'
The Wipers Times

NATTY TOY, PLUSH BREECHES AND A TOUR OF LOVELY BELGIUM
SPOOF ADVERTS
Western Front, 1916

In a post-mortem after the Great War, the German army high command concluded that defeat had been caused by, *inter alia*, the superior sense of humour of the British. To educate its diminished ranks in the British way of fun, the Reichswehr circulated a conflict-era Bruce Bairnsfather cartoon showing 'Old Bill' in a dug-out with a massive hole in the wall. A rookie is asking 'Old Bill', 'What made that?' 'Mice', replies Old Bill. In a footnote the German army felt obliged to explain: 'It was not mice; it was a shell.'

The German high command might not have got the joke, but they did get the point; it *was* the ability to laugh at the situation, at themselves, that pulled the British through.

The British satirical trench newspaper, *The Wipers Times*, was founded by two 'hostilities only' officers from the 12th Sherwood Foresters, Captain FJ Roberts MC and Lieutenant JH Pearson MC DSO, and printed on a press found in the ruins of Ypres. Or 'Wipers' as it was better known to the British army.

**THE
WIPERS TIMES.
OR
SALIENT NEWS.**

No 4. Vol. 2.   Monday. 20th March, 1916.   Price 50 Centimes.

HAS YOUR BOY A MECHANICAL TURN OF MIND?   YES!

–o–o–o–o–

**THEN BUY HIM A
FLAMMENWERFER
INSTRUCTIVE – AMUSING.**

–o–o–o–o–

**Both young and old enjoy.
This natty little toy.**

–o–o–o–o–

GUARANTEED ABSOLUTELY HARMLESS

–o–o–o–o–

Thousands Have Been Sold.

–o–o–o–o–

**Drop a postcard to Messrs. ARMY, RESEARCH and CO.,
when a handsome illustrated catalogue will be sent you.**

ARE YOU GOING OVER THE TOP?
IF SO BE SURE TO FIRST INSPECT OUR NEW LINE OF
VELVETEEN CORDUROY PLUSH BREECHES.

BE IN THE FASHION AND LOOK LIKE A SOLDIER.

ALL ONE PRICE, 9s. 11d.

THOUSANDS OF TESTIMONIALS FROM ALL FRONTS.

SEND FOR THESE AND ILLUSTRATED BROCHURE
ENTITLED:
**"Breeches And Their Wearers" Or
"Legs Make The Officer."**

Address: POND & CO., WULVERGHEM. Agents all along the line.

**ARE YOU TIRED, HOT & THIRSTY AFTER A LONG WALK?
YES! THEN DROP IN AT BUS FARM THE NEW TEA SHOP.**

–o–o–o–

**Tastefully Fitted.
General Attractions.
Walloon Waitresses.**

–o–o–o–

FAMOUS CRUMPET HOUSE. AIRY TEA ROOMS.
SPECIAL ACCOMMODATION FOR MOTORISTS.
SWITCHBACK NEAR BY.
TAKE THE TUBE OR GREEN 'BUS. PARTIES CATERED FOR
AND WEDDING BREAKFASTS ARRANGED.

–o–o–o–

TELEPHONE: 102, HOP.
TELEGRAMS: 'MOVING.'

TRY OUR NEW CIRCULAR TOUR.
EMBRACING ALL THE HEALTH RESORTS OF
LOVELY BELGIUM.

–o– o–o–

Books Of Coupons Obtainable From
R. E. Cruting & Co.,
London. Agents Everywhere.

–o–o–o–

Our expert Guides meet all trains, and our excellent system of
G. S. coaches will make you realize what travelling is.

–o–o–o–

BEAUTIFUL SCENERY ON ALL CIRCUITS.

−o−o−o−
NO SALIENT FEATURE OMITTED.
−o−o−o−
BOOK AT ONCE TO AVOID DISAPPOINTMENT.

'A white disc was pinned over his heart'
CAPTAIN T.H. WESTMACOTT

EXECUTIONS AT DAWN
WESTERN FRONT, 14 APRIL−21 JULY 1916

Westmacott served with the 1st Indian Cavalry Division. There were 346 Allied executions during the Great War, mostly for desertion.

14 April, 1916

I was staying with Bowring of the 51st Division, and we received orders to attend the execution of a deserter in the Cheshire Regiment. The man had deserted when his battalion was in the trenches and had been caught in Paris. He was sentenced to death, but the sentence was remitted, and he was sent back to his battalion. He did so well in the trenches that he was allowed leave to England. He deserted again, and after being arrested was sent back to his battalion in France, when he was again sentenced to death. This time he was shot. We got up at 3.30 a.m., and Bowring and I were driven to the HQ of the 5th Division, the car breaking down on the way. When we got to DHQ Coates, of the 15th Hussars, the APM had gone on with the firing party. We caught them up, and I found Coates, the firing party and a company of the Cheshires drawn up opposite a chair under a railway embankment. The condemned man spent the night in a house about half a mile away. He walked from there blindfolded with the doctor, the parson and the escort. He walked quite steadily on to parade, sat down in the chair, and told them not to tie him too tight. A white disc was pinned over his heart. He was the calmest man on the ground. The firing party was 15 paces distant. The officer commanding the firing party did everything by signal, only speaking the word 'Fire!' The firing party was twelve strong, six kneeling and six standing. Before the condemned man arrived, the firing party about turned after grounding arms, and the OC firing party and the APM mixed up the rifles and unloaded some of them.

On the word 'Fire!' the man's head fell back, and the firing party about turned at once. The doctor said the man was not quite dead, but before the OC firing party could finish him with his revolver he was dead, having felt nothing. The company was then marched off. The body was wrapped in a blanket, and the APM saw it buried in a grave which had been dug close by, unmarked and unconsecrated.

26 June, 1916

A Sowar in the 29th Lancers shot the Wordi Major (native Adjutant) of the Regiment dead. He then threw away his rifle, tore off most of his clothes, and rushed off to the HQ of the Lucknow Brigade, where he happened to catch General Morton Gage, the Brigadier, in the street. He told the General a long story, but as the General was British service he could not understand a word. The man was a Delhi policeman, and a Jat, who enlisted for the period of the war. He is a sulky kind of fellow but there is no doubt that the Wordi Major, who was an absolute rotter, goaded the wretched fellow to desperation.

After this date we moved down to the neighbourhood of Doullens for the battle of the Somme. Until the 13th of July the man was in my charge and I had to drag him about with DHQ until that date, very hard luck on the man. He behaved very well the whole time and one day he said to me, 'Sahib, I am quite certain now that I shall not be shot, as you have kept me so long.'

19 July

Had a long ride of about 28 miles to Villers Chatel, north of Aubigny, Yadram, the murderer, riding with me under escort the whole way. On arrival, orders came in for his execution.

20 July

Rode over to the Lucknow Brigade HQ and to the 29th Lancers and arranged everything including the place of execution.

Sent Yadram to the Regiment under escort to have the sentence promulgated. Gibbon, the Divisional Chaplain, was a great nuisance, as he obtained leave from the Divisional Commander to visit Yadram during the night. As Yadram was a Jat and not a Christian we all considered it a great piece of impertinence on Gibbon's part.

21 July

Got up at 2.45 a.m. and went over to the 29th Lancers with Gordon, the General's ADC, and Winckworth, my assistant. The Regiment was drawn up dismounted in hollow square with the firing party and the chair in front. The firing party consisted of twenty men, five from each squadron. They grounded arms and faced about and moved 3 paces to the rear, while I mixed up the rifles and unloaded some of them. Then they marched back and picked up their arms. The prisoner was then brought up under escort blindfolded with a white disc pinned over his heart, and he sat down in the chair. As Sergeant Walsh, my provost sergeant was tying him to the chair, he shouted in Hindustani, 'Salaam, O Sahibs! and Salaam, all Hindus and Mahometans of this regiment! There is no justice in the British Sirkar. I did this deed because I was abused. Those of you who have been abused as I was go and do the same, but eat your own bullet and do not be shot as I shall be.'

Then the OC firing party gave the signal, and the party came to the present, and on the word 'Fire' they fired a volley. The regiment and the firing party then faced about and marched off. Five bullets had gone through the disc, but the man still breathed, and I had to shoot him through the heart with my revolver, a horrid job. The grave had already been dug at the firing point, and Yadram was put straight into it and the grave was filled in and levelled by a fatigue party from the regiment.

Just under 40,000 British troops deserted during the Great War – a surprisingly small number, given that 5,700,000 men were put under arms, half of them conscripted. Some of the conscripts who deserted should clearly never have been sent to the front in the first place; when Private T. Keegan of the 11th Royal Scots went AWOL his unit described him to the military police as '17 . . . [of] poor intelligence . . . [and] in a childish way is easily frightened when spoken to'.

Like desertion, mutiny was conspicuous by its absence in the British army of 1914–18. There was a serious mutiny at the Étaples 'bull-rings' (base depots) in September 1917, and some 'strikes' in 1918 but nothing like the downing-of-arms that affected the armies of France and Germany. Moreover, the Étaples mutiny was not prompted by pacifism, or even war-weariness, so much as the 'petty tyranny' exercised there by NCOs and officers.

While bullying by the Étaples 'canarioo' (as the training staff were nicknamed for their yellow armbands) was loathed, most who passed through the camps recognised that their job as finishing schools for soldiers was necessary. In the bullrings Tommy was taught to kill, and kill well. Robert Graves, taking a turn as a bullring instructor, noted:

> Troops learned . . . that they must HATE the Germans and KILL as many of them as possible. In bayonet-practice, the men had to make horrible grimaces and utter blood-curdling yells as they charged. The instructors' faces were set in a permanently ghastly grin . . . 'In the belly! Tear his guts out!' they would scream, as the men charged the dummies. 'Now that upper swing at his privates with the butt. Ruin his chances for life! No more little Fritzes!'

There were other ways of killing Fritz aside from cold steel:

———◆———

*'we used a heavy sporting rifle . . . donated to the army
by British big-game hunters'*
LIEUTENANT STUART CLOETE

SNIPING
WESTERN FRONT, 1916

I spent most of the day in the trenches, checking snipers' reports, sniping myself and watching the German line from behind a heavy iron loophole plate with a high-powered telescope. We often saw Germans moving about a mile or more away. It gave me a curious feeling to watch them. Watching and reporting all movement was part of the sniper's job. I sent a report of what we had seen to Divisional Intelligence by runner every night. We looked for their snipers' posts and when we found them we tried to destroy them. There were no armour-piercing bullets then. So we used a heavy sporting rifle – a 600 Express. These heavy rifles had been donated to the army by British big-game hunters and when we hit a plate we stove it right in, into the German sniper's face. But it had to be fired from a standing or kneeling position to take up the recoil. The first man who fired it in the prone position had his collar-bone broken. I hit two Germans at long range – about four hundred yards – with telescopic sights, and fired at a good many others. My best sniper turned out, when his parents at last traced him, to be only fourteen years old. He was discharged as under age. He was the finest shot and the best little soldier I had. A very nice boy, always happy. I got him a military medal and when he went back to Blighty and, I suppose, to school, he had a credit of six Germans hit. He was big for his age and had lied about it when he enlisted under a false name, and then had had sufficient self-restraint to write to no one. I had noticed that he received no mail and wrote no letters but had never spoken to him about it. The snipers worked in pairs, one observer with a telescope and one with the rifle. They changed over every half hour as it is very tiring to use a telescope for a long period. In action the sniper's job was to work independently and try to pick off any enemy leaders he could see. That was what the Germans did to us and they had no difficulty as we wore officers' uniforms with long tunics, riding breeches, trench boots and Sam Browne belts. This was one reason why the officers' casualties were so high. The Germans had a further advantage in their sniping. With them it was done by their Jaeger battalions, picked sharpshooters who in peacetime had been gamekeepers and guides. They wore green uniforms insted of grey and were permanently stationed in one sector, so that they knew every blade of grass in front of them and spotted the slightest change; this gave them a big edge on us because we were moved quite often.

Cloete served with the King's Own Yorkshire Light Infantry.

'Twenty-seven men with faces blackened and shiny . . .'
LIEUTENANT SIEGFRIED SASSOON

NIGHT RAID

WESTERN FRONT, 25 MAY 1916

Sassoon, Royal Welch Fusiliers, won a Military Cross in the action below.

Twenty-seven men with faces blackened and shiny – Christy-minstrels – with hatchets in their belts, bombs in pockets, knobkerries – waiting in a dug-out in the reserve line. At 10.30 they trudge up to Battalion H.Q. splashing through mire and water in the chalk trench, while the rain comes steadily down. The party is twenty-two men, five N.C.O.s and one officer (Stansfield). From H.Q. we start off again, led by Compton-Smith: across the open to the end of 77 street. A red flashlight winks a few times to guide us thither. Then up to the front line – the men's feet making a most unholy tramp and din; squeeze along to the starting-point, where Stansfield and his two confederates (Sergeant Lyle and Corporal O'Brien) loom over the parapet from above, having successfully laid the line of lime across the craters to the Bosche wire. In a few minutes the five parties have gone over – and disappear into the rain and darkness – the last four men carry ten-foot light ladders. It is 12 midnight. I am sitting on the parapet listening for something to happen – five, ten, nearly fifteen minutes – not a sound – nor a shot fired – and only the usual flare-lights, none very near our party. Then a few whizz-bangs fizz over to our front trench and just behind the raiders. After twenty minutes there is still absolute silence in the Bosche trench; the raid is obviously held up by their wire, which we thought was so easy to get through. One of the bayonet-men comes crawling back; I follow him to our trench and he tells me that they can't get through: O'Brien says it's a failure; they're all going to throw a bomb and retire.

A minute or two later a rifle-shot rings out and almost simultaneously several bombs are thrown by both sides: a bomb explodes right in the water at the bottom of left crater close to our men, and showers a pale spume of water; there are blinding flashes and explosions, rifle-shots, the scurry of feet, curses and groans, and stumbling figures loom up from below and scramble awkwardly over the parapet – some wounded – black faces and whites of eyes and lips show in the dusk; when I've counted sixteen in, I go forward to see how things are going, and find Stansfield wounded, and leave him there with two men who soon get him in: other wounded men crawl in; I find one hit in the leg; he says O'Brien is somewhere down the crater badly wounded. They are still throwing bombs and firing at us: the sinister sound of clicking bolts seems to be very near; perhaps they have crawled out of their trench and are firing from behind their advanced wire. Bullets hit the water in the craters, and little showers of earth patter down on the crater. Five or six of them are firing into the crater at a few yards' range. The bloody sods are firing down at me at point-blank range. (I really wondered whether my number was up.) From our trenches and in front of them I can hear the mumble of voices – most of them must be in by now. After minutes like hours, with great difficulty I get round the bottom of the crater and back toward our trench; at last I find O'Brien down a very deep (about twenty-five feet) and precipitous crater on my left (our right as they went out). He is moaning and his right arm is either broken or almost shot off: he's also hit in the right leg (body and head also, but I couldn't see that then). Another man (72 Thomas) is with him; he is hit in the right arm. I leave them there and get back to our trench for help, shortly afterwards Lance-Corporal Stubbs is brought in (he has had his foot blown off). Two or three other wounded men are being helped down the trench; no one seems to know what to do; those that are there are very excited and uncertain: no sign of any officers – then Compton-Smith comes along (a mine went up on the left as we were coming up at about 11.30 and thirty (R.E.s) men were gassed or buried). I get a rope and two more men and we go back to O'Brien, who is unconscious now. With great difficulty we get him half-way up the face of the crater; it is now after one o'clock and the sky beginning to get lighter. I make one more journey to our trench for another strong man and to see to a stretcher being ready. We get him in, and it is found that he has died, as I had feared. Corporal Mick O'Brien (who often went patrolling with me) was a very fine man and had been with the Battalion since November 1914. He was at Neuve Chapelle, Festubert and Loos.

I go back to a support-line dug-out and find the unwounded men of the raiding-party refreshing themselves: everyone is accounted for now; eleven wounded (one died of wounds) and one killed, out of twenty-eight. I see Stansfield, who is going on all right, but has several bomb-wounds. On the way down I see the Colonel, sitting on his bed in a woollen cap with a tuft on top, and very much upset at the non-success of the show, and the mine disaster; but very pleased with the way our men tried to get through the wire.

'there came the sudden loud clattering at the front-door knocker that always meant a telegram'
NURSE VERA BRITTAIN

HOME FRONT
DEATH OF A BROTHER
15 JUNE 1916

Brittain, a Volunteer Auxiliary Detachment nurse, had already lost her fiancé to the war.

I had just announced to my father, as we sat over tea in the dining room, that I really must do up Edward's papers and take them to the post office before it closed for the weekend, when there came the sudden loud clattering at the front-door knocker that always meant a telegram.

For a moment I thought that my legs would not carry me, but they behaved quite normally as I got up and went to the door. I knew what was in the telegram – I had known for a week – but because the persistent hopefulness of the human heart refuses to allow intuitive certainty to persuade the reason of that which it knows, I opened and read it in a tearing anguish of suspense.

'Regret to inform you Captain E. H. Brittain M.C. killed in action Italy June 15th.'

'No answer,' I told the boy mechanically, and handed the telegram to my father, who had followed me into the hall. As we went back into the dining room I saw, as though I had never seen them before, the bowl of blue delphiniums on the table; their intense colour, vivid, ethereal, seemed too radiant for earthly flowers.

Then I remembered that we should have to go down to Purley and tell the news to my mother.

Late that evening, my uncle brought us all back to an empty flat. Edward's death and our sudden departure had offered the maid – at that time the amateur prostitute – an agreeable opportunity for a few hours' freedom of which she had taken immediate advantage. She had not even finished the household handkerchiefs, which I had washed that morning and intended to iron after tea; when I went into the kitchen I found them still hanging, stiff as boards, over the clothes-horse near the fire where I had left them to dry.

Long after the family had gone to bed and the world had grown silent, I crept into the dining room to be alone with Edward's portrait. Carefully closing the door, I turned on the light and looked at the pale, pictured face, so dignified, so steadfast, so tragically mature. He had been through so much – far, far more than those beloved friends who had died at an earlier stage of the interminable War, leaving him alone to mourn their loss. Fate might have allowed him the little, sorry compensation of survival, the chance to make his lovely music in honour of their memory. It seemed indeed the last irony that he should have been killed by the countrymen of Fritz Kreisler, the violinist whom of all others he had most greatly admired.

And suddenly, as I remembered all the dear afternoons and evenings when I had followed him on the piano as he played his violin, the sad, searching eyes of the portrait were more than I could bear, and falling on my knees before it I began to cry, 'Edward! Oh, Edward!' in dazed repetition, as though my persistent crying and calling would somehow bring him back.

'It was a lovely bright morning'
PRIVATE SIDNEY WILLIAMSON

THE SOMME

DAY ONE: OVER THE TOP WITH THE ROYAL WARWICKSHIRE REGIMENT

7.30 A.M. 1 JULY 1916

After a week's heavy shelling British troops went 'over the top' on the morning of 1 July along a 15 mile sector of the Western Front. They expected little opposition; instead they encountered a horizontal hail of machine-gun fire. Some 60,000 casualties were sustained in what was the bloodiest day ever to befall the British army. Their sacrifice secured 100,000 yards of ground.

Diary; 1 July 1916 [on the Somme]

It was a lovely bright morning, but the feelings of the men were tense. We had breakfast at 5.0 a.m., afterwards the officers were going round to see all the men and have a talk with us. The shelling was terrific and the Germans started to shell our lines. At 7.20 a mine was exploded under the German trenches. An officer detailed me and another soldier standing by me to carry forward with us a box containing a signalling lamp. At 7.30 a.m. whistles were blown and the attack started. What did I see! To the left as far as Gommecourt and to the right as far as Beaumont Hamel, lines of soldiers going forward as though on parade in line formation. Just 'over the top' the soldier helping me with the box stopped and fell dead. I had to go on but without the box. Lt Jones was the next officer I saw to fall, then CSM Haines was calling for me, he had been wounded. I reached the first German line and dropped into it where there were many German dead. The battlefield was nothing but shell holes and barbed wire, but now I noticed many dead and dying, and the line of soldiers was not to be seen. With no officers or NCO near I felt alone and still went forward from shell hole to shell hole. Later Cpl Beard joined me and he asked me to hold down a ground signalling sheet so that he could get a message to the observing aeroplane flying overhead. He asked for 'MORE BOMBS' and the Pilot of the aeroplane asked 'Code please'. This was flashed back and the aeroplane flew away.

Things were now getting disorganised and at this point we could not go any further. The machine-gun fire was deadly. And our bombs had all been used up. The Colonel of the Seaforths came up and took charge of all the odd groups of men belonging to various Regiments. He told us to dig ourselves in and eventually there must have been 50 or 60 men at this spot, and it all started from the one small shell hole Cpl Beard and myself were first in.

Now there was a lull in the fighting till 3.0 p.m. At one time a shout went up that we were surrounded by Germans, but they were Germans running from the dugouts in the first line and giving themselves up. I do not think they made it.

With Cpl Beard we started to get back to our lines shell hole by shell hole, but we soon got parted. I managed to reach the British lines at 7.30 p.m., but the sight that met my eyes was terrible. Hundreds of dead soldiers were everywhere, and the Germans kept up their heavy shelling. Met Sam and Bob Patterson in the trench, the only two of my own Battalion. Stayed in the British trench all night.

Behind the frontline, the staff at the Casualty Clearing Stations (CCS) tended to the wounded and the dying. The Reverend John Stanhope Walker was the chaplain at 21st CCS at Crombie, on the junction of the Ancre and Somme rivers, 1 July 1916:

We have 1,500 in and still they come, 3–400 officers, it is a sight – chaps with fearful wounds lying in agony, many so patient, some make a noise, one goes to a stretcher, lays one's hand on a forehead, it is cold, strike a match, he is dead – here a Communion, there an absolution, there a drink, there a madman, there a hot water bottle and so on – one madman was swearing and kicking, I gave him a drink, he tried to bite my hand, and squirted the water from his mouth into my face – well, it is an experience beside which all previous experience pales.

'Colonel Crawshay . . . saw me lying in the corner,
and they told him I was done for'
LIEUTENANT ROBERT GRAVES

REPORTED DEAD
THE SOMME
22 JULY 1916

One piece of shell went through my left thigh, high up, near the groin; I must have been at the full stretch of my stride to escape emasculation. The wound over the eye was made by a little chip of marble, possibly from one of the Bazentin cemetery headstones. (Later, I had it cut out, but a smaller piece has since risen to the surface under my right eyebrow, where I keep it for a souvenir.) This, and a finger-wound which split the bone, probably came from another shell bursting in front of me. But a piece of shell had also gone in two inches below the point of my right shoulder-blade and came out through my chest two inches above the right nipple.

My memory of what happened then is vague. Apparently Dr Dunn came up through the barrage with a stretcher-party, dressed my wound, and got me down to the old German dressing-station at the north end of Mametz Wood. I remember being put on the stretcher, and winking at the stretcher-bearer sergeant who had just said. 'Old Gravy's got it, all right!' They laid my stretcher in a corner of the dressing-station, where I remained unconscious for more than twenty-four hours.

Late that night, Colonel Crawshay came back from High Wood and visited the dressing-station; he saw me lying in the corner, and they told him I was done for. The next morning, 21 July, clearing away the dead, they found me still breathing and put me on an ambulance for Heilly, the nearest field hospital. The pain of being jolted down the Happy Valley, with a shell hole at every three or four yards of the road, woke me up. I remember screaming. But back on the better roads I became unconscious again. That morning, Crawshay wrote the usual formal letters of condolence to the next-of-kin of the six or seven officers who had been killed. This was his letter to my mother:

Dear Mrs Graves,   22.7.16
I very much regret to have to write and tell you your son has died
of wounds. He was very gallant, and was doing so well and is a
great loss.

He was hit by a shell and very badly wounded, and died on the
way down to the base I believe. He was not in bad pain, and our
doctor managed to get across and attend to him at once.

We have had a very hard time, and our casualties have been
large. Believe me you have all our sympathy in your loss, and we
have lost a very gallant soldier.

Yours sincerely,

G. Crawshay, Lt-Col.

Then he made out the official casualty list – a long one, because
only eighty men were left in the battalion – and reported me 'died
of wounds'. Heilly lay on the railway; close to the station stood the
hospital tents with the red cross prominently painted on the
roofs, to discourage air-bombing. Fine July weather made the
tents insufferably hot. I was semi-conscious now, and aware of my
lung-wound through a shortness of breath. It amused me to watch
the little bubbles of blood, like scarlet soap-bubbles, which my
breath made in escaping through the opening of the wound. The
doctor came over to my bed. I felt sorry for him; he looked as
though he had not slept for days.

I asked him: 'Can I have a drink?'

'Would you like some tea?'

I whispered: 'Not with condensed milk.'

He said, most apologetically: 'I'm afraid there's no fresh milk.'

Tears of disappointment pricked my eyes; I expected better of
a hospital behind the lines.

'Will you have some water?'

'Not if it's boiled.'

'It is boiled. And I'm afraid I can't give you anything alcoholic
in your present condition.'

'Some fruit then?'

'I have seen no fruit for days.'

Yet a few minutes later he returned with two rather unripe
greengages. In whispers I promised him a whole orchard when I
recovered.

The nights of the 22nd and 23rd were horrible. Early on the morning of the 24th, when the doctor came round the ward, I said: 'You must send me away from here. This heat will kill me.' It was beating on my head through the canvas.

'Stick it out. Your best chance is to lie here and not to be moved. You'd not reach the Base alive.'

'Let me risk the move. I'll be all right, you'll see.'

Half an hour later he returned. 'Well, you're having it your way. I've just got orders to evacuate every case in the hospital. Apparently the Guards have been in it up at Delville Wood, and they'll all be coming down tonight.' I did not fear that I would die, now – it was enough to be honourably wounded and bound for home.

Graves had a 'blighty one' – a wound serious enough for him to be taken back to Britain. Bert Steward, a 19-year-old rifleman with the 6th London Rifles, was another winner.

<hr />

'what seemed like a hammer blow hit me on the top left of my shoulder'
PRIVATE BERT STEWARD

A BLIGHTY ONE

WESTERN FRONT, 15 SEPTEMBER 1916

Zero hour, and my corporal made a little gesture at me, and we got out of the ditch and started to walk. I never saw him again.

Imagine us then rather like overladen porters going slow over a shockingly ploughed field in a man-made thunder storm. Hailstones of a lethal kind zipped past our heads. From behind us the bombardment from our own guns, which I had seen massed wheel to wheel, went on. To left and right men were moving forward in uneven lines. My plan was to walk alone and not get bunched up with others. I kept away from them. I soon found this easier. On each side some had disappeared. I saw only one tank – in a ditch with a broken track, like a dying hippopotamus, with shells bursting round it. I kept walking. I walked about half a mile. I reached the shelter of an embankment. With this solid mass between me and the enemy I felt safe.

The next moment was the luckiest of my life. I had walked all the way through a hail of bullets. I had been a slowly-moving target for the machine guns. The bullets had all missed, though narrowly, for parts of my tunic were in ribbons. Then, just as I had reached safety, as I thought, what seemed like a hammer blow hit me on the top of my left shoulder. I opened my tunic. There was a clean round hole right through the shoulder. A bullet! But where from? Then I realised I was getting enfiladed by some machine-gunner to my right, on my side of the embankment. I threw myself down, but not before another bullet struck my right thigh.

In the embankment was the entrance to a dugout. I crawled into it. It was occupied by Germans. None of them spoke. They were all dead.

There was parcels from home strewn about, cigarettes, black bread, eatables, and one huge German, lying face downwards, made a good couch to sit on. Now I was joined by two friends, one less lucky, a young lad from Liverpool, with a bullet through the stomach.

Here we were, in front of our front line. About a hundred yards back I could see tin hats bobbing about. The remnants of the cast-irons were manning an improvised front line among the shellholes. Beyond them, I thought, was England, home and beauty.

I had taken High Wood, almost by myself, it seemed. I had no further territorial ambitions. Indeed, what I now had in mind was to go as quickly as possible in the opposite direction, as soon as possible. Leaving the dugout, I ran for it, zigzagging to escape bullets (two were enough) and so fast that I toppled head-first on top of a rifleman who was almost as scared as I was. After he had recovered he told me how I could work my way along the line of shellholes to a dressing station. I went, keeping my head down; I was taking no chances. I had two bullet holes. If they had been drilled by a surgeon they could not have been located more conveniently. I was incredibly lucky. But another might spoil everything. I crawled along.

The dressing station was a captured German underground hospital, with entrance big enough for an ambulance, built like a fortress, furnished with tiers of wooden bunks. It was crowded with wounded, now being sorted out by our adjutant.

'Those who can run follow me, nobody with a leg wound,' he said. 'We have to move fast,' I was the first to follow. In and out of shellholes we went – a rough but rapid journey in the right direction – until we reached a sunken lane where a horse-drawn hooded cart waited to take a dozen of us an hour's trot nearer home . . .

The Canadian doctor looked like any other in his white coat. He turned out to be a saint. 'You've been very lucky,' he said in a kindly way. Then he explained that one bullet, almost incredibly, had found a narrow gap between collar-bone and shoulder-blade, and that neither of the two had touched muscle or bone. 'How old are you and how long have you been in the trenches?' he asked and, when I told him, he wrote on a card and gave it to the nurse.

Later I looked up at the card pinned to the chart above my bed. It was marked with a big B. What did it mean? A nurse hurrying by answered my question. She smiled as she said – 'It means Blighty.'

The Somme battle dragged on until mid-November 1916, by which time the British had sustained 420,000 casualties. German casualties were 650,000 killed and wounded.

<hr>

'It is too cruel to think my darling boy is gone for ever'
MRS PHIN

A BEREAVED MOTHER WRITES TO HER LATE SON'S COMMANDING OFFICER
GLASGOW, 4 DECEMBER 1916

Mrs Phin writes to Lieutenant Norman Collins, Seaforth Highlanders; Collins had earlier informed her of her son's death. Writing condolence letters was commonly agreed to be one of the worst duties to befall the frontline officer.

Dear Mr Collins
I now write to thank you for your kind letter of sympathy you so

kindly sent me on my sore Bereavement. It is too cruel to think my darling boy is gone for ever, I do miss his letters so much for he wrote to me regular and never grumbled. But it is a great comfort to me to hear from you and to speak so highly of him and I know very well that it is for a good cause we are fighting. But if only his sweet young life had only been spared I cannot realise he is gone and that I will never see him again.

Well dear Sir I hope and pray that you may get through all right and that your nearest and dearest may be spared the terrible blow that the sad news brings for it just breaks a mothers heart it's the worst I ever got whatever I hope you will over look the liberty I have taken in writing to you but I felt I must thank you. With all good wishes for your safety I remain.

Yours truly

M Phin

Collins, who lived to over a hundred, kept Mrs Phin's letter all his life.

'my boy I love you dearly'
CAPTAIN JOHN COULL

LAST LETTER HOME TO A SON
2 APRIL 1917

France 2.4. 17 1 pm

My dear boy Fred,

This is a letter you will never see unless your daddy falls in the field. It is his farewell words to you in case anything happens. My boy I love you dearly and would have greatly liked to get leave for a few days to kiss you and shake hands again, after a few months separation, but as this seems at the present moment unlikely, I drop you this few lines to say 'God bless you' and keep you in the true brave manly upright course which I would like to see you follow.

You will understand better as you get older that your daddy came out to France for your sakes and for our Empire's sake. If he died it was in a good cause and all I would ask of you dear boy, is that you will keep this note in memory of me, and throughout your life may all that is good attend you and influence you. May you be strong to withstand the temptations of life and when you come to the evening of your days may you be able to say with St Paul 'I have fought the good fight'.

Goodbye dear boy and if it is that we are not to meet again in this life, may it be certain that we shall meet in another life to come, which faith I trust you will hold on to and live up to.

I remain ever

Your loving Daddy

J.F. Coull

John Coull, 23rd Royal Fusiliers, was killed in action on the Western Front on 30 September 1918, just six weeks before war's end.

Epistolic farewells like Coull's were not unusual. Far from it. A letter 'to be opened only in the event of my death' was penned by most soldiers on entering the front lines. Coull's simply stands in for every soldier father's.

'It seemed as though my lungs were shutting up'
GUNNER WILLIAM PRESSEY

GAS!, MESSINES
WESTERN FRONT, 7 JUNE 1917

The Germans first used poison gas in October 1914, but so defective was its employment that no one on the Allied side noticed. Following the successful German gas-attack at Ypres on 22 April 1915, the British determined to deploy the weapon themselves; the first offensive use of gas by the British army came on 25 September 1915 at Loos.

Anti-gas devices were initially extemporized; handkerchiefs soaked in urine, then placed over the nose, were popular, though some British troops used women's sanitary towels dipped in bicarbonate of soda. Official smoke helmets were issued intermittently throughout 1915, and the improved PH helmet came into being in 1917, to be replaced by the box respirator.

We had been shooting most of the night and the Germans had been hitting back with shrapnel, high explosive and gas shells. With the terrific noise and blinding flashes of gunfire, if a lull occurred for only a few minutes and you were leaning against something, you had just to close your eyes and you were asleep. Nearing daylight we were told to rest. We dived into the dugout, I pulled off my tunic and boots and was asleep in no time at all.

I was awakened by a terrific crash. The roof came down on my chest and legs and I couldn't move anything but my head. I thought, 'So this is it, then.' I found I could hardly breathe. Then I heard voices. Other fellows with gas helmets on, looking very frightening in the half-light, were lifting timber off me and one was forcing a gas helmet on me. Even when you were all right, to wear a gas helmet was uncomfortable, your nose pinched, sucking air through a canister of chemicals. As I was already choking I remember fighting against having this helmet on.

The next thing I knew was being carried on a stretcher past our officers and some distance from the guns. I heard someone ask, 'Who's that?' 'Bombardier Pressey, sir.' 'Bloody hell.' I was put into an ambulance and taken to the base, where we were placed on the stretchers side by side on the floor of a marquee, with about twelve inches in between. I suppose I resembled a kind of fish with my mouth open gasping for air. It seemed as if my lungs were gradually shutting up and my heart pounded away in my ears like the beat of a drum. On looking at the chap next to me I felt sick, for green stuff was oozing from the side of his mouth.

To get air into my lungs was real agony and the less I got the less the pain. I dozed off for short periods but seemed to wake in a sort of panic. To ease the pain in my chest I may subconsciously have stopped breathing, until the pounding of my heart woke me up. I was always surprised when I found myself awake, for I felt sure that I would die in my sleep.

Wilfred Owen, Artists' Rifles, captured for ever the sheer terror of a gas attack in *Dulce et Decorum Est*, 1917:

> Gas! GAS! Quick boys! – An ecstasy of fumbling,
> Fitting the clumsy helmets just in time;
> But someone still was yelling out and stumbling,
> And floundering like a man in fire or lime . .

*   *   *

Dim, through the misty panes and thick green light,
As under a green sea, I saw him drowning.

* * *

In all my dreams, before my helpless sight,
He plunges at me, guttering, choking, drowning . . .

*'Then into a hut all white inside, with a row of white
operating tables down the centre . . .'*
CAPTAIN JOHN GLUBB

MEDICAL OPERATION
FRANCE, 21 AUGUST 1917

I sat on the table in the cellar, while they dressed my wound. The RAMC [Royal Army Medical Corps] orderly put some plug into my neck which stopped the bleeding. They also put a rubber tube in my wound, sticking out of the bandage. They told me there was no ambulance in Hénin and I should have to walk to Boiry-Becquerelle. We accordingly set out, I leaning on the medical orderly's arm. I was not looking forward to the long walk at all, but luckily the orderly remembered that there was some regimental medical officer, who lived in a dugout at the south end of the village. We turned in there and I sat down on a stone at the entrance to the dugout.

This doctor said it was all rubbish not getting an ambulance, and sent the orderly back to the dressing station to telephone to Heninel for one. He took my temperature and said that I was all right for the moment, but I heard him tell the orderly that it was a good thing they dressed me at once, or I should have been done for. I felt no anxiety about whether I should live or die, but I was very cold, and the broken pieces of jawbone in my mouth were unpleasant. I felt no pain.

I gave the doctor my name and unit, and told him that our camp was on the Neuville – Vitasse road, next to the battalion in reserve. I wrote down, 'Please let them know,' for I could not speak. I heard later that the doctor sent the company a telegram, saying that I was badly wounded and was not expected to live.

At last the ambulance arrived and we set off. I was horribly cold, which I conveyed to the medical orderly by signs and he put a blanket round me. We went through Boiry-Becquerelle to the main Casualty Clearing Station (No. 20 CCS) at Ficheux. Here they helped me out and into a chair, when a doctor came up and said, 'What's the matter here, old man?' and took off and redid my bandage. I was put into the 'pending operations' ward, and slept like a log till the morning.

Early next morning I was dressed for the slaughter in long woollen stockings and laid in a line of stretchers waiting for operating. Somebody gave me an injection of morphia, and then two orderlies came up and said, 'Come on, this one will do first.' So they picked up my stretcher and bore me out, along the duckboard walks, with a steady bobbing up-and-down motion. Lying on my back, I looked up at the blue sky and the white drifting clouds.

Then into a hut all white inside, with a row of white operating tables down the centre and white-aproned doctors and nurses moving about. They held up my stretcher and I crawled over on to the table and lay down. One or two of them came to look at me, and then the anaesthetist came up, and told me to breathe deeply through my nose. At a word from the surgeon, he put the mask on my face and I smelt that suffocating sickly smell of gas. Once or twice I felt I would suffocate and longed to pull it off. Then my head began to sing, and a tap of water which was dripping seemed to grow louder and louder. I began saying to myself 'I'm still awake! Yes, of course, I must be.' The tap grew louder and louder, and beat all through my head. For a moment, the man took off the mask, and a voice said, 'How old are you?' I tried to say twenty, and he put the mask back. The singing and the tap grew louder – and then nothing.

When I came round again, Dad was beside my bed. I was almost perfectly conscious at once, and I remember writing down on a piece of paper, 'This rather spoils our leave.' We were both due for leave to England and had been trying to arrange to go together on 24 August. Colonel Rathbone had telephoned II Army that morning to say I was hit.

When Dad came into the mess for lunch, his staff officers, Colonel Stevenson and Major de Fonblanque, told him they had a message for him, which they would tell him after lunch. Not suspecting anything, he had a good lunch, and then they told him that I had been hit and that they had ordered his car to be ready, knowing that he would want to come and see me. So he drove down at once, but he was not allowed to stay long.

I remained half alive for several days, lying still all day only semi-conscious. I asked for a book to read but found I could not read it. I had apparently nearly swallowed my tongue during the operation and, to prevent this, they had pierced my tongue and threaded a wire through it with a wooden rod on the end of it. This was extremely uncomfortable. A good deal of discharge came from my mouth, and I was very miserable, with my pillow always covered with blood and slime. I was later told that I looked very bad, with my mouth dragged down, discharging and filthy, and with my head and neck all bandages.

The CCS was made entirely of marquees and tents, and was comfortable, considering the circumstances. The officers' ward consisted of three or four marquees, placed side by side, with boarded floors, and rows of beds with coloured counterpanes, and looked neat and pretty.

Glubb, Royal Engineers, did not return to active service until late in 1918. After the war he served the Jordanian royal family, and as 'Glubb Pasha' commanded the Arab Legion.

'5.10.pm–5.15. Sleep'
CAPTAIN GEOFFREY BOWEN

TRENCH LIFE
A DAY IN THE LIFE OF AN OFFICER
WESTERN FRONT, 3 SEPTEMBER 1917

Bowen served with the 2nd Lancashire Fusiliers.

8 p.m. Started.
9.30 p.m. Arrived.
11 p.m. Company arrived.
11 p.m. – 3 a.m. Round the line.
3.15 a.m. – 4.15 a.m. Sleep.

4.15 a.m. – 6 a.m. Stand to.

6 a.m. – 9. Sleep.

9 a.m. – 9.30 a.m. Breakfast: bacon, eggs, tinned sausage.

9.30 a.m. – 10.10. Round line.

10.10 a.m. – 12. Reports etc.

12.30 p.m. Lunch: Steak, potatoes, beans, sweet omelette.

1.45 p.m. – 2.15. Daylight patrol.

2.15 p.m. – 2.30 Sleep.

2.30 p.m. 3.40. Gup [chat] with C.O.

4. pm. Tea, bread, jam.

4.30 p.m. – 4.35. Sleep.

4.35 p.m. – 5.10. Entertain "Bowes".

5.10 p.m. – 5.15. Sleep.

5.15 p.m. – 5.25. Trench Mortar Officer reports.

5.25 p.m. – 6.15. Sleep.

6.15 p.m. – 6.35. Entertain Brain and Padre.

6.35 p.m. – 7.30. Sleep.

7.30 p.m. – 8. Round line.

8 p.m. – 8.15 Dinner: Steak, potatoes, tinned fruit and custard.

8.15 p.m. – 9. Round line.

11.30 p.m. – 12.30 a.m. Sleep.

12.30 – 2.30 a.m. Intensive sniping.

2.30–5 a.m. Sleep.

'There followed a terrific roar, and the line vanished from sight behind a spouting cloud of smoke'
LIEUTENANT-COLONEL T.E. LAWRENCE

LAWRENCE OF ARABIA BLOWS UP A TRAIN ON THE HEJAZ RAILWAY
SEPTEMBER 1917

An archaeologist, Thomas Edward Lawrence joined the army in 1914, initially serving in intelligence before being attached to the Hejaz Expeditionary Force, an 'army' of Arab irregulars under Sheikh Feisal. 'Lawrence of Arabia's' exploits in the desert, such as the 'train job' here, became much romanticised (by himself, not least) but they did have the military benefit of tying down thousands of Turkish troops.

It might also be said that Lawrence's guerrilla warfare prefigured the hit-and-run raids of World War II specials forces such as Stirling's SAS and Popski's Private Army.

It took me nearly two hours to dig in and cover the charge: then came the difficult job of unrolling the heavy wires from the detonator to the hills whence we would fire the mine. The top sand was crusted and had to be broken through in burying the wires. They were stiff wires, which scarred the wind-rippled surface with long lines like the belly marks of preposterously narrow and heavy snakes. When pressed down in one place they rose into the air in another. At last they had to be weighted down with rocks which, in turn, had to be buried at the cost of great disturbance of the ground.

Afterwards it was necessary, with a sand-bag, to stipple the marks into a wavy surface; and, finally, with a bellows and long fanning sweeps of my cloak, to simulate the smooth laying of the wind. The whole job took five hours to finish; but then it was well finished: neither myself nor any of us could see where the charge lay, or that double wires led out underground from it to the firing point two hundred yards off, behind the ridge marked for our riflemen. . . .

The men with rifles posted themselves in a long line behind the spur running from the guns past the exploder to the mouth of the valley. From it they would fire directly into the derailed carriages at less than one hundred and fifty yards, whereas the ranges for the Stokes and Lewis guns were about three hundred yards. An Arab stood up on high behind the guns and shouted to us what the train was doing – a necessary precaution, for if it carried troops and detrained them behind our ridge we should have to face about like a flash and retire fighting up the valley for our lives. Fortunately it held on at all the speed the two locomotives could make on wood fuel.

It drew near where we had been reported, and opened random fire into the desert. I could hear the racket coming, as I sat on my hillock by the bridge to give the signal to Salem, who danced round the exploder on his knees, crying with excitement, and calling urgently on God to make him fruitful. The Turkish fire sounded heavy, and I wondered with how many men

we were going to have affair, and if the mine would be advantage
enough for our eighty fellows to equal them. It would have been
better if the first electrical experiment had been simpler.

However, at that moment the engines, looking very big, rocked
with screaming whistles into view around the bend. Behind them
followed ten box-wagons, crowded with rifle-muzzles at the windows and doors; and in little sand-bag nests on the roofs Turks
precariously held on, to shoot at us. I had not thought of two
engines, and on the moment decided to fire the charge under the
second, so that however little the mine's effect, the uninjured
engine should not be able to uncouple and drag the carriages away.

Accordingly, when the front 'driver' of the second engine was
on the bridge, I raised my hand to Salem. There followed a
terrific roar, and the line vanished from sight behind a spouting
column of black dust and smoke a hundred feet high and wide.
Out of the darkness came shattering crashes and long, loud
metallic clangings of ripped steel, with many lumps of iron and
plate; while one entire wheel of a locomotive whirled up suddenly
black out of the cloud against the sky, and sailed musically over
our heads to fall slowly and heavily into the desert behind. Except
for the flight of these, there succeded a deathly silence, with no
cry of men or rifle-shot, as the now grey mist of the explosion
drifted from the line towards us, and over our ridge until it was
lost in the hills.

In the lull, I ran southward to join the sergeants. Salem picked
up his rifle and charged out into the murk. Before I had climbed
to the guns the hollow was alive with shots, and with the brown
figures of the Beduin leaping forward to grips with the enemy. I
looked round to see what was happening so quickly, and saw the
train stationary and dismembered along the track, with its wagon
sides jumping under the bullets which riddled them, while Turks
were falling out from the far doors to gain the shelter of the
railway embankment.

As I watched, our machine-guns chattered out over my head,
and the long rows of Turks on the carriage roofs rolled over, and
were swept off the top like bales of cotton before the furious
shower of bullets which stormed along the roofs and splashed
clouds of yellow chips from the planking. The dominant position
of the guns had been an advantage to us so far.

When I reached Stokes and Lewis the engagement had taken another turn. The remaining Turks had got behind the bank, here about eleven feet high, and from cover of the wheels were firing point-blank at the Beduin twenty yards away across the sand-filled dip. The enemy in the crescent of the curving line were secure from the machine-guns; but Stokes slipped in his first shell, and after a few seconds there came a crash as it burst beyond the train in the desert.

He touched the elevating screw, and his second shot fell just by the trucks in the deep hollow below the bridge where the Turks were taking refuge. It made a shambles of the place. The survivors of the group broke out in a panic across the desert, throwing away their rifles and equipment as they ran. This was the opportunity of the Lewis gunners. The sergeant grimly traversed with drum after drum, till the open sand was littered with bodies. Mushagraf, the Sherari boy behind the second gun, saw the battle over, threw aside his weapon with a yell, and dashed down at speed with his rifle to join the others who were beginning, like wild beasts, to tear open the carriages and fall to plunder. It had taken nearly ten minutes.

I looked up-line through my glasses and saw the Mudowwara patrol breaking back uncertainly towards the railway to meet the train-fugitives running their fastest northward. I looked south, to see our thirty men cantering their camels neck and neck in our direction to share the spoils. The Turks there, seeing them go, began to move after them with infinite precaution, firing volleys. Evidently we had a half-hour respite, and then a double threat against us.

I ran down to the ruins to see what the mine had done. The bridge was gone; and into its gap was fallen the front wagon, which had been filled with sick. The smash had killed all but three or four and had rolled dead and dying into a bleeding heap against the splintered end. One of those yet alive deliriously cried out the word typhus. So I wedged shut the door, and left them there, alone.

Succeeding wagons were derailed and smashed: some had frames irreparably buckled. The second engine was a blanched pile of smoking iron. Its driving wheels had been blown upward, taking away the side of the fire-box. Cab and tender were twisted into strips, among the piled stones of the bridge abutment. It would never run again. The front engine had got off better: though heavily derailed and lying half-over, with the cab burst, yet its steam was at pressure, and driving-gear intact.

Our greatest object was to destroy locomotives, and I had kept in my arms a box of gun-cotton with fuse and detonator ready fixed, to make sure such a case. I now put them in position on the outside cylinder. On the boiler would have been better, but the sizzling steam made me fear a general explosion which would sweep across my men (swarming like ants over the booty) with a blast of jagged fragments. Yet they would not finish their looting before the Turks came. So I lit the fuse, and in the half-minute of its burning drove the plunderers a little back, with difficulty. Then the charge burst, blowing the cylinder to smithers, and the axle too. At that moment I was distressed with uncertainty whether the damage were enough; but the Turks later found the engine beyond use and broke it up.

The valley was a weird sight. The Arabs, gone raving mad, were rushing about at top speed bareheaded and half-naked, scream-ing, shooting into the air, clawing one another nail and fist, while they burst open trucks and staggered back and forward with immense bales, which they ripped by the rail-side, and tossed through, smashing what they did not want. The train had been packed with refugees and sick men, volunteers for boat-service on the Euphrates, and families of Turkish officers returning to Damascus.

There were scores of carpets spread about; dozens of mattresses and flowered quilts, blankets in heaps, clothes for men and women in full variety; clocks, cooking-pots, food, ornaments and weapons. To one side stood thirty or forty hysterical women, unveiled, tearing their clothes and hair; shrieking themselves distracted. The Arabs without regard to them went on wrecking the household goods; looting their absolute fill. Camels had become common property. Each man frantically loaded the nearest with what it could carry and shooed it westward into the void, while he turned to his next fancy.

Seeing me tolerably unemployed, the women rushed, and caught at me with howls for mercy. I assured them that all was going well: but they would not get away till some husbands delivered me. These knocked their wives off and seized my feet in a very agony of terror of instant death. A Turk so broken down was a nasty spectacle: I kicked them off as well as I could with bare feet, and finally broke free.

Next a group of Austrians, officers and non-commissioned officers, appealed to me quietly in Turkish for quarter. I replied with my halting German; whereupon one, in English, begged a doctor for his wounds. We had none: not that it mattered, for he was mortally hurt and dying. I told them the Turks would return in an hour and care for them. But he was dead before that, as were most of the others (instructors in the new Skoda mountain howitzers supplied to Turkey for the Hejaz war), because some dispute broke out between them and my own bodyguard, and one of them fired a pistol shot at young Rahail. My infuriated men cut them down, all but two or three, before I could return to interfere.

So far as could be seen in the excitement, our side had suffered no loss. Among the ninety military prisoners were five Egyptian soldiers, in their underclothes. They knew me, and explained that in a night raid of Davenport's, near Wadi Ais, they had been cut off by the Turks and captured. They told me something of Davenport's work: of his continual pegging away in Abdulla's sector, which was kept alive by him for month after month, without any of the encouragement lent to us by success and local enthusiasm. His best helpers were such stolid infantrymen as these, whom I made lead the prisoners away to our appointed rallying place at the salt rocks.

Lewis and Stokes had come down to help me. I was a little anxious about them; for the Arabs, having lost their wits, were as ready to assault friend as foe. Three times I had had to defend myself when they pretended not to know me and snatched at my things. However, the sergeants' war-stained khaki presented few attractions. Lewis went out east of the railway to count the thirty men he had slain; and incidentally, to find Turkish gold and trophies in their haversacks. Stokes strolled through the wrecked bridge, saw there the bodies of twenty Turks torn to pieces by his second shell, and retired hurriedly.

*'A few minutes later Dr Dunn temporarily resigned
from the Royal Army Medical Corps'*
PRIVATE FRANK RICHARDS

PASSCHENDAELE

26–27 SEPTEMBER 1917

Richards, Royal Welch Fusiliers, was one of the few 'Contemptibles' to survive four years on the front line. He consistently refused any form of promotion but was awarded both the DCM and MM.

In July 1917 the British commander, Field Marshal Douglas Haig, launched another of his 'big pushes', the third battle of Ypres, sometimes known as Passchendaele. Richards, returning from home leave ('every man of military age that I met wanted to shake hands with me and also ask for my advice on how to evade military service'), rejoined the regiment in time to go into 'the blood tub' on 26 September:

Our Brigade were in reserve and ready to be called upon at any moment. Orders were given that no fires were to be lit. September 26th, 1917, was a glorious day from the weather point of view and when dawn was breaking Ricco and I who were crack hands at making smokeless fires had found a dump of pick-handles which when cut up in thin strips answered very well. We soon cooked our bacon and made tea for ourselves and the bank clerk and architect, and made no more smoke than a man would have done smoking a cigarette. We had at least made sure of our breakfast which might be the last we would ever have.

At 8 a.m. orders arrived that the Battalion would move off to the assistance of the Australians who had made an attack early in the morning on Polygon Wood. Although the attack was successful they had received heavy casualties and were now hard pressed themselves. Young Mr Casson led the way, as cool as a cucumber. One part of the ground we travelled over was nothing but lakes and boggy ground and the whole of the Battalion were strung out in Indian file walking along a track about eighteen inches wide. We had just got out of this bad ground but were still travelling in file when the enemy opened out with a fierce bombardment. Just in front of me half a dozen men fell on the side of the track: it was like as if a Giant Hand had suddenly swept them one side. The Battalion had close on a hundred casualties before they were out of that valley. If a man's best pal was wounded he could not stop to dress his wounds for him.

We arrived on some rising ground and joined forces with the Australians. I expected to find a wood but it was undulating land with a tree dotted here and there and little banks running in different directions. About half a mile in front of us was a ridge of trees, and a few concrete pillboxes of different sizes. The ground that we were now on and some of the pillboxes had only been taken some hours previously. I entered one pillbox during the day and found eighteen dead Germans inside. There was not a mark on one of them; one of our heavy shells had made a direct hit on the top of it and they were killed by concussion, but very little damage had been done to the pillbox. They were all constructed with reinforced concrete and shells could explode all round them but the flying pieces would never penetrate the concrete. There were small windows in the sides and by jumping in and out of shell holes attacking troops could get in bombing range: if a bomb was thrown through one of the windows the pillbox was as good as captured.

There was a strong point called Black Watch Corner which was a trench facing north, south, east and west. A few yards outside the trench was a pillbox which was Battalion Headquarters. The bank clerk, architect and I got in the trench facing our front, and I was soon on friendly terms with an Australian officer, whom his men called Mr Diamond. He was wearing the ribbon of the D.C.M., which he told me he had won in Gallipoli while serving in the ranks and had been granted a commission some time later. About a hundred yards in front of us was a bank which extended for hundreds of yards across the ground behind which the Australians were. Our chaps charged through them to take a position in front and Captain Mann, our Adjutant, who was following close behind, fell with a bullet through his head. The enemy now began to heavily bombard our position and Major Poore and Mr Casson left the pillbox and got in a large shell hole which had a deep narrow trench dug in the bottom of it. They were safer there than in the pillbox, yet in less than fifteen minutes an howitzer shell had pitched clean in it, killing the both of them.

During the day shells fell all around the pillbox but not one made a direct hit on it. The ground rocked and heaved with the bursting shells. The enemy were doing their best to obliterate the strong point that they had lost. Mr Diamond and I were mucking-in with a tin of Maconochies when a dud shell landed clean in the trench, killing the man behind me, and burying itself in the side of the trench by me. Our Maconochie was spoilt but I opened another one and we had the luck to eat that one without a clod of earth being thrown over it. If that shell had not been a dud we should have needed no more Maconochies in this world. I had found eight of them in a sandbag before I left the wood and brought them along with me. I passed the other six along our trench, but no one seemed to want them with the exception of the bank clerk and architect who had got into my way of thinking that it was better to enter the next world with a full belly than an empty one.

The bombardment lasted until the afternoon and then ceased. Not one of us had hardly moved a yard for some hours but we had been lucky in our part of the trench, having only two casualties. In two other parts of the strong point every man had been killed or wounded. The shells had been bursting right on the parapets and in the trenches, blowing them to pieces. One part of the trench was completely obliterated. The fourth part of the strong point had also been lucky, having only three casualties. Mr Diamond said that we could expect a counter attack at any minute. He lined us up on the parapet in extended order outside the trench and told us to lie down. Suddenly a German plane swooped very low, machine-gunning us. We brought him down but not before he had done some damage, several being killed including our Aid Post Sergeant.

A few minutes later Dr. Dunn temporarily resigned from the Royal Army Medical Corps. He told me to get him a rifle and bayonet and a bandolier of ammunition. I told him that he had better have a revolver but he insisted on having what he had asked me to get. I found them for him and slinging the rifle over his shoulder he commenced to make his way over to the troops behind the bank. I accompanied him. Just before we reached there our chaps who were hanging on to a position in front of it started to retire back. The doctor barked at them to line up with the others. Only Captain Radford and four platoon officers were left in the Battalion and the Doctor unofficially took command.

We and the Australians were all mixed up in extended order. Everyone had now left the strong point and were lined up behind the bank, which was about three feet high. We had lent a Lewis-gun team to the 5th Scottish Rifles on our right, and when it began to get dark the Doctor sent me with a verbal message to bring them back with me, if they were still in the land of the living. When I arrived at the extreme right of our line I asked the right-hand man if he was in touch with the 5th Scottish. He replied that he had no more idea than a crow where they were, but guessed that they were somewhere in front and to the right of him. I now made my way very carefully over the ground. After I had walked some way I began to crawl. I was liable any moment to come in contact with a German post or trench. I thought I saw someone moving in front of me, so I slid into a shell hole and landed on a dead German. I waited in that shell hole for a while trying to pierce the darkness in front. I resumed my journey and, skirting one shell hole, a wounded German was shrieking aloud in agony: he must have been hit low down but I could not stop for no wounded man. I saw the forms of two men in a shallow trench and did not know whether they were the 5th Scottish or the Germans until I was sharply challenged in good Glasgow English. When I got in their trench they told me that they had only just spotted me when they challenged. The Lewis-gun team were still kicking and my journey back with them was a lot easier than the outgoing one.

I reported to the Doctor that there was a gap of about one hundred yards between the 5th Scottish Rifles and we; and he went himself to remedy it. The whole of the British Front that night seemed to be in a semi-circle. We had sent up some S O S rockets and no matter where we looked we could see our S O S rockets going up in the air: they were only used when the situation was deemed critical and everybody seemed to be in the same plight as ourselves. The bank clerk and I got into a shell hole to snatch a couple of hours rest, and although there were two dead Germans in it we were soon fast asleep. I was woke up to guide a ration party to us who were on their way. Dawn was now breaking and I made my way back about six hundred yards, where I met them. We landed safely with the rations.

Major Kearsley had just arrived from B Echelon to take command of the Battalion. The Brigadier-General of the Australians had also arrived and was sorting his men out. It was the only time during the whole of the War that I saw a brigadier with the first line of attacking troops. Some brigadier that I knew never moved from Brigade Headquarters. It was also the first time I had been in action with the Australians and I found them very brave men. There was also an excellent spirit of comradeship between officers and men.

We were moving about quite freely in the open but we did not know that a large pillbox a little over an hundred yards in front of us was still held by the enemy. They must have all been having a snooze, otherwise some of us would have been riddled. Major Kearsley, the Doctor and I went out reconnoitring. We were jumping in and out of shell holes when a machine-gun opened out from somewhere in front, the bullets knocking up the dust around the shell holes we had just jumped into. They both agreed that the machine-gun had been fired from the pillbox about a hundred yards in front of us. We did some wonderful jumping and hopping, making our way back to the bank. The enemy's artillery had also opened out and an hour later shells were bursting all over our front and in the rear of us.

A sapping platoon of one sergeant and twenty men under the command of The Athlete were on the extreme left of the bank, and the Major and I made our way towards them. We found the men but not the officer and sergeant, and when the Major inquired where they were they replied that they were both down the dug-out. There was a concrete dug-out at this spot which had been taken the day before. I shouted down for them to come up, and the Major gave the young officer a severe reprimand for being in the dug-out, especially as he knew our men had just started another attack. Our chaps and the 5th Scottish Rifles had attacked on our right about fifteen minutes previously. The Major gave The Athlete orders that if the pillbox in front was not taken in fifteen minutes he was to take his platoon and capture it and then dig a trench around it. If the pillbox was captured during that time he was still to take his platoon and sap around it. I felt very sorry for The Athlete. This was the first real action he had been in and he had the most windy sergeant in the Battalion with him. Although The Athlete did not know it, this sergeant had been extremely lucky after one of the Arras stunts that he had not been court-martialled and tried on the charge of cowardice in face of the enemy.

We arrived back at our position behind the bank. We and the Australians were in telephone communication with no one; all messages went by runners. Ricco, the bank clerk and the architect were running messages, the majority of our Battalion runners being casualties. Sealyham was still kicking and Lane was back in Bechelon; it was the first time for over two years he had been left out of the line. The Sapping-Sergeant came running along the track by the bank and informed the Major that The Athlete had sent him for further instructions as he was not quite certain what he had to do. The Major very nearly lost his temper and told me to go back with the Sergeant and tell him what he had to do. Just as we arrived at the sapping-platoon we saw some of our chaps rushing towards the pillbox which surrendered, one officer and twenty men being inside it.

The enemy were now shelling very heavily and occasionally the track was being sprayed by machine-gun bullets. I met a man of one of our companies with six German prisoners whom he told me he had to take back to a place called Clapham Junction, where he would hand them over. He then had to return and rejoin his company. The shelling was worse behind us than where we were and it happened more than once that escort and prisoners had been killed making their way back. I had known this man about eighteen months and he said, 'Look here, Dick. About an hour ago I lost the best pal I ever had, and he was worth all these six Jerries put together. I'm not going to take them far before I put them out of mess.' Just after they passed me I saw the six dive in one large shell hole and he had a job to drive them out. I expect being under their own shelling would make them more nervous than under ours. Some little time later I saw him coming back and I knew it was impossible for him to have reached Clapham Junction and returned in the time, especially by the way his prisoners had been ducking and jumping into shell holes. As he passed me again he said: 'I done them in as I said, about two hundred yards back. Two bombs did the trick.' He had not walked twenty yards beyond me when he fell himself: a shell-splinter had gone clean through him. I had often heard some of our chaps say that they had done their prisoners in whilst taking them back but this was the only case I could vouch for, and no doubt the loss of his pal had upset him very much.

During the afternoon the Major handed me a message to take to A Company, which consisted of the survivors of two companies now merged into one under the command of a young platoon officer. They had to advance and take up a position about two hundred yards in front of them. The ground over which I had to travel had been occupied by the enemy a little while before and the Company were behind a little bank which was being heavily shelled. I slung my rifle, and after I had proceeded some way I pulled my revolver out for safety. Shells were falling here and there and I was jumping in and out of shell holes. When I was about fifty yards from the Company, in getting out of a large shell hole I saw a German pop up from another shell hole in front of me and rest his rifle on the lip of the shell hole. He was about to fire at our chaps in front who had passed him by without noticing him. He could never have heard me amidst all the din around: I expect it was some instinct made him turn around with the rifle at his shoulder. I fired first and as the rifle fell out of his hands I fired again. I made sure he was dead before I left him. If he hadn't popped his head up when he did no doubt I would have passed the shell hole he was in. I expect he had been shamming death and every now and then popping up and sniping at our chaps in front. If I hadn't spotted him he would have soon put my lights out after I had passed him and if any of his bullets had found their mark it would not have been noticed among the Company, who were getting men knocked out now and then by the shells that were bursting around them. This little affair was nothing out of the ordinary in a runner's work when in attacks.

The shelling was very severe around here and when I arrived I shouted for the officer. A man pointed along the bank. When I found him and delivered the message he shouted above the noise that he had not been given much time; I had delivered the message only three minutes before they were timed to advance. During the short time they had been behind the bank one-third of the Company had become casualties. When I arrived back I could only see the Major. All the signallers had gone somewhere on messages and the Doctor was some distance away attending wounded men whom he came across. He seemed to be temporarily back in the R.A.M.C.

After four months of mud and blood, Haig called off the Passchendaele offensive; some 260,000 Allied casualties attested to the success of the German defensive line.

Then, in March 1918, the Germans tried a big push of their own: the Michael offensive. This storm of steel pushed the British Expeditionary Force back as much as forty miles. Haig issued an order on 11 April that: 'There is no other course open to us but to fight it out! Every position must be held to the last man.'

To divine the mood of the Army, GHQ surveyed soldiers' letters home:

You will probably have seen a few bits about us in the newspapers (Glorious Deeds!). If you ever hear anybody say that the troops are in excellent spirits just refer them to this battery. The sooner one side wins the better and we know who will win (*not us*).

* * *

It is no use being pessimistic Clara for I tell you we are bound to win with the men we have got. I have just seen a battalion of them going into the trenches. They look into the gates of Hell and laugh, this every day and night, and I tell you the boys of Britain cannot be beat.

* * *

Any one reading the papers can see that our Government is full of corruption, that is what has made a chap sick of the whole business out here, there are a good many out here my dear like myself fed up and don't care a damn which side wins. After four years and now we are being pushed back and no end in sight.

* * *

The night previous to our departure from the billet for the trenches we were all singing and a chap just remarked 'You would think we were going home instead of going into the arena', but this is where we beat Fritz; in dark days or bright, we don't lose heart, 'Jerry' may give us a smack today, but he will get a harder one tomorrow. Really I am so proud to be a British soldier and to be able to fight to the bitter end for British interest and it is the same with us all here.

They did fight to the bitter end. At Manchester Hill only 40 men from the 16th Battalion emerged from the defence alive and free; their commanding officer, Lieutenant-Colonel Elstob, was awarded the VC. Posthumously.

Under the strain of it all, however, some were going 'bomb happy'.

'this pathetic, scrabbling incoherent animal that had once been a British Staff Officer'
Captain Arthur Osburn

A SHELL-SHOCKED OFFICER
1918

It was a depressing experience. The shelter we were in had only been a temporary one, constructed for the crews of the German artillery before they had been driven back. So the side facing their line was naturally quite unprotected from their fire. Long abandoned and out of repair, a single hit would have undoubtedly brought the half-rotten 'roof' and tons of bricks and rubble down on top of us. We literally cowered in the mud, feeling quite helpless. Suddenly three men of the Brigade Signals appeared in the entrance carrying or rather dragging a Staff Officer. Breathlessly they flung him inside and, shouting something about 'the General's orders,' bolted out again. There was no chance of getting further explanations, for the piece of ground that lay between our shelter and the ladder leading underground to the good German dug-out which Brigade Headquarters had annexed was being well plastered with shell.

The Staff Officer, a biggish man, somewhere between twenty-five and thirty, lay moaning on the ground. We could find no wound. In the din I tried to question him, thinking he had been seized with a fit or with acute internal pain. But he only moaned and jibbered and shook his head, grovelling on the ground at my feet with his face pressed to the muddy floor. While I questioned him we were suddenly assailed by a more than usually heavy burst of shelling. A perfect hurricane of whizz-bangs, skimming just over the roof and bursting on a bank only about ten yards away, the splinters rattling on the roof or flying back through the entrance.

The grovelling object appeared now to be suddenly seized with a fresh access of terror. Wildly and incoherently he made efforts to conceal himself between the remains of a broken chair and the mud wall of the shelter. Then suddenly, spasmodically, he began to dig furiously with his fingers. The huddled men, mostly stretcher-bearers of the R.A.M.C., stared at him in amazement, the pink tabs on his collar, and a decoration on his smart uniform, seemed strangely inconsistent with this extraordinary behaviour. It was a case of complete loss of nerve and self-control. Driven mad with terror, slobbering and moaning, he clawed and scrabbled violently in the mud, his head under the chair. It was like a terrified and overrun fox going to ground, trying to dig his way back to safety through the very bowels of the earth. His behaviour was simply less than human. Extreme terror had driven him back through a thousand generations to some pre-human form of life. I suppose some cringing prehistoric half-human thing, making futile efforts to escape from rending beak and steely claw of hovering pterodactyl, may once have burrowed and behaved thus. Not wishing to have my men, who were in any case not enjoying the shelling, demoralized by this exhibition of terror from an officer, who had himself passed orders on to me, I made renewed attempts to quiet him. Above the roar of shelling I shouted in his ear:

'You're all right – safe here! Keep still – be quiet! In a moment, as soon as this shelling stops we'll carry you to an ambulance! Quite close! You'll go back – straight to the Base – Home – and have a long rest! Try and sit up and swallow some brandy.'

But one might as well have spoken to a mad dog. At last, the shelling abating a little, I got three of the biggest men I had with me to lay hold of this pathetic, scrabbling incoherent animal that had once been a British Staff Officer, and we tried to drag him, or carry him out. He resisted violently.

At last after several efforts we got rid of him. Halfway to the ambulance that would carry him to safety he tried to bolt back to us! The three men had to risk their lives to get him across the hundred and fifty yards of comparatively open ground and across a road into an old gun-pit where I had had a Ford motor-ambulance concealed. I do not know what became of him; possibly he never reached home alive, or perhaps he is in an asylum. Perhaps, recovered, he shoots partridges now in Norfolk, dines at Claridges, hunts with the North Cotswold, or keeps a chicken farm in Surrey. But when one thinks of how we treated this Staff Officer, and how, on the other hand, some poor, half-educated, blubbering ploughboy, whose nerves had likewise given way, and who was not much more than half this Staff Officer's age, was sent back to face the enemy or be shot for cowardice . . . But that is war. It must often be luck; it can never mean justice.

The Great War was the first in which British soldiers were understood to suffer damage beyond the purely physical; in 1916 'mental wards' were opened in base hospitals for cases of shell-shock and 'anxiety neurosis'. In 1921 65,000 British victims of shell-shock were still receiving disability pensions.

'the most remarkable feature of that day and night was the uncanny silence that prevailed'
CAPTAIN LLEWELYN EVANS

ARMISTICE
FRANCE, 11 NOVEMBER 1918

And then the war was over. Everywhere along the Western Front the German army was in rout. With the writing on the wall, written large and in blood, the German Supreme Command sued for peace.

November 11th. There had been so much talk of an armistice that a Brigade message in the morning telling us of its having been signed at 8 o'clock, and that hostilities were to cease at 11, fell somewhat flat. The event was anticlimax relieved by some spasmodic cheering when the news got about, by a general atmosphere of 'slacking off for the day', and by the notes of a lively band in the late afternoon. The men betook themselves to their own devices. There was a voluntary Service of Thanksgiving in the cinema which the Germans had built; the spacious building was quite full. The local civilians were overjoyed. They dug out some *drapeaux des Alliées* in astonishingly quick time. And they were hospitable with their poor means. They brewed an awful decoction of baked ground oats in place of coffee which had been

unobtainable for a long time. To me the most remarkable feature
of that day and night was the uncanny silence that prevailed. No
rumbling of guns, no staccato of machine-guns, nor did the roar
of exploding dumps break into the night as it had so often done.
The War was over.

Some 950,000 soldiers from Britain and the Empire died in the Great War. A whole
generation.

The 'War to end all Wars' did no such thing. There were always Britain's small
wars to fight, and the inter-war Tommy found himself in action in Ireland, Russia,
Iraq, Egypt and India and Burma.

'The decanters circulated again'
SECOND-LIEUTENANT JOHN MASTERS

REGIMENTAL MESS
INDIA, 1935

John Masters was commissioned into the 4th Prince of Wales's Own Gurkha Rifles
in 1935, just in time to see the Indian Army in all its old, cane-chair, gin-swilling
majesty:

A guest night was approaching, at which I would be ceremonially
'dined into' the regiment. Days ahead I started to worry over the
details of my dress and appearance. Biniram was neither excited
nor frightened, which makes his negligence the more
inexcusable. On the night my shirt was stiff and white as it could
be, my black bow tie beautifully tied, and my mess Wellingtons
polished like mirrors. After walking into the anteroom, I checked
at attention with the proper carefully rehearsed carelessness, and
said, 'Good evening, sir,' to the senior officer present. Alas, I had
two fly buttons undone.

Major and Brevet Lieut.-Colonel David Murray-Lyon, D.S.O.,
M.C. – more usually known as M.L. – said, 'Good evening,
Masters. Stars in the east, I see. Good lord, that doesn't matter.
Do 'em up. Well, this is the last time you'll be a regimental
guest until you get married, so make the best of it. What d'you
want?'

'A gimlet, please, sir.' 'Orderly, *yota* gimlet, *yota* gin-mixie-vermouth-cherry. Jim, can the C.O. come in tonight?'

'No, sir, he's held up at Dalhousie. You're the senior dining member.'

The room was full of officers. Many voices arose.

'Orderly, *dwui siano* whisky-soda.' '*Mero lagi pani.*' '*Ek* gimlet.' '*Dwui* sherry.' '*Tin thulo* whisky-soda.'

The orderly listened and said amiably, '*Huzoor, sahib!*'

The voices continued. 'Heard the latest about Sheepers? He persuaded some girl that . . .'

'Take Austria, now. *They* don't care, they're *gemütlich*. German in a way, but sort of carefree . . .'

'It's all very well for you, but we machine-gunners have work to do while you're bumsucking round battalion office. 7157 ought to be promoted and then there's 7493 too, and as for 6701 . . .'

'. . . Christmas Week in Lahore. The Boy's bought a racehorse. He gave me a tip for . . .'

'. . . crossed the Baralacha just ahead of a blizzard and came down through Zingzingbar behind forty Tibetans from the Patseo sheep fair. Stank like badgers, but one of them was a wonderful old boy. Lectured me on . . .'

'6573? That's Sarbdhan, isn't it? The one who got hit in the bottom in 'thirty-one?'

'Yes, but it wasn't his fault, you ass.'

A small Gurkha wearing bottle-green full-dress uniform marched into the room, saluted, and said, '*Sahib, khana tay yar chha.*'

M. L. said, 'Are we all here? Oh, you again, James, late as usual.'

'Good evening, sir. My watch – damned clock.'

Out on the green lawn under the lights the band struck up 'The Roast Beef of Old England,' and we straggled into the dining-room. The officers who chose to sit at the head and foot of the table became the president and vice-president respectively, for the meal. No one else had any special place except that the senior dining member sat half-way down the table to the president's left, with the principal guest immediately on his right. On this night M. L., the second-in-command of the battalion, was the senior dining member, and I was the principal and only guest.

I accepted a glass of sherry and looked around, while cautiously toying with the hors d'œuvres. Outside, now that we were all seated, the band started on selections from *The Mikado*. The Gurkha in full dress, the three black chevrons on his right sleeve hardly visible against the dark-green cloth, stood immobile behind the president's chair. He was Machhindra, the mess havildar. The candlelight gleamed warmly on his wrinkled bronze face and glinted in his eyes as he glanced around the table and at the bearers who were serving up the food.

Around me the conversation rippled in comfortable waves. People spoke to me sufficiently to keep me in the current, and M. L. saw to it that my glass was never empty. I, on the other hand, saw to it that the level of the champagne in the glass did not go down too fast, for the disastrous June Ball of 1933 was much in my mind. Before I realized that the meal had progressed so far, the bearers were clearing the table. The decanters of port, sherry, madeira, and whisky circulated clockwise from the president. The orderlies took our water glasses away. This has been done in most messes since the day of King George I. Secret sympathizers with the Stuart cause would drink to the health of 'the King,' but would pass their wine glasses over their water glasses as they spoke, thus changing the toast from Hanoverian George to Stuart James or Charles, who were in exile in France – 'the king over the water.'

The president rang a tiny bell, a silver replica of the regimental war memorial. We fell silent. The president rose to his feet and said quietly, 'Mr Vice, the King Emperor.'

The vice-president rose, glass in hand, and said, 'Gentlemen, the King Emperor.'

We all stood up and drank the King Emperor's health.

The president sat down, turned to the mess havildar, and asked him to invite the bandmaster in for a drink. Little Mr Adams entered and agreed to have a glass of port with the president. This was an invariable custom, but he managed to look shyly gratified at the invitation. As there was no place on our Establishment for a bandmaster of any sort, let alone a British one, we paid his salary from the Band Fund, which was principally supported by subscriptions from the officers.

While Mr Adams was still sitting there the president caught M. L.'s eye. The president nodded at the mess havildar, and

Machhindra went out of the room. By now cigars and cigarettes were alight all round the table, and the decanters had made a second circuit.

A high, droning roar arose in the garden outside, and I started in my seat with alarm. Then high whines superimposed themselves upon the roar. I would have said then, in 1935, that the noise sounded like a hurricane a-building, but now I would describe it as an approaching squadron of jets. The mingled noises grew louder. I paled and looked around the table, ready to dive under it if anyone else showed a sign of doing so. But the officers went on with their talk, albeit now they had to bellow at one another above the din.

Machhindra flung open the double doors behind the president. Hard on his heels the noise burst upon us and overwhelmed us, and with it, one behind another in single file, came the four bagpipers who were causing it. The leader swung his shoulders and began to march around the table; the others followed. All wore rifle-green full dress. Silk banners hung from two of the pipes, one green, one pale silver.

I did not think I liked bagpipes, and their noise was very loud indeed. I crouched lower in my chair, but not too noticeably, for it was already clear that M.L. was a Highland fanatic and an expert bagpiper. He looked up keenly now, listening sharply to every note from each pipe, a slight frown creasing his rugged face as blurred fingering or a false grace note displeased him. The smoke curled to the ceiling from the cigarette held up rather high between his strong fingers. He smoked only his own special oval cigarettes of peculiar pungency, made in Aden by a Greek merchant, stamped with our crest, and sent to him in boxes of five hundred. I looked at the pipe programme in its little silver stand in front of him, and saw that they were playing the quick march of the first set, 'The Green Hills of Tyrol.'

The steady unison broke. 'The Green Hills' is one of the few pipe tunes that has a 'second' part, and now our pipe-major dropped into it. Suddenly the haunting minor harmony infused the steady cadence with a sad magic. As suddenly the plane on which I was experiencing the events of the evening moved from the directly seen to the indirectly felt, from the outside to the inside, from the senses to the spirit.

They had taken me into this family, and I felt the comradeship of those who had come before me to this table and been received into this home. I saw their graves on the banks of the Euphrates, in the Afghan snows, under the poplars beside the *pavé* to Neuve Chapelle, on the Russian steppes, in the seas and the mountains and the hills – oh, the green hills, the green hills . . .

The candlelight shone on the centrepiece. There, set on an ebony stand formally carved to represent waves, a Chinese junk rode, nose down, over the smooth surface of the table. Its silver-woven sails bellied to the imagined wind, its masthead pennants streamed forward, its tiny cannon peered out among the silver cordage, its helmsman stood steady at the tiller above the high stern. In front of the president stood a silver statuette of a Gurkha – Naik Chandsing Thapa of ours. It was in 1905 that he was a naik, and in that same year (the second of my father's service in India, the last of my great-uncle's) the 1st Gurkhas had given us this statuette of him. An earthquake had destroyed their home station of Dharmsala, and a party of ours, Chandsing among them, went to the rescue. Dharmsala is thirty-five miles from Bakloh by precipitous mountain paths. Every man of our rescue party had been given a pick, shovel, or crowbar and told to find his own way to Dharmsala as fast as he could. They all arrived before nightfall that same evening.

Farther down the table a monstrosity of Victorian craftsman-ship, only less ornately symbolic than the Albert Memorial, sent its pillars and cupids writhing towards the ceiling. In its vast shadow rested a delicate vase presented to us by Lord Curzon, the Viceroy of that time, in 1900. More silver gleamed everywhere – cups, candelabra, ashtrays, beakers; and on the wall hung presentation shields of wood and silver, and between the shields were the heads, horns, tusks, and skulls of animals.

This was our family's home. Here were the beautiful things any family picks up over the years. Here were the horrors presented by Aunt Hattie and kept on display because Aunt Hattie is a nice old thing and no one wants to offend her. (Our Aunt Hattie was usually the Maharajah of Nepal.) Here were purely sentimental pieces, meaningless to anyone outside the family, military equivalents of locks of hair – medals, swords, and photographs; the unspeakable watercolour old Colonel Snodgrass did the night the mess tent burned down after the battle of Umbeyla. Or was it Ali Masjid?

The pipers finished the set – slow march, quick march, strathspey, and reel – and marched out. While we banged on the table in applause Machhindra placed the quaich in front of the president. This was a small, shallow silver bowl with stub handles. The president half filled it with neat Scotch whisky, and Machhindra took it to M. L. The pipe-major marched in, halted with a clash of boots beside M. L.'s chair, turned to face the table, and saluted. M. L. rose to his feet, handed him the quaich, and picked up his own glass. All the others remained seated but took their glasses in hand, and I followed suit. The pipe-major raised the quaich in front of his face with both hands, looked round at us over the brim, and shouted '*Taggra raho!*' ('Good health!'). He poured the whisky down his throat in one easy motion till it was all gone, and went on turning over the quaich until he could kiss the bottom with a loud smack. Then he reversed it again, bowed his head, and handed it back to M. L. All the officers cried out, '*Taggra raho!*' raised their glasses, and drank to the pipe-major.

The decanters circulated again. The solo piper marched in and played a set. M. L. was in serious doubt whether he should be given a drink, as he had been careless with his grace notes. Finally he relented, and again we answered, '*Taggra raho,*' to the piper's salute. The band struck up on the lawn, now playing 'In a Monastery Garden.' (They could also play a brass-band arrangement of Beethoven's Fifth.)

M. L. said, 'Drink up, and we'll go into the anteroom.' No one could leave the table until I did, for I was a regimental guest. The president and vice-president could not leave until everyone else had.

In the anteroom we slowly gathered again. Two captains sprawled in chairs, their long legs up, arguing good-humouredly about music. M. L. pressed a glass of brandy and soda on me. Someone began to do tricks on the mantelpiece. The orderlies were giggling, and Moke had one of their caps on. M. L. was in good form, and it looked as though a real party was developing. I began to join in.

Then I collected my wits. I was a regimental guest. Therefore no one might leave the mess until I did. I thanked M. L. for the regiment's hospitality, stiffened to attention, and said, 'Good night, sir.'

I thought I saw a momentary gleam of approval in M. L.'s eye as he said, 'Good night, Masters.'

Perhaps I had learned something already – a little self-discipline. I went out, and alone, to bed. But it wasn't lonely in the deserted bungalow, though I could hear the party going on in the mess until three in the morning.

For all its apparent easy-living, the Indian Army could still fight; shortly after Masters' regimental mess it defeated the Pathans on the North-West Frontier.

In Europe, meanwhile, the Second World War was in dress rehearsal.

'a bullet shot past my ear with a vicious crack'
MILITIAMAN GEORGE ORWELL

SPANISH CIVIL WAR
DUCKING A FASCIST BULLET
JANUARY 1937

The writer George Orwell was one of several hundred leftist sympathisers from Britain who volunteered to fight for the elected Spanish republic against Franco's fascists. Most volunteers joined the International Brigade, but Orwell joined the Trotskyist militia, the POUM.

The road wound between yellow infertile fields, untouched since last year's harvest. Ahead of us was the low sierra that lies between Alcubierre and Zaragoza. We were getting near the front line now, near the bombs, the machine-guns, and the mud. In secret I was frightened. I knew the line was quiet at present, but unlike most of the men about me I was old enough to remember the Great War, though not old enough to have fought in it. War, to me, meant roaring projectiles and skipping shards of steel; above all it meant mud, lice, hunger, and cold. It is curious, but I dreaded the cold much more than I dreaded the enemy. The thought of it had been haunting me all the time I was in Barcelona; I had even lain awake at nights thinking of the cold in the trenches, the stand-to's in the grisly dawns, the long hours on sentry-go with a frosted rifle, the icy mud that would slop over my boot-tops. I admit, too, that I felt a kind of horror as I looked at the people I was marching among. You cannot possibly conceive what a rabble we looked. We straggled along with far less cohesion than a flock of sheep; before we had gone two miles the rear of the column was out of sight. And quite half of the so-called men were children – but I mean literally children, of sixteen years old at the very most. Yet they were all happy and excited at the prospect of getting to the front at last. As we neared the line the boys round the red flag in front began to utter shouts of 'Visca P.O.U.M.!' 'Fascistas-maricones!' and so forth – shouts which were meant to be war-like and menacing, but which, from those childish throats, sounded as pathetic as the cries of kittens. It seemed dreadful that the defenders of the Republic should be this mob of ragged children carrying worn-out rifles which they did not know how to use. I remember wondering what would happen if a Fascist aeroplane passed our way – whether the airman would even bother to dive down and give us a burst from his machine-gun. Surely even from the air he could see that we were not real soldiers?

As the road struck into the sierra we branched off to the right and climbed a narrow mule-track that wound round the mountain-side. The hills in that part of Spain are of a queer formation, horseshoe-shaped with flattish tops and very steep sides running down into immense ravines. On the higher slopes nothing grows except stunted shrubs and heath, with the white bones of the limestone sticking out everywhere. The front line here was not a continuous line of trenches, which would have been impossible in such mountainous country; it was simply a chain of fortified posts, always known as 'positions', perched on each hill-top. In the distance you could see our 'position' at the crown of the horseshoe; a ragged barricade of sand-bags, a red flag fluttering, the smoke of dug-out fires. A little nearer, and you could smell a sickening sweetish stink that lived in my nostrils for weeks afterwards. Into the cleft immediately behind the position all the refuse of months had been tipped – a deep festering bed of breadcrusts, excrement, and rusty tins.

The company we were relieving were getting their kits together. They had been three months in the line; their uniforms were caked with mud, their boots falling to pieces, their faces mostly bearded. The captain commanding the position, Levinski by name, but known to everyone as Benjamin, and by birth a Polish Jew, but speaking French as his native language, crawled out of his dug-out and greeted us. He was a short youth of about twenty-five, with stiff black hair and a pale eager face which at this period of the war was always very dirty. A few stray bullets were cracking high overhead. The position was a semi-circular enclosure about fifty yards across, with a parapet that was partly sand-bags and partly lumps of limestone. There were thirty or forty dug-outs running into the ground like rat-holes. Williams, myself, and Williams's Spanish brother-in-law made a swift dive for the nearest unoccupied dug-out that looked habitable. Somewhere in front an occasional rifle banged, making queer rolling echoes among the stony hills. We had just dumped our kits and were crawling out of the dug-out when there was another bang and one of the children of our company rushed back from the parapet with his face pouring blood. He had fired his rifle and had somehow managed to blow out the bolt; his scalp was torn to ribbons by the splinters of the burst cartridge-case. It was our first casualty, and, characteristically, self-inflicted.

In the afternoon we did our first guard and Benjamin showed us round the position. In front of the parapet there ran a system of narrow trenches hewn out of the rock, with extremely primitive loopholes made of piles of limestone. There were twelve sentries, placed at various points in the trench and behind the inner parapet. In front of the trench was the barbed wire, and then the hillside slid down into a seemingly bottomless ravine; opposite were naked hills, in places mere cliffs of rock, all grey and wintry, with no life anywhere, not even a bird. I peered cautiously through a loophole, trying to find the Fascist trench.

'Where are the enemy?'

Benjamin waved his hand expansively. 'Over zere.' (Benjamin spoke English – terrible English.)

'But *where?*'

According to my ideas of trench warfare the Fascists would be fifty or a hundred yards away. I could see nothing – seemingly their trenches were very well concealed. Then with a shock of dismay I saw where Benjamin was pointing; on the opposite hill-top, beyond the ravine, seven hundred metres away at the very least, the tiny outline of a parapet and a red-and-yellow flag – the

Fascist position. I was indescribably disappointed. We were nowhere near them! At that range our rifles were completely useless. But at this moment there was a shout of excitement. Two Fascists, greyish figurines in the distance, were scrambling up the naked hill-side opposite. Benjamin grabbed the nearest man's rifle, took aim, and pulled the trigger. Click! A dud cartridge; I thought it a bad omen.

The new sentries were no sooner in the trench than they began firing a terrific fusillade at nothing in particular. I could see the Fascists, tiny as ants, dodging to and fro behind their parapet, and sometimes a black dot which was a head would pause for a moment, impudently exposed. It was obviously no use firing. But presently the sentry on my left, leaving his post in the typical Spanish fashion, sidled up to me and began urging me to fire. I tried to explain that at that range and with these rifles you could not hit a man except by accident. But he was only a child, and he kept motioning with his rifle towards one of the dots, grinning as eagerly as a dog that expects a pebble to be thrown. Finally I put my sights up to seven hundred and let fly. The dot disappeared. I hope it went near enough to make him jump. It was the first time in my life that I had fired a gun at a human being.

Now that I had seen the front I was profoundly disgusted. They called this war! And we were hardly even in touch with the enemy! I made no attempt to keep my head below the level of the trench. A little while later, however, a bullet shot past my ear with a vicious crack and banged into the parados behind. Alas! I ducked. All my life I had sworn that I would not duck the first time a bullet passed over me; but the movement appears to be instinctive, and almost everybody does it at least once.

Orwell failed to duck all the bullets coming his way; he was wounded in May 1937 and invalided back to Britain.

Two years later, it wasn't only volunteers from the British left who were fighting fascism.

On the late summer's morning of Sunday 3 September, 1939, prime minister Neville Chamberlain informed the nation over the wireless that hostilities with Germany had commenced.

Unlike 1914, there were no flag-waving crowds in 1939; people now knew what to expect from total war. Inside the regular army, the mood was largely this-is-what-we-are-paid-for phlegmatic, although the major who wrote that 'thank goodness old Chamber-bottom has not given into Hitler again' was far from alone in his relief to be at war instead of appeasement.

Initially, the Second World War hardly involved Britain. Hitler was busy in the East of Europe. People talked of a 'Phoney War'; the troops sang 'We're going to hang out the washing on the Siegfried Line' and more propaganda leaflets were dropped than bombs. For the British army, the false war was a godsend; run down since its glory days of 1918, it needed time to fill out its thin khaki ranks; reservists were recalled, territorials mobilised, volunteers accepted and the first conscripts from the 1939 National Service Act brought into the training depots.

The Phoney War did not last, of course. In April 1940 Hitler invaded Norway and Denmark. And then the real war reached Western Europe.

➤●◄

'My God, how few of us stood up'
SERGEANT L.D. PEXTON

THE BATTLE OF FRANCE
SERGEANT PEXTON IS CAPTURED
21 MAY 1940

At 4.30 a.m. on 10 May more than 1,800 Wehrmacht Panzers began filing through the supposedly impenetrable Ardennes forest – thus neatly avoiding France's defensive pride and joy, the Maginot Line – and into the open country beyond. Rushing to meet the German juggernaut were the French, Belgians – and the 13 divisions of the British Expeditionary Force.

For the Tommies the advance through north France and Flanders was like tracing a path through history; they went past Waterloo and the battlegrounds of the First World War. Indeed, some of the BEF had even served on the self-same territory in 1914–18.

In 1940, however, there was to be no miracle on the Marne, no turning back of the German host. But it wasn't for want of the British soldier trying:

Diary 15 May 1940

[Cambrai, Northern France] Stood to at 3.30 a.m. Very quiet up to 4.15. German spotting plane came over pretty low. 6.30 a.m. First taste of bombers. 68 of them all trying to create hell upon earth together. What a day – just about blew us all out the ground. Got shelled all day too. Getting very warm round here now. Don't mind the bombs so much as the planes' machine-guns. They're wicked.

16 May

Stood to again at dawn. Quiet. Told they had come through Luxemburg with four armoured divisions, but that they could only last till Sunday with petrol. '*Must* hold them at all costs.' Still more shelling. Cambrai must be in a mess by now. Got some more bombs today.

17 May

Dawn again. Lovely morning. Can't believe that war is anywhere near. Refugees still pouring out of Cambrai. I am only fifty yards from the main Cambrai–Arras road. Big steel bridge not far from my dug-out. Heard from Coy Commander today that Engineers will blow it up if he gets too near.

18 May

Stood to again. Pretty cold this morning. Spotter came over again at 4.30 a.m. Started getting a bit deeper into Mother Earth ready for his mates to come. They came all right. One hundred and seventeen bombers and fighters. Quite sticky while it lasted. The village that was in our rear just isn't now. Fighters began to machine-gun from the main road. What a mess. Be glad when night comes.

19 May

2.45 a.m. Hell of a bang. They have blown the bridge up. He must be advancing again. Shells coming all over the place. Just in front of our position. Hope when he lifts he goes well over our heads. Lots of dud shells coming. Went to see the bridge at 9.30 a.m.: Lots of dead there – must have gone up with it. Took a chance in between shells and dived in cafe. Got a bottle of Rum and two bottles of Vin Rouge. Didn't stay long. Good job, as cafe went west five minutes later. Direct hit. Shells are giving us some stick now, 12 noon. Afraid we shall have to retire soon. Can't hold tanks with rifles or bren-guns. 4 p.m. We HAVE to hold on till 8 p.m. and then retire. Roll on 8 p.m. It's been hell all day. Air battles have been worth looking at though. Got out at 8 p.m. and marched 6 kilometres and got some lorries. Arrived at small village at 3 a.m.

20 May

Slept till 8 a.m. Went out of barn to see what was happening and if possible scrounge some grub. Found that some grub was going on in one of the lorries but had to wait for the next party. Don't know where they are going. Refugees still coming through from somewhere. Saw two men running down the road. Refugees said they were Parachutists. Captain Martin and myself called on them to halt but they didn't. Not immediately. Dropped them. Both dead when we got to them. 10 a.m. Fun began. Germans came from nowhere. Properly surprised us. Got down to it in the open and fought for all we knew how. Getting wiped out this time all right. Got back out of the farm buildings, and he's sending everything he has at us. 11 a.m. Still holding out and there's a bit of a lull. Kid on my right will keep sticking his head up above the clover. He's sure to get his soon, I'm thinking. Can't really remember much about the next hour. Remember the order 'Cease fire' and that the time was 12 o'clock. Stood up and put my hands up. My God, how few of us stood up. German officer came and spoke in English. Told to pick up the wounded and carry them to the road. There aren't many that need carrying. We have to leave our dead. Took us off the road into another field. I expected my last moments had come and lit a fag. Everyone expected to be shot there and then. Patched up our wounded as best we could and were taken back about two miles. Stayed the night in a Roman Catholic church. Learned that this village is called Ficheaux. Note: out of appr. 1,400 men only 425 spent the night in this church.

21 May

Roused out of it at 6 a.m. and put on road. I'm just beginning to realize that I'm a prisoner. We have had nothing to eat since Sunday and today is Tuesday. My water-bottle is empty now. Hope they give us something to eat soon. Got nothing to eat today.

On the same day that Pexton was captured, the Germans had reached the Channel, cutting the Allied army in two. Encircled, the remnants of the BEF retreated on Dunkirk, where began the most famous evacuation in British history.

⇒•◄

'The fellows laid down on open beaches with the bombs
falling alongside us . . .'
Private Jack Toomey

PRIVATE JACK TOOMEY IS EVACUATED FROM DUNKIRK
1 June 1940

Toomey, 42nd Postal Unit, writes to his cousins after his evacuation from Dunkirk; 224,584 other British troops, and 112,546 Franco-Belgian troops, were successfully taken off the beaches and brought to Britain by the Royal Navy and an armada of civilian craft. The BEF survived to fight another day.

Dear Folks,

Just a line to let you know that I am still knocking about, had a letter from Mum this morning and was glad to hear that Aunt Edie was a lot better.

Things up here aren't too bad, we are billeted in a British Legion Club – beer downstairs blankets upstairs. An air raid warning twice nightly but such things don't bother us veterans who have been bombed from dawn to dusk nearly every day for three weeks, well, not much anyway.

Would you like to hear all about the War straight from the horses mouth. You wouldn't, good 'cos you are going to . . .

Never look a dive-bomber in the face, Bill, cos if you do you can bet your sweet life things are going to hum soon, but pray and pray hard and run, run like hell for the nearest ditches and dive into them. I got quite used to diving in the end, could make a flat dive from the middle of the road or a power dive from a lorry in one motion. Well, after the bombers had gone and we took stock of the wreckage and found we were all alive, they came back and threw out leaflets for our use.

Then came the order to move and a rumour had it that we were making for Dunkirk. Off we went, about half-a-mile in front of Jerry, after an hour we stopped and everyone went into the ditch, that is, except another bloke and myself who were jammed in the back of the lorry. We could hear M.G. fire and thought it was a quiet shoot up by Jerry planes but when tracer shells started coming through the roof of our lorry, I knew I was wrong. Two shells took a knapsack from the box next to my head and threw it out of the back looking like cotton waste, another went past my ear so close that I felt the wind of it. All the time M.G. bullets were smacking and rickshetting off the struts. I just sat and gave up all hope of coming out of that lorry alive. However I heard a noise of a tank chugging past the lorry and the shooting stopped for us. The bloke driving the tank saw us in the lorry and calmly tossed a hand grenade under the tailboard! After it had gone off and we found we were still alive we came out of that lorry with our hands in the clouds. There are pleasanter ways of committing suicide than fighting five tanks, an armoured wireless car and a plane, with a rifle. Well, they took us prisoners and while we were looking after the wounded the French opened fire and we were between the two fires, so back into the ditch we went. The main body of prisoners were run off to a nearby village. We lay in the ditch in a thunderstorm for two hours and then went back to our own lines. So much for my 'escape', more of a case of getting left behind. The engine of our wagon was so shot up that it fell out when we pressed the self starter. We managed to get a tow from our Ordance and after ten hours we slung it into the ditch. We had got separated from our crowd and were alone in the middle of the night in France or was it Belgium, anyway we were lost, so we just ambled on until something came along – it did – one of our artillery crowds so we joined the arty for a spell. Then as dawn came up we found the main Dunkirk road and what a jam, after about ten hours of stopping and starting driving into ditches and back into lorries we got near Dunkirk, and here we had to dash thru' a barrage of shrapnel so we slammed the old bus into top and went flat-out down the road. When all was clear and we were on the outskirts of Dunkirk we stopped on a long raised road with the canal on either side and nice big trees sheltering us from the air. We got out and looked up – there were about seventy bombers (German make, naturally, we hadn't seen one of our planes for three weeks!!!) knocking hell out of the docks or what was left of them. From there to the beaches and they were black with troops waiting to go aboard only there were no boats. They gave us a raid that afternoon and evening and the following day they gave us a raid that lasted from dawn till dusk, about 17 hours. The fellows laid down on open beaches with the bombs falling alongside us, lucky it was sand, it killed the effect of the bombs. At the end of the day there were about 8 fellows killed and injured out of about 100,000.

The following day dawn broke and we saw the most welcome sight of all about a dozen destroyers off the beaches and more coming up – boats of all shapes and sizes, barges, Skylarks, lifeboats and yachts. Fortunately the day was cloudy and misty, the bombers only came once and as they came low beneath the clouds the Navy let 'em have it. They slung up everything, the guns, I never saw this action, I was scrounging for a drink, we hadn't had water for a fortnight it was too risky to drink and all we could get was champagne and wines. Spirits only made me thirstier. However on this morning I had a drink of vin blanc and had to sit down. I was drunk as a lord, the last time I had anything to eat was about three days off, and on an empty stomach the wine had a devastating effect. That evening we went aboard after making dash after dash up the jetty to dodge shrapnel – Jerry had got close enough for his light artillery to shell us.

We got aboard and started, there were about 800 of us on one small destroyer. The Navy rallied round and dished out cocoa, tins of bully, and loaves of new bread. This was the first grub some of us had for nearly four days and the first bread we had for a fortnight.

When we were about an hour's run off Dover and thought we were safe a bomber came down and slammed three bombs at us – missed us by six feet and put all the lights out downstairs. We got to Dover at 2 am and climbed aboard a train, we were still scared to light cigarettes, a light on the beaches meant a hail of bombs, and we just drowsed, at Reading we got out and shambled to the road outside, it was about 8 am and people just going to work stopped and stared, we must have look a mob, none of us shaved or wash for a week, our uniform was ripped and torn, with blood and oil stains. I had no equipment bar a tin hat and gas mask, a revolver I picked up from somewhere stuck out of my map pocket.

One or two old dears took one look at us and burst into tears. I dont blame them, I frightened myself when I looked into a mirror.

They had buses to run us to the barracks, we could just about shuffle to them, we were so done up. At the barracks breakfast was waiting and they apologised because it was tinned salmon and mashed potatoes, we, who had been on half or no rations for nearly three weeks were too busy eating. After grub we slept for a few hours and had dinner, got paid and changed our money to English, changed our uniform for a clean lot, had a shave, shampoo, haircut, and bath and breezed out for a drink of beer. We stayed here for a week and went to Bournemouth to be re-equipped. At Bournemouth, three Spitfires roared overhead one day just above the pier and over the beach. I was on the beach, laying flat on my face before you could say 'Scarp'. I just couldn't help it. Leaves a self preservation instinct or something.

From there we were sent up to here, nothing much has happened, we work in the P.O. doing much the same as we do in civilian life. They, the army, did try to get us out of it into the country under canvas but we told them we couldn't work without a post office near us so they let us stay.

Thus ends my little bit of the epic of the battle of Northern France and Dunkirk.

The times were rather tough and altho' I was scared stiff for three weeks it was something I wouldn't want to have missed. My only regret was that one of our Rover Scouts was left behind.

Still, c'est la guerre.

Chin, chin,

Love to all,

Jack.

After the Fall of France, military minds concentrated on protecting the Isles from the Germans, now just 22 miles away across the Channel. A call for Local Defence Volunteers (LDV), men aged between 16–65 who were not eligible for service in the full-time army, raised 300,000 men in a fortnight. Churchill, always a man for the grand touch, promptly rechristened the LDV the Home Guard. The populace just as quickly dubbed them 'Dad's Army'.

Not everyone in the army, however, was on the defensive in summer 1940. Colonel Dudley Clarke RA, recalling the success of T.E. Lawrence's guerrilla campaign in the desert in 1917–18, persuaded the Chief of the Imperial General

Staff to sponsor offensive raids by small numbers of highly trained troops.

The commando concept was born. One of the earliest raids was on the Lofoten Islands in occupied Norway, from where the Germans imported the bulk of the fish oil they used in the making of explosives.

'far and away the most interesting, lively and instructive
half-day of my whole life'
BOMBADIER EVAN JOHN

COMMANDO RAID ON THE LOFOTEN ISLANDS
NORWAY, 12 MARCH 1941

Bombadier Evans's letter of running commentary on the Lofoten raid was for his wife.

I had a beastly dream last night – that I was reading a telegram to say that you had been badly injured in an air-raid and were hoping I could come and see you in a London hospital. It is a good thing I am not superstitious, and that my contempt for psycho-analysis doesn't extend to disbelief in its most obvious proposition – that suppressed anxieties become the realities of dreamtime.

It is somehow rather flattering, as well as comforting to go out on deck and see our escort of men-o'-war humming along around us. But I haven't seen a seal yet!

Monday, 12 noon

Tomorrow is the day of landing. The time 06.45, three-quarters of an hour before Arctic dawn. They are serving out the rifle ammunition now, the grenades (which are filthy dangerous things) not till the last moment.

I don't feel at all Arctic, having missed my seals and my Northern Lights. It is now misty and drizzly outside (which is what we want – aeroplanes being our chief and perhaps only danger). But is often as misty and drizzly in England, and it is no colder than I've known it often there.

Now I must get my ammunition.

5.30

Last daylight before attack. Last daylit preparations. Sailors tapping and testing davits. Colonel Elström is inspecting Norskers with their *ruksaks* full of soap, cigarettes, coffee, etc. His *Inspektjon* interrupts a conversation I was having with a very nice middle-aged Norwegian, and also a game of chess I was playing with my handsome young sailor. I jot down the state of the game, and try to tell him, in faltering and inaccurate Norsk, the story of the two French officers in Napoleon's army: they began a game of chess in Moscow in 1812; it was interrupted by the order to retreat from the burning city; one of them wrote down the state of the game on the back of an old envelope, saying, 'We'll finish it when we meet again'; they didn't meet again till after the Retreat (and what a Retreat! Close on half a million souls dying of wounds, hunger, frostbite or drowning in the Beresine); but they did run across each other in a Berlin café next spring, and one of them pulled out his old envelope, reset the game, and insisted on finishing it. I tell my Norwegian that we shall do the same, but after our Advance, in some kaffe-hus in Oslo.

Unfortunately, I have already spoilt the whole business. I have lost the bit of paper on which I wrote the position down!

It also occurs to me that if there are to be explosions tomorrow, and Norwegian civilians to be moved out of the danger zone, I had better know the Norsk way of saying: 'For your own safety.' A sailor supplies it. 'For din egen sikkerhet,' if I'm spelling it right. I like 'sikker' for 'safe' or 'sure'. It reminds me of Bruce's 'make siccar'.

It is clearing up a little. Fresher, but not at all cold. Things begin to get exciting.

Well, we've all been waiting for this since last August and now it's come, we are all glad. Maybe it's a good thing that our first venture is likely to be a tame one. And perhaps it won't be! Too excited and interested to be at all frightened.

Overnight shave and wash – cold water, Arctic Circle, but no discomfort. Feel very fit. Must now say good night.

I am getting too fond of this unconscionably long letter to like

the prospect of having to destroy it on the altar of 'Security'. I may
have to. If I don't, here it is – the record of gradual approach to
possible battle as felt by one who has never yet seen a man die,
never even seen a dead man.

Of course I'm not taking it ashore. We're not allowed to take
any written papers ashore, for fear of death or capture. But I am
taking ashore my Army Book 156 (blank) in case I get a few
moments to scribble something down.

Tuesday 5.15 (scribbled in boat)

It is just light enough to write. We are packed sardine-wise and
half asleep, being embarked in more than enough time. It is calm
and clear twilight. In spite of the latitude, season of the year and
early morning hour. I don't need gloves, though in an open boat
at sea!

We are beginning to move in earnest. I can see nothing except
a saxe-blue sky, a gull, and occasionally the mast-heads of the
man-of-war leading us.

Some spray coming in which is cold!

Whole silhouette of man-of-war. She is slowing down and we
are passing her. I have seldom seen anything so dramatic and
beautiful – every spar and rope clean-cut against the blue, every
man standing rigid and motionless at his gun or instrument.

On land, Svolvaer

Bang-banging everywhere. Presumably demolition, plus (?) men-
o'-war sinking German trawlers.

A perfectly lovely morning. Beautiful little mountain peaks,
pink in sunlight, round a rather picturesque little town.

8.00 a.m.

Guarding half-wrecked office.

Sapper has put one charge of explosive on safe and made a
hole in it. But safe still resists and he has gone for more H.E. We
don't want sappers so much as burglars!

No Germans this side of water. Must be dead or captured

t'other side, because crowd is parading with Norwegian flag, cheering, etc.

09.00 a.m.

The safe is being a b—y nuisance. I don't know the Norsk for sledgehammer so have drawn this for a Norwegian, and made him produce required sledgehammer to batter door.

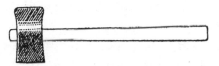

Meanwhile the sapper is prizing it with a whale-harpoon harpoon head!

10.00

Safe open. Little of interest. £5 worth of notes and coppers – to be returned to firm. Fine blaze in adjoining factory and yard.

We have captured one German soldier, a nasty-looking little twerp in a green uniform; he is smiling sheepishly and seems rather pleased to be captured. Officer has taken camera from him and is photographing fire.

Large crowd of Norsk children collecting. Much fraternisation.

It *has* been very tame. Little danger now unless from air, or torpedo on return.

12.00

Back on S.S. *Domino* with many recruits for Norsk army and navy in England, 100–200 prisoners, mainly sailors, but one flying officer and some soldiers. All objectives achieved. One casualty on our side – an officer has wounded himself with his own revolver. So it has been a mere tea party for us, and all the heroics look a little silly.

4.00

All, or nearly all, is over. Norway is invisible to the left (PORT!). The last of the Lofotens sliding past on the right (STARBOARD!), looking like gigantic fairy icebergs in the evening sun.

When I say 'nearly all' there are still torpedoes and (for an hour or two of daylight still) aeroplanes. *Apropos* of the latter, I've just had a nasty false alarm. I had been handing back the last of our ammunition to the powder magazine through a manhole in the floor; round me some men were engaged on the very ticklish business of extracting fuses from hand grenades, on an extremely crowded mess deck. I had barely left it to go above when I heard a loud explosion and rushed back, expecting to find the place a shambles. They were still quietly un-fusing grenades and the bang was one of our anti-aircraft guns firing at a single German plane.

This has now vanished, and the sky is clear.

Speaking of crowded mess decks – we were not too badly off on the voyage out, better than on the *Ludo*. We have now a lot of prisoners (the officers, naval and air force, looking like ridiculous stiff caricatures of Nazis, in impossibly starched uniforms), soldiers, airmen, the rest German mercantile marine and Norsk quislingites. We have also some 100 Norsk recruits for the loyal navy and army. We are turned off our mess deck to make room for the prisoners; are supposed to eat (50 of us) where another 50 men were and are still eating, and to sleep in a passage entrance to the officers' mess. No other solution, and no one to blame, except the prisoners for letting themselves be caught!

Well, it has been far and away the most interesting, lively and instructive half-day of my whole life. I can hardly believe it is only this morning, admittedly early this morning, that we were looking up at that gloriously silhouetted warship and then gliding silently into the still unsuspecting harbour of Svolvaer. I only wish I had had time to scribble down some more impressions on the spot.

———◆·◆———

'Four of my tanks were blazing infernos'
CAPTAIN ROBERT CRISP

TANK ACTION AT SIDI REZEGH
WESTERN DESERT, 28 NOVEMBER 1941

The spill over of the Second World War into Africa was primarily caused by the territorial ambitions of Hitler's ally, Mussolini. Alas for the new would-be Roman emperor his army was repelled in Egypt on 9 December 1940 by Britain's Western Desert force, who then rolled the Italians 400 miles back towards Libya.

In all probability, the war in the desert would have ended there and then had not Hitler sent Mussolini a shining knight in tank armour. Erwin Rommel. For eighteen months the conflict in North Africa swung viciously back and forth along the coastal strip. Some of the fiercest tank fighting in the war occurred around Sidi Rezegh airfield, south of Tobruk, during Operation Crusader; the 'Honey' referred to by Crisp, 3rd Royal Tank Regiment, was an M3 light cavalry tank.

As my Honey edged up to the final crest I was immediately aware of the dense throng of transport in front of me. The Trigh was black and broad and moving with packed trucks and lorries. Over it all hung a thick, drifting fog of dust so that only the nearest stream of vehicles was clearly discernable. There was not a panzer in sight. The tail of the enemy column was just on our right front, and it looked as though we could not have timed it better. The Germans gave no sign of having seen us, or of being aware of our tanks poised for the strike within a thousand yards of them. They moved slowly westwards wondering, no doubt, what the devil Rommel thought he was playing at with these mad rushes up and down the desert, and beefing like hell about the dust.

I looked approvingly to right and left, where the rest of the squadron were lined up following the curve of the contour. From each turret top poked the head and shoulders of the commander, eyes glued to binoculars trained on that enemy mass. It must have been quite a sight to somebody only a week out from base camp in England. I got on the air to the C.O. with a quick, formal announcement that 'C' Squadron was in position and ready. From my left the other squadron did the same. Within a minute the reply came: 'Hullo JAGO, JAGO calling. Attack now. Alec sends a special message "Go like hell and good luck". Good luck from me too. JAGO to JAGO, off.'

The order went through all the intercoms, from commander to crew: 'Driver, advance. Speed up. Gunner, load both guns.' The Honeys positively leapt over the top of the ridge and plunged down the steady incline to the Trigh. I knew my driver, who was getting used to this sort of thing, would have his foot hard down on the accelerator, straining his eyes through the narrow slit before him to stationary and bewildered; many lying on their sides or backs with wheels poking grotesquely upwards. Dark figures of men darted wildly about.

Even as I watched, a great lorry went plunging down the escarpment out of control; it struck some outcrop and leapt high in the air, somersaulting to the bottom in a fantastic avalanche of earth, rock and scrub and odd-shaped bundles of men integrated with jagged pieces of wood and metal. The concentration of transport in the wadi below was a wonderful target. I said quickly into the mouthpiece: 'Both guns. Men and vehicles. Fire with everything you've got.'

The bullets went zipping inches above the heads of the three immovable figures in front of the tank. They never twitched a muscle. When the 37-mm. cannon suddenly went off they jumped involuntarily, but none of them turned their heads or gave any indication that I could see of fear or curiosity. They just stood there, three backs and three pairs of arms while the tracers went streaming in flat, straight lines into the dusty turmoil below. I wondered idly where the rest of the Honeys were, and if they were having as good a time as mine was.

Suddenly there was a fearful bang, and simultaneously I was drenched from head to foot in an astonishing cascade of cold water. For a moment or two I was physically and mentally paralysed. I just could not believe that anything like that could happen. Then realisation came swiftly and terribly . . . the water tins on the back of the tank had been hit. It could mean only one thing. As I looked backwards I was already giving the order to the gunner to traverse the turret as fast as he bloody well could. In one comprehensive flash I saw it all, and the fear leapt up in me. Not fifty yards away a 50-mm. anti-tank gun pointed straight at the Honey, pointed straight between my eyes. Beyond it were other guns and then as the dust drifted over the scarp the sight I had dreaded most – a number of motionless Honeys and the huddled figures of black-bereted men crouched on the sand or stretched out in the agony of death.

It took less than a second for the whole scene and its awful meaning to register in my mind. I could see the German gunners slamming the next shell into the breech as the turret whirled. I yelled 'On. Machine gun. Fire.' In the same moment I saw the puff of smoke from the anti-tank gun and felt and heard the strike on the armour-plating. Quickly I looked down into the turret. A foot or two below me the gunner was staring at his hand, over which a dark red stain was slowly spreading. Then he gave a scream and fell grovelling on the floor. In the top right hand corner of the turret a jagged hole gaped, and through it, like some macabre peepshow, I could see the gun being reloaded. I knew that in another few seconds I would be dead, but something well beyond reason or sanity impelled my muscles and actions.

I leaned down and pulled the trigger, and kept my finger there until the gun jammed. God knows where the bullets went. Twice I felt the Honey shudder and the second time more water came pouring in. When the Browning stopped and my mind leapt about searching for some ways to stay alive I suddenly saw the slim chance. If the tank would move at all, and we could drop over the edge of the escarpment, we would be out of sight of those blasted anti-tank guns. I could see them framed in that jagged hole, the gunners working feverishly, their faces strained and vicious. I said urgently into the mike: 'Driver, advance. Over the edge. Quick!'

Nothing. I thought 'My God, Whaley's had it. We've all had it,' and screamed down into the turret 'Driver advance. For Christ's sake advance!' Then I saw what had happened. In falling, the gunner had jerked back on the intercom leads to the driver's earphones. The cords had tightened round his neck, pulling him backwards over the driving seat and half-strangling him. He wrestled frantically with his earphones and ripped them off. He didn't need them to hear my panic bellowing.

I felt the gears engage, and for a split second the world stood still. Then the engine revved, and the Honey heaved forward and dropped with a violent crash over the escarpment. In the turret we were hurled about like corks, and then the bouncing stopped and we rode smoothly down the slope. We were out of sight of the guns on top of the escarpment, and with a great rush of unbelief I knew we were going to get away with it. The three German motor-cyclists still stood motionless. The tank could not have missed them by more than a few inches, yet they still had their hands in the air. Down in the driving compartment Whaley was wrestling with the sticks to keep the tank on a diagonal course that would take him to the bottom of the slope away from the enemy. When the ground levelled out a bit I ordered him to turn right to run into a little wadi that offered a safe way out to the south. We were travelling with the turret back to front, and I prodded the operator with my foot as he bent over the prostrate gunner and indicated to him that I wanted the turret traversed back to the normal position. While he was turning the handle I could not resist a last backward look at those three men. Incredibly, they were still standing as we had left them. I began to think they had become literally petrified with fright and would stay there down the centuries in some miraculous monument.

So much had happened in a few minutes, or a few hours it might have been, and I had looked so closely into the valley of the shadow, that I found it difficult to return to reality. I just could not fully absorb our situation. I had to grip the hardness of the armour-plating and see the familiar figures of the tank crew to realise that we were still alive, and that we were going to stay alive. The gunner lay there groaning in pain and sobbing in fear. There was nothing much wrong with him, and I shouted at him roughly to pull himself together. My thoughts went out to the rest of the squadron. Where were they? What had happened to them? Were they all dead? It was something I had to find out.

We were chugging along casually through the deserted silence of the wadi. It was uncanny after the tumult and terror just behind us, and the thought kept on intruding that we were no longer on earth, that we were driving in some ghost tank on another level of existence . . . that we were all dead. When I put the mouthpiece to my lips I was half-prepared to hear no voice come out. The unreality persisted when the Honey swung right in response to my order, and moved slowly up the slope to the crest. As soon as my eyes were above the lip of the escarpment we halted, and the full picture of horror burst on me immediately.

Not much more than 500 yards away, like a projection on a cinema screen, lay the battlefield. My eyes lifted to the tall black columns, leaning slightly with the wind, and followed them down to the Honeys gasping smoke. Four of my tanks were blazing infernos; three others just sat there, sad and abandoned. A line of anti-tank guns with their crews still manning them expectantly, lined the edge of the drop. The whole scene was silhouetted sharply against the yellow clouds of dust which rose in a thick fog from the wadi bank. I could see many men running about between guns and tanks and vehicles. My heart ached as I picked out the familiar bereted figures of our own troops, huddled in disconsolate groups or being shepherded by gesticulating Germans.

Was there nothing I could do? My mind moved round the prospect of a sudden charge into that line of anti-tank guns, over-running them before they could get their sights on me. If I had had a gunner to fire the Browning, perhaps I might have. As it was I was grateful for the opportunity of rejecting it as impossible, and so prolonging my life and those of my crew. But who knows? It might have come off.

As a concession to my own great distress and impotency I stood up on the turret and waved my beret. There was a chance that some gunner, operator or driver, one of the commanders perhaps, might have been lying crouched in the scrub, waiting for the night or the unbidden moment to make a break for it. But it was more of a gesture of complete despair, and when I heard the whishing past my ears, followed by the quick barking of the machine guns, I dropped back into the turret. I said wearily over the intercom: 'O.K., Whaley. There's nothing we can do. Let's go back.'

We followed the wadi southwards as it grew shallower and shallower, eventually disgorging us unobtrusively on to the plateau over which we had charged so bravely ... when? ten minutes ago? an hour ago? today? yesterday? and how many lives ago? My wrist-watch was staring me in the face as we paused on the rim of the depression. The hands pointed to 17 minutes past one. 17 minutes.

In the desert men sometimes longed for action. Anything to break up the monotony of life in the featureless terrain. One soldier, Private R. Crimp, 7th Armoured Division, wrote:

The desert, omnipresent, so saturates consciousness that it makes the mind as sterile as itself ... Nothing in the landscape to rest or distract the eye; nothing to hear but roaring truck engines; and nothing to smell but carbon exhaust fumes and the reek of petrol. Even food tastes insipid, because of the heat, which stultifies appetite. The sexual urge, with nothing to stir it, is completely dormant ... The most trivial actions, such as cleaning the sand off weapons, making a fire or brew, or, when you're lying down by the truck, moving position into the patch of shade ... seem utterly not worthwhile and require a tremendous effort to perform . . . Then, of course, there are the flies. Lord Almighty, that such pests should ever have been created! . . . At the moment of writing there are five crawling over my hands and I'm spitting as many again away from my mouth.

Back in Britain, training continued for the latest batches of call-ups.

⇒•◦•⇐

'This is the safety-catch, which is always released/
With an easy flick of the thumb'
PRIVATE HENRY REED

NAMING OF PARTS

1942

To-day we have naming of parts. Yesterday,
We had daily cleaning. And to-morrow morning,
We shall have what to do after firing. But to-day,
To-day we have naming of parts. Japonica
Glistens like coral in all of the neighbouring gardens
   And to-day we have naming of parts.
* * *

This is the lower sling swivel. And this
Is the upper sling swivel, whose use you will see
When you are given your slings. And this is the piling swivel,
Which in your case you have not got. The branches
Hold in the gardens their silent, eloquent gestures,
   Which in our case we have not got.
* * *

This is the safety-catch, which is always released
With an easy flick of the thumb. And please do not let me
See anyone using his finger. You can do it quite easy
If you have any strength in your thumb. The blossoms
Are fragile and motionless, never letting anyone see
   Any of them using their finger.
* * *

And this you can see is the bolt. The purpose of this
Is to open the breech, as you can see. We can slide it

Rapidly backwards and forwards; we call this
Easing the spring. And rapidly backwards and forwards
The early bees are assaulting and fumbling the flowers:
   They call it easing the Spring.

*   *   *

They call it easing the Spring; it is perfectly easy
If you have any strength in your thumb: like the bolt,
And the breech, and the cocking-piece, and the point of balance,
Which in our case we have not got; and the almond-blossom
Silent in all of the gardens and the bees going backwards and
forwards,
   For to-day we have naming of parts.

Henry Reed served with the RAOC, before pneumonia forced a transfer to the Government Code and Cipher School at Bletchley.

Training was a chore ameliorated by friendship. To an even greater extent than Kitchener's New Army, the volunteer-cum-conscript army of the Second World War was a lesson in democracy and comradeship. A people's army. In the history of the British soldier, only Cromwell's Ironsides had been so politically radical.

Some things about the British soldier remained unchanged. Like his forebears the Tommy of the Second World War sang. Irreverently.

> Hitler, he's only got one ball,
> Goring's got two, but very small.
> Himler's got something similar,
> Poor old Goebbels' got no balls at all.

When the Tommies ran out of their own songs, they nicked the Germans' 'Lili Marlene'. Paratroopers were even heard to sing the SS favourite, the Horst Wessel.

———➤◆◄———

'I strode through the snow trying to look like a Prussian'
LIEUTENANT AIREY NEAVE

ESCAPE FROM COLDITZ

GERMANY, 5 JANUARY 1942

Schloss Colditz was the POW camp to which the Germans sent the 'bad boys', the serial escapers among the Allied prisoners.

On the morning of 5 January 1942 Luteyn and I were ready to escape. We held a conference with Pat Reid and 'Hank' Wardle and decided to try immediately after the nine o'clock *Appell* that evening. Our compasses, maps and a small bundle of notes were ready for hiding inside our bodies. The uniforms were now intact beneath the stage and our civilian clothes had so far escaped detection in their 'hide'. In a moment of supreme confidence, I collected the addresses of relatives of my companions. Then flushed and excited, I lay down to sleep throughout the afternoon and early evening.

A few minutes before nine I went down to the courtyard, when the snow was falling lightly. The turrets cast long shadows in the light of the moon and the steep walls enfolded me for what I believed to be the last time. There was once more the eternal sound of hundreds of men taking their meagre exercise in clogs. I stood waiting for the *Appell*, eyeing the Dutch contingent where Luteyn was waiting ready to join me. We wore cardboard leggings painted with black polish. I wore my usual combination of battledress and sweater, and my Army boots, being brown, were also darkened with black polish. Underneath I had my 'civilian clothes' with a pair of R.A.F. trousers. I had an over-powering sense that this was my last evening in the castle. The certainty grew with every minute, making me composed and determined.

There was a sharp order of dismissal and, mingling with the dispersing prisoners, Pat Reid, 'Hank' Wardle, Luteyn and I hurried quickly into the senior officers' quarters. In the darkness of the theatre we felt our way beneath the stage, then carefully prised up the loose floor-boards. Pat Reid lifted the trap called 'Shovewood', which on its underside was whitewashed, disguising the hole in the ceiling of the passage below. I could see the strong, determined lines on his face as he worked in the glow of a cigarette-lighter. The trap removed, the mattress-cover rope was let down through the hole in the ceiling. Cautiously we climbed down, holding the boxes of uniforms, and landed with soft bumps on the floor of the passage.

The bright lights from the courtyard shone through the cobwebbed windows in the outer wall of the passage. Treading softly in our socks, we reached the door of the gate-bridge. Pat Reid, shining his lighter on the lock, swiftly picked it. It opened without a sound, for he had oiled the hinges earlier in the week. We were in the half-light of a narrow corridor. We walked quietly across it and stopped at the door that led to the guard-house.

The German uniform overcoats were unpacked in silence and we put them over our workmen's clothes, leaving our battledress in the boxes. As we pulled on our boots there was no sound except the grating of Pat Reid's wire searching in the lock. A minute passed, and suddenly came fear and exasperation. The door would not open. Beneath our feet we could hear the creaking of the gates and the voices of sentries changing guard. We stood motionless, fully dressed as German officers, and waited with pounding hearts. Pat Reid spoke in a hoarse whisper:

'I'm afraid I can't get it open!'

He continued turning the wire in the lock. I could hear the wire rasping against the rusty metal as he tried again and again to open it. Ten minutes passed in terrible suspense. Through the cobwebbed window I could see the snow falling. I folded my arms and waited. Suddenly there was the noise of old hinges creaking. A quick snap and the door swung open, showing us the dim interior of the attic.

'Good luck,' said Pat Reid, and shook hands.

We waited till the door was locked behind us and we could no longer hear his muffled steps. Then we crept carefully to the top of stone spiral stairs at an open door on the other side of the attic. A wireless in the guard-room on the ground floor was playing organ music. It was the moment to go down, for the music was loud. We walked quickly down the first flight of stairs, past the door of the officers' mess on the first floor where a light showed beneath. We waited, then stepped confidently down through darkness, into the passage beside the guard-room. The guard-room door was half open, and I caught a glimpse of German uniforms inside, as we marched smartly into the blinding whiteness of the snow under the arc-lights.

The testing time had come. I strode through the snow trying to look like a Prussian. There stood the sentry, the fallen snow covering his cap and shoulders, stamping his feet, just as I had pictured him. He saluted promptly, but he stared at us, and as our backs were turned I felt him watching. We walked on beneath the first archway and passed the second sentry without incident.

Then, between the first and second archways, two under-officers talking loudly came from the *Kommandantur*. They began to march behind us. I felt Luteyn grow tense beside me. I clasped my hands behind my back with an air of unconcern. I might have been casually pacing an English parade ground. In a moment of excitement I had forgotten my part. 'March with your hands at your sides, you fool,' came a fierce sharp whisper from my companion.

Again I saw the bicycles near the clock tower. Could they be ridden fast in this thick snow? We passed beneath the tower, saluted by the sentry, and came to the fateful wicket-gate. As Luteyn opened it I watched the under-officers, their heads bowed to the driving snow, march on across the moat bridge. Down we went into the moat, stumbling and slipping, until we reached its bed. A soldier came towards us from the married quarters. He reached us, stopped and stared deliberately. I hesitated for a moment ready to run, but Luteyn turned on him quickly and in faultless German said crossly, 'Why do you not salute?'

The soldier gaped. He saluted, still looking doubtful, and began to walk up the side of the moat towards the wicket-gate. We did not look back but hastened up to the path on the far side, and, passing the married quarters, came to the high oak paling which bordered the pathway above the park. We were still within the faint glare of searchlights. Every moment that we stayed on the pathway was dangerous. Lifting ourselves quickly over the paling, we landed in thick snow among the tangle of trees. My cardboard belt was torn and broken and with it into the darkness vanished the holster.

Groping among the trees we struggled through frozen leaves down the steep bank and made for the outer stone wall. It was five minutes before we were at the bottom of the slope. Helped by Luteyn, I found a foothold in the stones of the wall and sat astride the coping. The wall, descending steeply with the tree-covered slope, was shrouded in snow and ice. Each time that I tried to pull Luteyn on top, I lost my foothold and slid backwards through the steep angle of the wall. Then, with numbed hands, I caught him beneath the armpits and, after great efforts, hoisted him up beside me. For a minute we sat breathless in the cold air clinging to the coping, and then jumped a distance of twelve feet. We fell heavily on the hard ground in the woods outside the castle grounds. I was bruised and shaken and frightened. I stood leaning against a tree looking at Luteyn. Another minute passed in the falling snow.

'Let's go,' I said, and we began to climb towards the east, seeking the direction of Leisnig, a small town six miles away.

Luteyn and Neave reached neutral Switzerland four days later.

Just under 200,000 British and Commonwealth soldiers were captured and imprisoned by the Germans in the Second World War. 'Home runs' like those of Luteyn and Neave were rare. Officially, it was a soldier's duty to try and escape, but only 5 per cent of prisoners were inveterate escapers; however, almost the whole of the remainder aided and abetted escape attempts. For the POW, the 'war behind the wire' consisted largely of a long struggle against depression and hunger.

There were distractions. 'Other ranks' POWs were used as cheap labour by the Germans, but few POWs objected since it enabled bartering with German civilians. A few POW labourers even managed to seduce the German women they were working alongside.

Of course, it was perfectly possible for a British soldier at home to be incarcerated, should he infract military regulations.

***

'The cell . . . must have been built in anticipation of Houdini'
GUNNER TERENCE ('SPIKE') MILLIGAN

DETENTION
14 SEPTEMBER 1942

We were alerted for a practice shoot at Sennybridge Camp in Wales. Burdened down with kit, I decided to hide my rifle in the rafters of the hay-loft. 'That's a good idea,' said patriotic Edgington. The short of it was several other patriots did the same. And it came to pass, that after we had gone thence, there cometh a Quarter Bloke, and in the goodness of his heart he did inspect ye hay-loft, and woe, he findeth rifles, and was sore distressed, where-upon he reporteth us to the Major, who on Sept. 14th, 1942, gaveth us fourteen bloody days detention. For some reason all the other 'criminals' were sent to our RHQ at Cuckfield, but I was sent to Preston Barracks, Brighton, alone, no escort, Ahhhh, they trusted me. At Brighton station, I tried to thumb a lift; I got one from an ATS girl driving a General's Staff car. She dropped me right outside Preston Barracks. As the car stopped, the sentry came to attention, then *I* got out. I reported to the sergeant I/C Guardroom. 'Welcome to Preston Barracks,' he said.

'You're welcome to it too,' I replied.

'Now,' he said, 'from now on you keep your mouth shut and your bowels open.'

Then he gave me a cup of tea that did both. He stripped me of all kit, leaving essentials like my body. The cell, my God! it must have been built in anticipation of Houdini. Seven foot by six foot, by twenty foot high, stone floor, small window with one iron bar, up near the ceiling, wooden bed in the corner. The door was solid iron, two inches thick, with a small spy-hole for the guard. No light. 'You go to sleep when it gets dark, like all the good little birdies do,' said the sergeant. 'Make yourself comfortable,' he said, slamming the cell door. Every day, a visit from the orderly officer, a white consumptive lad who appeared to be training for death. 'Got everything you want?' he said. 'No, sir, I haven't got a Bentley.' I grinned to let him know it was a joke, that I was a cheery soul, and not downhearted. It wasn't the way he saw it. He pointed to a photo of my girl by my bed. 'That will have to go,' he said.

'Yes sir, where would you like it to go? I think it would go nice on the piano.'

'Put it out of sight.'

'But it's my fiancée sir.'

'Photographs are *not allowed*.' He was starting to dribble.

'What about statues sir?'

He lost his English 'cool'. 'Sergeant – put this man under arrest.'

'He's already under arrest sir,' said Sarge.

'Well give him extra fatigues for being impertinent!'

I planned revenge. I cut my finger-nails. On his next visit I placed them in a cigarette lid.

'What are those?'

'Finger-nails sir.'

'Throw them away.'

'They are my fiancée's sir.'

'Throw them away.'

'Very good sir.'

The next time he visited I had cut a small lock of my hair, tied a small bow on it and placed it on my bed.

'What's that?'

'A lock of hair sir.'

'Throw it away.'

'It's my fiancée's sir,' etc. etc.

The last one I planned was with an artificial limb, but the officer never visited me again. He was drafted overseas, and killed during an air raid on Tobruk; a NAAFI Tea Urn fell on his head.

My duties were not unpleasant.

1) Reveille 0600. Make tea for the Guard. Drink lots of tea.

2) Collect blackberries along the railway bank for Sergeants' Mess Tea.

3) In pouring rain, shovel two six-foot-high piles of coke into 'One Uniform Conical Heap'. (A Bad Day.)

4) Commissioned to draw a naked Varga Girl for Guard Room. (A Good Day.)

5) Trip to beach to collect winkles for Sergeants' Mess Tea.

6) Weed Parade Ground by hand. (Bloody Awful Day.)

7) Commissioned to draw Varga Girl for Sergeants' Mess. (Another Good Day.)

8) Oil all locks and hinges at Preston Barracks, sandpaper door of cell, prime, undercoat, and paint gunmetal black.

9) Drive Major Druce-Bangley to Eastbourne (his driver taken ill with an overdose of whisky) to have it off with his wife in house on seafront.

After fourteen days I was sent back to Hailsham – I arrived to find the whole Battery boarding lorries – yes! 'Prepare to move' again! With my kit I jumped into a fifteen hundredweight, making it a sixteen hundredweight.

'Where are we going?'

'I don't know, it's another secret destination,' said Sergeant Dawson.

Three hours later, we were back to square one. Bexhill.

'I wish they'd make their fucking minds up,' said Sergeant Dawson.

'Look Sarge, they're moving us about to make us look a lot,' said Gunner Tome.

'We look a lot,' said Dawson, 'a lot of cunts.'

'Give us a merry song, Sarge,' I said, running for cover.

Gunner Milligan was bound for North Africa, where the pendulum of the desert war was about to stop swinging. On 23 October 1942 the British Eighth Army, under the newly appointed General Bernard Montgomery, opened the battle of El Alamein. Watching the first troops go into action was Michael Carver of the Royal Tank Corps:

Suddenly the whole horizon went pink and for a second or two there was perfect silence, and then the noise of the 8th Army's guns hit us in a solid wall of sound that made the whole earth shake ... Then we saw a sight that will live forever in our memories – line upon line of steel-helmeted figures with rifles at the high port, bayonets flashing in the moonlight, and over all the wailing of the pipes ... As they passed they gave us the thumbs up sign, and we watched them plod on towards the enemy lines, which by this time were shrouded in smoke.

——◦◦◦——

'I did not agree with ... snatching little gobbets of glory for the regiment'
LIEUTENANT KEITH DOUGLAS

EL ALAMEIN
A POET THROWS AWAY THE CHANCE OF A MILITARY CROSS
2 NOVEMBER 1942

Presently an infantry patrol, moving like guilty characters in a melodrama, came slinking and crouching up to my tank. A corporal, forgetting his attitude for the time being, leant against the tank, saying: 'You see them Jerry derelicts over there, them two?' He indicated the two burnt-out tanks to our right front and added: 'They've got a machine-gun in that right-hand one. We can't get up to them. They open up on us and pin us down, see?' 'Well, what would you like us to do?' 'I should have thought you could run over the buggers with this,' he said, patting the tank.

'Well, we'll see. I'll have to ask my squadron leader.' I indicated his tank, 'Will you go over and tell him all about it?' 'Very good, sir,' said the corporal, suddenly deciding that I was an officer. He departed. His patrol, who had been slinking aimlessly round in circles, waiting for him, tailed on behind him.

Andrew's instructions were of the kind I was beginning to expect from him. 'See what you can do about it. See if you can get those chaps out of it. But be very careful. I don't want you to take any risks.' I interpreted this to mean: 'If you make a mess of it, I wash my hands of you,' and opened the proceedings by ordering Evan to spray the area of the derelict with machine-gun fire.

The machine-gun, however, fired a couple of desultory shots, and jammed; Evan cleared and re-cocked it. It jammed again. A furious argument followed, Evan maintaining that the trouble was due to my not passing the belt of ammunition over the six-pounder and helping it out of the box. I pointed out that the belt was free on my side. Our understanding of each other was not helped by the fact that while I was speaking into the i/c microphone, Evan removed his earphones because they hampered his movements. He then shouted to me, disdaining the microphone, words which I could not hear through my heavy earphones. At length the conversation resolved itself into a shouting match. Evan became more and more truculent, and I ordered the driver to begin advancing slowly towards the enemy. This had the effect I wanted. Evan stopped talking, and applied himself feverishly to mending the machine-gun. After about a hundred yards I halted and scrutinized the derelict through my glasses. I could see no movement. I wondered what the crew of the machine-gun felt like, seeing a tank slowly singling them out and advancing on them. Evan was stripping the gun in the bad light and confined space of the turret, skinning his fingers, swearing and perspiring. At this moment Andrew's voice spoke in my ear, saying airily that he was going to refuel: 'Nuts five, I'm going back to the N.A.A.F.I. for lemonade and buns. Take charge. Off.' So now I was left to my own devices.

Looking down for a moment at a weapon-pit beside us, I saw a Libyan soldier reclining there. He had no equipment nor arms, and lay on his back as though resting, his arms flung out, one knee bent, his eyes open. He was a big man: his face reminded me of Paul Robeson. I thought of Rimbaud's poem: 'Le Dormeur du Val' – but the last line:

Il a deux trous rouges au côté droit

was not applicable. There were no signs of violence. As I looked at him, a fly crawled up his cheek and across the dry pupil of his unblinking right eye. I saw that a pocket of dust had collected in the trough of the lower lid. The fact that for two minutes he had been lying so close to me, without my noticing him, was surprising: it was as though he had come there silently and taken up his position since our arrival.

Evan's swearing approached a crescendo. 'I'll have to take the bastard out,' he said. 'It's the remote control's bust. I'll fire it from the trigger.' We got the biscuit tin off the back of the tank and mounted the gun on it loose, on the top of the turret. From this eminence, as we advanced again, Evan sprayed earth and air impartially, burning his fingers on the barrel casing, his temper more furious every minute. At length he succeeded in landing a few shots round the derelict tank. A red-faced infantry sub-altern ran up behind us, and climbed on to the tank. He put his hands in his pocket and pulled out two grenades, the pins of which he extracted with his teeth. He sat clutching them and said to me: 'Very good of you to help us out, old boy,' in a voice much fiercer than his words. We were now only about thirty yards from the derelict, and saw the bodies of men under it. They did not move.

'There they are!' cried the infantryman suddenly. A few yards from the left of the tank, two German soldiers were climbing out of a pit, grinning sheepishly as though they had been caught out in a game of hide and seek. In their pit lay a Spandau machine-gun with its perforated jacket. So much, I thought with relief, for the machine-gun nest. But men now arose all round us. We were in a maze of pits. Evan flung down the Besa machine-gun, cried impatiently, 'Lend us your revolver, sir,' and snatching it from my hand, dismounted. He rushed up and down calling 'Out of it, come on out of it, you bastards,' etc. The infantry officer and I joined in this chorus, and rushed from trench to trench; I picked up a rifle from one of the trenches and aimed it threateningly, although I soon discovered that the safety-catch was stuck and it would not fire. The figures of soldiers continued to arise from the earth as though dragons' teeth had been sown there. I tried to get the prisoners into a body by gesticulating with my useless rifle. To hurry a man up, I pointed a rifle at him, but he cowered to the ground, like a puppy being scolded, evidently thinking I was going to shoot him on the spot. I felt very embarrassed, and lowered the rifle: he shot away after his comrades as though at the start of a race. I began to shout: 'Raus, raus, raus,' with great enthusiasm at the occupants of some trenches further back, who were craning their necks at us in an undecided way. Evan unluckily discouraged them by blazing off at them with a Spandau which he had picked up, and some high explosive began to land near the tank, which was following us about like a tame animal. Evan now found a man shamming dead in the bottom of a pit and was firing at his heels with my revolver, swearing and cursing at him. Another German lay on the ground on his back, occasionally lifting his head and body off the ground as far as the waist, with his arms stretched stiffly above his head and his face expressive of strenuous effort, like a man in a gymnasium. His companions gesticulated towards him and pointed at their heads, so that I thought he had been shot in the head. But when I looked more closely, I could see no wound, and he told me he was ill. Two of them assisted him away.

From the weapon pits, which were crawling with flies, we loaded the back of the tank with Spandaus, rifles, Luger pistols, Dienstglasse, the lightweight German binoculars, British tinned rations and the flat round German tins of chocolate.

As the main body of the prisoners was marched away under an infantry guard, the high explosive began to land closer to us. I did not feel inclined to attack the further position single-handed, so I moved the tank back and tacked it on to the column of prisoners. The mortar stopped firing at us, and some of the infantry climbed on to the tank to ride back. I reported over the air that we had taken some prisoners.

'Nuts five, how many prisoners?' asked what I presumed to be Andrew's voice. 'Nuts five wait. Off.' I said, counting, 'Nuts five about figures four zero. Over.' 'Bloody good. Most excellent.'

Apparently it was the Colonel talking. 'Now I want you to send these chaps back to our Niner' – he meant the Brigadier – 'so that you'll get the credit for this.' This was unfortunately more than my conscience would stand. I felt that all the work had been done by Evan and the infantry officer, and said so. This was a bad thing to say to Piccadilly Jim, because it showed him that I did not agree with him about snatching little gobbets of glory for the regiment whenever possible. The infantry were in another Brigade, as Piccadilly Jim knew. Evan said: 'You were a bloody fool to say that, sir. You've as good as thrown away an M.C.' I said shortly that if I had, it was an undeserved one.

The reaction on me of all this was an overpowering feeling of insignificance. I went over to the infantry officers who were searching the prisoners and said: 'You did most of the dirty work, so you'd better take them back to your Brigade.' The one who had ridden on my tank replied. 'Yes, we had orders to,' in such a supercilious way that I almost decided to insist on my right to escort them after all. The man with a bad head was lying groaning on the ground. He clutched his head and waved it from side to side. I think perhaps he had ostitis: the pain made him roll about and kick his legs like a baby.

The turret, after the removal of the Besa, and our leaping in and out of it, was in utter confusion. During our struggles with the machine-gun the bottom of an ammunition box had dropped out, and the belt of it was coiled everywhere. The empty belt fired from the biscuit box mounting had fallen in whorls on top of this. The microphones, spare headphones, gunner's headphones and all their respective flexes were inextricably entwined among the belts. Empty cartridge and shell cases littered the floor. On the surface of this morass of metal reposed the Besa itself, and an inverted tin of Kraft cheese, which had melted in the sunlight. I rescued a microphone and a pair of headphones, and got permission to retire and reorganize. On my way back I was to call at the Colonel's tank. This I duly did, but my ears were singing so loudly that I could scarcely hear his kind words. As soon as the tank moved away from the prisoners, we were again fired on by a mortar, which followed us as we moved back, dropping shells consistently a few yards behind us. We brewed up in dead ground to the enemy behind a ridge; the mortar continued to search this ground with fire, but never got nearer than thirty yards, and that only with one shot.

We examined our trophies, and were shocked to find that the infantry had stolen all our German binoculars while enjoying our hospitality as passengers on the tank. We all bitterly reproached them, and I regretted ever having wished to give them extra credit. We had left, however, a large stack of machine-guns and rifles, which we dumped. Three Luger pistols, which we kept: these are beautiful weapons, though with a mechanism too delicate for use in sandy country. There were a few odds and ends of rations, cutlery, badges, knives, etc., which we shared out, eating most of the extra rations there and then in a terrific repast, with several pints of coffee. At last I decided we ought to rejoin the squadron, and reported we were on our way back.

On the day that Douglas was annoying Piccadilly Jim, Montgomery was directing 'two hard blows' at the hinges of the German line at El Alamein. Rommel prepared to retreat but was forbidden to do so by Hitler. The Afrika Korps made desperate bids to plug the gaps in their defence – including throwing HQ staff into them – but it was not enough. There was no option but withdrawal, Hitler's orders not withstanding. Moving through the battlefield in the wake of the German retreat, Keith Douglas came upon scene upon scene of tragedy:

The men with me were walking along bent double as though searching the ground. I said to them, 'It's no good ducking down. If you're going to be hit you'll be hit. Run across the open ground. Run.' They began to trot reluctantly, and I ran ahead. Presently I saw two men crawling on the ground, wriggling forward very slowly in a kind of embrace.

As I came up to them I recognized one of them as Robin, the RHA Observation Officer whose aid I had been asking earlier in the day: I recognized first his fleece-lined suede waistcoat and polished brass shoulder titles and then his face, strained and tired with pain. His left foot was smashed to pulp, mingled with the remainder of a boot. But as I spoke to Robin saying, 'Have you got a tourniquet, Robin?' and he answered apologetically, 'I'm afraid I haven't ...' I looked at the second man. Only his clothes distinguished him as a human being, and they were badly charred. His face had gone: in place of it was a huge yellow vegetable. The eyes blinked in it, eyes without lashes, and a grotesque huge mouth dribbled and moaned like a child exhausted with crying.

Robin's mangled leg was not bleeding: a paste of blood and sand, or congealed slabs of blood, covered it. I thought it would be better left as it was than bandaged, now that the air had closed it. 'I'll go on back,' I said, 'and get hold of something to pick you up, a scout car or something. Stay here.' I ran on. Before I had gone a hundred yards I was ashamed: my own mind accused me of running to escape, rather than running for help. But I hurried on, determined to silence these accusations by getting a vehicle of some kind and bringing it back, in the face of the enemy if necessary.

Douglas survived the North African campaign but was killed during the battle for Normandy.

El Alamein was more than the turning point of the war in the desert; it was the turning point of the war against Hitler.

⟶⊸◈⊷⟵

'That when I fall – if fall I must – My soul may triumph in the dust'
BOMBARDIER L. CHALLONER, ANONYMOUS

A POEM AND A PRAYER
WESTERN DESERT, DECEMBER 1942–FEBRUARY 1943

From *Poems from the Desert*, an anthology of verse written by members of the Eighth Army on active service in North Africa.

In the Desert To-day

What did I see in the desert to-day,
In the cold, pale light of the dawn?
I saw the Honeys creaking out,
Their brave, bright pennants torn;
And heads were high against the sky,
And faces were grim and drawn.

* * *

What did I see in the desert to-day,

Where the frantic lizard runs?
The song of death was shouted forth
As the gunners manned the guns.
The men who'd pledged for Motherland
Their freedom and their lives,
Swore as they sweated in the smoke
To man the Twenty-fives.

*   *   *

What did I see in the desert to-day,
Beside the rocks and the sand?
I saw the squadrons in the sky
Of Bomber and Fighter Command.
I heard the thunder of their work,
I saw their lightning stroke,
And far across the skyline came
The rolling clouds of smoke,
Whilst incoherent in their rage
The chattering Bredas spoke.

*   *   *

What did I see in the desert to-day,
Beside the sand and the rocks,
Where the distance fades into misty grey
And the shimmering mirage mocks?
I saw the lonely hare
Leap from the hidden form,
As the crashing notes of the One-o-fives
Foretold the coming storm.
I saw the startled plovers rise
From the wadi by the well,
And quick among the tortured scrub
Scampered the light gazelle,
When the clangour of our armour rose
Insistent in the west,
And, fluttering, the spent A.P.'s
Came bounding o'er the crest.

*   *   *

What did I see in the desert to-day?
Relics of what had died.
The pale, enamelled shells of snails

Wherein the spiders hide,
And the dark, fast-rusting shells of hate
Lie shattered side by side.

* * *

What did I see in the desert to-day,
As the sun dropped, angry, red,
Out of the golden western sky?
The smoke still rose ahead,
And the last of the fighters from patrol
Over our lines had sped,
And the sands had folded into their void
The last of their unknown dead.

* * *

What did I see in the desert to-day—
Anything new in the 'Blue'?
I found a crevice in the rocks
Where a single violet grew,
As fresh as in woods and lanes of home—
The green fields once we knew.
And I saw the Faith in the eyes of men,
And I knew their hearts were true.

L. CHALLONER
Bombardier

A Soldier – His Prayer

(This anonymous poem was blown by the wind into a
slit trench at El Agheila during a heavy bombardment.)

Stay with me, God. The night is dark,
The night is cold: my little spark
Of courage dies. The night is long;
Be with me, God, and make me strong.

* * *

I love a game. I love a fight.
I hate the dark; I love the light.
I love my child; I love my wife.
I am no coward. I love Life,

* * *

Life with its change of mood and shade.
I want to live. I'm not afraid,
But me and mine are hard to part;
Oh, unknown God, lift up my heart.

* * *

You stilled the waters at Dunkirk
And saved Your Servants. All your work
Is wonderful, dear God. You strode
Before us down that dreadful road.

* * *

We were alone, and hope had fled;
We loved our country and our dead,
And could not shame them; so we stayed
The course, and were not much afraid.

* * *

Dear God, that nightmare road! And then
That sea! We got there – we were men.
My eyes were blind, my feet were torn,
My soul sang like a bird at dawn!

* * *

I knew that death is but a door.
I knew what we were fighting for:
Peace for the kids, our brothers freed,
A kinder world, a cleaner breed.

* * *

I'm but the son my mother bore,
A simple man, and nothing more.
But – God of strength and gentleness,
Be pleased to make me nothing less.

* * *

Help me, O God, when Death is near
To mock the haggard face of fear,
That when I fall – if fall I must–
My soul may triumph in the Dust.

ANONYMOUS

The anonymous writer of 'A Soldier – His Prayer' spoke for hundreds of thousands
in the army in his hope that post-war Britain would be a 'kinder world' of moral and

national regeneration. If it was a People's War, it stood to reason and emotion that there should be a People's Peace of 'fair shares' to follow it.

Before the dawning of the New Jerusalem, however, there were still sacrifices to be made, many of them in the 'forgotten war' in the Far East. There the British soldier encountered a professional killer who, unlike the British, was expert at jungle warfare: the Japanese. Malaya and Burma, both British colonies, had fallen to the Japanese in their great 1942 advance after Pearl Harbor. Not that these defeats unduly perturbed the British soldier. As Field Marshal Slim, commander of the 14th Army, pointed out: 'In his long career [he, the British Soldier] has suffered so many disasters, won so many victories, that neither the one nor the other unduly depresses or elates him. Come what may, he holds to his inflexible confidence in ultimate victory'.

To achieve that ultimate victory in the Far East, the British were obliged to rethink their attitude to the jungle; instead of treating it as a no-go zone, they had to learn that the jungle was neutral. The 'Chindits' of General Orde Wingate were among the first to do so.

'Duncan was the first to . . . have gone to his death at my instance'
MAJOR BERNARD FERGUSSON

THE DEATH OF A FRIEND
BURMA, 3 APRIL 1943

In 1943, Fergusson commanded No. 5 Column of Orde Wingate's special force Chindits on their 1,000-mile-behind-Japanese lines expedition into Burma. 'Chindit' was derived from the Burmese mythical creature the 'chinthe'.

We had learned that the village, which was not shown on the map, was called Zibyugin; and that the Japs were in Pumpri and Lonpu; but it was essential to know more than that before we pushed on. We wanted information on which to decide, not only our immediate future, but our whole future policy: whether to go east or north . . .

John, Duncan and I discussed for an hour what our best course was to be, and we came to the conclusion that we must get more information, and if possible more food from the village. If their reports about the country further east were favourable, then we could pass from village to village all through the Kachin country, with no worries about food, and with continuous information about enemy movements and dispositions. We agreed that it was more than likely that the Japs would not have tumbled to our presence in the neighbourhood, and that they were unlikely to come into the village so early in the morning unless they were going to move on elsewhere. We thought that a patrol should go into a village, and that one o'clock would be the best time for it. Duncan volunteered to go, and to my grief I let him.

We had some tea about half-past twelve, and then Duncan got up and slowly prepared for the patrol. He had chosen to accompany him Maung Kyan, Gilmartin, and one of the commando platoon, Stevenson. Duncan left behind his maps, but took his pack: he had always disapproved of people leaving their packs behind when they went on patrol. I watched, lying on my back but propped up on my elbows. At last he was ready.

'Well, I'm off', he said. 'If I get into trouble, I'll fire my rifle. So Long!'

'Good luck', I said; and off he went.

The hands of my watch seemed to turn desperately slowly during the next hour. They showed two o'clock when Pepper, who was sentry, burst through the bushes.

'I just heard two shots, sir', he said.

I leaped to my feet and listened; so did John. There was a moment's silence, and then with terrible distinctness we heard three more. We stood a long time, but heard nothing.

Ages later I said to John, 'They might have been killing a couple of pigs.'

'It's possible,' he said; 'but do you really think so?'

It was at five o'clock that Maung Kyan and Stevenson got back. They had been wandering round in circles. I talked to Stevenson and John to Maung Kyan.

The patrol had gone into the village, and advanced cautiously to the first house. All was quiet. Duncan climbed the steps and disappeared into the building. He had come out again almost immediately with a Kachin who by agitated gesture was urging silence on them all. At that moment a Burmese, probably a Jap guide, came round the corner, and seeing the patrol began shouting. Duncan and the others ran for the jungle and reached a *chaung* on the fringe of it. There he faced the village, from which the Japs were running towards them, and thew himself on to the ground in a firing position.

'You run on back,' he said. 'I'll cover you and join you.'

Gilmartin flung himself down beside Duncan, and that was the last they saw.

I waited till dawn next morning, and then marched miserably away to the north-west. I had stopped being a passenger and become the column commander again. As I marched, there came into my head the lines:

> He is gone on the mountain,
>   He is lost to the forest,
> Like a summer-dried fountain,
>   When our need was the sorest.
> The font, reappearing,
>   From the raindrops shall borrow,
> But to us comes no cheering,
>   To Duncan no morrow!
> Fleet foot on the correi,
>   Sage council in cumber,
> Red hand in the foray,
>   How sound is thy slumber!

I had lost many friends already in the war, but Duncan was the first to have fallen so near me, and the only one to have gone to his death at my instance . . . All the way back to India, I seemed to see his broad shoulders, his powerful arm slashing at the jungle, his bush hat tilted back on his head; and at the halts to hear his talk, the infectious laugh which wrinkled his face, the absurd bamboo pipe which he had made with his *kukri*. And in moments of stress, I seemed almost aware of the old sage counsel.

Lieutenant Duncan Menzies had been tied to a tree by the Japanese and shot.

Overall, losses on the first Chindit expedition were 1,000 men, a third of the total sent off. Yet for all the hardship and fatalities incurred the expedition was a success: after the first Chindit expedition, the British soldier in the Far East no longer felt himself outclassed in jungle fighting by the Japanese. The boost to morale was incalculable.

Some 210 of the 1,000 losses on the expedition were men taken prisoner; of these 168 were murdered or starved to death by the Japanese. There was nothing exceptional about such a fate; the Japanese were uniformly barbaric in their treatment of British and Allied POWs.

——◆●◆——

'they literally beat one man to death'
PRIVATE JEFFREY ENGLISH

ONE FOR EVERY SLEEPER
A POW ON THE BURMA-SIAM RAILWAY
MAY 1943

English was captured by the Japanese in the fall of Singapore, 1942; a year later he was put to work building the Burma-Siam railway. Two out of every three Allied POWs on the railway died from starvation, disease or mistreatment. One for every sleeper laid.

At our previous camp the ration parties had been drawn from the semi-sick, but here *all* men not bedded down had to go on the working parties to the cutting, and so the afternoon ration parties had to be found from the now off-duty night shift. A man would work or be going to and from work for the best part of fourteen hours, do a four-hour ration fatigue, and have only six hours out of twenty-four for feeding, cleaning himself up, and sleeping.

For the first week or so, when we still had over 300 'fit' in the combined Anglo-Australian camp, each individual only got two ration fatigues a week. It would have been even less, but of course one half of our 300 were on the day shift, and only the other half were on the unhappy night shift.

On three pints of rice a day, all this, of course, was impossible and flesh and blood could not stand the strain; and in addition to the overwork we had dysentery and other diseases spreading at a frightening pace. As the numbers of 'fit' men dwindled, the burden carried by the remainder consequently grew, until after only a few weeks the fitter men were doing all five ration fatigues a week as well as working the night shift in the cutting, and only having two days a week of real rest. As they gradually cracked up, more unfortunates, just past the crisis of their exhaustion or illnesses but in no way fully recovered, would be forced out in their place, lasting in their turn perhaps three or four days before they themselves had to be replaced by yet others not quite so ill.

Just as this gruelling programme put that at our previous camp in the shade, so did the new Nip Engineers make the last lot look like gentlemen. There, they had generally beaten only those whom they caught flagging or had somehow provoked their precariously balanced ill-humour; but here they beat up indiscriminately, beating every man in a gang if they wanted it to go faster, and two of them in particular were simply blood-thirsty sadists.

They were known to us as 'Musso' and 'The Bull', and they seemed to compete amongst themselves as to who could cause the most hurt. They were both on the night shift, and both would come on duty with a rope's end strapped to the wrist. These they plied liberally, and they also carried a split-ended bamboo apiece, whilst Musso in particular would lash out with anything which came handy, such as a shovel. Every morning two or three men would come back to camp with blood clotted on their faces and shoulders or matted in their hair, whilst others would return with puffy scarlet faces but no eye lashes or eye brows, these having been burnt off where they'd had a naked acetylene flare waved slowly across the eyes – a favourite trick of another Nip known to us as 'Snowdrop'.

They drove the men on, not just to make them work, but as a cruel master drives a beast of burden to force it on to further efforts greater than it can manage; and one would see half a dozen men staggering along with an 18-foot tree trunk, or rolling an outsize boulder to the edge of the cutting, with the Nip running alongside lashing out at them or kicking their knees and shin and ankles to keep them going.

Frequently men fainted, and to make sure that they weren't shamming, the Nip would kick them in the stomach, ribs or groin. If the man still didn't move, the favourite trick was to roll him over face downwards, and then jump up and down on the backs of his knees, so as to grind the kneecaps themselves into the loose gravel. If he fell on his side, a variation was to stand on the side of his face and then wriggle about, grinding and tearing his undercheek in the gravel: and as a way of telling a faked faint from a real one, both of these methods are, believe me, highly efficacious.

On one occasion a man was beaten up so badly by the Nips that they thought he wouldn't live, and so they got four prisoners and told them to bury him under a heap of rocks. The prisoners observed that he wasn't yet dead, but the Nips indicated that that didn't matter – they could bury him alive. It was only after a great deal of persuasion by a spunky Australian officer (who naturally took a personal bashing for his trouble, but didn't let that deter him) that the Nips eventually changed their minds and let the man be carried back to camp. He was carried on a stretcher, and came round later, but the beating had sent him almost off his head; he disappeared into the jungle and we couldn't find him for two days. On the third day he crept in for food; but he was now quite mental and became a gibbering idiot at the mere sight of a Nip. Had we bedded him down in a hospital tent, he could very well have simply popped off again; and so we found him a job in the cook-house where he would be working with others, and he worked there for a shaky fortnight before he packed it in and died.

At the next camp up the road, at Hintok, whence we sometimes drew our rations, they literally beat one man to death. He was discovered resting in the bushes down at their cutting when he ought to have been working, and the Nips took him down to the cutting in front of all the other prisoners and gave him a terrific beating up. He fainted once or twice, and was brought round by the usual Nip methods; and they continued in this way until they could bring him round no more. He wasn't quite dead yet, and was carried back to camp: but although he regained consciousness he avoided going out again on the next shift by the simple device of dying.

The Hintok Nips were on much of a par with our own Musso and The Bull: and another pretty case arose from the familiar story of the Nips demanding a working party of 120 men when the most that Hintok could muster was 105. The Nips went into the hospital tent and brought out the first fifteen of those bedded down, all of whom were dysentery cases, some of them in a very bad way indeed. They were forced to join the parade, and they set off for the cutting. One man in particular was very, very bad, but no one was allowed to lag behind and help him get along, and after several collapses he at last could go no further.

He arrived back at the camp dragging himself through the mud on his hands and knees, and was put back into the hospital: but when the Nips returned that night they knew that they'd been one short all day. They dug him out from the hospital, supported by a man on either side as he could no longer stand by himself, and then with all the typical gallantry of the Japanese, they started in and beat him up. He lay writhing on the ground whilst they beat and kicked him senseless, and although they left him breathing he was dead within two hours.

In a similar case at our own camp, three men, all very sick, passed out on the way to work, and Musso sent the squad officer back to bring them down. They were rounded up and shepherded in, and Musso, as they approached, rushed forward and started beating them with a stout bamboo. He broke the first bamboo on one of them, seized another one and broke that one too, and then got a pick handle and used it as a two-handed club. He bashed them unmercifully, and then ordered them to pick up a length of rail from the light railway, and carry it over to the rock face. It being the night shift, there was no overhead scorching sun to add to their woes; but he ordered them to hold the length of rail above their heads.

No matter how he beat them, they couldn't get it above their heads, but at last they got it to chest level, and there he kept them holding it for the best part of twenty minutes. Every time they sagged he laid in with the pick-handle, and as they couldn't even ward off the blows with their hands they were in a horrible state by the time he let them go.

That same night Musso further distinguished himself. A fellow called 'B——' (I'll just call him that lest his widow might read this) had been holding a chisel and his mate missed with his sledgehammer and crushed B——'s hand. Musso blamed B—— for not holding the chisel upright, and instead of knocking him off work and letting him have his broken fingers set, he put him onto the job of turning the big crank which worked one of the generators floodlighting the cutting. The handle was far too heavy for him to turn with his one good hand, so that he had to use the bleeding pulp of his crushed hand as well. Musso stood over him, and every time he flagged and the lights dimmed, he was beaten with a bamboo. He was kept at it for nearly an hour, during which time he twice fainted; but when he fainted for the third time he didn't come round. He was helped back to camp at the end of the shift, and he died a week later from cholera, from which he had probably already been sickening when Musso did his stuff on him.

Musso, mark you, was merely a private soldier – a private soldier under no restraint or the exercise of any control by his superiors. His was one of the few names which we managed to find out and retain – he was Superior Private Kanaga – and I must confess to having shed not a single tear when I learnt, after the war, that both he and The Bull were hanged after trial by the War Crimes Commission. What happened to Snowdrop I never learnt.

By the end of only three weeks at this new camp we were at the end of our tether. In our part of the camp alone we had fifty dead, 150 bedded down in hospital, and only fifty working; and the Australians had comparable figures but over double the size of ours.

Even the Nips realized that something had got to be done, for the men they still had were dropping of exhaustion: although they had tried to keep them going by sheer brutality alone, there comes a time when any amount of flogging seems preferable to more work.

The Nips had a bright idea. They explained that the fit working men needed more food than did those bedded down in hospital, which seemed eminently logical. The shine went off the ball, however, when they further explained that the way in which they would introduce the differential would be to keep the rations for the fit men exactly as they were   but would reduce the hospital to two meals a day.

——◆◆◆——

'NEVER AGAIN SHALL WE SEPARATE'
Private Thomas Smithson

POSTCARD FROM A POW
Taiwan, 1943

Smithson, imprisoned by the Japanese on Taiwan, writes to his wife on a postcard issued by the Imperial Japanese Army.

MY DEAREST EILEEN
RECEIVED CARDS AND LETTER'S. HAPPY TO KNOW YOU WELL AND EVERYONE AT HOME. DEAREST I MISS YOU MORE EACH DAY. NEVER AGAIN SHALL WE SEPARATE. ALL I ASK OF THIS WORLD IS MY OWN LITTLE COTTAGE AND REMAINDER OF MY LIFE IN YOUR SWEET COMPANIONSHIP. GOD BLESS YOU, DEAR.
LOVE, EVER, YOURS TOM

'Its highlight was an interview with a psychiatrist'
Rifleman Alex Bowlby

OFFICER SELECTION
1943

I had volunteered for the Army – I hadn't fancied being called up – and this, plus the fact of my having been to one of the public schools which the regiment preferred its officers from, automatically ear-marked me as a potential officer. This upset my platoon sergeant even more than my arms-drill. One bleak November morning he could stand it no longer. The squad was practising gas-drill. I had hidden myself in the back rank but the Sergeant had turned the squad round. When everyone else had replaced their respirators I was still wrestling with the head-piece. The eye of the Sergeant was upon me. Desperately I rammed home the head-piece. When I buttoned up the respirator it bulged like a pregnant serpent. The Sergeant moved in for the kill. Unbuttoning the respirator he replaced it correctly. Then he thrust his face into mine.

'If you ever get a commission my prick's a bloater!'

A week later I was sent to a War Office Selection Board. Its highlight was an interview with a psychiatrist. I thought this would be fun. When I entered his room I had to stop myself giggling. He motioned me to sit down, and continued to correct papers (we had all answered a word-association test). After five minutes' silence I no longer found anything funny about the interview. After ten minutes I felt like screaming.

The psychiatrist suddenly looked up from the papers. He stared at me until I had to look down.

'You were unhappy at school, are extremely self-conscious, and find it difficult to concentrate. Correct?'

I nodded dumbly, wondering how on earth he did it.

'Both your parents are neurotic, aren't they?'

'I–I don't know.'

'H'm. Have you ever had a woman?'

'No.'

'Do you want to?'

'Of course!'

The psychiatrist gave me another long stare. I ended up looking at the floor.

'What do you like most in life?'

'Poetry, I suppose.'

'Why?'

'Because it's part of my ideals.'

'What ideals?'

'I don't quite know how to explain. I suppose my ideals are what I believe in.'

'What do you believe in?'

'Helping other people. Doing what I feel is right.'

The psychiatrist leant across the table.

'What would your feelings be if you bayoneted a German?'

This was much better.

'I'd feel sorry for him. I don't think he would have caused the war any more than I did.'

The psychiatrist frowned.

'Well, what would you feel if *you* were bayoneted by a German?'

'A great deal of pain.'

'Yes, but *what else?*'

I couldn't think of anything else.

'Nothing.'

The psychiatrist glared at me. I stared back. We looked at each other until I felt dizzy.

'You should avoid going out alone at nights,' he said finally.

I nearly burst out laughing. But he hadn't quite finished.

'And if you don't give up these so-called ideals of yours you'll go mad within eighteen months.'

I was so shaken I couldn't speak. Finally I said: 'But what shall I do?'

'That's up to you.'

When I got out of the room I fainted.

For some weeks afterwards my nerves were all to bits. I lived for letters from a friend who slowly convinced me that the psychiatrist was talking through his hat.

The War Office was keen on the use of psychiatrists, not only to select officers but to train them. Even public schoolboys, whom the War Office believed to be inherent leaders, required 'man management' advice from psychiatrists on how to handle the citizen-in-uniform of 1939–45, who was discernibly more independent-minded than his First World War counterpart.

Alex Bowlby later fought in the Italian campaign. As a rifleman, not an officer.

———◈◈◈———

'waiting – waiting – waiting'
SERGEANT NELL

ONE MAN'S WAR
LIFE IN A GERMAN POW CAMP
1 JANUARY 1944–21 JUNE 1944

Nell was captured at Mersa Matruh in June 1942; he was liberated in April 1945.

New Year's Day 1944

They can't win. Hitler is losing lives for nothing. We heard yesterday that the Russians have launched an offensive of 300,000 men. The Russian steam-roller. May it roll everything before it. An
· educational scheme is afoot. At first I enrolled for English,

Electricity and Psychology, but have since changed to the London Matriculation Course. I wonder, can I do it? How much longer is the war going to last? I could put up with fighting but this endless turning over of days in a POW camp, waiting – waiting – waiting. When is it going to end?

5 February

I went to the theatre this evening and saw the play *Boy Meets Girl*. When a man is dressed as a woman he looks astoundingly like the authentic article. None of us have been on speaking terms with a woman for some time; perhaps that has something to do with it. It is almost two years since I even spoke to a woman. Letters!!! Three of them, two from Eve and one from Father. At long last I have got letters from my darling Eve. Oh, Evie, my sweet.

20 February

My thirtieth birthday. But I kept it a secret. I am worried about Gerry. He has fallen to pieces because he has failed (in his own estimation) as a writer. Since last June he has been working on a novel and now he finds that he can't carry on. He is distressed and eating next to nothing. Eve wonders if I have changed much. I wonder how much she has changed and in what ways? I take for granted that she will be much prettier. I wonder if she can cook yet? Oh, Evie, my darling, if you knew this terrible longing I have for you. A little boy may cry for what he wants. Poor Eve, she doesn't know it, but for some time I am going to be her baby. What a delightful mother I am going to have. Eve, my darling – or shall I say 'Mummy'?

Later. I think the Germans are worrying about the war. They have issued three blankets to every Russian prisoner and have given them coal. It is rather late in the day to be humane. Thousands of Russians have died of TB as a result of malnutrition by the Germans. They actually hope that their treatment of hapless POWs will be forgotten. British and French prisoners are treated well but the other nationalities get no more consideration than animals. As I lay listening to the drone of hundreds of planes and the explosion of their bombs, I thought of the children and old people, terrified and being maimed and killed and rendered homeless. And then I thought of Eve.

26 April

At the bath-house today I saw some Russians who had just bathed. They were naked, waiting for their bodies to dry in the air (they have no towels). What a ghastly sight they were, nothing but skin and bone. Their skin was stretched tightly over their ribs, their stomachs were distended like bladders, there was no flesh where their buttocks should have been. It would be inconceivable that human beings could treat their fellow man as the Germans are treating the Russians were we not here to see it. And I was in the same condition once. May-day is a National holiday to celebrate their National Socialist Party's coming into power. It will be their last celebration.

. . . I am thirty years of age and going bald, what will Eve think when she sees me? There is nothing but a spiritual link between us and the war would seem to be slowly but surely breaking it. And I am sure my heart will break with it . . . The *Camp* – that propaganda paper for POW's – has shown us the type of temporary house to be supplied to people in Britain after the war. It is made of steel and has four rooms. Not very big but it will do until proper houses are provided. I wonder if Eve and I shall get one? Oh, how I long for the day when we can live together!

21 June

A man has just been shot and killed. He was reaching through the fence to pick some wild strawberries when a German soldier drew his pistol and shot him . . . Writing! Mine is getting worse. We write, they say, as we live. I am nervous so I must write nervously . . . If I weren't a prisoner I could be with my Eve. It makes me wild when I think of it. Eve is very sweet in her last letter. She asks me to marry her as soon as I get home. Gosh! I never knew that the time would come when a girl would ask *me* to marry her! Letters are so few and far between. They are next important to food – they *are* spiritual food for us prisoners. I want Evie all day . . . I have agreed with her regarding our not having children until we have our own home. Our children must not be left to chance as I was. My childhood was a mild form of Hell. Roll on peace and the scaffold for the Nazis.

———————

'the Japs were only 50 yards away'
MAJOR J. WINSTANLEY

KOHIMA

BURMA, 4–20 APRIL 1944

Kohima, a village in the Naga Hills, marks the furthest point reached by the Japanese in their assault on India. The small British and Commonwealth garrison defending the village consisted mainly of the 4th Royal West Kents, a battalion of Assam Rifles and two companies of the Burma Regiment. Attacking them was the entire Japanese 31st division. Major Winstanley commanded B Company 4th Royal West Kents at Kohima:

Our position on Garrison Hill was on the fringe of the Tennis Court, and included a mound above the Tennis Court occupied by my right-hand platoon, my middle platoon in the Club House, with my left hand platoon holding a bank that fell away from the Tennis Court. The Tennis Court was 'no man's land'. On the other side the ground fell away – that's where the Japs were. The Japs were only 50 yards away.

The battle took place on the Tennis Court – we shot them on the Tennis Court and grenaded them on the Tennis Court. We held the Tennis Court against desperate attacks for five days. We held because I had instant contact by radio with the guns, and the Japs never seemed to learn how to surprise us. They used to shout in English as they formed up, 'give up'. So we knew when an attack was coming in. One would judge just the right moment to call down gun and mortar fire to catch them as they were launching the attack, and by the time they were approaching us they were decimated. They were not acting intelligently and did the same old stupid thing again and again. We had experienced fighting the Japs in the Arakan, bayonetting the wounded and prisoners. So whereas we respected the Afrika Korps, not so the Japanese. They had renounced any right to be regarded as human, and we thought of them as vermin to be exterminated. That was important – we are pacific in our nature, but when we are aroused, we fight quite well. Also our backs were to the wall, and we were going to sell our lives as expensively as we could. Although we wondered how long we could hang on, we had no other option. We had no idea we were confronted by a whole Jap division and outnumbered some ten to one. We had no thought of surrender at any level; we were too seasoned soldiers for that. We couldn't taunt the Japanese back as we couldn't speak Japanese, but there were some JIFs on the other side, and we taunted them in English.

The other weapon that was so effective were grenades used by Victor King's platoon who showered them with grenades as they formed up. As Kohima was a depot, we didn't lack grenades, but we were very short of 3-inch mortar bombs. We were supplied from the air, and much of the loads went to the Japs. They had captured British 3-inch mortars, and most of the mortar bombs dropped for our use fell into enemy hands.

We had a steady toll of casualties mainly from snipers. Showing yourself in daylight resulted in being shot by a sniper. They also used their battalion guns in the direct fire role, in morning and evening 'hates'. This caused mayhem among the wounded lying in open slit trenches on Garrison Hill, so that many were killed or re-wounded. We heard that 2 Div were being flown in to relieve us, and we could hear the sound of firing to our north, as the division fought its way down to us. But it seemed to take ages.

After five days I was relieved on the Tennis Court by the Assam Regiment and moved to Hospital Spur. The Tennis Court position held, the Kuki Picket changed hands several times. We were in a filthy state.

The fighting at Kohima was amongst the most intense and personal endured by British troops in the Second World War. One VC awarded at Kohima, to Lance Corporal JP Harman of the Royal West Kents, was for a plain, old-fashioned bayonet charge. Private H. Norman witnessed it:

Lance Corporal Harman . . . volunteered to go on a one man bayonet attack past our pit to clear the Japs off our feature. He went down past our pit and killed some Japs. He was covered by

> Sgt Tacon who . . . killed a Jap who [was] just going to throw a grenade at Harman. Harman killed the rest of the Japs, but instead of running back as we were shouting for him to do, he walked back calmly, and the inevitable happened.

Before dying Harman said, 'I got the lot – it was worth it'.

There was little opportunity to bury Harman and the other dead at Kohima, which came to resemble an abattoir. On one trip to collect water, Private Norman 'kept falling over dead bodies which were black and decaying . . . As we passed through the hospital the smell was overpowering. Colonel Young had designed a large pit covered by a tarpaulin which he used as an operating theatre, but hundreds of wounded were lying in open pits and this area was continually being mortared and shelled day and night . . .'

After the war, a memorial to the dead was erected at Kohima. On it was inscribed the legend:

> When you go home
> Tell them of us and say
> For their to-morrow
> We gave our to-day

Four thousand British and Commonwealth troops gave their to-days at Kohima.

'our torches illuminated the interior of the car –
the bewildered face of the general'
CAPTAIN W. STANLEY MOSS

THE KIDNAPPING OF GENERAL KREIPE
CRETE, 26 APRIL 1944

Moss, along with fellow SOE operative Paddy Leigh Fermor, was parachuted into Crete to organise partisan resistance to the German garrison on the island; on 26 April 1944 the duo pulled off their greatest escapade, the abduction of the garrison's commanding officer.

> We scrambled out of the ditch on to the road. Paddy switched on his red lamp and I held up a traffic signal, and together we stood in the centre of the junction.

In a moment – far sooner than we had expected – the powerful headlamps of the General's car swept round the bend and we found ourselves floodlit. The chauffeur, on approaching the corner, slowed down.

Paddy shouted, 'Halt!'

The car stopped. We walked forward rather slowly, and as we passed the beams of the headlamps we drew our ready-cocked pistols from behind our backs and let fall the life-preservers from our wrists.

As we came level with the doors of the car Paddy asked, *'Ist dies das General's Wagen?'*

There came a muffled *'Ja, ja'* from inside.

Then everything happened very quickly. There was a rush from all sides. We tore open our respective doors, and our torches illuminated the interior of the car – the bewildered face of the General, the chauffeur's terrified eyes, the rear seats empty. With his right hand the chauffeur was reaching for his automatic, so I hit him across the head with my cosh. He fell forward, and George, who had come up behind me, heaved him out of the driving-seat and dumped him on the road. I jumped in behind the steering-wheel, and at the same moment saw Paddy and Manoli dragging the General out of the opposite door. The old man was struggling with fury, lashing out with his arms and legs. He obviously thought that he was going to be killed, and started shouting every curse under the sun at the top of his voice.

The engine of the car was still ticking over, the hand-brake was on, everything was perfect. To one side, in a pool of torchlight in the centre of the road, Paddy and Manoli were trying to quieten the General, who was still cursing and struggling. On the other side George and Andoni were trying to pull the chauffeur to his feet, but the man's head was pouring with blood, and I think he must have been unconscious, because every time they lifted him up he simply collapsed to the ground again.

This was the critical moment, for if any other traffic had come along the road we should have been caught sadly unawares. But now Paddy, Manoli, Nikko, and Stratis were carrying the General towards the car and bundling him into the back seat. After him clambered George, Manoli, and Stratis – one of the three holding a knife to the General's throat to stop him shouting, the other two with their Marlin guns poking out of either window. It must have been quite a squash.

Paddy jumped into the front seat beside me.

The General kept imploring, 'Where is my hat? Where is my hat?'

The hat, of course, was on Paddy's head.

We were now ready to move. Suddenly everyone started kissing and congratulating everybody else; and Micky, having first embraced Paddy and me, started screaming at the General with all the pent-up hatred he held for the Germans. We had to push him away and tell him to shut up. Andoni, Grigori, Nikko, and Wallace Beery were standing at the roadside, propping up the chauffeur between them, and now they waved us good-bye and turned away and started off on their long trek to the rendezvous on Mount Ida.

We started.

The car was a beauty, a brand-new Opel, and we were delighted to see that the petrol gauge showed the tanks to be full.

We had been travelling for less than a minute when we saw a succession of lights coming along the road towards us; and a moment later we found ourselves driving past a motor convoy, and thanked our stars that it had not come this way a couple of minutes sooner. Most of the lorries were troop transports, all filled with soldiery, and this sight had the immediate effect of quietening George, Manoli, and Stratis, who had hitherto been shouting at one another and taking no notice of our attempts to keep them quiet.

When the convoy had passed Paddy told the General that the two of us were British officers and that we would treat him as an honourable prisoner of war. He seemed mightily relieved to hear this and immediately started to ask a series of questions, often not even waiting for a reply. But for some reason his chief concern still appeared to be the whereabouts of his hat – first it was the hat, then his medal. Paddy told him that he would soon be given it back, and to this the General said, '*Danke, danke.*'

It was not long before we saw a red lamp flashing in the road before us, and we realized that we were approaching the first of the traffic-control posts through which we should have to pass. We were, of course, prepared for this eventuality, and our plan had contained alternative actions which we had hoped would suit any situation, because we knew that our route led us through the centre of Heraklion, and that in the course of our journey we should probably have to pass through about twenty control posts.

Until now everything had happened so quickly that we had felt no emotion other than elation at the primary success of our venture; but as we drew nearer and nearer to the swinging red lamp we experienced our first tense moment.

A German sentry was standing in the middle of the road. As we approached him, slowing down the while, he moved to one side, presumably thinking that we were going to stop. However, as soon as we drew level with him – still going very slowly, so as to give him an opportunity of seeing the General's pennants on the wings of the car – I began to accelerate again, and on we went. For several seconds after we had passed the sentry we were all apprehension, fully expecting to hear a rifle-shot in our wake; but a moment later we had rounded a bend in the road and knew that the danger was temporarily past. Our chief concern now was whether or not the guard at the post behind us would telephone ahead to the next one, and it was with our fingers crossed that we approached the red lamp of the second control post a few minutes later. But we need not have had any fears, for the sentry behaved in exactly the same manner as the first had done, and we drove on feeling rather pleased with ourselves.

In point of fact, during the course of our evening's drive we passed twenty-two control posts. In most cases the above-mentioned formula sufficed to get us through, but on five occasions we came to road blocks – raisable one-bar barriers – which brought us to a standstill. Each time, however, the General's pennants did the trick like magic, and the sentries would either give a smart salute or present arms as the gate was lifted and we passed through.

————◆————

'This was the supreme moment – the final reckoning with the Monastery'
MAJOR FRED MAJDALANY

CASSINO
THE END
ITALY, 16–18 MAY 1944

The Allies invaded the Italian mainland at Salerno, south of Naples, on 9 September 1943 and from there slugged northwards towards Rome.

Monte Cassino was the centrepiece of the German's defensive 'Gustav Line', which dominated the Liri Valley and thus the approach to Rome itself. Not since 536 AD had an army taken Rome from the south. To conquer Monte Cassino required Western Europe's largest land battle of the Second World War. The first Allied attack on Monte Cassino went in on 17 January 1944; the ultimate attack started on 16 May 1944.

Major Fred Majdalany served with the Lancashire Fusiliers.

07.10 hours. Time to get ready. The shouts of the sergeant-majors. Jokes and curses. The infantry heaving on to their backs and shoulders their complicated equipment, their weapons and the picks and shovels they have to carry, too, so that they can quickly dig in on their objective. The individuals resolving themselves into sections and platoons and companies. Jokes and curses.

'Able ready to move, sir.'

'Baker ready to move, sir.'

'Charlie ready to move, sir.'

'Dog ready to move, sir.'

The column moved off along the track we'd taken the previous night. It was Tuesday morning. It was the fifth day of the offensive. In England the headlines were announcing that the Gustav Line was smashed except for Cassino and Monastery Hill. 'Except' was the operative word. That was our job now. To break through and cut off Cassino and the Monastery.

On the stroke of nine there was an earth-shaking roar behind us as four hundred guns opened fire almost as one. With a hoarse, exultant scream four hundred shells sped low over our heads to tear into the ground less than five hundred yards in front, bursting with a mighty antiphonal crash that echoed the challenge of the guns. It was Wagnerian.

From then on the din was continuous and simultaneous: the thunder of the guns, the hugely amplified staccato of the shell-bursts close in front, and the vicious overhead scream that linked them with a frenzied counterpoint. And sometimes the scream became a whinny, and sometimes a kind of red-hot sighing, but most of the time it was just a scream – a great, angry baleful scream. The fury of it was elemental, yet precise. It was a controlled cyclone. It was splendid to hear, as the moment of actual combat approached.

The makers of films like to represent this scene with shots of soldiers crouching dramatically in readiness, and close-ups of tense, grim faces. Whereas the striking thing about such moments is the matter-of-factness and casualness of the average soldier. It is true that hearts are apt to be thumping fairly hard, and everyone is thinking, 'Oh, Christ!' But you don't in fact look grim and intense. For one thing you would look slightly foolish if you did. For another you have too many things to do.

The two leading companies were due to advance exactly eight minutes after the barrage opened. So those eight minutes were spent doing such ordinary things as tying up boot laces, helping each other with their equipment, urinating, giving weapons a final check, testing wireless sets to make certain they were still netted, eating a bar of chocolate. The officers were giving last-minute instructions, marshalling their men into battle formations, or having a final check-up with the tank commanders with whom they were going to work.

Those who were not in the leading companies were digging like fiends, for they knew that the temporary calm would be quickly shattered as soon as the tanks and the leading infantry were seen emerging from it.

Meanwhile the barrage thundered on, and to its noise was added the roar of the Shermans' engines. A great bank of dust and smoke welled slowly up from the area the shells were pounding, so that you couldn't see the bursts any more. The sputtering of the 25-pounders rippled up and down the breadth of the gun-lines faster than bullets from a machine-gun, so numerous were they.

At eight minutes past nine they moved. Geoff led his company round the right end, Mark led his round the left end of the bank which concealed us from the enemy in front. Then the Shermans clattered forward, with a crescendo of engine-roar that made even shouted conversation impossible. The battle was on.

Geoff and Mark were to reach the start-line in ten minutes, at which time the barrage was due to move forward two hundred yards. Geoff and Mark would edge us as close to it as possible – perhaps within a hundred and fifty yards, and they'd wait until it moved on again, and then, following quickly in its wake, their bayonets and Brens would swiftly mop up any stunned remnants that survived. And while they were doing this the protective Shermans would blast with shells and machine-guns any more distant enemy post that sought to interfere.

Then the barrage would move forward another two hundred yards. The process would be repeated until the first objective had been secured – farm areas in each case. Then Kevin, who would soon be setting off, would pass his company through Geoff's and assault the final objective, the code word for which was 'Snowdrop'. When Kevin wirelessed 'Snowdrop' the day's work would be largely done. Highway Six would be only two thousand yards away.

To-day was crucial. To-day would decide whether it was to be a break-through or a stabilized slogging-match here in the flat entrance to the Liri Valley, with our great concentrations of men and material at the mercy of the Monastery O.P.

The Boche reacted quickly. Within a few minutes of our barrage opening up the shells started coming back. The scream of their shells vied with the scream of ours. Salvo after salvo began to rain down on the farms and the groves to our rear, where our supporting echelons were massed ready to follow in the wake of the assault. The sun's rays, growing warmer every minute, cleared the last of the morning mist. The Monastery seemed to shed the haze as a boxer sheds his dressing-gown before stepping into the ring for the last round. Towering in stark majesty above the plain, where the whole of our force was stretched out for it to behold. This was the supreme moment – the final reckoning with the Monastery.

Mortar-bombs began to land on the crest immediately in front. The bits sizzled down on our positions. Ahead the machine-guns were joining in. The long low bursts of the Spandaus: and the

Schmeissers, the German tommyguns that have an hysterical screech like a Hitler peroration. There were long answering rattles from the Besas of the Shermans. Then the *Nebelwerfers*, the six-barrelled rocket-mortars, as horrific as their name . . . The barrels discharge their huge rockets one at a time with a sound that is hard to put into words. It is like someone sitting violently on the bass notes of a piano, accompanied by the grating squeak of a diamond on glass. Then the clusters of canisters sail through the air with a fluttering chromatic whine, like jet-propelled Valkyries . . . There were several regiments of them facing us, and the existing cacophony was soon made infinitely more hideous by scores of Valkyries. They were landing well behind. For the time being the Boche were concentrating everything on the farms and the woods, that were crammed with concentrations of trucks and tanks and supplies of all kinds.

'You may as well push off now, Stuart,' John said. A minute later the fourth company moved round the right end of the bank and went the way of the others. The first of the prisoners came in. Six paratroops. Able Company's. Four large blond ones and two little dark ones. They were sent straight back.

Smoke-shells were being poured on to Monastery Hill now in a frantic effort to restore the mist. They had some effect, but they couldn't blot it out. The barrage seemed to get a second wind and the guns seemed to be firing faster than ever. The German shells were taking their toll of the rear areas. Four farms were on fire. We could see three ammunition-trucks blazing. Three more prisoners: one wounded, the other two helping him along. A grinning fusilier in charge. Some wounded in from Baker Company. All walking cases. Running commentary from tank liaison officer – 'Rear Link'. He sits in a Honey tank at our H.Q. and acts as wireless link between the squadron fighting with us in front and the tanks' regimental head-quarters. 'Both companies moving well. Machine-gun has opened up on Baker Company. Freddie Troop moving round to cope.' The sharp crack of the Shermans' seventy-fives, and a burst of Besa that seems to go on for ever. That must be Freddie Troop 'coping'.

'Okay now,' says Rear Link. 'On the move again.'

The *Nebelwerfers* have quietened down. They're easy to spot. Perhaps the counter-battery boys have got on to them. Our turn now. They're shelling our ridge as well as mortaring it. Some close ones. Rear Link has news. How Troop reports that five men have just come out of a building it has been blasting for five minutes and surrendered. Able Company report all's well. Baker report all's well. Charlie Company, following up, report all seems to be well in front, some wounded on the way back from Able. Three shells just above us. A signaller is hit.

The barrage ends. The effect is like the end of a movement in a symphony when you want to applaud and don't. From now on the guns will confine themselves to steady visitations on the enemy's rear. Unless the infantry want something hit. In which case the whole lot will switch in a very few minutes on to the place the infantry want hit. The infantry want something hit now. The voice on the wireless says, 'Two machine-guns bothering me from two hundred yards north of Victor Eighty-two. Can you put something down?' John tells Harry, who is eating a sandwich. Harry gets on the wireless and says, 'Mike target – Victor Eighty-two – north two hundred – five rounds gun-fire.' The shells scream over. Harry says, 'We may as well make sure.' He orders a repeat. The voice on the wireless says, 'Thanks. That seems to have done the trick. They're not firing any more.' Harry finishes his sandwich.

Rear Link has been deep in conversation with the left-hand troop commander. Rear Link thinks the companies have reached the first objective. No, not quite. It is all right on the left. But the right company seems to have run into something. Trouble from a farm. Tanks moving round to help. A lot of firing, ours and theirs. Rear Link says the tanks are pouring everything they've got into the farm. Twelve more prisoners – they look more shaken than the others. They had a bad spot in the barrage. Rear Link asks the troop commander how the battle is going on the right. The troop commander says it is a bit confused. A platoon is moving round to a flank. The farm seems to be strongly held. A reserve troop has joined in. A tank has been hit and has 'brewed up'. Baker on the left report that they are on their first objective. Charlie report they are moving up to pass through Baker. The *Nebelwerfers* again. Not as many as before. Some of them, at any rate, have been discouraged by the counter-battery fire. They seem to be going for the Bailey a mile back on the main track. Our anti-tank guns are in that area waiting to be called forward. Hope they are all right. Get Charles on the wireless and ask him. Charles says two trucks hit. One man killed and ten wounded. It has been all right since the first shelling. Able Company report that they are now firmly on first objective. Some casualties getting the farm. But they've killed a lot of Germans, and got eleven prisoners. They're digging in. The tanks are protecting their right, which seems horribly open. The tanks are in great form. They won't stop firing. They are spraying everything that could possibly conceal a German.

It has become very unhealthy behind our ridge. They are still mainly hitting the top of it. So long as they stay up there it won't be too bad. But there is always a nasty uncertainty about it. If they add a few yards to the range they'll be landing right among us. One or two have already come half-way down the slope.

Rear Link getting excited again. He's been talking to one of the troop commanders. Rear Link says Charlie appear to be on their objective. Can he signal 'Snowdrop' to his R.H.Q.? John says, 'No, not yet.' Rear Link gets another message from the tanks. Rear Link says Charlie have started to dig in. Can he signal 'Snowdrop'? John says, 'No. They haven't consolidated yet.' Kevin reports that he has arrived and is digging in. He says he has sent back more prisoners. More wounded, more prisoners, more *Nebelwerfers*, more shells, and the Monastery horribly clear. Rear Link has another conversation with the tanks. 'How about "Snowdrop", sir?' Rear Link almost pleads. 'Not yet,' John says. 'Not until they have consolidated.'

They're shelling us hard now. Not on the crest any more, but just over our heads and to our right. It is a different battery. They seem like 105s. They are coming over in eights. About every thirty seconds. The hard digging earlier in the morning is paying a good dividend. The last three salvoes landed right on our mortars, but they are well dug in and they get away without a single casualty. None of the shells has landed more than thirty yards from the command post. It is very frightening. Kevin on the wireless. Charlie Company are being counter-attacked with tanks. More shells on us. Twelve this time. Two of them within twenty yards. Behind, fortunately. Harry has taken a bearing on the guns and passed it back to the counter-battery people. Kevin on the wireless again. The leading Boche tank has got into a hull-down position fifty yards from his leading platoon. He has had some casualties. Our tanks trying to deal with it but hampered by very close-wooded country and a sunken lane that is an obstacle. Boche infantry are edging forward under cover of the fire from their tanks. More shells on the command post. The same place still. If they switch thirty yards to their left we've had it. That is the frightening thing. Wondering if they'll make a switch before they fire again. The accuracy of the guns is their downfall. John tries to get Kevin on the wireless. The signaller cannot get through. His toneless signaller-voice goes on saying, 'Hello Three, hello Three, hello Three, hello Three.' But he cannot get an answer. A closer shell blasted me against the bank. It is a queer feeling when you are brought to earth by blast. There is an instant of black-out, then sudden consciousness of what has happened: then an agonized wait for a spasm of pain somewhere on your person. Finally, a dull reactionary shock as you slowly discover you are intact. The signaller's voice again, 'Cannot – hear – you – clearly – say – again – say again – that's – better – hear – you – okay.' Kevin on the wireless. There is a tank deadlock. The rival tanks are now very close, on opposite sides of the same shallow crest. If either moves the other will get it the second the turret appears above the crest. The German cannot be outflanked. He has chosen his position cunningly. The sunken lane protects him. Kevin has had more casualties. More shells on the command post. Intense machine-gun fire from the direction of Kevin's company. Not a vestige of haze round the Monastery. This is the climax. No word from Kevin. John saying, 'Are you through to Charlie Company yet?' The signaller-voice tonelessly persevering: 'Hear my signals, hear my signals, hello Three . . . hear you very faintly . . .' Then, after an eternity, 'Through now, sir. Message for you, sir.' It is Kevin on the wireless. A fusilier has knocked out the tank with a Piat. It has killed the crew. The tank is on fire. The others are withdrawing. The infantry are withdrawing. Charlie Company are getting some of them as they withdraw. The counter-attack is finished. Consolidation may proceed. The tension is broken.

It went from mouth to mouth. 'Bloke called Jefferson knocked out the tank with a Piat. Bloody good show! Bloke called Jefferson knocked out the tank with a Piat. Bloody good show! Bloody good show – bloke called Jefferson . . .' It passed from one to another till all the signallers knew, the stretcher-bearers, and the mortar crews, and the pioneers: and the anti-tank gunners waiting some way behind, and some sappers who were searching for mines along the track verges. Till the whole world knew. 'A chap called Jefferson . . .'

Kevin on the wireless. 'No further attacks. Consolidation completed.'

'Get on to Brigade,' John said, 'and report "Snowdrop".'

'Snowdrop,' the Adjutant told Brigade.

'Snowdrop,' Brigade told Division.

'Snowdrop,' Division told Corps.

'Snowdrop,' Corps told Army.

In all the headquarters all the way back they rubbed out the mark on their operations maps showing our position in the morning and put it in again twelve hundred yards farther forward, on the chalk-line called 'Snowdrop'. It was ten past two. The battle had been going for six hours.

'Command post prepare to move,' John said.

We advanced in extended order through the long corn, as the ground was completely flat and without cover. The smell of the barrage still lingered, and the lacerated ground testified to its thoroughness. Wondering how many of the farms away to the right were still occupied by Boche; wondering how many machine-guns were concealed in the woods and the olive groves which stretched across the front a thousand yards ahead. Wondering if anyone had spotted our wireless aerials, which are impossible to conceal, and which always give away a head-quarters.

There wasn't a vestige of cover in the half-mile stretch to where the reserve company had dug in. There was still a lot of firing in front, mainly from the tanks. They were taking no chances with the open right flank. They were dosing all the farms in turn. With nine tell-tale wireless aerials swaying loftily above the heads of the sweating signallers who carried the sets on their backs, we pushed on quickly through the long corn, wishing it was a good deal longer. And the Monastery watched us all the way.

As soon as the command post was established in the area of the reserve company, John went forward to where Kevin's company were, and he took me with him. They had turned the area into a compact little strong-point. It had to be compact, because there were fewer than fifty of them left out of ninety who had set off in the morning. Besides which, the country was so thick with trees that you couldn't see more than fifty yards ahead. They had adapted some of the excellent German trenches to face the other way. Some were reading the highly-coloured magazines left behind by the Boche. These were filled with lurid artists' impressions of the Cassino fighting bearing such captions as 'Our paratroop supermen defying the Anglo–American hordes in living Hell of Cassino'. They were all on that level. There was one copy of a sumptuous fashion magazine, which seemed slightly incongruous, and suggested that the Rhine-maidens weren't all the drab blue-stockings the Nazis made them out to be. There was one of the famous new steel pill-boxes: an underground three-roomed flatlet, which included a well-stocked larder. Only its small, rounded, steel turret protruded above the ground, and this was skilfully camouflaged.

A few yards away Jefferson's tank was still burning. They were all talking about Jefferson. They were all saying he saved the company. The tank had wiped out a section at sixty yards' range, and was systematically picking off the rest of the company in ones and twos until fewer than fifty were left. Then Jefferson, on an impulse, and without orders, snatched up a Piat and scrambled round to a position only a few yards from the tank. Unable to get in a shot from behind cover, he had stood up in full view of the enemy and fired his weapon standing up, so that the back-blast of the exploding bomb knocked him flat on his back. Then he had struggled to his feet and aimed a shot at the second tank – but the tank was hurriedly pulling back, and with it the Boche infantry. It was one of those things that aren't in the book. Jefferson was typical of the best Lancashire soldiers – quiet and solid and rather shy, yet able in an emergency to act quickly without seeming to hurry. Such men are nice to have around in battles. It was one of those deeds the full implications of which don't really strike you till some time later, then leave you stunned and humble.

The next day, 18 May, the Germans on Monte Cassino raised the white flag of surrender. Two thousand British troops perished in the Cassino battle. So much for the popular idea that the campaign in Italy was a 'dodge' from the upcoming invasion of occupied France. The troops in Italy sang, with full irony:

> We're the D-Day Dodgers, out in Italy,
> Always on the vino, always on the spree,
> Eighth Army skivers and the Yanks.
> We go to war, in ties like swanks,
> We're the D-Day Dodgers, in sunny Italy . . .
>
> * * *
>
> Looking round the hillsides, through the mist and rain,
> See the scattered crosses, some that bear no name.
> Heartbreak and toil and suffering gone,
> The boys beneath, they slumber on.
> They are the D-Day Dodgers, who'll stay in Italy.

D-Day, the Allied invasion of occupied France, came on 6 June 1944.

'The farmer and his wife wanted us to stay and drink'
PRIVATE JAMES BYROM

D-DAY
A BRITISH PARATROOPER LANDS IN NORMANDY
1 A.M., 6 JUNE 1944

Four years after Dunkirk, the British (now accompanied by Americans, Free French, Poles and Canadians) returned to France in the largest amphibious operation of all time. Preceding the 5,000 craft crossing the Channel were the airborne divisions, with the British 6th Airborne Division tasked with protecting the eastern flank of the invasion beaches. The paratroopers, faces blackened, and fantastically encumbered by equipment, began dropping into Normandy just after midnight on the 5th.

Byrom served with the Parachute Medical Service.

A shadow darted from a nearby tree, and I was joined in the open by the huge sten-gunner with the black face. The whites of his eyes gleamed in the moonlight, and for all my weariness I found myself on the verge of giggles.

'You speak the lingo, tosh? All right, then, you go up and knock on the door, and we'll give you coverin' fire. I'll stay 'ere and my mate'll creep round the other side of the yard so's to cover you proper.'

A dog barked at my approach. From the corner of my eye I could see a stealthy figure flit from behind a haystack into the shadow of the barn door. There was no answer to my first knock. The household was obviously fast asleep. I knocked louder, and this time I heard a scurrying on the stairs and a sudden clamour of French voices. Footsteps approached the door, withdrew, hesitated, then approached again. The door opened.

On the way I had been searching for suitable words with which to introduce ourselves – some calming, yet elegant phrase worthy of the French gift of expression and of their infallible flair for the dramatic moment. But at the sight of the motherly, middle-aged peasant the gulf of the years disappeared, and I might have been back in 1939, an English tourist on a walking tour dropping in to ask for a glass of cider and some camembert.

'*Excusez-nous, Madame. Nous sommes des parachutistes anglais faisant partie du Débarquement Allié.*'

There was a moment of scrutiny, then the woman folded me in her arms. The tears streamed down her face, and in between her kisses she was shouting for her husband, for lamps, for wine. In a moment I was carried by the torrent of welcome into the warm, candle-lit kitchen. Bottles of cognac and Calvados appeared on the table, children came clattering down the wooden stairs, and we found ourselves – an evil-looking group of camouflaged cut-throats – surrounded and overwhelmed by the pent-up emotions of four years. The farmer and his wife wanted us to stay and drink, to laugh and cry and shake hands over and over again. They wanted to touch us, to tell us all about the Occupation, and to share with us their implacable hatred of the Boche. It seemed that the moment so long awaited could not be allowed to be spoilt by realities, till every drop of emotion was exhausted. I was nearly as much affected as they were. Warmed by the fiery trickle of Calvados, I rose to this – certainly one of the greatest occasions of my life – so completely that I forgot all about the Drop, all about the marshes and the battery. It was the sight of my companions, bewildered by all this emotion and talk, automatically drinking glass after glass, that suddenly reminded me of what we had come for. I began politely to insist on answers to questions which had already been brushed aside more than once: Where were we? How far away were the nearest Germans? Once more the questions were ignored. '*Ah, mon Dieu, ne nous quittez pas maintenant! Ah, les pauvres malheureux! Ils sont tous mouillés!*'

It was moving and exasperating. At last I managed to get what we wanted – a pocket compass and a promise of escort to the hard road through the marshes to Varaville.

'Day of hell. Counter-attack'
SERGEANT G.E. HUGHES

DIARY OF AN INFANTRYMAN IN NORMANDY
6–24 JUNE 1944

At 7 a.m., an hour after the American landings, the British seaborne forces touched down on Sword, Gold and Juno beaches. Their reception was curiously mixed. Some waded to shore to be greeted by attractive mademoiselles with flowers, others were mown down by German machine-gun fire in a manner reminiscent of the trenches in 1916. Such was the lot of Sergeant GE Hughes' Hampshire Regiment.

Diary, 6 June 1944
06.00 Get in LCA [Landing Craft Assault]. Sea very rough. Hit the beach at 7.20 hours. Murderous fire, losses high. I was lucky T[hank] God. Cleared three villages. Terrible fighting and ghastly sights.

June 7
Still going. Dug in at 02:00 hrs. Away again at 05.30. NO FOOD. Writing few notes before we go into another village. CO out of action, adjutant killed. P Sgt lost. I do P Sgt['s job]. More later.

June 8
07.30, fire coming from village. Village cleared. Prisoners taken. Night quite good but German snipers lurking in wood. Had 2 hrs' sleep. Second rest since the 6th.

June 9

06.30 hrs went on wood clearing. Germans had flown. Only one killed for our morning's work. We are now about 8 to 10 miles inland. Promoted to Sgt.

June 10

Joan darling, I have not had you out of my thoughts. T[hank] God I have come so far. We have lost some good men. Our brigade was only one to gain objectives on D-Day.

The French people give us a good welcome. Had wine.

June 11

Contact with enemy. Lost three of my platoon. Very lucky T[hank] God. Only had 5 hours sleep in 3 days.

June 12

This day undescrible [sic] mortar fire and wood fighting. Many casualties. T[hank] God I survived another day.

June 13

Just had my first meal since Monday morning. Up all night. Everyone in a terrible state. I keep thinking of u.

June 14

Counter-attack by Jerry from woods. Mortar fire. 13 of my platoon killed or missing. After heavy fighting yesterday CSM also wounded, also Joe. O[fficer] C[ommanding] killed. I am one mass of scratches. Advanced under creeping barrage for 3 miles. Drove Jerry back. It is hell. 3 Tiger tanks came here, up to lines during night.

June 16

[resting] Received letter from home. Wrote to Joan and Mum.

June 17

[resting]

June 18

Day of Hell. Counter-attack.

June 19
Day of Hell. Counter-attack.

June 20
Day of Hell. Advanced. Counter-attacked.

June 21
Quiet day. We have been fighting near Tilley [Tilly]. Bayonet charge. Shelled all day. Letters from home.

June 22
Out on patrol. Got within 35 yards of Tiger before spotting it. Got back safely T[hank] God. Shelled to blazes. Feeling tired out.

June 23
No sleep last night. Exchanged fire, out on patrols all day, went on OP for 4 hours. Stand-to all night. Casualties.
   Just about had enough.

June 24
Had to go back to CCS [Casualty Clearing Station]. Malaria.

———◆◆———

'We will love you for ever'
VARIOUS

GRAVESTONE EPITAPHS, BRITISH COMMONWEALTH CEMETERIES
RYES AND BAYEUX
NORMANDY, FRANCE, 1944

Private A. Richards, Hampshire Regiment
I wonder why you had to die without a chance to say goodbye.
Eileen and family.

Private F.A. Kelly, Devonshire Regiment
Beloved/Your Duty Bravely Done/Rest in Peace/Mum

Trooper A.J. Cole, 61st Regiment, Recce Corps, RAC
The Dearest Daddy and Husband in the World. We will love you
for Ever, Darling.

Perhaps the most telling measure of the bloodiness of the Normandy campaign was
that the tables used by the British to forecast battle casualties had to be extended
in mid-campaign to include a new category of fighting: Double Intense.

⸻⸱⸱⸻

'By morning I had to issue more Bensedrine to face the dawn attack'
LIEUTENANT EM MACKAY

ARNHEM
A BRIDGE TOO FAR
HOLLAND, 17–26 SEPTEMBER 1944

With Normandy lost, the Germans withdrew to defensible positions on the great
waterways of northwest Europe, the Rhine, the Meuse and the Scheldt. To breach
the new German line, the Allies launched Operation Market Garden, a massive
airborne assault on the bridges along the Eindhoven–Arnhem road. These secured,
so the plan went, Allied armour could drive into Arnhem – and thence into Germany
itself.

Unfortunately for the British 1st Airborne Division, dropped the far side of the
Arnhem bridge, the 9th and 10th SS Panzer Divisions were refitting in the locality
after their mauling in Normandy.

Monday
We still had six hours to go till dawn. I made a hurried
reconnaissance of the school. It had a basement, two floors and
an attic, and I decided to fight the battle from the first-floor,
merely holding the basement and ground-floor, and to observe
from the attic. I had fifty men (seven wounded), one other
lieutenant, six Bren guns, plenty of ammunition and grenades,
and a certain amount of explosive; no anti-tank weapons, very
little food, and only the water in our water-bottles; no medical
supplies except morphia and field dressings.

There was a breathing-space of an hour before the next attacks
were made: two were driven off before dawn. During lulls we went
out and collected one or two wounded paratroops from the area.

Dawn was heralded by a hail of fire from the house we had been driven out of a few hours previously. As it was only 20 yards away, our positions on the northern face of the school became untenable for anything but observation. As soon as it was fully light, we could see the exact positions held by the enemy next door. They very foolishly remained in them, and it was easy to form a plan to eliminate them. One machine-gun was fired by remote control from one end of our northern face. It drew all the fire, while from the other end we opened up with two Bren guns, and killed all the machine-gun crews. More of the enemy attempted to recover the guns, and were immediately eliminated. The time was now 8 am.

Meanwhile a battle seemed to be developing round our southern face. The Germans were putting in a strong attack on the house 60 yards south of us, and against a small force holding the other corner of the cross-roads on the opposite side of the street. A great deal of firing was going on and tracers were flashing all around. Someone was firing a light ack-ack gun straight down the street. It was all very confusing. No one seemed to know who was who. We joined in with our southern machine-guns as best we could. The battle seemed to be reaching a climax about 9.30 when a cry came from one of the west rooms to say an armoured car had just gone past the window.

I rushed over and was in time to see a second go by. The ramp was on a level with our first-floor, with its edge about 12 yards away. We could do nothing against these armoured cars, having no anti-tank weapons. However, after five had gone by, some armoured half-tracks tried to sneak through. These have no roof on them and so were dead meat. The first went by with a rush, but we managed to land a grenade in it. The second came on with its machine-guns blazing, and a man beside me was killed before we could stop it by killing the driver and co-driver. The crew of six tried to get out and were shot one by one, lying round the half-track as it stood there in the middle of the road.

This caused the remaining half-tracks to stop just out of view, and gave me a breathing-space to organise a system for their elimination. Ten minutes later two came on together, firing everything they had, in an attempt to force the passage. As they passed the one that was already knocked out, we shot the driver and co-driver of the leading half-truck. The driver must have been only wounded, as he promptly put it in reverse, and collided with the one behind. They got inextricably entangled, and we poured a hail of fire into the milling mass, whereupon one went on fire.

As the crew tried to get out of both, they were promptly killed. The score was beginning to mount. Another tried to take advantage of the billowing smoke to get through. It was similarly dealt with and there were no survivors. There appeared to be a lull, when suddenly I heard a clanking just below me. It was about 5 feet away and I looked straight into its commander's face. I don't know who was the more surprised. It must have climbed down the side of the ramp and was moving down a little path, 9 feet wide, between it and the school.

His reaction was quicker than mine; for with a dirty big grin he loosed off three shots with his luger. The only shot that hit me smashed my binoculars, which were hanging round my neck. The boys immediately rallied round, and he and his men were all dead meat in a few seconds. The half-track crashed into the northern wing of the school.

There was a further lull of about half an hour, when another half-track came down the ramp at full speed. The driver was promptly killed. The vehicle swung right, rushed down the side of the ramp, crashed head-on into the southern wing, just below us, where the rest of the crew were dispatched. While this was going on, another nosed out from behind the burning trio on the road. The same system was employed, and another eight Germans joined the growing pile. We were doing well, and our casualties were comparatively light.

It was nearing mid-day, and although there was a certain amount of clanking in the distance, no further attempt was made to force a crossing from the south. In any case the bridge was now blocked by burning vehicles. This lull was too good to last. Ten minutes later, with a sighing sound, fifteen mortar bombs landed on and around us. I could hear fire orders being given in English from the other side of the ramp, and realised we were being mortared by our own side. Leaning out of the nearest window, I gave vent to some fruity language at the top of my voice, the authenticity of which could not be doubted. The mortaring stopped.

To clinch matters, we let loose our old African war-cry of 'Whoa Mahomet.' This had an immediate effect, and was taken up by all the scattered points and houses round the bridge. The firing died down, and soon the air was ringing with the sound. Morale leapt up. Throughout the succeeding days this was the only means of telling which buildings were being held. It was one thing the Germans, with all their cleverness, could not imitate . . .

Tuesday
. . . Suddenly there was an appalling explosion in the south-west corner room. I rushed over with my batman. It seemed to be full of debris and someone was groaning in a corner. There was a blinding flash, and the next thing I remember was someone shaking me and slapping my face. I had been blown across the room, and was half buried under a pile of fallen brickwork. The whole south-west corner of the school, plus part of the roof, had been blown away. Everyone had become a casualty, and, by the time I was brought round, had been carried below, including my batman, who was blinded.

I found out later that the weapon that wrought this havoc was an anti-tank projector, which threw a twenty-pound bomb. The enemy failed to follow up his advantage, many of the boys being dazed by the explosions. We were given a breathing-space, but not for long.

Twenty minutes later, on looking out of a window, I was amazed to see a dozen Germans below me, calmly setting up a machine-gun and a mortar. They were talking and were evidently under the impression that all resistance in the house had ceased. A hurried reconnaissance revealed that we were entirely surrounded by about sixty Germans, at the range of some 10 feet, who were unaware of our existence.

It seemed too good to be true. All the boys were tee'd up at their windows, grenades ready with the pins out. On a signal, grenades were dropped on the heads below. This was followed up instantly by all our machine-guns and sub-machine-guns (six Brens and fourteen Stens) firing at maximum rate. The boys, disdaining cover, stood up on the windowsills, firing machine-guns from the hip. The night dissolved in sound, the din was hideous, the heavy crash of the Brens mixed with the high-pitched rattle of the Stens, the cries of wounded men, punctuated by the sharp explosions of grenades, and swelling above it all the triumphant war-cry, 'Whoa Mahomet'.

It was all over in a matter of minutes, leaving a carpet of field-grey round the house, together with a few machine-guns and mortars . . .

Wednesday

By morning I had to issue more Bensedrine to face the dawn attack. No one had now had any sleep for seventy-two hours. The water had given out twelve hours ago and the food twenty-four hours ago. As expected, with dawn the tanks came rolling up from the water-front, with infantry supporting. We were now alone on the east of the bridge. Every house was burnt down, with the exception of the one on the opposite corner of the cross-roads, which was in German hands.

We drove off three attacks in two hours. The school was now like a sieve. Wherever you looked you could see daylight. The walls were no longer bullet-proof, rubble was piled high on the floors, laths hung down from the ceilings, a fine white dust of plaster covered everything. Splattered everywhere was blood: it lay in pools in the rooms, it covered the smocks of the defenders, and ran in small rivulets down the stairs. The men themselves were the grimmest sight of all: eyes red-rimmed for want of sleep, their faces, blackened by fire-fighting, wore three days' growth of beard. Many of them had minor wounds, and their clothes were cut away to expose a roughly fixed, blood-soaked field-dressing. They were huddled in twos and threes, each little group manning positions that required twice their number. The only clean things in the school were the weapons. These shone brightly in the morning sun, with their gleaming clips of ammunition beside them. Looking at these men I realised I should never have to give the order 'These positions will be held to the last round and the last man.' They were conscious of their superiority. Around them lay four times their number of enemy dead.

By ten o'clock the enemy gave up their attempts to take the school by storm. They concentrated on the force now under the arches of the bridge, about eighty men, nearly all that remained of the original four hundred. These were eliminated by about two o'clock, when our last cry of 'Whoa Mahomet' was answered by silence. We were now the last organised position holding out near the bridge. It was a matter of time before we succumbed . . .

Montgomery ordered the 1st Airborne to withdraw across the river on the night of the 25th September. Only 2,400 men out of 9,000 got away.

'He might have been submitting to field punishment rather than the act of love'
SERGEANT NORMAN LEWIS

SOLDIERS IN A NEOPOLITAN BROTHEL
ITALY, 4 OCTOBER 1944

Norman Lewis served in the Field Security Police.

Somewhere a few miles short of Naples proper, the road widened into something like a square, dominated by a vast semi-derelict public building, plastered with notices and with every window blown in. Here several trucks had drawn up and our driver pulled in to the kerb and stopped too. One of the trucks was carrying American Army supplies, and soldiers, immediately joined by several from our truck, were crowding round this and helping themselves to whatever they could lay hands on. Thereafter, crunching through the broken glass that littered the pavement, each of them carrying a tin of rations, they were streaming into the municipal building.

I followed them and found myself in a vast room crowded with jostling soldiery, with much pushing forward and ribald encouragement on the part of those in the rear, but a calmer and more thoughtful atmosphere by the time one reached the front of the crowd. Here a row of ladies sat at intervals of about a yard with their backs to the wall. These women were dressed in their street clothes, and had the ordinary well-washed respectable shopping and gossiping faces of working-class housewives. By the side of each woman stood a small pile of tins, and it soon became clear that it was possible to make love to any one of them in this very public place by adding another tin to the pile. The women kept absolutely still, they said nothing, and their faces were as empty of expression as graven images. They might have been selling fish, except that this place lacked the excitement of a fish market. There was no soliciting, no suggestion, no enticement, not even the discreetest and most accidental display of flesh. The boldest of the soldiers had pushed themselves, tins in hand, to the front, but now, faced with these matter-of-fact family-providers driven here by empty larders, they seemed to flag. Once again reality had betrayed the dream, and the air fell limp. There was some sheepish laughter, jokes that fell flat, and a visible tendency to slip quietly away. One soldier, a little tipsy, and egged on constantly by his friends, finally put down his tin of rations at a woman's side, unbuttoned and lowered himself on her. A perfunctory jogging of the haunches began and came quickly to an end. A moment later he was on his feet and buttoning up again. It had been something to get over as soon as possible. He might have been submitting to field punishment rather than the act of love.

Five minutes later we were on our way again. The tins collected by my fellow travellers were thrown to passers-by who scrambled wildly after them. None of the soldiers travelling on my truck had felt inclined to join actively in the fun.

'the summit and culmination of my military life'
LIEUTENANT COLONEL JOHN MASTERS

REFLECTONS ON WAR AND LEADERSHIP ON THE ROAD TO MANDALAY

BURMA, MARCH 1945

Out there in the jungle, down by Mandalay,
A few forgotten soldiers slowly fight their way,
They dream of the girls they left back home,
And soon they hope to cross the foam
To see their land and loved ones . . .
From *Down by Mandalay* (sung to the tune of 'Lili Marlene'), Anonymous

After the battles of Imphal and Kohima, the 'forgotten army' in Burma began a dramatic advance against the Japanese; by early March 1945 the 19th Indian Division, commanded by Major-General TW ('Pete') Rees was nearing Mandalay. Lieutenant-Colonel John Masters was the 19th Division's general staff officer.

We passed Madaya, over half-way to Mandalay. That night a cipher-office check [message carrier] handed me a message. I glanced at it, then at the battle map, swore, and went to Pete. I said, 'There's a message here that I don't think you'll want to see, sir. It's from Corps. I can lose it.'

Pete smiled – 'You'd better give it to me. Thank you all the same, though.'

I handed it to him. Corps had ordered all its three divisions to hold back one brigade no more than twenty miles from Shwebo, to be ready at hand in case of a Japanese counterattack.

Pete said, 'Come along to my tent.' Recognising the symptoms, I went first to my own bivouac and got my whisky. In Pete's tent, beside a table, the hurricane lantern burning between us, Pete said, 'What am I going to do about this? It's absolute nonsense.'

I agreed. Shwebo was on the other side of the Irrawaddy, twenty miles west of the river. To obey the order we'd have to pull a brigade out of the advance and send it back to Singu. Shwebo was certainly vital, since it contained the airfields which were receiving our supplies, but . . .

Pete said, 'The way to defend Shwebo is to keep attacking as hard as we can, so that the Japs don't have troops to spare, or time to think of sending them back there.'

Obviously, but I wondered why Pete was so upset, why he needed so badly to talk to me. He said, 'You know I've lost one division already from saying what I think . . .'

I didn't know. He gave me the details, munching angrily on a slice of a cake. It was in the Western Desert in 1942, at the time of Rommel's big advance. Pete, commanding the 10th Indian Division – the division which contained Willy Weallens and the 2/4th Gurkhas – had not approved of his corps commander's plan, and had told him so. The corps commander replied that if he had no confidence in the plan he could hardly carry it out effectively, and summarily relieved him of the command of the division. Pete had been right, as usual, for when the Germans attacked dispositions were proved to be unsound.

Pete said, 'Should I have kept my mouth shut? It was a bad plan, but it was my division, and I knew it, and I could have fought it better than anyone else. Perhaps if I had been there, it would have held . . .'

The message from Corps lay on the table. I thought of the time, last year, when I had so strongly felt that my brigade should continue to operate in the Pinlebu area, on the tactics it knew best. I said Pete must do what he thought was right regardless of the consequences. They could only try to relieve him of command again, and I did not think Slim would accept that.

Pete nodded slowly. He said he would take no action on the order. If anyone was going to destroy the momentum of this attack, it was not going to be Pete Rees. He would fly back the next day and protest personally to the corps commander. He sat, thinking. He would have to go back twenty miles by jeep to the nearest airstrip, then by light plan to Shwebo. He would be away at least six hours. I asked which brigadier was to command the division during that time, as he would have to be called in from his brigade, and be given time to make his own arrangements.

Pete said with a twinkle, 'No brigadier, Jack. They've all got their hands full. You are. You can reach me on the radio if you have to.'

The next morning, after he drove off, I drew a deep but somewhat grumbling breath and took Tactical Headquarters forward. Commanders always resent staff officers and vent on them the helpless anger they are often bound to feel at their superior's orders. If any of the brigadiers chose to protest that what they were being told to do was impossible, I would be in a nasty spot indeed. So would they when Pete came back, but that was another story.

Those six hours were the summit and culmination of my military life. Knowing Pete's mind so intimately, I did not have to hesitate when faced by the few moments demanding positive decision. The leading brigade met opposition at such and such a point; I told the brigadier to attack as soon as he could, and passed the next brigade round him. Twice the C.R.A. came with artillery problems, but I had only to forecast my next moves, and leave the detailed solutions to him. Once a brigadier came, but it was Jumbo Morris of 62, who had wanted me to get back 111

Brigade soon after the Chindit campaign, he already having been given this 'normal' brigade in 19 Division – and he cheerfully agreed with my order and went off and did it. Twice the dialled face of the radio tempted me in moments of petty crisis. I had only to pick up the microphone and ask for Daddy, and all would be well. The familiar gentle voice would tell me I was doing well, solve the problem, and I would be covered. I managed not to do it, telling myself furiously that if I couldn't command a division for a few hours, after all I had seen and done, I'd better go back to being a Brigade Major.

In the afternoon Pete returned, having won his fight with Corps, and the sight of his face, beaming with pleasure at what we had achieved in his absence, was enough reward. The experience itself made me understand even more fully Lee's saying that it is fortunate war is so terrible, otherwise men would love it too much. The 19th Indian Infantry Division numbered about 1,000 officers, 14,000 men, and 180 guns, besides its trucks and tanks. This whole mass of strength and skill and courage, of flesh and steel, reacted like a sword in the hand.

In the evening of 10 March the 4th Ghurkhas stormed Mandalay Hill, only to find that it was riven with underground chambers containing hold-out Japanese soldiers. Masters recorded: 'A gruesome campaign of extermination began, among the temples of one of the most sacred places of the Buddhist faith. Sikh machine-gunners sat all day on the flat roofs, their guns aimed down the hill on either side of the covered stairway. A Sikh got a bullet through the brain five yards from me. Our engineers brought up beehive charges, blew holes through the concrete, poured in petrol, and fired a Verey light down the holes. Sullen explosions rocked the buildings and Japanese rolled out into the open, on fire but firing. Our machine-gunners pressed their thumb pieces. The Japanese fell, burning.'

Final victory in the Far East was still four months away, but in Europe the end was nearer. On 23 March British and Canadian soldiers of the 21st Army Group finally crossed the Rhine into Germany itself; the Americans had crossed days earlier to the South. In the East the Russians were steam-rollering towards the Oder. Germany disintegrated. On 5 May Field-Marshal Montgomery took the formal surrender of all German sea, land and air forces in Holland, Denmark and north-west Germany.

'it doesn't seem possible . . . that we have at last won the war'
PRIVATE JACK CLARK

VE DAY
A SOLDIER WRITES HOME
HOLLAND, 8 MAY 1945

8 May 1945   *2058212 Clark J*
                                              B Troop 190 Bty
                                              143 Field Reg. RA
                                              B.L.A.

My Own Darling Olive,
Wasn't it wonderful news darling? In fact it seems all too good to
be true. Today – VE Day is the day we have been waiting for for as
many years but even so it doesn't seem possible somehow that we
have at last won our War. I suppose you were tremendously
excited and happy when you heard the news at home but its hard
to explain really and it may sound funny but it didn't somehow
make much impression on us when we first heard the
capitulation. That was at twenty to eight on Friday the 4th of May
and only concerned our part of the front – Holland and Northern
Germany. It didn't seem to make a lot of difference at first. We
had just come in from the O.P. and were due to go out on a
practise scheme in the morning as we were pretty browned off. It
was an English speaking civilian who came and told us and he
must have thought us a pretty poor lot because, we didn't take
much notice but just went on cleaning our Carrier! Later on in
the evening we went over to the Gun Position and did a bit of
celebrating. For this purpose we dug out our Rum Bottle and
drank the contents between the four of us and a double ration
which was issued to mark the occasion as well! Outside all around
and as far as you could see the sky was full of lights, parachute
flares, and illuminating flares of all colours. There were lines of
tracer bullets and bofors shells streaming across the sky and in
fact it was a real Guy Fawkes night. That was when I wrote that
letter form to you and it is signed by our carrier crew – the driver,
the other driver op, the officer and his assistant.
    After this we had to spit and polish everything in preparation

for the big march forward. Whilst we were waiting yesterday morning to move off dressed in our Sunday best with all the vehicles shining and our webbing scrubbed white we received the news from Regimental Headquarters that all resistance everywhere had ceased. This was before it was broadcast on the wireless. Our job is to go on into Holland and round up and disarm the Germans mostly S.S. troops and send them back to Germany. We started yesterday midday and came into the German lines about 25 miles. All along the roads the civilians were lined up cheering and waving flags and wearing orange shirts and ties and the girls orange dresses and ribbons and painted on the trees and walls were big slogans 'Welcome' and 'We Thank You'. We have come as far as' DOORN where you remember the Kaiser was held captive since the last war. You will find this place on the map quite easily and I will be able to let you know exactly where we are in future as we have been told we can now do this. We expect to be here for about a week then are going on into Germany as Occupation troops.

It's funny here really for there are Jerries all over the place and all of them fully armed. We came into our Billet about seven o'clock yesterday evening and it was occupied by Jerries up to an hour of us arriving. Our advance party came along and told them to clear out so they just packed up and moved about 200 yards away and there they are. They ride around on bikes with rifles on their backs and some of them actually had the nerve to come and ask us for cigarettes today! You don't need a very vivid imagination to guess what our answer was. It seems so strange that everything could have altered so much in 24 hours just by the signing of a piece of paper.

On the wireless this morning we heard the official announcement of VE Day and that everyone, all over the world was celebrating it. We had no opportunity of celebrating at all and nothing to celebrate with literally not even water because the water supply has been off all day and only just come on again. Out here we always said that when Victory came the only people who would have the opportunity of celebrating would be those who did no fighting but I suppose that's just hard luck and we don't begrudge anyone who feels happy and has a good time these days.

We have a fine billet here, a large detached house in the

middle of a pine forest just outside Doorn. It's been a lovely day and wonderfully peaceful and quiet. Now it is evening and the sun is just going down – Darling this would be such a wonderful place to go walking with you just you and I together with no more worries and fears for each other.

I have your three lovely letters nos. 72, 73 and 74 which has just arrived. Although I love reading your sweet words so much Darling it will be wonderful when we no longer have to write letters to each other but can speak our words of Love and Adoration to each other.

I am on duty from midnight until four o'clock as I'm going to bed now and will join you again in four hours time. You will be sleeping whilst I am writing so Sleep Well Darling and God Bless you and bring quickly the moment when we shall be lying together in each others arms once again for I love you and long for your Love to the very depths of my heart.

With the surrender of Japan on 14 August 1945 the Second World War came to its end. More than 198,000 British soldiers had perished during its course.

If there were any hopes that the 1939–45 conflict would be *the* war to end wars they were rudely and quickly shattered. Since 1945 there has only been one year in which a British serviceman has not died in the line of duty. That year was 1968.

'*Call me CORPORAL. You shithead*'
PRIVATE TONY THORNE

NATIONAL SERVICE
BASIC TRAINING
1950s

Between 1947 and 1963 more than two million men passed through National Service, the only period of peacetime conscription in British history. Tony Thorne 'got some in' with the Royal West Surreys and, as subaltern, with the East Surreys.

Our squad, No 1 Squad, was all in the same barrack room under the watchful eye of Cpl Prudence. There were eighteen in all, excluding the Führer, who also had a bed in the same room. All the original truckload that had travelled down from Guildford was in No 1 Squad and we were joined by the larger part of another truckload which had come in from Edgware. Of the total eighteen we were divided about equally between ex-public school types, 'the lah dee fockin' dah lot' as the Corp called us, and another group of equally nondescript recruits.

There were no less than three Irishmen. Their only interest in serving in the British army was subversion and they did not show much interest in that. They kept their own company to the exclusion of all else and indulged in conspiratorial conversation. Their principal method of subversion was to disobey every instruction. It was never very clear to the rest of us how much of this was a deliberate plot and how much of it was the exercise of a natural talent. But, either way, it served the purpose of deflecting some of Cpl Prudence's anger away from other incompetents in the squad, of whom there were several.

The little plumber was still with us. It turned out that his name was Reg Plummer, which seemed appropriate. He also turned out to be a cracking good little soldier and a cracking good little colleague as well. Within a few days his kit was almost as well bulled as Prudence's. He just had that natural skill with his hands that made light work of spit and polish. His pack and his pouches stood in their correct position atop his metal wardrobe, squared off, erect and creamily Blanco'd. His blankets were always folded into a perfect square. But much more important, he was full of help and advice to all around him. He showed the giant Simon Gillett how to iron the pimples off his enormous boots. He tried and failed to mould the devout Tony Swinson's beret into the shape of his head. Poor Swinners was one of God's people, but his beret simply declined to answer his prayers. As Reg Plummer entreated, 'It's no good all that praying. It's just turning your beret into a fockin' halo.'

And it was a fact. However much Swinners, and indeed all of us, including Cpl Prudence, tried, his beret just refused to take shape. Even after ten weeks Swinners was still parading with a thing like a frisbee on his head.

The rest of the squad included some other very cheerful cockneys, full of humour and life, and some very dull and sullen figures, who made it pretty clear that they resented the Army and everything and every one associated with it.

Down my end of the room I was fortunate; first and foremost because Cpl Pru was down the other end. But also, and I would come to appreciate this even more, because I had two great mates on either side.

Webby found the whole kit thing quite easy. Within a few days his boots began to acquire that peculiar gleam we all sought and he began to turn into something beginning to look like a soldier. He was also able to find the time to laugh at my efforts. In a pattern that repeated itself all around the room, Webby got his kit up to scratch and then turned to help me. He spent almost as much time on my boots as he did on his own. As a joint effort my kit slowly began to pass muster. I could never aspire to the best in the squad, but, after many hours of unremitting toil, I just began to take shape.

On the other side was John Farrar, old Grandad himself. He had been a big star in his school cadet force and he rapidly emerged as one of the real luminaries of No 1 Squad. In addition he had that maturity which comes with twenty-one years. He also turned into a latter-day-saint. As we all sweated and panicked over our wretched boots and kit, John would tour the barrack room often well into the night. Like Henry V on the night before Agincourt, John Farrar mingled with the troops and administered to the sick and faint of heart. With a spit here and a polish there, old Grandad would make his rounds, encouraging everyone, always finding a word of praise for even the most disastrous efforts.

There was a terrible ordeal three times a day. This was called 'mess', which is a well-chosen Army word for meals. In our case it was not necessarily all that appropriate because the food at Howe barracks was not at all bad. But meals were nevertheless a terrible ordeal. This was because of the inspection that took place before each meal rather than the meal itself.

A shout of 'Mess' from the corridor outside our barrack room was the signal for us to grab our knife, fork and spoon, together with our white china drinking mug and race outside. There the ordeal began. We were required to line up in single file holding our white china mugs at the high port. This inspection was a Biggy. All three squads would be lined up in the corridor and this inspection would call for at least two, and sometimes even three, corporals. When we were all assembled, the pantomime began.

Cpl Jones pulls up opposite me. He peers into my spotless white china mug.

' 'Ere look at this, Cpl Prudence.'

Cpl Prudence scurries alongside Cpl Jones.

'What's this in there?' shrieks Prudence, pointing his little index finger inside my mug.

'Er, it's the bottom of my mug.'

'CORPORAL! Call me CORPORAL. You shithead. What's that in your fockin' mug? You . . .'

'Er nothing, CORPORAL.'

Prudence to Jones, leering. 'What's that in that mug, Corporal?'

'Sheeet!' screams Jones. ' 'E's got shit in his mug.'

Prudence to me, 'Now what's in that fockin' mug soldier?'

'Shit, CORPORAL.'

'Louder,' scream Prudence and Jones in unison. 'Louder.'

'SHIT, CORPORAL,' I scream.

'Blimey,' says Prudence to Jones, ' 'E's got shit in his mug.'

Jones peers into my mug much as Sir Lancelot would have peered into the Holy Grail. 'What are we going to do about it Corporal?' He asks earnestly of his colleague.

'Smash it. Smash it,' they cry out gleefully together. Then they fight each other to grab the mug from my hand and hurl it down onto the concrete floor where it smashes into a thousand pieces.

New mugs had to be purchased from the quarter-master's store and the stock market saw the price of North Staffordshire Potteries Ltd move to new heights daily.

This ritual was repeated three times a day, every day and the corporals never tired of it. Often the corridor looked like a snowstorm. Twice I bought a brand new mug and had it smashed the same day. On one occasion the whole of No 3 Squad had their mugs smashed. Mug-smashing was a perk of Corporaldom and they loved it.

National servicemen were not exempt from frontline duty. During the sixteen years of National Service 2,912 servicemen were killed in action, 395 of them National servicemen. The bulk of the dead came during one war. Korea.

'one tiny figure, throwing grenades, firing a pistol . . .'
MAJOR ANTHONY FARRAR-HOCKLEY

THE GLOSTERS AT IMJIN RIVER
LIEUTENANT CURTIS ATTACKS A MACHINE-GUN NEST
KOREA, 23 APRIL 1951

The communist regime of North Korea launched a major offensive in the Korean War on 22 April 1951, breaking through the line held by the United Nations west of Chungpyong Reservoir. The situation was saved only by the stand of the Gloucestershire Regiment at Imjin river; although ultimately overwhelmed, the Glosters' action broke one arm of the North Korean advance.

Lieutenant Philip Curtis was awarded the VC for the action below.

The dawn breaks. A pale, April sun is rising in the sky. Take any group of trenches here upon these two main hill positions looking north across the river. See, here, the weapon pits in which the defenders stand: unshaven, wind-burned faces streaked with black powder, filthy with sweat and dust from their exertions, look towards their enemy with eyes red from fatigue and sleeplessness; grim faces, yet not too grim that they refuse to smile when someone cracks a joke about the sunrise. Here, round the weapons smeared with burnt cordite, lie the few pathetic remnants of the wounded, since removed: cap comforters; a boot; some cigarettes half-soaked with blood; a photograph of two small girls; two keys; a broken pencil stub. The men lounge quietly in their positions, waiting for the brief respite to end.

'They're coming back, Ted.'

A shot is fired, a scattered burst follows it. The sergeant calls an order to the mortar group. Already they can hear the shouting and see, here and there, the figures moving out from behind cover as their machine-guns pour fire from the newly occupied Castle Site. Bullets fly back and forth; overhead, almost lazily, grenades are being exchanged on either side; man meets man; hand meets hand. This tiny corner of the battle that is raging along the whole front, blazes up and up into extreme heat, reaches a climax and dies away to nothingness – another little lull, another breathing space.

Phil is called to the telephone at this moment; Pat's voice sounds in his ear.

'Phil, at the present rate of casualties we can't hold on unless we get the Castle Site back. Their machine-guns up there completely dominate your platoon and most of Terry's. We shall never stop their advance until we hold that ground again.'

Phil looks over the edge of the trench at the Castle Site, two hundred yards away, as Pat continues talking, giving him the instructions for the counter attack. They talk for a minute or so; there is not much more to be said when an instruction is given to assault with a handful of tired men across open ground. Everyone knows it is vital: everyone knows it is appallingly dangerous. The only details to be fixed are the arrangements for supporting fire; and, though A Company's Gunners are dead, Ronnie will support them from D Company's hill. Behind, the machine-gunners will ensure that they are not engaged from the open, eastern flank. Phil gathers his tiny assault party together.

It is time; they rise from the ground and move forward up to the barbed wire that once protected the rear of John's platoon. Already two men are hit and Papworth, the Medical Corporal, is attending to them. They are through the wire safely – safely! – when the machine-gun in the bunker begins to fire. Phil is badly wounded: he drops to the ground. They drag him back through the wire somehow and seek what little cover there is as it creeps across their front. The machine-gun stops, content now it has driven them back; waiting for a better target when they move into the open again.

'It's all right, sir,' says someone to Phil. 'The Medical Corporal's been sent for. He'll be here any minute.'

Phil raises himself from the ground, rests on a friendly shoulder, then climbs by a great effort on to one knee.

'We must take the Castle Site,' he says; and gets up to take it.

The others beg him to wait until his wounds are tended. One man places a hand on his side.

'Just wait until Papworth has seen you, sir–'

But Phil has gone: gone to the wire, gone through the wire, gone towards the bunker. The others come out behind him, their eyes all on him. And suddenly it seems as if, for a few breathless moments, the whole of the remainder of that field of battle is still and silent, watching amazed, the lone figure that runs so painfully forward to the bunker holding the approach to the Castle Site: one tiny figure, throwing grenades, firing a pistol, set to take Castle Hill.

Perhaps he will make it – in spite of his wounds, in spite of the odds – perhaps this act of supreme gallantry may, by its sheer audacity, succeed. But the machine-gun in the bunker fires directly into him: he staggers, falls, is dead instantly; the grenade he threw a second before his death explodes after it in the mouth of the bunker. The machine-gun does not fire on three of Phil's platoon who run forward to pick him up; it does not fire again through the battle: it is destroyed; the muzzle blown away, the crew dead.

'the only sensation at the time was of a mild tapping on the front of the chest'
CORNET AUBERON WAUGH

NATIONAL SERVICE
AN ACCIDENTAL SHOOTING
CYPRUS, JUNE 1958

At the time of Waugh's self-inflicted injury, Cyprus was being fought over by its Greek and Turkish inhabitants. Waugh served with the British component of the United Nations peace keeping force on the island.

My troop was sent to take up a position between the Turkish village of Guenyeli and the Greek village of Autokoi on the Nicosia-Kyrenia road, to discourage reprisal raids and generally keep them apart. On patrol, we always travelled with a belt in the machine guns of the armoured cars, but without a bullet in the breech. The medium machine guns we had trained on, called Bisa, needed two cocking actions to put a bullet in the breech. The Browning .300, which we had in Cyprus, needed only one. It is most probable that I cocked the gun in a moment of absent-mindedness, but that did not explain subsequent events which were the result of excessive heat and a faulty mechanism. I had noticed an impediment in the elevation of the machine gun on my armoured car, and used the opportunity of our taking up positions to dismount, seize the barrel from in front and give it a good wiggle. A split second later I realized that it had started firing. No sooner had I noticed this, than I observed with dismay that it was firing into my chest. Moving aside pretty sharpish, I walked to the back of the armoured car and lay down, but not before I had received six bullets – four through the chest and shoulder, one through the arm, one through the left hand.

My troop corporal of horse, who had been on patrol between the two villages, arrived back at that moment and swore horribly at my driver, whom he imagined to be responsible. In fact nobody had been in the armoured car, as I explained from my prone position. I was rather worried and thought I was probably going to die, as every time I moved the blood pouring out of holes in my back, where the bullets had exited, made a horrible gurgling noise. To those who suffer from anxieties about being shot I can give the reassuring news that it is almost completely painless. Although the bullets caused considerable devastation on the way out, the only sensation at the time was of a mild tapping on the front of the chest. I also felt suddenly winded as they went through a lung. But there was virtually no pain for about three quarters of an hour, and then only a dull ache before the morphine began to take effect.

The machine gun had shot nearly the whole belt – about 250 rounds – into the Kyrenia road, digging an enormous hole in the process, before being stopped by Corporal Skinner, who showed great presence of mind by climbing into the armoured car's turret from behind. In the silence which followed, Corporal of Horse Chudleigh came back to me, saluted in a rather melodramatic way as I lay on the ground and said words to the effect that this was a sorry turn of events. He was a tough Bristolian parachutist and pentathlete. On this occasion he looked so solemn that I could not resist the temptation of saying: 'Kiss me, Chudleigh.'

Chudleigh did not spot the historical reference, and treated me with some caution thereafter. At least I *think* I said 'Kiss me, Chudleigh.' This story is denied by Chudleigh. I have told the story so often now that I honestly can't remember whether it started life as a lie.

As I was being lifted into the military ambulance with more

horrible gurgles he said: 'I don't expect you will be needing your pistol any more,' and removed it from my holster. It was a 9 millimetre Browning automatic, in short supply and much prized by those, like Chudleigh, who had been issued only with a .38 Smith and Wesson revolver.

The Blues medical officer was a Catholic and an old Downside boy. He accompanied me in the ambulance to hospital and read the De Profundis to me on the way. This struck me as rather gloomy, although there was nothing else to do, but not nearly as gloomy as the surgeon, Colonel John Watts, who prepared to operate immediately for the removal of a lung, spleen and two ribs. Feeling quite happy as the morphine took effect and fortified, as they say, by the last rites of the Church in the shape of an Irish priest to whom I took an instant dislike, I said to Colonel Watts in as nonchalant a tone as I could muster:

'Tell me, Colonel, what chance do you actually think I have of pulling through?

He fixed me with his cool blue eyes and said: 'I think you've got a very good chance.'

I felt as if an icy hand had been placed over my heart, but more even than terror I felt fury.

'What do you fucking *mean* I've got a good chance? You're supposed to say I will be out of bed the day after tomorrow.'

I later learned that none of them thought I would survive, but Colonel Watts performed brilliantly, taking out the lung, spleen and ribs in a hospital whose general standard of equipment, as I later realized, was somewhere around that of a cottage hospital in the Soviet Union.

I woke up after the operation in the stiffling heat of the general surgical ward, delighting Colonel Watts, when he told me that he had removed my spleen, by asking whether that would improve my temper. I was heavily doped and in great pain, with severe difficulty in breathing, but my chief irritation was the ward wireless which, because there were other ranks present, had to be played full blast all day.

—➤◆◄—

'I cock my rifle and the place goes quiet'
LIEUTENANT A.F.N. CLARKE

NORTHERN IRELAND
MIDNIGHT ON THE SHANKILL
JULY 1973

British troops entered Northern Ireland in 1969 to maintain peace between the
Protestant and minority Catholic communities. AFN Clarke served as a platoon
commander with 3rd Battalion The Parachute Regiment.

Funny things happen in the dead of night in the Shankill.

Standing around in the Ops. Room looking through the
personalities file, when a call comes through on the radio. A
panic voice, indistinct amid the crackle of static. Immediately the
whole atmosphere changes. The stand-by section commander,
half-asleep in his chair, suddenly wide awake and half-way out of
the door to get the section ready and Saracen fired up. Within
two minutes they are sitting in the Saracen and I've joined them
with the information that a patrol has been ambushed in the
Shankill Road. No other information bar the exact location.

'Straight down to the Shankill, turn left and up to the Agnes
Street junction. Go like hell.' I'm shouting into the driver's ear
above the roar of the engine.

'When we get there, I'm dropping three of you off short of the
turn and want you down in fire positions covering the rear. Jimmy,
take the other three round the immediate area. There's a back-up
on its way as soon as they get a Pig out to pick them up.' Shouted
orders. Thumping heart. Eyes wide in expectation. Cocked
weapons. Holy fuck, this is it!

There's a grey Morris 1800 in the middle of the street.
Confusion. A Military Policeman kneeling beside the front wing.
Another appearing from a doorway.

'What the fuck are you doing here?'

'We were just doing a routine car patrol, checking on stolen
vehicles.'

'You were what?' I'm incredulous. I don't believe my ears. Two
M.P.s casually driving down the Shankill in the middle of the
night in a civilian car in full uniform.

'Oh, forget it. What happened?'

'As we were driving along, we were fired at from down there.' Pointing away to the south of the road. 'We stopped and returned the fire.'

'Did you hit anything?'

'No.'

'How many rounds?'

'They fired about four or five, I think. My mate loosed off his magazine.'

'What, the whole lot?'

'Yes.'

Thirty-odd rounds sprayed into the darkness. What would they have done if the gunmen had stayed around for a second go? Crap-hats.

Jimmy's returned from his snoop around and found nothing. Not even a sign of life in the vicinity. Anti-climax. Another fucking anti-climax. The tension screw winds a little tighter.

The lads are giving the monkeys hell. The back-up patrol has arrived along with the O.C., the C.O., the Battalion Ops. officer and God knows what else. If only they would all stay out of the way and let us get on with it. The new C.O. in particular is being a pain in the arse. Career stamped all over himself like a cheap tattoo. A boring little man with a boring little mind.

How is it that we are controlled by a lot of fucking idiots? For some reason the best officers never get to the top positions. It certainly gets to the men, and the image of the chinless wonder drinking gin and tonic in the Mess is further enhanced by guys like this one. We've got a good Battalion with great soldiers and some really good officers, and then there is this clown.

I manage to get my guys back into the Saracen and we are meandering slowly back to Leopold Street via the back streets in low gear at high revs. The high-pitched whine of the Saracen in low gear is shattering, and guaranteed to wake even the heaviest of sleepers. Wake up you bastards! If we don't sleep you don't. A couple of guys walking down the street with a girl. Great!

Pile out of the Saracen, rifles levelled.

'Assume the position. Hands on the wall, fingers spread, now get those legs apart. Afraid you'll drop something?'

The girl is standing still, not saying a word. All our questions meeting no response. They're more afraid of what the 'boys' will do to them than what we have to offer. Soon change that, sunbeam. The dull thud of an idly swung baton up between the legs. Gasp of pain.

'Who told you to move, cunt.' Baton swings again, cracking hard onto a kneecap. Shrug from the tom in my direction. 'Looked as if he was going to hit you, boss.'

A body search with hands up hard between the legs. Squeezing testicles. Tears in the eyes. Fear in the eyes. Hopelessness in the face, turning slowly to anger and hard resolve. That's good, mate, get angry, try something. Better still, go tell your mates.

'What are you doing with these two specimens, love? Why not come back with us? Bet they don't know what it's for. Nice girl like you.'

Hungry-eyed toms, with open crudeness, visually undressing the girl.

'Is she a good fuck, mate? Do a good blow job, does she?' Chuckles and laughter.

'O.K. lads, you've had your fun, back in the vehicle. Let's go.' Back to Leopold Street. Back to the cocoon. Back to the freaky non-talk of people grouped together for too long, to a private world behind a blanket stretched over the opening of a bunk, to the constant banter and false bravado.

The 'street' is the reality and the unreality. The centre of the universe, the beginning and the end of time. The whole spectrum of all human existence in full living colour written on the walls, scored with the thump of explosive, photographed in the mind of a diseased body. Replayed every day, relived with boredom. We live in the commercial break of a battered building. Selling our morality to ourselves over and over again, with the help of war books, films, T.V. and sleep. Don't think of the rights and wrongs, just let the beast rise and enjoy the primeval passion.

An Army sniper who had just shot and killed a terrorist on the street was asked by a woman reporter what it was like to shoot someone.

'You just squeeze this little thing here,' he said. She went away with the wrong impression, but no doubt just what she wanted to hear. The soldier sadly shaking his head. We are here to create the news for a hundred poised pens and ready cameras. To provide a nation with its quota of violence, to give people the chance to shake their heads, others to organise marches, pressure groups and all the other paraphernalia of a well-organised growing industry. Northern Ireland is an industry, providing reporters with the opportunities to further their already stagnant careers, for social workers to martyr themselves on the unsympathetic conscience of an unimaginative nation. An entertainment without interlude. To hell with the lot of you.

The O.C. has us into the briefing room again. A club raid is on tonight. Great, comes the cry.

'Tony, your platoon with the Int. Section and C.S.M. We are not going to inform the R.U.C. until you are on the way. By the time they inform the club, you will be in there.'

Major, we love you!

It has been suspected that on a number of occasions when the R.U.C. have been informed prior to a raid, a tip-off has found its way to the target concerned. So now we have stopped letting them know until we are actually going through the front door. This method has led to the success of finding enormous amounts of arms and ammunition and other goodies. We don't trust any bugger, sometimes not even ourselves.

Club raid. Fantastic. Fantastic. This is going to be fun.

There is a woman living in a house just across the street from the location and it is obvious that as soon as a pile of Landrovers and Pigs and Saracens move off into the night that something is afoot and the word will spread like wildfire through the area. So we take it casually, and move out with two Landrovers as the main attack force first, the Pigs with the troops for the cordon to follow a little later. We are then going to join up and hit the club at the same time.

It's difficult to keep the excitement to a quiet level. All the toms wanting to be part of the action and in the raid group. No such luck lads, the first people through the door will be the C.S.M. and Hookey, being the biggest. Or at least that was the plan. Everything is going smoothly, gliding gently down the street to meet up with the Pigs. As soon as the vehicles enter the street that the club is in, the U.V.F. sentries will have warned the occupants of a patrol in the area. We've got to be real fast.

We turn into the street. Foot flat down on the accelerator and hurtle towards the club. Watch as the sentries dive into the door. All chaos and noise now. Pig slewing across the road disgorging soldiers who take up their positions, sealing off the junction and stopping all pedestrians.

Hookey and the C.S.M. pile out of the front seat, me right behind thinking now that I would much rather be a spectator. Too late.

Hookey hits the door with a flying kick and bounces back into the street. Fury doubled, he and Brian attack it with crowbars and finally break in where the noise of screams from the women and yelling abuse from the men, mixed with flying bottles, glasses, chairlegs and whatever else is available, hits you like a wall. Some guy tries to crown me with a broken whisky bottle. I try to get my baton into a swinging position and eventually have to club him with my S.L.R.

Hookey's biting a bloke's nose virtually in half, and Brian's swinging lustily with his baton, yelling all the while. Two of my men manage to get to the rear of the club and the physical resistance begins to falter under the viciousness of the onslaught. More soldiers come in from the street, but there's still a little fighting going on. I cock my rifle and the place goes quiet.

'Right you bastards. Men on the floor, spread, women over on the right-hand side and for Christ's sake, shut up.'

Some semblance of order now returning to the place. Bloody faces, spilled beer, broken bottles and glasses litter the floor. Sobbing women, shaking youths, cramped into this tiny den of hate and violence. The Pigs commandeered from other areas have arrived, and we start shuffling the human cargo up to Castlereagh for interrogation. Brian is standing over a guy seated in a chair in the middle of the room. He is very casually splashing whisky over a large split in the guy's skull, and then with great care and deliberation, starts to stitch him up.

'Where did you learn that, Brian?'

'On my D. Company medics. course. We spent a day on wounds and stitching.' Doctor for a day. Expert in an instant. That's Belfast.

The tension has lifted somewhat and eases a bit more when one of the drunks, hitherto unnoticed, struggles to his feet and starts singing, slurring all the words together. A couple of the toms pick it up and before long there is quite a little sing-song. A brief connection through the gulf. Pigs are trundling off down the road one after another with pasty, blurry faces staring unfocused out of the back doors. Some still giving vent to their discomfort, hands tied together with the plastic tourniquets with non-slip grips. Very efficient and easier to carry around than handcuffs.

Outside, the cordon is working well except for one bugger screaming about maltreatment, only to get another wallop over the head with a baton and collapse insensible on the pavement.

'What's going on out here, for fuck's sake?' I ask.

'Just some cunt trying to get through the cordon saying that he is the local U.D.A. man around here and that he wants to see someone in authority. I tell him he's going nowhere and he starts to get naughty. So I belted him.'

Fair enough, thinks I, and have a look at this guy. He's only one of the most influential blokes in the area, isn't he. Well, this will certainly keep the pot boiling for a little longer. There is certainly enough yelling and screaming going on out here, with cries of: 'Why don't you do this in the Ardoyne instead of picking on poor innocent people?'

'We like to share it around. Don't want you all to feel you're missing something,' replies a tom.

Images of a political rally. Switch off the sounds and watch the mouths work, the fists shake, the eyes piercing like the sniper's bullet, knowing that all these people would, at this moment, gladly see you die. Not in the unreality of a news bulletin, but in the flesh, now.

Sullen-faced youths on the periphery watching, gauging the feelings, counting down the time to positive action. The old game of 'He knows that I know that he knows that I know.' Chess with the lives of young teenage soldiers, fodder to sop the appetite of a thousand frustrated souls.

It's taken two hours to lift all the males from the club up to Castlereagh and we are just tidying up, searching the premises and generally making a nuisance of ourselves. Well, one thing is for sure, it's going to take them a long time to get this back together. Their bar stock liberally spread all over the floor, wiped off the shelves by a 'careless' baton or rifle. Doors hanging off their hinges, tables and chairs broken, mirrors smashed, and the toms enjoying every moment of it.

Outside, the crowd gradually drifting away, muttering like a giant animal. The R.U.C. constables, who arrived late, are away in the background, not wanting any part of the proceedings. Most of them are Prots. anyway, so don't want the local community to have any reason to be upset with them. None of the lads in our Company will have much to do with them, knowing the extent of their pay and overtime, plus the suspicion of graft from the Prot. areas to turn a blind eye on certain occasions and to keep them informed as to what the Army are going to hit next. There is also the feeling that we are here running their war, getting killed to protect them from it. Going into areas that they just do not penetrate. Memories of taking an R.U.C. constable into the Ardoyne for the first time in four years. Memories of the look on his face, the smell of fear, the suspicion of damp at the crutch. All this and an eight-man patrol just to guard him. It's your war – get on with it.

The search finished, the team get into their Pig and drive slowly away up the road towards the Crumlin. The rest of us start to pack up, taking care because it is at this stage that you become most vulnerable to attack. Everything going smoothly. Just a minor disturbance with some kids flinging bottles, quickly taken care of, and a semblance of peace returns to the area, floating on an undercurrent of increasing tension and hate.

***

'Go. Go. Go.'
SOLDIER I

THE SAS RELIEVE THE SIEGE AT PRINCES GATE

LONDON, 5 MAY 1980

The Iranian embassy in London was taken over by Arab gunmen on 30 April 1980; six days later the terrorists began shooting embassy staff held hostage. At that point the British government ordered a waiting counter-terrorist team from 22 SAS to storm the embassy building.

We took up a position behind a low wall as the demolition call sign ran forward and placed the explosive charge on the Embassy french windows. It was then that we saw the abseiler swinging in the flames on the first floor. It was all noise, confusion, bursts of submachine-gun fire. I could hear women screaming. Christ! It's all going wrong, I thought. There's no way we can blow that charge without injuring the abseiler. Instant change of plans. The sledge-man ran forward and lifted the sledge-hammer. One blow, just above the lock, was sufficient to open the door. They say luck shines on the brave. We were certainly lucky. If that door had been bolted or barricaded, we would have had big problems.

'Go. Go. Go. Get in at the rear.' The voice was screaming in my ear. The eight call signs rose to their feet as one and then we were sweeping in through the splintered door. All feelings of doubt and fear had now disappeared. I was blasted. The adrenalin was bursting through my bloodstream. Fearsome! I got a fearsome rush, the best one of my life. I had the heavy body armour on, with high-velocity plates front and back. During training it weighs a ton. Now it felt like a T-shirt. Search and destroy! We were in the library. There were thousands of books. As I adjusted my eyes to the half-light – made worse by the condensation on my respirator eyepieces – the thought occurred to me that if we had blown that explosive charge we might have set fire to the books. Then we would really have had big problems: the whole Embassy would have been ablaze in seconds.

The adrenalin was making me feel confident, elated. My mind was crystal clear as we swept on through the library and headed for our first objective. I reached the head of the cellar stairs first, and was quickly joined by Sek and two of the call signs. The entry to the stairs was blocked by two sets of step-ladders. I searched desperately with my eyes for any signs of booby traps. There wasn't time for a thorough check. We had to risk it. We braced ourselves and wrenched the ladders out of the way.

Mercifully there was no explosion. The stairs were now cleared and we disappeared into the gloom of the basement. I fished a stun grenade out of my waistcoat and pulled the pin. Audio Armageddon, I thought as I tossed the grenade down into the darkness. We descended the stairs, squinting into the blinding flashes for any unexpected movement, any sign of the enemy, and then we were into the corridor at the bottom. We had no sledge, no Remington with us, so we had to drill the locks with 9-milly, booting the doors in, clearing the rooms methodically as we went along. Minutes turned into seconds; it was the fastest room clearance I'd ever done.

It was when I entered the last room that I saw the dark shape crouched in the corner. Christ! This is it, I thought. We've hit the jackpot. We've found a terrorist. I jabbed my MP5 into the fire position and let off a burst of twenty rounds. There was a clang as the crouched figure crumpled and rolled over. It was a dustbin!

Nothing, not a thing. The cellars were clear. I was now conscious of the sweat. It was stinging my eyes, and the rubber on the inside of the respirator was slimy. My mouth was dry and I could feel the blood pulsing through my temples. And then we were off again, no time to stop now, up the cellar stairs and into the Embassy reception area. As we advanced across the hallway, there was smoke, confusion, a tremendous clamour of noise coming from above us. The rest of the lads, having stormed over the balcony at the front and blasted their way into the first floor of the building with a well-placed explosive charge, were now systematically cleaving the upper rooms, assisted by a winning combination of the stunning effect of the initial explosion, the choking fumes of CS gas, the chilling execution of well-practised manoeuvres and the sheer terror induced by their sinister, black-hooded appearance. We were intoxicated by the situation. Nothing could stop us now.

Through the gloom I could see the masked figures of the other team members forming into a line on the main staircase. My radio earpiece crackled into life. 'The hostages are coming. Feed them out through the back. I repeat, out through the back.'

I joined a line with Sek. We were six or seven steps up from the hallway. There were more explosions. The hysterical voices of the women swept over us. Then the first hostages were passed down the line. I had my MP5 on a sling around my neck. My pistol was in its holster. My hands were free to help the hostages, to steady them, to reassure them, to point them in the right direction. They looked shocked and disorientated. Their eyes were streaming with CS gas. They stumbled down the stairs looking frightened and dishevelled. One woman had her blouse ripped and her breasts exposed. I lost count at fifteen and still they were coming, stumbling, confused, heading towards the library and freedom.

'This one's a terrorist!' The high-pitched yell cut through the atmosphere on the stairs like a screaming jet, adding to the confusion of the moment. A dark face ringed by an Afro-style haircut came into view; then the body, clothed in a green combat jacket, bent double, crouched in an unnatural pose, running the gauntlet of black-hooded figures. He was punched and kicked as he made his descent of the stairs. He was running afraid. He knew he was close to death.

He drew level with me. Then I saw it – a Russian fragmentation grenade. I could see the detonator cap protruding from his hand. I moved my hands to the MP5 and slipped the safety-catch to 'automatic'. Through the smoke and gloom I could see call signs at the bottom of the stairs in the hallway. Shit! I can't fire. They are in my line of sight, the bullets will go straight through the terrorist and into my mates. I've got to immobilize the bastard. I've got to do something. Instinctively, I raised the MP5 above my head and in one swift, sharp movement brought the stock of the weapon down on the back of his neck. I hit him as hard as I could. His head snapped backwards and for one fleeting second I caught sight of his tortured, hate-filled face. He collapsed forward and rolled down the remaining few stairs, hitting the carpet in the hallway, a sagging, crumpled heap. The sound of two magazines being emptied into him was deafening. As he twitched and vomited his life away, his hand opened and the grenade rolled out. In that split second my mind was so crystal clear with adrenalin it zoomed straight in on the grenade pin and lever. I stared at the mechanism for what seemed like an eternity, and what I saw flooded the very core of me with relief and elation. The pin was still located in the lever. It was all over, everything was going to be okay.

But this was no time to rest, this was one of the most vulnerable periods of the operation, the closing stages. This is where inexperienced troops would drop their guard. The radio crackled into life. 'You must abandon the building. The other floors are ablaze. Make your way out through the library entrance at the rear. The Embassy is clear. I repeat, the Embassy is clear.'

I joined Sek and we filed out through the library, through the smoke and the debris. We turned left and headed back for number 14, past the hostages, who were laid out and trussed up on the lawn ready for documentation, past the unexploded explosive charge, past the discarded sledgehammer and other pieces of assault equipment – all the trappings of battle in the middle of South Kensington. It was 8.07 p.m.

As we made our way through the french windows of number 14, the Gonze, ex-Para, a new boy in the regiment from one of the other call signs, removed his respirator and asked the Irish police sergeant on duty at the door what the Embassy World snooker score was. A look of total disbelief spread across the policeman's face and he just stood there shaking his head from side to side.

I crossed the room to my holdall and as I began pulling off my assault equipment I could feel the tiredness spreading through my limbs. It wasn't just the energy expended on the assault, it was the accumulation of six days of tension and high drama, of snatched sleep in a noisy room, of anxiety and worry over the outcome of the operation. I looked to my left. The Toad had just returned. He looked tired, his face was flushed and he was out of breath. He looked at me and shook his head. 'I'm getting too old for this sort of thing.'

'So am I,' I replied.

Within fifteen minutes most of the team members had stripped off their assault kit, packed it into their holdalls and parcelled their MP5s into plastic bags to be taken away for forensic examination. Before moving out through the front door of number 14 to the waiting Avis hire van, we had a dramatic visit from Home Secretary William Whitelaw, old Oyster Eyes himself. He stood before us, tears of joy unashamedly running down his cheeks, wringing his hands in relief. He thanked the assembled team members for what they had done for the country that day. 'This operation will show that we in Britain will not tolerate terrorists. The world must learn this.' It was a fine personal gesture and rounded the operation off perfectly.

——●◆●——

'Under the intense heat my hands enlarged and the skin peeled off'
CAPTAIN HILARIAN ROBERTS

FALKLANDS WAR
SIR GALAHAD IS HIT BY AN EXOCET MISSILE
8 JUNE 1982

One of the last remnants of Empire, the Falkland Islands were invaded by Argentina on 2 April 1982. In resolute response, the Conservative government of the day dispatched a task force southwards to fight the last solo campaign of the British army.

Argentine resistance was bitter. An early taste came on 8 June when Argentine aircraft attacked British troopships riding at anchor in Fitzroy Sound, East Falkland. Captain Hilarian Roberts of the Welsh Guards was on the tank deck of the RFA *Sir Galahad* when an exocet missile struck:

It's an extraordinary thing but there was just an instant of complete unease, which is a bit uncanny really, because everything was still going on as before. Then my Platoon Sergeant, Roberts 32, just shouted, 'Get down, get down!' I hadn't heard any planes or anything like that, but I went straight to the ground. There was this rather dull, all-embracing crack, a terrifically enveloping thud, and a huge flame ahead where all these people had been sitting. It just billowed straight over me and I experienced an extraordinary slow-motion feeling of being burnt and watched my hands become the colour of those rather sickly white-grey washing-up gloves. Under the intense heat my hands enlarged and the skin peeled off like talons of wax. It was amazing, it couldn't have taken long, it must have been so quick, but I saw it like a slow-motion film. Then I found my hair on fire and with these useless hands I was trying to put my hair out!

All sorts of extraordinary things were happening so quickly and I felt complete resignation. I thought, 'Well, that's it, it's finished, it's all over.' I was just enveloped in smoke and the smell of burnt flesh, but there was no sort of anger, just the feeling that it's over, finished. Then I suppose some sort of instinct to survive took over because suddenly I thought, 'I'm not dead and I'm damn well not going to die now.' By now the blast had gone over and there was black smoke beginning to billow up terrifically at our end. It was, of course, a dead end. Well, there were one or two people in the smoke and the flames, but there was no way you could get to them. I saw a man burning in the most extraordinary way – he was like a human torch.

I'd be dead if I hadn't been flat on the ground. The blast went right over the top of me; otherwise I would still be down there. The blast could have thrown anything at you. In fact, I was completely and utterly covered in feathers from an exploding sleeping bag. If it had been anything heavy I would have gone. The combat trousers saved my legs because they don't burn much; if I'd been wearing plastic or lightweight trousers, I would have burnt. Fortunately I just sort of had burn holes from things that had fallen on me; they had gone through to the skin and I remember the extraordinary sight of just a frizz of wool – the rest of my jumper had vanished.

I got up and could see very little, really. I knew there was one way out, the one upstairs way, and I moved towards it, thinking, 'What can I do?' I couldn't touch anything. My hands, my God they hurt, they really hurt. I felt, 'What on earth can I do?' because this was where you, as an officer, had to do something. I heard CQMS Morgan shouting, 'Keep calm, one at a time, keep calm,' in complete darkness. It was strange but tremendously reassuring. So I just repeated what he was saying, over and over again. All the while and in front of me they were putting out people still on fire; there must have been about ten or fifteen of them. For us in the smoke, in that bottleneck, the only way out was up the stairs and there was that awful feeling that if they didn't keep completely calm, someone would stumble or get caught and there would be chaos. A lot of people were in my state, rather shocked and hands sort of dripping and faces beginning to blacken all over. By now the skin of my hands had just vanished and was lying in terrible grey straggles. We were going up the stairs very slowly and we got stuck in a sort of dead end and had to back out to get up again but no-one panicked – they behaved really beautifully, of that there is no question. There was a lot of shouting but it wasn't panic-struck shouting, because if anybody had got really panicky, we just wouldn't have got out at all. Eventually, we did get out. It couldn't have taken very long, a couple of minutes, I think, but it felt a lot longer. We came staggering out onto the deck, and then I suppose the adrenalin, the immediate instinct to get out, began to wear off. My God, you felt as sick as a dog. But there was this marvellous thing as well, seeing people whom you knew you had to encourage – it's such a great advantage to have something to do instead of just sitting there. I didn't see anybody on the deck who performed badly.

'His eyes closed. He died then and there'
LANCE-CORPORAL VINCE BRAMLEY

MOUNT LONGDON
13–14 JUNE 1982

Lance-Corporal Vince Bramley served with 3rd Battalion The Parachute Regiment in the Falklands War.

In the half light of false dawn I could now hear shouting all down the hill. Some guys were screaming like mad. One voice went right through me – the scream of a man who knows he is about to die. All over the hill people were shouting, 'Medic, medic.'

I was about to crawl from my hole when another shell hit the ground. I hadn't even heard it coming. I fell on my face and stayed there for a few seconds. Another shell landed nearby. This time a shower of dirt fell on my back. I crawled back into my hole and curled up again, waiting. My body shook uncontrollably. The shells landed in thick salvoes, the noise and explosions around me making my head spin as if someone were banging it against a wall. I willed it to stop, but the shells carried on landing around me. Then, this second bombardment within minutes ended as suddenly as it had begun. The last shell landed further down the hill. After a few minutes many of us began to crawl from our hiding places. Standing on a rock, I looked down the hill. In the early-morning mist I could see troops walking and running in all directions. Some guys were carrying wounded lads down towards the FAP. The screaming of the wounded was everywhere.

About twenty-five metres away I saw a lad half dragging himself down the hill, holding his leg. He had no webbing, no helmet, but his weapon was still in his free hand. I searched about me frantically. I had to help someone, but who first? I picked up and replaced my webbing. SLR in hand, I made my way towards the guy dragging his leg. As I reached him the OC screamed, 'Support teams on me, support teams on me.'

The lad looked at me with pitiful eyes. I recognized him from B Company. He'd obviously been wounded for some time, as the blood on his leg was now dried and dark. He rested against a rock. When I reached him I crouched to look at his leg. I was about to help him when he said, 'You'd better go, mate. Your boss is screaming for you. Besides, it's your turn over there now.'

'OK,' I said.

Quickly turning around, I made my way to where the OC was standing in his original spot. As I reached him, with all my kit, Tommo, Johnny and a few others joined us.

'Where's the rest?' shouted the OC.

'I saw a few carrying wounded down the hill, sir,' said Tommo.

'For fuck's sake, we've a bloody task to do. How many here?'

Tommo did a quick head check. 'Eight, sir.'

'OK, follow Sergeant Pettinger. He will lead you to our new positions.'

Sergeant Pettinger stood there, his eyes showing strain. He was an excellent soldier, and many had great respect for him. As part of D Company he knew the hill better than most, from previous recces.

'Right,' he said. 'Keep well behind me. It's hell up front still – they're crawling out of bunkers now, so watch yourselves.'

I quickly fixed my bayonet. I was standing right next to Sergeant P when he turned on his heels and started to half run, half trot through a small gap in some crags. I immediately followed him. Tommo and Johnny were behind me as we all squeezed through. I can remember the OC shouting behind us, 'Move, move. Their artillery will soon be here again.'

Sergeant P waited only for me to squeeze myself through the gap before he took off again. After we had gone about four or five steps a hand dropped out of the rocks, grabbing at my ankle and denims. The shock of it made us jump. Instantly, Sergeant P was back with me. We both looked at my feet. Still holding my denims was a wounded Argie. His eyes were staring at me; pleading perhaps, full of sorrow? Sergeant P shouted, 'Step back, Brammers.'

I tried to step back, but the wounded soldier tightened his grip on me. I leaned back as Sergeant P pointed his weapon and fired two bullets into the man's head, the noise of his weapon echoing around the small gap. Tommo and Johnny were behind me now. The Argie's head bounced quickly as the two rounds entered him. His eyes rolled to the back of his head and his mouth opened to release a trickle of blood and saliva, which ran down his chin on to his shirt collar. At the same time, his hand gave up its grasp on my denims and dropped on to my boot. I flicked my boot as if I was playing football. His hand and arm dropped across his body and from his mouth came a low whistle of air, mixed with blood. All this took seconds, but it seemed a lifetime to me. Each detail remains with me today. The sight of this guy dying at my feet shocked me. But I was growing harder. Although shaken, I felt no remorse at that time. The deadly game of war lay at my feet; only I mattered.

The rights and wrongs of war can never be argued from the armchair. Decisions are made on the spot, questions asked afterwards. That lone Argie could have been rigged to a booby-trap, or even armed. The kill was done quickly and professionally. I felt that I should have acted as quickly as Sergeant P.

'Come on, move!' he shouted.

We all took off behind him. The small gap ended about five or six steps later and we broke out into a clearing. Across the skyline I saw some guys walking through the mist, which was now lifting. They had fixed bayonets. In groups of two or three they were searching around. Sergeant P and I stood together for several seconds, while the rest of the eight guys left from the platoon broke out into the clearing as well. A shell screamed in, landing just as we all hit the ground. As we picked ourselves up Sergeant P shouted at us to move and we ran further into the clearing.

My first view of the surrounding area in the clearing was one of total bedlam. Bodies lay everywhere, wounded and dead alike. I could see four or five Argentinians clumped together across our pathway, twisted in their final positions, now beginning to rot. One had an arm hanging off. Another had half his head missing; the brains lay to one side, like spilled minced meat.

A bullet hit the rock above my head and I ducked – not that it would have made any difference. A member of B Company was firing a sub-machine-gun at the area where the enemy was still holding out.

Sergeant P screamed an order to follow him. As we trotted further into the clearing we had to jump over the twisted pile of corpses. My mind never was, nor has since been, so alert. Adrenalin was rushing through my body so quickly that I felt I was floating with an excitement mingled with fear.

A little farther into this clearing lay three or four Argentinians, shaking visibly, close together on the ground. We half ran, half walked through a deadly, sickening area of death. They looked up as we arrived. All had been seriously wounded, and were moaning and crying. One held up his hands across his eyes and shouted, 'Mama.' I felt he thought that we were, or I was, about to shoot him. He went on calling for his 'Mama' in a low wail.

Some lads from B Company were pushing a few prisoners to join the three or four already on the ground. One prisoner held his head in both hands. As he was thrown to the ground he released his hands to break his fall and I saw that his ear was missing. A gunshot wound was also visible on his left knee. It had been bandaged, but the bandage was loose and trailed from the wound. Blood ran down from his ear and from his leg. He hit the ground and began to cry like the others.

One Argentinian sat in a trance, his eyes wide and staring at nothing. Tears ran down his face, the only sign that he was alive. None of them moved; all looked like they expected to be shot by us. But we ran past. The whole area was littered with weapons, helmets, clothing, food and ammo.

After running through this clearing I noticed some B Company lads covering and firing into some rocks ahead of us. A lance-corporal screamed, 'They're breaking!' He then fired off six or seven shots at what must have been fleeing enemy soldiers. Some others joined him, their SLRs echoing around the clearing.

My mind buzzed, my eyes searched and checked every crag. I felt I was floating, as if it was all a dream. At the same time I was completely ready to meet my own death. I felt that luck was the only way I would survive now.

A few bullets whizzed overhead and smashed into the rocks. A corporal shouted that Tumbledown was firing at us. We ran into a tight gap in the path and all came to an abrupt halt, as it was a dead end. Four or five bodies lay sprawled there, close together. This time they were our own men: the camouflaged Para smocks hit my eyes immediately. CSM Wicks was standing over them like a guardian, screaming at some of his men to cover the further end of the path and a small crest. The CSM and Sergeant P exchanged quick words. I wasn't listening; my mind was totally occupied with looking into the crags for the enemy. I turned and looked at our own lads, dead on the ground, mowed down when they tried to rush through this gap. I felt both anger and sadness. The CSM's face showed the strain of having seen most of his company either wounded or shot dead. That night's fighting was written in every line of his face.

We all doubled back into the clearing we had just run through. We spread out and waited for our next move. A wounded Argentinian lay to my right, about ten metres away. He had been hit in the chest and screamed as he held the wound. A lad from B Company ran across the clearing at him and ran his bayonet through him. The screaming Argentinian tried to grab the bayonet from him before it took his life. Our lad screamed, 'Shut up, shut up, you cunt!'

The enemy soldier died as the bayonet was withdrawn. The lad walked back to his seat among the rocks, as if nothing had happened.

To my right three Argentinians were crying with their heads in their hands. Were they the dead man's friends? At their feet lay one of our lads, moaning in pain as a medic attended to him. I could see his back was peppered with shrapnel. I swung to my left and fell against some rocks. I now felt the shock of it all coursing through my body. I wailed softly, my throat feeling like I wanted to choke. My eyes watered and I shook my head to force myself into reality. But this was reality. I looked for Bob and Johnny. I couldn't see Bob, but Johnny was there, staring right at me. Our eyes met, telling each other that we felt the end had come.

A lad resting with his rifle pointed towards Tumbledown turned and fell into a tight ball, curling himself up as he hit the ground screaming, 'Incoming, incoming.'

We all dropped to the ground, crawling behind rocks wherever

we could. The first shell went over us, on to the west side of the
mountain. Then the shells started to creep towards us and one
thumped into the clearing, hitting a rock about thirty metres
away. The ground shook as if we'd been hit by an earthquake,
shrapnel pierced the ground or bounced off rocks all around us.
Grant Grinham screamed out as shrapnel hit his leg. Two of his
mates were pulling him into better cover as the shells rained
around us again. This time, when an Argentinian cried out no
one went to his aid. Soon after, Corporal Stewart McLaughlin was
hit in the back by shrapnel. He was later killed by a direct mortar
hit as he was being taken to a first aid post.

I lay there trembling as the shells roared over us. Each
explosion shook more fear into us. The barrage ended after ten
or fifteen shells had landed on different parts of the mountain.

I crawled from behind my rock. I stood up, then fell against
the rock that some lads were running around as they tried to get
the wounded lad out of this deadly area and to the FAP. In front
of me a B Company lad was sitting beside a wounded Argentinian.
They rested together as if they were watching a game.

---

*'More than anything I felt the pinch of no longer
having my friends around me'*
LANCE-CORPORAL VINCE BRAMLEY

THE SOLDIER RETURNS HOME
JULY 1982

Back in my quarters I started to fight a completely different war,
against boredom. The first thing I did was to throw open all the
windows, because the claustrophobia I felt almost made me ill.
The wind came rushing in, much to my relief, but not Karon's.
Within an hour I had to go out and walk about. Karon and I
walked around Salisbury shopping, but still the people annoyed
me as they crowded together, pushing and shoving.

That night I was restless, sweating and walking about the
house. I sat for two or three hours by the open windows in the
lounge. I couldn't stop thinking of how the lads who had been hit
by shrapnel or bullets were coping.

Next day we went home to Aldershot. A banner hanging from the front top window of our house saying 'Welcome Home' was touching, but somehow embarrassing. I didn't want anyone to know where I had been. I started to grow a beard on this six-week leave, to hide my identity as a soldier.

What hit me most was that I really hated the leave at first. It was so fucking boring. There was no way I could relax. If I had been asked to go and do a tour of duty in Ireland I would have gone. More than anything I felt the pinch of no longer having my friends around me. We had been together so tightly over the last few months that it was as if now I had severed an arm. The buddy-buddy system that we had needed to literally survive wasn't there any more and the sheltered life now seemed to me far too boring to endure.

I made a point of not talking about my experiences to any member of my family, including my wife. But I do remember sitting up in bed one evening, turning to my wife and giving her a very mild insight into what had really happened. I was sick to death of the press's views and of the publicity of a country still high on the war. I told Karon what had happened to Denzil and Jones. The blank look she gave me, with a half smile, told me she wasn't interested and couldn't understand me at all. I never said anything again. I tried to look at it from her point of view instead. She was sick of the war, of the army and of me going away. Whenever I bumped into one of the lads I seemed more at home and relaxed talking our private language with him than I did with civvies and my own family. If I had had my own way I would have gone on the biggest bender ever, but I knew that was the easy way out. I remember buying the LP 'The Friends of Mr Cairo' by Vangelis. That record had been played daily to us over the intercom on the *Canberra* on the journey down. The track 'I'll Find My Way Home' had been an instant hit with the troops.

The days at home turned into weeks. I finally returned to camp with many other Paras who had chosen to help unload the *Elk* in Plymouth of all the remaining 3 Para equipment. Next day came notice of a further six weeks' leave. It was sending me nuts.

Karon and I moved into new quarters in Aldershot. Setting up the new home gave me something to do for a while. As I walked into town on the first morning after our arrival, the sun was out and kids were playing in the small swing park. It was a typical summer's day, quiet and nice. All of a sudden a jet fighter flew over us with a scream and I ducked and was halfway into a doorway before I realized it was peacetime now. Karon looked at me, half giggling. I smiled to cover the embarrassment that engulfed me.

━━━◆◆◆━━━

'On I stumbled for another hour. My dehydration was making me choke and gag'
CORPORAL CHRIS RYAN

GULF WAR
THE ONE THAT GOT AWAY
24–31 JANUARY 1991

Corporal Ryan was inserted, by helicopter, 100 miles north-west of Baghdad as part of a roadwatch team from 22nd Special Air Service Regiment. The eight-team, code-named Bravo Two Zero, lying up in cold, featureless desert was quickly compromised and in a running fight to get away from Iraqi forces became separated, caught or killed. Only Ryan escaped to safety.

Never in my life had I been so exhausted. Often on selection and afterwards I thought I had pushed myself to my limit – but this was something else. I had sunk to an altogether different plane of tiredness and debilitation. The temptation to stop and rest was almost irresistible, but I knew that if I did I would never reach the border before my body gave out.

Helping me, I'm sure, were the years of training that I'd put in: not just the physical fitness which I'd built up, but the mental toughness, which life in the SAS had given me. Always competing with other guys as good as or better than myself, always determined to come out on top, I had learnt to push myself beyond what seemed to be possible. I was used to being hurt, and knew that I simply had to walk through the pain.

I couldn't fall back on religious belief to sustain me, because I didn't have any. As a child I'd gone to Sunday school, but only because someone would read us a story and we played games. In school proper I'd had religion thrown down my neck until I was sick of it; but as an adult I found I was unable to believe in God, seeing how much misery and disease and poverty there are in the world. At the same time, I think that humans do need to believe in something or someone. When you're in trouble you'll always cry for somebody – whether it's God, your mother or your wife. In those dire straits I believed in my wife and child – and the person who dragged me out of it was Sarah [Ryan's daughter].

Without warning, the hallucinations began again. Suddenly, out in the middle of the black Iraqi night, there she was, walking in front of me, dressed in the purply-blue top and yellow bottoms, all covered in dots, that she'd worn at Christmas. The image I had of her, and the angle from which I could see her, were exactly the same as they'd been in Hereford. As I hobbled over the rocks and gravel, she somehow kept ahead of me, toddling on, leading the way through the dark. There seemed to have been a complete reversal of roles. Now she was the one who had confidence; I was the one who was afraid. Time and time again I heard her say, 'Daddy, do it.' Her voice was so clear that I thought I could pick her up in my arms. Time and time again I reached out to touch her. I felt that if I could catch hold of her hand, she would pull me out of trouble. Throughout that endless night I was on the verge of tears when I found I could not reach her. And yet, even when I realised she was not there, I knew that it was only the thought of her, and my need to see her again, that were keeping me going.

Towards the end I was stopping and resting on my feet. Because they were so agonising if I sat down, I took to reading my map standing up – which was not a good idea, as my torch was up in the air instead of close to the ground. I'd walk until I was really knackered, then prop myself against something so that I kept the pressure on my feet.

I was so far gone that when I reached some houses I was on the point of giving in. 'If only I were in England!' I thought. 'There'd be milk bottles standing on the doorstep, and a milk-float coming past in the morning.' How many bottles of milk could I have drunk straight down?

I watched the houses for a while. They were only small places, but I'd find water in them, for sure, and food. Suddenly I decided

I'd had enough. 'Bollocks to it,' I thought. 'I'll go in, and if I have to, I'll do the people in there. I'll get something to drink and take their vehicle.'

I slid along one side of the nearest house, and found a window in the wall. It had iron bars down it, with a hessian curtain inside. Music was being played inside the room, and a candle or oil-lamp was flickering. I went past the window and reached the front of the building. Outside the door stood a car. 'Now!' I thought. 'Just let the keys be in it!' As I came round the corner I looked down, and there was a blasted dog, lying outside the door. The moment I saw it, it saw me and went berserk, barking frantically. Back I scuttled, along the side of the house, and away off into the wadis. The dog came out, and more dogs from the other buildings joined it. They followed me for about a hundred metres, barking like lunatics, then stopped. Oh for Turbo, I thought. He'd sort them.

Up in the wadis, I came to a railway line, scrabbled under it through a culvert, and was back in the desert. With a jolt I realised that this must be the same railway that Stan and I had crossed all those nights earlier. If only we'd tabbed straight along it, we'd have been out of Iraq days ago.

Galvanised by my latest fright, I kept walking, walking, walking. According to my calculations, I should have been passing Krabilah on my right, but there was no sign of the town. What I didn't realise was that every house had been blacked out because of the war, and that I had already gone clean by the place in the dark.

I reached a refuse heap, where loads of burnt-out old cans had been dumped in the desert, and sat down among them to do yet another map-study. I couldn't work things out. Where was the town, and where was the communications tower which the map marked? Where, above all, was the bloody border?

I started walking again, on the bearing, and as I came over a rise I saw three small buildings to my front. With the naked eye I could just make them out: three square bulks, blacked out. But when I looked through the kite-sight, I saw chinks of light escaping between the tops of the walls and the roofs. As I sat watching, one person came out, walked round behind, reappeared and went back indoors. I was so desperate for water that I went straight towards the houses. Again, I was prepared to take out one of the inhabitants if need be. I was only fifty metres away when I checked through the kite-sight again and realised that the buildings were not houses at all, but sand-bagged sangars with wriggly tin roofs. They formed some sort of command post, and were undoubtedly full of squaddies. Pulling slowly back, I went round the side and, sure enough, came on a battery of four anti-aircraft positions.

If I'd walked up and opened one of the doors, I'd almost certainly have been captured. Once more the fright got my adrenaline going and revived me.

On I stumbled for another hour. My dehydration was making me choke and gag. My throat seemed to have gone solid, and when I scraped my tongue, white fur came off it. I felt myself growing weaker by the minute. My 203 might have been made of lead, such a burden had it become, so much of the strength had ebbed from my arms. My legs had lost their spring and grown stiff and clumsy. My ability to think clearly had dwindled away.

At last I came to a point from which I could see the lights of a town, far out on the horizon. Something seemed to be wrong. Surely that couldn't be Krabilah, still such a distance off? My heart sank: surely the border couldn't still be that far? Or was the glow I could see that of Abu Kamal, the first town inside Syria, some twenty kilometres to the west? If so, where the hell was Krabilah? According to the map, Krabilah had a communications tower, but Abu Kamal didn't. The far-off town *did* have a bright red light flashing, as if from a tower – and that made me all the more certain that the place in the distance was Krabilah.

Morale plummeted once more. Like my body, my mind was losing its grip. What I *could* make out was some kind of straight black line, running all the way across my front. Off to my left I could see a mound with a big command post on it, sprouting masts. Closer to me were a few buildings, blacked out, but not looking like a town.

I sat down some 500 metres short of the black line and studied the set-up through the kite-sight. Things didn't add up. With Krabilah so far ahead, this could hardly be the border. Yet it looked like one. I wondered whether it was some inner frontier-line which the Iraqis had built because of the war, to keep people back from the border itself. Suddenly I thought of the Int guy back at Al Jouf, unable to tell what the border looked like. 'What an arsehole!' I thought. 'He should have known. That's his fucking job.'

Whatever this line ahead of me might be, all I wanted to do was get across it. I was gripped by a terrific sense of urgency, but I forced myself to hold back, sit down and observe it. 'This is where you're going to stumble if you don't watch out,' I told myself. 'This is where you'll fall down. Take time over it.'

There I sat, shivering, watching, waiting. A vehicle came out of the command post and drove down along the line – an open-backed land-cruiser. Directly opposite my vantage-point two men emerged from an observation post, walked up to the car, spoke to the driver, jumped in, and drove off to the right. It looked as if the Iraqis were putting out roving observers to keep an eye on the border. I couldn't tell whether this was routine, or whether they suspected that enemy soldiers were in the area; but after a few minutes I decided that the coast was clear, and I had to move.

At long last I came down to the black line. Creeping cautiously towards it, I found it was a barrier of barbed wire: three coils in the bottom row, two on top of them, and one on top of that. Having no pliers to cut with, I tried to squeeze my way through the coils, but that proved impossible: barbs hooked into my clothes and skin and held me fast. I unhooked myself with difficulty, and decided that the only way to go was over the top. Luckily the builders had made the elementary mistake, every twenty-five metres, of putting in three posts close to each other and linking them together with barbed wire. Obviously the idea was to brace the barrier, but the posts created a kind of bridge across the middle of the coils. I took off my webbing and threw it over, then went up and over myself, sustaining a few lacerations but nothing serious.

Still I could not believe I was clear of Iraq. The barrier seemed so insignificant that I thought it must only be marking some false or inner border, and that I would come to the true frontier some distance further on. The real thing, I thought, would be a big anti-tank berm, constructed so that vehicles could not drive across. Maybe this was why I had no feeling of elation; for days I had been thinking that, if I did manage to cross the frontier, it would be the climax of my journey, but now I felt nothing except utter exhaustion.

With my webbing back in place, I set off yet again on the same bearing. Never in my life, before or since, have I pushed myself so hard. I think I was brain-dead that night, walking in neutral, moving automatically, stumbling grimly onwards. Once or twice Sarah returned to keep me company and lead me, but mostly I dragged myself on without hearing, seeing or thinking.

In the end I could go no further. I simply had to sit down and rest. I took my weapon off my shoulder, and just as I was lifting the night-sight from where it hung round my neck, I seemed to click my head, and felt what I can only describe as a huge electric shock. I heard a noise like a ferocious short-circuit – *krrrrrrk* – and when I looked down at my hands, there was a big white flash.

The next thing I knew I was sitting in the same place, but I couldn't tell if I had been asleep, or unconscious, or what. I was aware that time had passed, but had no idea how much. Nor did I know what had happened to me. But it was a weird feeling, to have been out of the world for a while.

I got my kit back on and stood up. This time my feet were real torture, and I was barely able to totter forwards until they went numb again.

It was still dark. The night seemed very long. Nothing for it but to keep going. Was I in Syria or Iraq? Couldn't tell. Better steer clear of the odd house, then, because every one had a dog. What would I do when it got light? Didn't know. Couldn't think. Should be in Syria.

I woke up a bit when I found I was crossing vehicle tracks – many wheel marks imprinted in dry mud. Then after a while I thought I heard something behind me. As I turned to look, the same phenomenon hit me again: a big crack of static in the head and a blinding flash. This time I woke up on the ground, face-down, and I said to myself, 'Jesus! You picked a stupid place to fall asleep. Get a grip.'

On my feet again, I checked my weapon to make sure I hadn't pushed the muzzle into the ground as I fell, and went forward once more. Now I was walking towards a red light, which never seemed to get any brighter. I would approach the next crest in the ground thinking, 'When I get there, the light will be close in front of me.' But that never happened. The glow must have been miles away.

All this time, although I did not know it, I was drawing away from Krabilah, which lay down to my right in the darkness. I had walked clean past it without seeing the least sign of it. But that was hardly surprising, because things were becoming blurred now. I was in and out of wadis, staggering on. I was on a flat area with more tracks. Presently I came to the wall of one wadi and had another attack: a big crack in my head, the same *krrrrrk* of static, a flash . . .

The next thing I knew, I came round to find my nose blocked and aching. How long I had been unconscious I could not tell. But dawn had broken, so I presumed that an hour had gone by, at least. In my compass-mirror I saw that blood had run down my cheeks and neck, matting in the stubble. Somehow I'd fallen flat on my face.

I propped myself against the rock wall. If ever I had come close to dying, it was then. I seemed to have nothing left. My strength had gone, and with it the will to move. I lay back with my head resting against the rock, feeling almost drunk. Now that daylight had come, I knew I ought to lie up. But no – I couldn't last another day without water. For minutes I sat there in a heap. Then I got out my precious flask and drank the last little sip of whisky. It tasted horrible, like fire. I was so dehydrated that it burnt all the way down into my stomach, and left me gasping and desperate, so that I wished I'd never drunk it.

Then suddenly, to my indescribable relief, out of the wadi wall came Paul, the guy in Bravo One Zero who'd burnt his hand before we left. He was dressed in green DPM, not desert gear, and stopped about twenty feet away from me.

'Come on, Chris,' he said, 'hurry up. The squadron's waiting for you.'

It seemed perfectly normal that the squadron should be there. Painfully I levered myself to my feet with the 203 and shuffled down the wadi, expecting to see the rest of the guys lined up, sorting themselves out, ready for the off. In my mental picture, everyone was in as bad a state as I was – knackered, but preparing to go. Yet when I came round the corner, there was nobody in sight.

To this day I swear that Paul walked out in front of me. I

thought I was *compos mentis*, and seemed to know what was happening. I knew I'd passed out. I knew I had fallen and hit my nose – but now I was fully conscious and alert again. I even heard the sound of Paul's boots as he came towards me over the gravel in the wadi bed, and for a few moments I thought my nightmare was over. I thought help and salvation had come. Far from it. I was still on my own. Disappointment dealt another crippling blow to my morale. What the hell was I to do now?

I sat down, trying to get myself together. It was early morning on Thursday 31 January. I'd been on the run for eight days and seven nights. It was ten days since my last proper meal, six days since I'd finished my biscuits, three since I'd had any water. My body wasn't going to last another day.

In a futile gesture I pulled out my TACBE, switched it on and let it bleep away. Then I looked up and realised that in the middle distance, about a kilometre away, there was a barn or house – a combination of both, standing out on a rise in the middle of scruffy fields in which rocks poked up out of the bare grey earth.

As I stood watching, a man came out of the house and walked away with a herd of goats. The people living in that barn must have water. I decided that I had to get some, whatever the cost. If I was in Syria, the people might be friendly. If I was still in Iraq, I was going to have to threaten to kill them, get a drink, and carry on. I'd made up my mind: I was going in there, and I'd kill everybody if need be.

Ryan was in Syria, a Coalition ally. Ryan, who was awarded the Military Medal for his exploit, had walked 117 miles to freedom.

' *"Don't worry about the bullets: I've got an umbrella."* '
ANONYMOUS

OBITUARY
DIGBY TATHAM-WARTER, *DAILY TELEGRAPH*
30 MARCH 1993

Digby Tatham-Warter, the former company commander, 2nd Battalion, Parachute Regiment, who has died aged 75, was celebrated for leading a bayonet charge at Arnhem in September 1944, sporting an old bowler hat and a tattered umbrella.

During the long, bitter conflict Tatham-Warter strolled around nonchalantly during the heaviest fire. The padre (Fr Egan) recalled that, while he was trying to make his way to visit some wounded in the cellars and had taken temporary shelter from enemy fire, Tatham-Warter came up to him, and said: 'Don't worry about the bullets: I've got an umbrella.'

Having escorted the padre under his brolly, Tatham-Warter continued visiting the men who were holding the perimeter defences. 'That thing won't do you much good,' commented one of his fellow officers, to which Tatham-Warter replied: 'But what if it rains?'

By that stage in the battle all hope of being relieved by the arrival of 30 Corps had vanished. The Germans were pounding the beleaguered airborne forces with heavy artillery and Tiger tanks, so that most of the houses were burning and the area was littered with dead and wounded.

But German suggestions that the parachutists should surrender received a rude response. Tatham-Warter's umbrella became a symbol of defiance, as the British, although short of ammunition, food and water, stubbornly held on to the north end of the road bridge.

Arnhem was the furthest ahead of three bridges in Holland which the Allies needed to seize if they were going to outflank the Siegfried line. Securing the bridge by an airborne operation would enable 30 Corps to cross the Rhine and press on into Germany.

As the first V2 rocket had fallen in Britain earlier that month, speed in winning the land battle in Europe was essential. In the event, however, the parachutists were dropped unnecessarily far from the bridge, and the lightly armed Airborne Division was attacked by two German Panzer divisions whose presence in the area had not been realised: soldiers from one of them reached the bridge before the British parachutists.

Tatham-Warter and his men therefore had to fight their way to the bridge, capture the north end, try to cross it and capture the other side. This they failed to do.

At one point the back of Tatham-Warter's trouserings was

whipped out by blast, giving him a vaguely scarecrow-like appearance instead of his normally immaculate turnout. Eventually he was wounded (as was the padre), and consigned to a hospital occupied by the Germans.

Although his wound was nor serious Tatham-Warter realised that he had a better chance of escape if he stayed with the stretcher cases. During the night, with his more severely wounded second-in-command (Capt A. M. Frank), he crawled out of the hospital window and reached 'a very brave lone Dutch woman' who took them in and hid them. She spoke no English and was very frightened, but fed them and put them in touch with a neighbour who disguised them as house painters and sheltered them in a delivery van, from where they moved to a house.

Tatham-Warter then bicycled around the countryside, which was full of Germans, making contact with other Arnhem escapees (called evaders) and informing them of the rendezvous for an escape over the Rhine.

On one of these trips, he and his companion were overtaken by a German staff car, which skidded off the muddy road into a ditch. 'As the officers seemed to be in an excitable state,' he recalled, 'we thought it wise to help push their car out and back on to the road. They were gracious enough to thank us for our help.'

As jobbing painters, Tatham-Warter and Frank aroused no suspicions by their presence in the home of the Wildeboer family (who owned a paint factory), although the area abounded with Gestapo, Dutch SS and collaborators. Even when four Panzer soldiers were billeted on the Wildeboers, they merely nodded and greeted each other on their comings and goings.

Eventually, with the help of the Dutch Resistance, Tatham-Warter assembled an escape party of 150, which included shot-down airmen and even two Russians. Guided by the Dutch, they found their way through the German lines, often passing within a few yards of German sentries and outposts.

Tatham-Warter suspected that the Germans deliberately failed to hear them: 30 Corps had been sending over strong fighting patrols of American parachutists temporarily under their command, and the Germans had no stomach for another bruising encounter.

In spite of Tatham-Warter's stern admonitions, he recalled that his party sounded more like a herd of buffaloes than a secret escape party. Finally, they reached the river bank where they were ferried over by British sappers from 30 Corps and met by Hugh Fraser (then in the SAS) and Airey Neave, who had been organising their escape.

Tatham-Warter was awarded the DSO after the battle.

Allison Digby Tatham-Warter was born on May 26 1917 and educated at Wellington and Sandhurst. He was destined for the Indian Army but while on the statutory year of attachment to an English regiment in India – in this case the Oxford and Bucks Light Infantry – he liked it so much that he decided to stay on. He formally transferred to the regiment in 1938.

He had ample opportunity for pig-sticking: on one occasion he killed three wild boar while hunting alone. The average weight of the boars was 150lb and their height 32in. He also took up polo – which he called 'snobs' hockey' – with considerable success.

In 1939 he shot a tiger when on foot. With a few friends he had gone to the edge of the jungle to make arrangements for the reception of a tiger the next evening. As they were doing so, they suddenly noticed that one had arrived prematurely. They shinned up the nearest tree, accompanied by some equally prudent monkeys.

When the monkeys decided it was safe to descend the party followed, only to find that the tiger was once more with them. This time Tatham–Warter, who was nearest, was ready, but it was a close shave.

In 1942 the Oxford and Bucks became glider-borne. This was not exciting enough for Tatham-Warter, however, and in 1944 he joined the Parachute Regiment.

'He was lusting for action at that time,' John Frost (later Major-General) recalled of Tatham-Warter, 'having so far failed to get in the war. There was much of "Prince Rupert" about Digby and he was worth a bet with anybody's money.'

Tatham–Warter's striking appearance was particularly valuable when the British were fighting against impossible odds at Arnhem. For within the perimeter were soldiers from other detachments, signals, sappers and gunmen, who would not know him by sight as his own men would, but who could not fail to be inspired by his towering figure and unflagging spirit of resistance.

Brigadier (later Gen Sir Gerald) Lathbury recalled that Tatham-Warter took command of 2 Para 'when the Colonel was seriously wounded and the second-in-command killed . . . he did a magnificent job, moving around the district freely and was so cool that on one occasion he arrived at the door of a house simultaneously with two German soldiers – and allowed them to stand back to let him go in first.'

In 1946 Tatham-Warter emigrated to Kenya where he bought and ran two large estates at Nanyuki. An ardent naturalist, he organised and accompanied high-level safaris and was an originator of the photographic safari. He also captained the Kenya Polo team (his handicap was six), and judged at horse shows (he had won the Saddle at Sandhurst). During the Mau Mau rebellion he raised a force of mounted police which operated with great success.

In later years Tatham-Warter took up carpentry and became highly skilled at inlaid work. Fishing and sailing were his other recreations.

In Richard Attenborough's controversial film about Arnhem, *A Bridge Too Far*, the character based on Tatham-Warter was played by Christopher Good.

In 1991 Digby Tatham-Warter published his own recollections, *Dutch Courage and 'Pegasus'*, which described his escape after Arnhem and paid tribute to the Dutch civilians who had helped him. He often revisited them.

He married, in 1949, Jane Boyd; they had three daughters.

March 30 1993

'. . . *if you are ferocious in battle, remember to be magnanimous in victory*'
LIEUTENANT-COLONEL TIM COLLINS

IRAQ II
EVE OF BATTLE SPEECH
KUWAIT, 19 MARCH 2003

Lieutenant-Colonel Collins was the Commanding Officer of the 1st Battalion The Royal Irish Regiment during the second conflict in the Persian Gulf.

'We are going to Iraq to liberate and not to conquer. We will not fly our flags in their country. We are entering Iraq to free a people – and the only flag that will be flown in that ancient land will be their own. Show respect for them.

'The enemy knows this moment is coming too. Some have resolved to fight and others wish to survive. Be sure to distinguish between them. There are some who are alive at this moment, who will not be alive shortly. Those who do not wish to go on that journey, we will not send; as for the others, I expect you to rock their world. Wipe them out if that is what they choose. But if you are ferocious in battle, remember to be magnanimous in victory.

'Iraq is steeped in history; it is the site of the Garden of Eden, of the Great Flood and the birthplace of Abraham. Tread lightly there.

'In the near future you will see things that no man could pay to see, and you will have to go a long way to meet a more decent, generous and upright people than the Iraqis. You will be embarrassed by the hospitality they will offer you, even though they have nothing. Don't treat them as refugees in their own country. Their children will be poor. In years to come they will know that the light of liberation in their lives was brought by you.

'If there are casualties of war, then remember that when they got up this morning and got dressed they did not plan to die this day. Allow them dignity in death. Bury them with due reverence and properly mark their graves.

'It remains my foremost intention to bring every single one of you out alive. But there may be those among us who will not see the end of this campaign. We will put them in their sleeping bags and send them back. There will be no time for sorrow.

'The enemy should be in no doubt that we are his Nemesis and we are bringing about his rightful destruction. There are many regional commanders who have stains on their souls and they are stoking the fires of hell for Saddam. He and his forces will be destroyed for what they have done to their people. As they die, they will know that it is their deeds that have brought them to this place. Show them no pity. It is a big step to take another human life. It is not to be done lightly. I know of men who have taken life needlessly in other conflicts. I can assure you that they live with the mark of Cain upon them.

'If someone surrenders to you, remember that they have that right in international law, and ensure that one day they go home to their family. The ones who wish to fight . . . well, we aim to please. Remember, however, that if you harm your regiment or its history by over-enthusiasm in killing, or cowardice, know that it is your family who will suffer. You will be shunned unless your conduct is of the highest order, for your deeds will follow you down through history. We will bring shame on neither our uniforms nor our nation.

'As for chemical and biological weapons, I believe the threat is very real. We know that the order to use these weapons has been delegated down to regional commanders. That means he has already taken the decision to use them. Therefore it is not a question of if, it is a question of when they attempt this. If we survive the first strike, we will survive the attack.

'As for ourselves, let's bring everyone home safely and leave Iraq a better place for us having been there. Our business now is north. Good luck.'

'two individual acts of great heroism by which he saved the lives of his comrades'
ANONYMOUS

IRAQ II
PRIVATE JOHNSON BEHARRY WINS THE VICTORIA CROSS
1 MAY – 11 JUNE 2005

The Victoria Cross citation for 25136865 Private Johnson Gideon Beharry, Princess of Wales's Royal Regiment:

Private Beharry carried out two individual acts of great heroism by which he saved the lives of his comrades. Both were in direct face of the enemy, under intense fire, at great personal risk to himself (one leading to his sustaining very serious injuries). His valour is worthy of the highest recognition.

In the early hours of 1st May 2004 Beharry's company was ordered to replenish an isolated Coalition Forces outpost located

in the centre of the troubled city of Al Amarah. He was driver of
a platoon commander's Warrior armoured fighting vehicle. His
platoon was the company's reserve force and was placed on
immediate notice to move. As the main elements of his company
were moving into the city to carry out the replenishment, they
were re-tasked to fight through a series of enemy ambushes in
order to extract a foot patrol that had become pinned down
under sustained small arms and heavy machine gun fire and
improvised explosive device and rocket-propelled grenade attack.

Beharry's platoon was tasked over the radio to come to the
assistance of the remainder of the company, who were attempting
to extract the isolated foot patrol. As his platoon passed a
roundabout, en route to the pinned-down patrol, they became
aware that the road to the front was empty of all civilians and
traffic – an indicator of a potential ambush ahead. The platoon
commander ordered the vehicle to halt, so that he could assess
the situation. The vehicle was then immediately hit by multiple
rocket-propelled grenades. Eyewitnesses report that the vehicle
was engulfed in a number of violent explosions, which physically
rocked the 30-tonne Warrior.

As a result of this ferocious initial volley of fire, both the
platoon commander and the vehicle's gunner were incapacitated
by concussion and other wounds, and a number of the soldiers in
the rear were also wounded. Due to damage sustained in the blast
to the vehicle's radio systems, Beharry had no means of
communication with either his turret crew or any of the other
Warrior vehicles deployed around him. He did not know if his
commander or crewmen were still alive, or how serious their
injuries might be. In this confusing and dangerous situation, on
his own initiative, he closed his driver's hatch and moved forward
through the ambush position to try to establish some form of
communications, halting just short of a barricade placed across
the road.

The vehicle was hit again by sustained rocket-propelled
grenade attacks from insurgent fighters in the alleyways and on
rooftops around his vehicle. Further damage to the Warrior from
these explosions caused it to catch fire and fill rapidly with thick,
noxious smoke. Beharry opened up his armoured hatch cover to
clear his view and orientate himself to the situation. He still had

no radio communications and was now acting on his own initiative, as the lead vehicle of a six Warrior convoy in an enemy-controlled area of the city at night. He assessed that his best course of action to save the lives of his crew was to push through, out of the ambush. He drove his Warrior directly through the barricade, not knowing if there were mines or improvised explosive devices placed there to destroy his vehicle. By doing this he was able to lead the remaining five Warriors behind him towards safety.

As the smoke in his driver's tunnel cleared, he was just able to make out the shape of another rocket-propelled grenade in flight heading directly towards him. He pulled the heavy armoured hatch down with one hand, whilst still controlling the vehicle with the other. However, the overpressure from the explosion of the rocket wrenched the hatch out of his grip, and the flames and force of the blast passed directly over him, down the driver's tunnel, further wounding the semi-conscious gunner in the turret. The impact of this rocket destroyed Beharry's armoured periscope, so he was forced to drive the vehicle through the remainder of the ambushed route, some 1,500 metres long, with his hatch opened up and his head exposed to enemy fire, all the time with no communications with any other vehicle. During this long surge through the ambushes the vehicle was again struck by rocket-propelled grenades and small arms fire. While his head remained out of the hatch, to enable him to see the route ahead, he was directly exposed to much of this fire, and was himself hit by a 7.62mm bullet, which penetrated his helmet and remained lodged on its inner surface.

Despite this harrowing weight of incoming fire Beharry continued to push through the extended ambush, still leading his platoon until he broke clean. He then visually identified another Warrior from his company and followed it through the streets of Al Amarah to the outside of the Cimic House outpost, which was receiving small arms fire from the surrounding area. Once he had brought his vehicle to a halt outside, without thought for his own personal safety, he climbed onto the turret of the still-burning vehicle and, seemingly oblivious to the incoming enemy small arms fire, manhandled his wounded platoon commander out of the turret, off the vehicle and to the safety of a nearby Warrior. He then returned once again to his vehicle and again mounted the exposed turret to lift out the vehicle's gunner and move him to a position of safety. Exposing himself yet again to enemy fire he returned to the rear of the burning vehicle to lead the disorientated and shocked dismounts to safety. Remounting his burning vehicle for the third time, he drove it through a complex chicane and into the security of the defended perimeter of the outpost, thus denying it to the enemy. Only at this stage did Beharry pull the fire extinguisher handles, immobilising the engine of the vehicle, dismount and then move himself into the relative safety of the back of another Warrior. Once inside Beharry collapsed from the sheer physical and mental exhaustion of his efforts and was subsequently himself evacuated.

Having returned to duty following medical treatment, on 11 June 2004 Beharry's Warrior was part of a quick reaction force tasked to attempt to cut off a mortar team that had attacked a Coalition Force base in Al Amarah. As the lead vehicle of the platoon he was moving rapidly through the dark city streets towards the suspected firing point, when his vehicle was ambushed by the enemy from a series of rooftop positions. During this initial heavy weight of enemy fire, a rocket-propelled grenade detonated on the vehicle's frontal armour, just six inches from Beharry's head, resulting in a serious head injury. Other rockets struck the turret and sides of the vehicle, incapacitating his commander and injuring several of the crew.

With the blood from his head injury obscuring his vision, Beharry managed to continue to control his vehicle, and forcefully reversed the Warrior out of the ambush area. The vehicle continued to move until it struck the wall of a nearby building and came to rest. Beharry then lost consciousness as a result of his wounds. By moving the vehicle out of the enemy's chosen killing area he enabled other Warrior crews to be able to extract his crew from his vehicle, with a greatly reduced risk from incoming fire. Despite receiving a serious head injury, which later saw him being listed as very seriously injured and in a coma for some time, his level-headed actions in the face of heavy and accurate enemy fire at short range again almost certainly saved the lives of his crew and provided the conditions for their safe evacuation to medical treatment.

Beharry displayed repeated extreme gallantry and unques-
tioned valour, despite intense direct attacks, personal injury and
damage to his vehicle in the face of relentless enemy action.

'Budd was declared MIA'
MAJOR JAMES LODEN

AFGHANISTAN
FIGHTING THE TALIBAN
AUGUST 2006

Major Loden served with 3 Para in the Afghanistan province of Helmand at the time
of the emails below:

I have a Co[mpan]y G[rou]p here although we are lacking
manpower. Desperately in need of more helicopters.

Attacks consist of regular rocket, mortar, RPG and small arms on
the fire base, plus fairly heavy fire fights out on the ground.

The Toms are getting to grips with their core business of mouse
hole charges, barmines and grenades for buildings, and all direct
fire weapons for the assault.

The RAF have been utterly utterly useless. In contrast USAF have
been fantastic.

I have a couple of soldiers who I have concerns about after some
heavy contact . . . Even now with our own artillery firing they look
very frightened and slow to react.

There is a fine line between giving them time to accept what has
happened and adjust, and gripping them hard and forcing them
to focus.

In this next email Loden praises the bravery of Corporal Bryan Budd, who was killed
in action on 20 August.

Budd saw the enemy 25 metres in front behind a bush line, and using hand signals organised his section to attack.

As he went forward the landrover on the left was ambushed, despite this he led his section forward with heavy fire personally accounting for at least 2 enemy.

Sadly he and 3 of his section were hit although one was only in the body armour. As the section pulled back in the face of heavy fire, no-one saw Budd was down.

The other 2 casualties were pulled back, and shortly afterwards Budd was declared MIA. The pl comd and 3rd section had made their way forward, and tried to advance forward to find Budd but they were driven back under heavy fire.

The platoon radio op took a round in the chest but was saved by the body armour. The platoon commander received some shrapnel in his backside but continued.

The CSM made another trip out and back on the Quad bike to collect the third casualty, this time coming under fire himself but continuing nonetheless.

By now they could see the Taliban were rushing weapons out of a mosque hidden in depth. We began to engage them with mortars. At about the same time the enemy engaged us with mortars, and were clearly getting the base plate bedded in as their rounds began to creep closer.

It was around an hour since he (Cpl Budd) had been hit, and initially had no pulse. He was given CPR and moved as quickly as possible.

The CSM raced out on the Quad bike and retrieved him, but the doctor was unable to save him.

The 2 platoons were trickling towards us now clearly exhausted, and if there ever needed to be a justification for the 2 miler this was it.

Those of us on the fire support tower were shouting at them to keep running and spread out because of the enemy mortar fire. They were all exhausted and scared, but I think the physicality of it was a real eye opener.

The contact on 20 Aug proves once again the old lesson, that all arms and services must be fit and capable of basic weapon skills and fieldcraft.

There were many people on that day who will go unrecognised, but simply volunteered immediately to go out as part of the reinforcements regardless of rank or experience.

*   *   *

Ref emotion there has been plenty of tears which as you know is all rather humbling.

I have followed the same line as far as keeping them together, and injecting humour where possible.

As for facts I have been in the field since July 27th and have only had 3 days with no contact so fairly constant.

[Referring to attack helicopters] The bottom line is that there are not enough of them.

[Then, referring to air support during a fight with the Taliban] Harrier couldn't identify and fired rockets that just missed Coy HQ compound.

Pl Comd decided to continue to move, but as the enemy closed up he put in a snap ambush and slowed them up with a heavy rate of fire.

Thankfully no casualties, lots of ammo expended!

'every night I had a photo of you on my headboard . . .
so you could look over me as I slept'
GUNNER LEE THORNTON

IRAQ II
LAST POST
SEPTEMBER 2006

Gunner Thornton, 12th Regiment Royal Artillery, was mortally wounded on patrol in Al Qurna on 5 September 2006. He had volunteered for the mission less than 24 hours after his best friend, Stephen Wright, was killed by a roadside bomb.

Gunner Thornton was due to marry his fiancée, Helen O'Pray, in August 2008. The letter below, addressed to Helen O'Pray, was written by Gunner Thornton 'in case of my death'.

Hi babe,

I don't know why I am writing this because I really hope that this letter never gets to you, because if it does that means I am dead. It also means I never had time to show you just how much I really did love you.

You have shown me what love is and what it feels like to be loved. Every time you kissed me and our lips touched so softly I could feel it. I got the same magical feeling as our first kiss.

I could feel it when our hearts get so close they are beating as one. You are the beat of my heart, the soul in my body; you are me because without you I am nothing.

I love you Helen. You are my girlfriend, my fiancée and my best friend. You are the person I know I could turn to when I needed help, you are the person I looked at when I needed to smile and you are the person I went to when I needed a hug.

When I am away it is like I have left my soul by your side. You have shown me so much while you have been in my life that if I lost you I could not live. You have shown me how to live and you have shown me how to be truly happy. I want you to know that every time I smile that you have put it there. You make me smile when others can't, you make me feel warm when I am cold.

You have shown me so much love and so much more. I want you to know how much you mean to me. You are my whole world and I love you with all my heart.

You are my happiness. There is no sea or ocean that could stop my love for you. It is the biggest thing I have ever had.

When I say I love you I am trying to say . . . that you make me feel warm and great about myself, you make me smile and laugh every day. You make time to talk to me and listen to what I have to say. I know God put me and you on this earth to find each other, fall in love and show the rest of the world what true love really is.

I know this is going to sound sad but every night I spent away I had a photo of you on my headboard. Each night I would go to bed, kiss my fingers, then touch your face. I put the photo over my bed so you could look over me as I slept. Well, now it is my turn to look over you as you sleep and keep you safe in your dreams.

I will always be looking over you to make sure you're safe. Helen, I want to say something and I mean this more than I ever did before. You were the love of my life, the girl of my dreams.

Just because I have passed away does not mean I am not with you. I'll always be there looking over you keeping you safe. So whenever you feel lonely just close your eyes and I'll be there right by your side. I really did love you with all I had. You were everything to me.

Never forget that, and never forget I will always be looking over you. I love you, you are my soul mate.

Love always and forever. Lee.

SOURCES AND PERMISSIONS

The author gratefully acknowledges permission to reproduce copyright material in this book. The author has made every effort to secure the necessary permissions, and apologises in advance for any errors or omissions. Queries regarding the use of material should be addressed to the author c/o the publishers.

Alexander, Alexander ('A Flogging'), from *The Life of Alexander Alexander*, ed. John Howell Blackwood, Edinburgh, 1830

Ancell, Samuel ('A Drunken Soldier'), from *A Circumstantial Journal of the Long and Tedious Blockade and Siege of Gibraltar, from the Twelfth of September, 1779. To the Third day of February, 1783*, Liverpool, 1785

Anonymous ('Agincourt: The view from the ranks'), from *Henrici Quinti Angliae Regis Gesta*, ed. B. Williams, English Historical Society, 1850

Anonymous ('The Soldier's Catechism'), quoted in *The English Soldier*, John Laffin, Sutton Publishing, 2004

Anonymous Officer ('Dettingen: The Platoon-Fire of the Royal Welch Fusiliers'), quoted in *Echoes of Old Wars: Personal and Unofficial Letters and Accounts of Bygone Battles, both by Land and Sea: by Those Who Were There 1513–1854*, comp. C. Field, Herbert Jenkins Ltd., 1934

Anonymous (American War of Independence: Bunker Hill: 'The Soldier's Song'), quoted in *The Rambling Soldier*, ed. Roy Palmer, Kestrel Books, 1977

Anonymous Officer ('The Taking of Seringpatam'), quoted in *Echoes of Old Wars: Personal and Unofficial Letters and Accounts of Bygone Battles, both by Land and Sea: by Those Who Were There 1513–1854*, comp. C. Field, Herbert Jenkins Ltd., 1934

Anonymous ('Barrack Room Blues'), quoted in *The Rambling Soldier*, ed. Roy Palmer, Kestrel Books, 1977

Anonymous ('Rules for Soldiers' Wives'), adapted from *Sir John Moore's System of Training*, JFC Fuller, Hutchinson, 1924

Anonymous ('Scarlet Fever'), quoted in *The Rambling Soldier*, ed. Roy Palmer, Kestrel Books, 1977

Anonymous Marine ('The Soldier's Battle: Inkerman'), quoted in *Echoes of Old Wars: Personal and Unofficial Letters and Accounts of Bygone*

Battles, both by Land and Sea: by Those Who Were There 1513–1854, comp. C. Field, Herbert Jenkins Ltd., 1934

Anonymous ('Obituary: Digby Tatham-Warter'), from the *Daily Telegraph*, 30 March 1993. Copyright © 1993 *Daily Telegraph*. Reprinted by permission

Anonymous ('Iraq II: Private Johnson Beharry Wins the Victoria Cross'), *London Gazette*, 17 March 2005. Reprinted by permission of the TSO/HMSO Licencing

Ashurst, George ('Troops on Furlough'), from *My Bit: Lancashire Fusilier at War 1914–18*, ed. R. Holmes, Crowood, 1987. Copyright © 1987 the Estate of George Ashurst. Reprinted by permission of the publishers

Atkyns, Richard ('The Difficulty of Killing Sir Arthur Heselrige'), from *Richard Atkyns and John Gwyn*, ed. P. Young and N. Tucker, Longmans, 1967

Bell J. F. ('Sergeant Bell Loses His Foot'), from *True World One Stories*, Robinson, 1997 (Originally published as *Everyman at War*, edited by C. B. Purdom, 1930)

Blackader, Colonel ('Diary: The Battle of Malplaquet'), from *Life and Diary*, ed. A. Crichton, H. B. Baynes, 1824

Blakeney, Robert ('Nivelle: Wounded'), *A Boy in the Peninsular War*, ed. Julian Sturgis, Murray, 1899

Bland, Bill ('Last Post'), unpublished letter, Imperial War Museum. Reprinted by permission of Mrs M. Mace

Blatchford, Robert ('First Drill'), from *My Life in the Army*, *Daily Mail*, 1910

Bowlby, Alex ('Officer Selection'), from *The Recollections of Rifleman Bowlby*, Leo Cooper Ltd, 1969. Copyright © 1969 Alex Bowlby. Reprinted by permission

Bowen, Geoffrey ('Trench Life: A Day in the Life of an Officer'), quoted in *Hot Blood & Cold Steel*, ed. Andy Simpson, Tom Donovan Publishing Ltd, 1993. Copyright © 1993 Tom Donovan Publishing and A. Simpson

Bramley, Vince ('Mount Longdon', 'The Soldier Returns Home'), from *Excursion to Hell*, Bloomsbury, 1991. Copyright © 1991 Vince Bramley, Republished as *Forward to Hell*, John Blake, 2006. Reprinted by permission of John Blake Publishing Ltd

Brittain, Vera ('Home Front: Death of a Brother'), from *Testament of Youth*, Virago, 1978. Copyright © 1970 Literary Executors of the Estate of Vera Brittain, Mark Bostridge and Timothy Brittain-Catlin

Brooke, Rupert ('The Declaration of War: Thoughts of a Soldier Poet'), quoted in *Echoes of Wars*, Robert Giddings, Bloomsbury Publishing, 1992

Bulstrode, Sir Richard ('Edgehill: A Cavalier in Action'), from *Memoirs and Reflections upon the reign and government of King Charles I and King Charles I*, 1721

Byrom, James ('D-Day: A British Paratrooper Lands in Normandy'), from *Unfinished Man*, Chatto & Windus, 1957. Reprinted by permission of David Higham Associates

Challoner, L. et al ('A Poem and a Prayer'), from *Poems from the Desert*, foreword General Montgomery, George G. Harrap & Co. Ltd., 1944

Churchill, Winston ('Omdurman: The 21st Lancers Charge the Dervishes'), from *My Early Life*, Heinemann, 1930. Copyright © the Estate of Winston Churchill. Reprinted by permission of Curtis Brown

Churchyard, Thomas ('Thomas Churchyard Under Siege'), adapted from *A General Rehearsal of Wars*, 1579

Clark, Jack ('VE Day: A Soldier Writes Home'), quoted in *Last Letters Home*, Tamasin Day-Lewis, Macmillan, 1995. Copyright © 1995 Tamasin Day-Lewis

Clarke, A. F. N. ('Northern Ireland: Midnight on the Shankill'), from *Contact*, Pan, 1984. Copyright AFN Clarke, 1983

Cloete, Stuart ('Sniping'), from *A Victorian Son: An Autobiography*, Collins, 1972

Cobbett, William ('The NCO's Lot'), from *The Progress of a Ploughboy to a Seat in Parliament*, ed. William Reitzell, Faber & Faber, 1933

Collins, Tim ('Gulf War II: Eve of Battle Speech'), *Rules of Engagement*, Headline, 2005. Copyright © 2005 Tim Collins

Cooper, John Spencer ('The War of 1812: The Battle of New Orleans'), from *Rough Notes of Seven Campaigns*, Spellmount, 1997

Cothe, William ('A Soldier's Letter'), from *Echoes of Old Wars: Personal and Unofficial Letters and Accounts of Bygone Battles, both by Land and Sea: by Those Who Were There 1513–1854*, comp. C. Field, Herbert Jenkins Ltd., 1934

Coull, John ('Last Letter Home to a Son'), unpublished letter, Imperial War Museum

Crisp, Robert ('Tank Action at Sidi Rezegh'), from *Brazen Chariots*, Frederick Muller, 1959. Copyright © 1959 Robert Crisp. Reprinted by permission of Jonathan Crisp

Crompton, G. ('Albuera: The French Attack'), *Echoes of Old Wars: Personal and Unofficial Letters and Accounts of Bygone Battles, both by Land and Sea: by Those Who Were There 1513–1854*, comp. C. Field, Herbert Jenkins Ltd., 1934

Cromwell, Oliver, ('Civil War: Death of a Nephew at Marston Moor, 'The Storming of Drogheda'), from *Cromwell's Letters and Speeches*, ed. Thomas Carlyle, Chapman & Hall, 1845

Dacre, Lord ('Scorched earth, Ambush and Sheep-stealing'), from *Original Letters Illustrative of English History*, vol. iv, ed. Henry Ellis, Dawson, 1969

Davies, Rowland ('The Battle of the Boyne'), from *Journals*, Volume LXVIII, 1857

Demuth, Norman ('Joining Up'), quoted in *Forgotten Voices of the Great War*, Max Arthur, Ebury, 2002. Reprinted by permission of the Random House Group Ltd

Denore, Bernard ('Western Front: The Retreat from Mons'), from *True World One Stories*, Robinson, 1997 (Originally published as *Everyman at War*, edited by C. B. Purdom, 1930)

Douglas, Keith ('El Alamein: A Poet Throws Away the Chance of a Military Cross'), from *Alamein to Zem Zem*, ed. Desmond Graham, Oxford University Press, 1979. Reprinted by permission of Faber & Faber

English, Jeffrey ('One for Every Sleeper: A POW on the Burma-Siam Railway'), from *One for Every Sleeper*, Robert Hale Ltd, 1989. Copyright © 1989 Jeffrey English. Reprinted by permission of Robert Hale Ltd

Etherington, Harry ('Broken Square at Abu Klea'), quoted in *Told from the Ranks: Recollections of Service during the Queen's Reign by Privates and Non-Commissioned Officers of the British Army*, ed. E. Milton Small, A. Melrose, 1897

Evans, Llewellyn ('Armistice'), from *The War The Infantry Knew: A Chronicle of Service in France & Belgium*, J. C. Dunn, P. S. King & Son, 1938

Farquhar, George ('The Recruiting Officer'), from *The Recruiting Officer*, ed. John Ross, A&C Black, 1991. Copyright © 1973 Ernest Benn Limited

Farrar-Hockley, Anthony ('The Glosters at Imjin River: Lieutenant Curtis Attacks a Machine Gun Nest'), from *The Edge of the Sword*, Muller, 1954. Copyright © 1954 Anthony Farrar-Hockley. Reprinted by permission of Sutton Publishing Ltd

Fergusson, Bernard ('The Death of a Friend'), from *Beyond the Chindwin*, Corgi, 1957. Reprinted by permission of Pen and Sword Books Ltd

Fielder, B. J. ('Love Letter to a Wife'), unpublished letter, Imperial War Museum

Fred ('One Man's War: A Letter Home to Mother'), unpublished letter, National Army Museum

Gibbon, Edward ('Mr Edward Gibbon in the Militia'), from *Autobiography*, 1796

Glubb, John ('Medical Operation'), from *Into Battle*, Cassell, 1975

Grattan, William ('Storming the Breaches at Ciudad Rodrigo'), from *Adventures with the Connaught Rangers, 1809–1814*, ed. Charles Oman, Edward Arnold, 1902

Graves, Robert ('Joining Up', 'Rats, Suicides, Patrols and Factoring Risk: The Subaltern's War, 'Reported Dead'), from *Goodbye to All That*, Penguin Books, 1960. Copyright © 1929, 1957 Robert Graves. Reproduced by permission of Carcanet Press Ltd

Green, Osman ('Boer War: Gunner Green is Captured by Boer Commandos'), from *My Reminiscences of the Latter Part of the Boer War and Guerrilla War from 1900 to 1902*, nd

Gregory, William and John Warkworth ('Guns and the Wars of the Roses'), quoted in *English Historical Documents 1327–1585*, ed. A. R. Myers, Eyre & Spottiswoode, 1975

Greenwell, Graham ('Shelled'), from *An Infant in Arms*, L. Dickson & Thompson, 1935. Reprinted by permission of Penguin UK

Grenfell, Julian ('A Happy Warrior'), quoted in *Salute the Soldier*, ed. Eric Bush, George Allen & Unwin, 1966

Hall, Edward ('The Journey of Spurs'), from *Edward Hall's Chronicle*, ed. Charles Whibley, T. C. & E. Jack, 1904

Harris, Benjamin ('Stern Duty: Rifleman Harris is Detailed for a Firing Squad', 'The Peninsular War: Plundering A Dead French Soldier', 'Suffering, Despair and Iron Discipline: Scenes from the Retreat to Vigo', 'The Expedition to Walcheren'), from *The Recollections of Rifleman Harris*, ed. H. Curling, 1848

Holme, Randle ('Inferno: Inside the Siege of Chester'), quoted *www.bbc.co.uk/radio4/history/voices/voices_chester.shtml*

Holwell, J. Z. ('The Black Hole of Calcutta'), from *The Annual Register*, 1758

Hook, Henry ('The Stand at Rorke's Drift'), quoted in *Imperial Echoes*, ed. R. Giddings, Leo Cooper, 1996

Hopkins, John ('Crimea: Winter in the Trenches', 'Crimea: Sergeant John Hopkins Writes Home After the Fall of Sevastopol'), from *Letters Received During the Crimean War from John Hopkins*, nd

Hostell, Thomas ('Petition of an Agincourt Veteran'), translated and adapted from *Original Letters Illustrative of English History*, ed. Henry Ellis, vol. I, Harding, Triphook and Lepard, 1827

Hughes, G. E. ('Diary of an Infantryman in Normandy'), unpublished diary, Imperial War Museum

Hulse, Sir Edward Westrow ('Western Front: The Christmas Truce'), quoted in *The Albatross Book of English Letters*, ed. the Earl of Birkenhead, Albatross Verlag, 1936

Humphreys, Thomas ('Boer War: Spion Kop'), quoted in *Marching to the Drums*, ed. Ian Knight, Greenhill, 1999

I, Soldier ('The SAS relieve the Siege at Prince's Gate'), from *Soldier 'I' SAS*, Paul Kennedy, Bloomsbury, 1989. Copyright © 1989 Michael Paul Kennedy. Reprinted by permission of Bloomsbury plc

John, Evan ('Commando Raid on the Lofoten Islands'), from *Lofoten Letter*, William Heinemann, 1941. Copyright © 1941 Evan John

Kipling, Rudyard ('Tommy'), from *Barrack Room Ballads*, Methuen, 1899

Knox, John ('The Death of General Wolfe on the Heights of Abraham'), from *Journal of John Knox*, vol. II, Champlain Society, nd

Lawrence, T. E. ('T. E. Lawrence Blows Up a Train on the Hejaz Railway'), from *The Essential T. E. Lawrence*, sel. David Garnett, Penguin, 1956

Lawrence, William from *A Dorset Soldier*, ed. Eileen Hathaway, Spellmount, 1993

Lewis, Norman ('Soldiers in a Neopolitan Brothel'), from *Naples '44*, Collins, 1978

Loden, James ('Afghanistan: Fighting the Taliban'), from http://news.sky.com/sky news/0,,30100-1234864,00.html

Mackay, E. M. ('Arnhem: A Bridge Too Far'), from *Royal Engineers' Journal*, Vol. LXVII. Reprinted by permission of the Corps and Institution of Royal Engineers

MacMullen, J. ('Reasons for Enlistment in the Army'), from *Camp and Barrack Room: or, the British Army as it is*, 1846

Majdalany, Fred ('Cassino: The End'), *The Monastery*, The Bodley Head, 1945

Marlborough, Duke of ('Blenheim: The Commander's View'), from *The Complete History of Spain*, 1707

Martindale, Adam ('The Reluctant Soldier'), from *The Life of Adam Martindale*, ed. R. Parkinson, Chetham Society, 1845

Masters, John('Regimental Mess'), from *Bugles and a Tiger*, Cassell, 2002. Copyright © 1956 The Estate of John Masters; ('Reflections on War and Leadership on the Road to Mandalay') from *The Road Past Mandalay*, Michael Joseph Ltd © 1961 Bengal-Rockland Inc

Miller, David ('Just Bullet and Dirt: The Infantryman's War in South Africa'), quoted in *The Great Boer War*, B. Farwell, Harper & Row, 1972

Milligan, Terence ('Spike', 'Detention'), from *Monty: His Part in My Victory*, Michael Joseph, 1976. Copyright © 1976 Spike Milligan. Reprinted by permission of Spike Milligan Productions Ltd

Mole, Edwin ('Edwin Mole Takes the King's Shilling', 'A Farewell to Arms'), from *A King's Hussar*, ed. H. Compton, Cassell, 1893

Molloy, J. ('The Ruthven Redoubt: Sergeant Molloy Refuses to Surrender'), quoted in *Britain at Arms*, ed. Thomas Gilby, Eyre & Spottiswoode, 1953

Montgomery, Hugh ('The Astonishing Victory: The Infantry at Minden'), quoted in *History of the King's Own Yorkshire Light Infantry*, Colonel H. C. Wylly, Lund Humphries, nd

Moss, W. Stanley ('The Kidnapping of General Kreipe'), from *Ill Met By Moonlight*, Harrap, 1950

Neave, Airey ('Escape from Colditz'), from *They Have Their Exits*, White Lion, 1973. Reprinted by permission of Pen and Sword Books Ltd

Nell, Sgt. ('One Man's War: Life in German POW Camp'), quoted in *Private Words*, ed. Ronald Blythe, Viking, 1991

O'Neill, John ('The Sinking of the HMS Troopship Birkenhead'), quoted in *Rank and File*, ed. T. H. McGuffie, Hutchinson, 1964

Osburn, Arthur ('A Shell Shocked Officer'), from *Unwilling Passenger*, Faber & Faber, 1932

Orwell, George ('Spanish Civil War: Ducking a Fascist Bullet'), from *Homage to Catalonia*, Gollancz, 1938. Copyright © the Estate of Eric Blair 1938, 1953. Reprinted by permission of A. M. Heath & Company

Owen, Susan ('A Letter to a Soldier Husband'), quoted in *By the Sword Divided*, John Adair, BCA, 1983

Parker, Robert ('Malplaquet: The Royal Irish Regiment Engages Irishmen in Service of the French'), from *Journal*, 1706

Parsons, Private R. ('Private Parsons Finds His Brother's Body on the Battlefield'), from *Reminiscences of a Crimean Veteran of the 17th Foot Regiment*, Kendal, 1905

Pexton, L. D. ('Sergeant Pexton is Captured'), unpublished diary, Imperial War Museum. Reprinted by permission

Poyntz, Sydnam ('An English mercenary Abroad'), adapted from *The Relation of Sydnam Poyntz, 1624–1636*, Camden Third Series, vol. xiv, 1908

Reed, Henry ('Naming of Parts'), from *A Map of Verona*, Jonathan Cape, 1947. Copyright © 1947 Henry Reed. Reprinted by permission of OUP

Reresby, Sir John ('Murder, Mutiny and Mayhem'), quoted in *English Historical Documents*, vol. viii, 1660–1714, ed. A. Browning, Eyre & Spottiswoode, 1953

Richards, Frank ('Joining Up', 'Passchendaele'), from *Old Soldiers Never Die*, Anthony Mott Ltd., 1983

Roberts, Frederick ('Indian Mutiny; Lieutenant Roberts Survives a Point Blank Shooting'), from *Forty One Years in India*, Bentley, 1898

Roberts, Hilarian ('Falklands War: Sir Galahad is Hit by an Exocet Missile'), from *Above All, Courage*, Max Arthur, Sidgwick & Jackson Ltd, 1985. Copyright © 1985 Max Arthur. Reprinted by permission of David Higham Associates

Robertson, George ('One Man War: Letters Home'), quoted in *Everyone a Witness*, A. F. Scott, White Lion, 1970

Roe, Edward ('Trench Life'), from *Diary of an Old Contemptible*, ed. Peter Downham, Pen & Sword Military, 2004. Reprinted by permission of Pen and Sword Books Ltd

Ross, Private ('Ramillies; Private Ross is Wounded by a Shell . . . and Discovered to be a woman'), from *The Life and Adventures of Mrs Christian Davies, commonly call'd Mother Ross*, 1743

Royal Dragoon ('War of the Spanish Succession: Prisoner of the Spanish', 'War of the Spanish Succession: Defeat at Brihuega'), adapted from *Special Publication No. 5 of the Society for Army Historical Research*, 1938

Ryan, Chris ('The One That Got Away'), from *The One That Got Away*, Ted Smart, 1995. Copyright © 1995 Chris Ryan. Reprinted by permission of the Random House Group Ltd

Ryder, John ('One Man's Sikh Wars: Death March, Close Combat'), from *Four Years' Service in India*, by a Private Soldier, 1853

Sassoon, Siegfried ('Night Raid'), from *Diaries 1915–18*, ed. Rupert Hart-Davis, Faber & Faber, 1983. Copyright © 1983 George Sassoon. Reprinted by permission of the Estate of Siegfried Sassoon and Faber & Faber

'71st', A Soldier of the '71st' ('First Action', 'A Discharged Soldier's Farewell to His Family'), from *Journal of a Soldier of the Seventy-First Regiment, Highland Infantry, from 1800 to 1815, including particulars of the battles of Vimiera, Corunna, Vittoria, The Pyrenees, Toulouse, Waterloo etc*, 1822; ('Waterloo: On the Morning of the Battle A Comrades Foresees His Death', 'Waterloo: After Battle'), from *Journal of a Soldier of the 71st or Glasgow regiment . . . from 1806–1815*, Leo Cooper, 1975

S.H. ('Diary of a Garrison Soldier Under Siege'), quoted in *The Oxford Book of Military Anecdotes*, ed. Max Hastings, Oxford University Press, 1985

Shipp, John ('A Redcoat, A Fight and a Hair-do', 'Convoy to India'), from *Memoirs of the Extraordinary Career of John Shipp, late a Lieutenant in His Majesty's 87th Regiment*, 1829

Smith-Dorrien, Horace ('Fix Bayonets and Die Like British Soldiers Do!. Isandhlwana'), quoted in *The Penguin Book of War*, ed. John Keegan, Viking, 1999

Smithson, Thomas ('Postcard from a POW'), unpublished letter, Imperial War Museum

Steward, Bert ('A Blighty One'), from the *Guardian*, September, 1990

Thompson, Leonard ('A Suffolk Farmboy Buries the Dead at Gallipoli'), quoted in *Akenfield*, Ronald Blythe, Allen Lane, 1969

Thorne, Tony ('National Service: Basic Training'), from *Brasso, Blanco & Bull*, Robinson, 2000. Copyright © 1998, 2000 Tony Thorne. Reprinted by permission of Constable and Robinson Ltd

Thornton, Lee ('Iraq II: Last Post'), from the *Daily Telegraph*, 23 September, 2006

Tomkinson, William ('The Peninsular War: Diary of a Cavalry Officer'), from *The Diary of a Cavalry Officer in the Peninsular War and Waterloo Campaign*, ed. James Tomkinson, Swann Sonnenschein & Co., 1895

Toomey, Jack ('Private Jack Toomey is Evacuated from Dunkirk'), unpublished letter, Imperial War Museum

Verney, Sir Edmund ('Arms, Absence, and Medicine: The Worries of a Father Soldier'), from *Verney Papers*, vol. II, ed. J. Bruce, Camden Society, 1853

Waugh, Auberon ('National Service: Accidental Shooting'), from *Will This Do?*, Century, 1991. Copyright © 1991 Auberon Waugh. Reprinted by permission of PFD

Waller, William ('Friends by the Sword Divided'), quoted in *By the Sword Divided*, John Adair, Century Publishing Co. Ltd, 1983

Warkworth, John ('The Wars of the Roses: Fog and Treachery'), adapted from *Chronicles of the White Rose*, Bohn, 1843

Webb, Thomas et al ('Soldiers Demand Their Pay'), from *Original Letters Illustrative of English History*, ed. Henry Ellis, vol. iv, Harding, Triphook and Lepard, 1827

Westmacott, T. H. ('Executions at Dawn'), unpublished diary, Imperial War Museum

Wharton, Nehemiah ('English Civil War: Nehemiah Wharton Skirmishes, Starves and Plunders'), from *Archaeologia*, vol. xxv, 1853

Wheatley, Edmund ('An Infantry Ensign at Waterloo'), from *Wheatley Diary*, ed. C. Hibbert, Longmans, 1964

Wickins, Charles ('Indian Mutiny: The Relief of the Residency'), from 'The Indian Mutiny Journal of Private Charles Wickins, 9th Regiment', *Journal of the Society for Army Historical Research*, vols. xxxv & xxxvi, 1957 & 1958

Wightman, James ('Crimean War: The Charge of the Light Brigade'), from 'One of the "Six Hundred" in the Balaclava Charge', *The Ninteenth Century* magazine, May, 1892

Williamson, Sidney ('The Somme: Day One: Over the Top with the Royal Warwickshire Regiment'), unpublished diary, Imperial War Museum. Reprinted by permission of Vanessa Williamson

Winstanley, J. ('Kohima'), unpublished sound recording, Imperial War Museum. Reprinted by permission of the Sound Archive, IWM

Wipers Times ('Natty Toy, Plush Breeches and a Tour of Lovely Belgium: Spoof Adverts'), from *The Wipers Times*, intro. Malcolm Brown, Little Books Ltd, 2006

INDEX